A Sociology of
Food and Nutrition

To Ivan Germov and Jan Williams
for fostering our academic development

A Sociology of
Food and Nutrition

The Social Appetite

Edited by John Germov and Lauren Williams

OXFORD
UNIVERSITY PRESS

OXFORD
UNIVERSITY PRESS

253 Normanby Road, South Melbourne, Victoria, Australia 3205
Oxford University Press is a department of the University of Oxford.
It furthers the University's objective of excellence in research, scholarship,
and education by publishing worldwide in

Oxford New York

Athens Auckland Bangkok Bogotá Buenos Aires Cape Town Chennai
Dar es Salaam Delhi Florence Hong Kong Istanbul Karachi Kolkata
Kuala Lumpur Madrid Melbourne Mexico City Mumbai Nairobi Paris
Port Moresby São Paulo Shanghai Singapore Taipei Tokyo Toronto Warsaw
with associated companies in Berlin Ibadan

OXFORD is a registered trade mark of Oxford University Press
in the UK and certain other countries

National Library of Australia
Cataloguing-in-Publication data:

A sociology of food and nutrition: the social appetite.
  Bibliography.
  Includes index.
  ISBN 0 19 550609 X.

  1. Food—Australia—Social aspects. 2. Food habits—
  Australia—Social aspects. 3. Nutrition—Australia—Social
  aspects. 4. Sociology—Australia. I. Germov. John. II.
  Williams, Lauren.

301

Edited by Lucy Davison
Cover design by design rescue
Typeset by Desktop Concepts Pty Ltd. Melbourne
Printed through Bookpac Production Services, Singapore

Foreword

The study of food and eating has been one of the fastest-growing areas in sociology since the 1980s. The essays collected here in *A Sociology of Food and Nutrition* bear ample witness to the vitality and wide scope of the new sub-discipline of the sociology of food. It is plainly an academic speciality whose time has come. Yet it is worthwhile to ask two questions:

- Why did sociologists, until fairly recently, pay little attention to food and eating, which are, after all, universal human activities requiring social organisation, and which are indeed more urgent necessities for people's survival than even sex?
- And why is the subject now so much the centre of sociological attention?

The lack of systematic attention given to food in the sociological classics is striking. Look up the word 'Diet' in an index to the works of Karl Marx, and you will find that it refers to a political assembly. To be fair, Marx's collaborator Friedrich Engels recorded a great deal of nauseating detail about the food of the poor in *The Condition of the Working Class in England* in 1845, and the nutritional aspects of poverty continued to receive attention in such empiricist classics as the works of Charles Booth and Seebohm Rowntree in Britain. After his experiences in the Russian Revolution, Pitirim Sorokin wrote a remarkable study of *Hunger as a Factor in Human Affairs*, although it remained unknown until its publication in English in 1975. At the other end of the social scale, in 1899 Thorstein Veblen drew attention in *The Theory of the Leisure Class* to lavish food and drink as means of social display by the wealthy. And a little later Norbert Elias wrote the famous section of *The Civilising Process* dealing with changing table manners among the European secular upper classes (though he said little about food as such). For the beginnings of serious theoretical interest in food, one can look to Herbert Spencer and Émile Durkheim, both of whom paid attention to the remarkable way in which all human groups taboo—and feel revulsion towards—the consumption of particular potential sources of nourishment, which are factually available to them but which they strictly avoid eating. Spencer's and Durkheim's interests were subsequently pursued more by their anthropological than by their sociological progeny. By the 1960s and 1970s, food was at the centre of structuralist theory, especially in the writings of Claude Lévi-Strauss and Mary Douglas. In the 1980s, food was in turn central to anthropology's turning away from structuralism. Marvin Harris—a controversial maverick among anthropologists—published *Good to Eat*, a hard-hitting polemic against structuralism, in which he sought to crack the tough old nut of explaining food avoidances, such as the Jewish taboo on pork and the Hindu taboo on beef, in materialist, developmental, and instrumental terms (the possibility of which Douglas had denied). And Sidney Mintz, in *Sweetness and Power*, showed how the British and American sweet tooth had been created in connection with the growth of sugar plantations and long-distance commerce in sugar.

By this time, sociologists were listening. But why had they neglected food as a topic for research for so long? Prestige has always played a part in the popularity of research topics. For most of this century, the prestigious topics tended to be stratification and class inequality, politics and power, industry, organisations and bureaucracy. All were in some sense masculine concerns. The inequality between the sexes was taken for granted, while that between social strata was not; work was mainly a man's world, the home and the kitchen a woman's. Leisure, culture, consumption—and food—were widely considered to be peripheral and even frivolous concerns. I would certainly not wish to present the women's movement of recent decades as the sole cause of the new interest in the study of the social aspects of food and eating. There is more to it than that. The shift from the primacy of production to the primacy of consumption was noted as early as 1950 by David Riesman in his classic *The Lonely Crowd*, and the thought was developed further by Daniel Bell and other theorists of post-industrial and post-modern society in the 1970s and 1980s. Whatever one calls it—post-industrial, postmodern, or consumer society—its rise cannot be entirely reduced to the changing balance of power between the sexes. Sport, for instance, was traditionally a mainly masculine preserve, yet it was once considered just as peripheral and frivolous an interest as eating and cooking. It probably suffered because it was seen as separate from the 'serious' world of work. But feminism has undoubtedly had a profound effect on the sociological enterprise as a whole. It is especially evident in the emergence not just of a vibrant sociology of food, but also of the sociologies of the body and of consumption—all of them intertwined with each other, as this book demonstrates.

One sign of the times is that sociological studies of food have in various ways come to be important vehicles for developing theoretical arguments (and the prestige of theorising and of an upper caste of theorists within sociology should never be underestimated). In *All Manners of Food*, I sought among other things to apply Elias's theory of civilising processes to the social shaping of appetite, as well as extending his account of court society to understanding the development of differences in culinary cultures between England and France. More ambitiously, in *Distinction*—voted in 1998 to be one of the ten most influential sociological books of the twentieth century—Pierre Bourdieu demonstrated how the field of food links up with many other areas of 'taste' (music, literature, furnishings, art . . .) in the deployment of cultural capital. Claude Fischler, in *L'Homnivore*, showed the long-term significance of human omnivorousness in the development of society. Alan Warde's *Consumption, Food and Taste* tackles, through modern food habits, the central issues of 'consumer society'. George Ritzer made a sociological best-seller out of *The McDonaldization of Society*, in which the hamburger chain becomes a metaphor for the hyper-rationalisation of contemporary society as a whole. And in *Sociologies of Food and Nutrition*, Wm. Alex McIntosh has produced a textbook through which students could be introduced to most of the main issues of current social theory solely through the study of food.

A Sociology of Food and Nutrition pulls together all of these strands in one volume. John Germov and Lauren Williams have persuaded many of the leading sociologists of food and nutrition from around the world to contribute chapters, and they are grouped to form a coherent treatment of the major issues: gender, the body, culture and class, public policy in the face of the industrialisation of food supply, and food in the context of the emerging global society.

Stephen Mennell

Contents

Acknowledgments

We would like to say thank you to the following people: the contributors who were so professional in their dealings with us and for their high-quality chapters; Jane a'Beckett for her patient assistance and particularly for being such a diligent and meticulous checker of references; Deidre Wicks for her inspirational sociological insights on food; and Joanne Ikeda and her colleagues for the size-acceptance tenets reproduced in chapter 12. Our gratitude to Jill Lane, our publisher, for her unfailing support of this project, and to the OUP staff, especially Maggie Way, Lucy Davison, and Steve Randles. And finally we thank our students, whose interest in and enthusiasm for a sociology of food and nutrition have been the stimulus for this book.

And on a personal note, thanks go to our family and friends: John's father Ivan and sister Roz; Lauren's parents Jan and Merve, and sisters Julie and Kim, who have coped so well with their own challenges in recent times. To our partners, Sue Jelovcan and Greg Hill, who have each supported both of us in a multitude of ways. And to the staff at the café that provided our 'working lunches', where food and work naturally intertwined, providing a fusion of the gastronomic and the intellectual as Cajun chicken foccacia, Italian mineral water, and espresso coffee competed for space on a table with drafts of the manuscript.

Despite the fact it is probably not the 'done thing', we would like to thank each other: this book has been a true collaboration, involving the complementarity of our skills and energy levels, making this project an enjoyable experience.

John Germov and Lauren Williams

The University of Newcastle

June 1998

All quotations used on the part openings have been taken from N. Sherrin 1995, *The Oxford Dictionary of Humorous Quotations*, Oxford University Press, Oxford.

The author and publisher are grateful to the following copyright holders for granting permission to reproduce various extracts and photographs in this book: the *Australian Journal of Nutrition and Dietetics* and the author for extract from Colin Binns, 'A Letter from America', *Australian Journal of Nutrition and Dietetics*, vol. 47, no. 2, 1990, p. 58; The Body Shop International PLC for photograph of the 'Ruby' advertising campaign; *Cleo* magazine for the covers of the January 1973, 1983, and 1993 issues; Guardian and Observer News Services and the author for extract from Tim Radford, 'Why Meat Will Soon Be Off the Menu', *Guardian Weekly*, 28 April 1998; Pine Forge Press for extract from George Ritzer, *The McDonaldization of Society*, pp. xii–xiii, © 1993 by Pine Forge Press, New York; Sage for extract from U. Beck, *Risk Society: Towards a New Modernity*, Sage, London, 1992, p. 132; South End Press for extract from P. Idemudia and S. Kole, 'World Bank Takes Control of UNCED's Environmental Fund', in K. Danaher (ed.), *50 Years is Enough: The Case against the World Bank and the International Monetary Fund*, South End Press, Boston, 1994; *Who Weekly* magazine for the cover of the 27 May 1996 issue. Every effort has been made to trace the original source of all material reproduced in this book. Where the attempt has been unsuccessful, the author and publisher would be pleased to hear from the copyright holder concerned to rectify any omission.

Contributors

John Coveney is in the Department of Health at Flinders University in Adelaide, where he lectures to students in nutrition and dietetics, medicine, and environmental health. His research projects have included an examination of the emergence of the discipline of nutrition in Australia, especially as a public health problem (presented as a doctoral thesis), an ethnographic exploration of family food habits, and a critical analysis of environmental issues related to the food supply. He is the author of a number of publications, including the book *Vegetarian Food and Children* (with Rhonda Mooney).

Pat Crotty is a senior lecturer in nutrition at Deakin University in Geelong. She initially trained as a dietitian, but later as a public health nutritionist. Pat's interests are in the area of social nutrition and the intersection of nutrition with the social sciences. This has recently led to a book on the social construction of dietary advice and a study of the Mediterranean diet as a guide to good nutrition. Recent publications include *Good Nutrition? Fact and Fashion in Dietary Advice*.

John Duff is a lecturer in sociology at Edith Cowan University in Perth. His research interests include the political economy of health care systems and health policy, and the sociology of ecological sustainability. Current research projects include a comparison of health payment systems in Australia and Singapore, and a study of the adoption of sustainable timber production on Australian farms. Recent publications include *Nutrition Research: Setting the Agenda for the 'New' Public Health* (PhD thesis) and 'Eating Away at the Public Health: A Political Economy of Nutrition', in C. Waddell and A. Petersen (eds), *Just Health: Inequality in Illness, Care and Prevention*.

John Germov is a lecturer in sociology at the University of Newcastle. John is author of *Get Great Marks for Your Essays*, co-author of *Get Great Information Fast* (with Lauren Williams), and editor of *Second Opinion: An Introduction to Health Sociology*. He is an associate investigator with the Australian Longitudinal Study of Women's Health, and his current research interests involve dieting women and size acceptance, the social implications of food biotechnology, and public-sector restructuring. John has been an executive member of The Australian Sociological Association (TASA) since 1995, during which time he has established the TASA website and email discussion list.

Joanne Pakel Ikeda, is the Cooperative Extension Nutrition Education Specialist and a lecturer in the Department of Nutritional Sciences at the University of California, Berkeley. She teaches nutrition education and counseling to dietetics students, and health education for teachers in the Graduate School of Education at UCB. Her research is on the foodways and dietary quality of minority populations living in California. She has done community participatory research with Mexican-American, Native American, Vietnamese-American, and Hmong-American communities throughout California. Her publications include 'Hmong American Food Practices, Customs, and Holidays' and 'Nutrition Education in a Culturally Pluralistic Society'.

Karen S. Kubena is Professor in the Human Nutrition Section of the Department of Animal Science, Texas A&M University. She also serves as Associate Dean for Academic Programs, College of Agriculture and Life Sciences. Research interests have included nutrition through the life cycle, metabolism of magnesium, and the role of dietary fat in cardiovascular disease. She is a registered dietitian and teaches courses in nutrition and the life cycle, and in nutrition and disease. A member of the editorial boards for the *Journal of the American Dietetic Association* and *Magnesium Research*, Dr Kubena is also a member of the American Society for Nutritional Sciences, the American Society for Clinical Nutrition, and the American Dietetic Association.

Mark Lawrence is a nutritionist and epidemiologist with 14 years' experience working in public health nutrition. During his 4 years as Senior Nutritionist at the Australia New Zealand Food Authority, he represented Australia at the United Nation's Codex Alimentarius Committee meetings in Bonn and Ottawa, chairing a Codex working group on health and nutrition claims. Currently, Mark is undertaking a PhD evaluating folate fortification of food products as a case study of public health policy development and implementation. Recent publications include: 'Regulatory and Legal Aspects of Functional Foods: The Australian Perspective' (with C. Preston) and 'Functional Foods and Health Claims: A Public Health Policy Perspective' (with M. Rayner).

Terry Leahy is a senior lecturer in the Department of Sociology and Anthropology at the University of Newcastle. Among other things, he teaches the subject 'Environment and Society'. He is presently engaged in a study of the attitudes of Australians to environmental issues and to environmental politics, based on in-depth interviews with individuals and focus groups. He has a long-standing interest in permaculture and intends to go on to conduct research into the use of permaculture in developing countries. A recent publication in the area of environment and society is 'Some Problems of Environmentalist Reformism'.

Lydia Martens, is lecturer in sociology at the University of Stirling (United Kingdom), having previously worked as researcher at the University of Lancaster. Her research interests span the areas of gender, work (broadly defined), and consumption. She is author of *Exclusion and Inclusion: The Gender Composition of British and Dutch Work Forces*.

Wm Alex McIntosh is Professor in the Departments of Sociology and Rural Sociology at the Texas A & M University and is also a member of the Faculty of Nutrition. His *Sociologies of Food and Nutrition* was published by Plenum in 1996. He contributed 'World Hunger as a Social Problem' to *Eating Agendas* (1995), 'Social Support, Stress, and Platelet Status of the Elderly' to *Applied Social Science* (1996), and 'An Application of the Health Belief model to Reduction in Fat and Cholesterol Intake' to *Wellness Behavior* (1995).

Stephen Mennell is Professor of Sociology at University College Dublin (The National University of Ireland, Dublin). From 1990 to 1993 he was Professor of Sociology at

Monash University, Australia. His many books include *All Manners of Food: Eating and Taste in England and France from the Middle Ages to the Present* and *Norbert Elias: Civilisation and the Human Self-Image.*

Anne Murcott is Professor of Sociology of Health at South Bank University, London. Her research interests include the sociology of health and illness, sociology of food, diet and culture, and ethnology. She was director of The Nation's Diet, a 1.6 million pound social science research program and editor of the book based on the program, *The Nation's Diet: The Social Science of Food Choice* (1998).

Elizabeth Murphy is a senior lecturer in the School of Social Studies at the University of Nottingham. She is Director of a project, funded by the British Economic and Social Research Council, entitled 'A Longitudinal Study of the Food Choices Made by Mothers on Behalf of Infants and Young Children'. She is the joint author of 'Food Choices for Babies' in *The Nation's Diet: The Social Science of Food Choice*. She has also recently directed a review of the application of qualitative methods to health care research. Her previous research has been concerned with lay concepts of health and illness—in particular, chronic illness.

Susan Parker is a research fellow in the School of Social Studies at the University of Nottingham. She specialises in the interviewing of women and has worked on many projects including an investigation of women's consultation experiences with their general practitioners and a study of women employees in British High Street banks. She is currently employed on a project, funded by the British Economic and Social Research Council, entitled 'A Longitudinal Study of the Food Choices Made by Mothers on Behalf of Infants and Young children'. She is the joint author of 'Food Choices for Babies' in *The Nation's Diet: The Social Science of Food Choice*. She has recently contributed a literature review on data analysis to a report on qualitative research methods.

Christine Phipps worked as a research assistant at Loughborough University on a project, funded by the British Economic and Social Research Council, concerned with credit use among young adults. She was subsequently a research fellow in the School of Social Studies at the University of Nottingham on a project funded by the British Economic and Social Research Council, and entitled 'A Longitudinal Study of the Food Choices Made by Mothers on Behalf of Infants and Young Children'. She is joint author of 'Food Choices for Babies' in *The Nation's Diet: The Social Science of Food Choice.*

Jane Potter is a community dietitian at Toronto Community Health Centre in Newcastle, Australia, who studied sociology as part of her degree. She has worked on a variety of community nutrition projects and has an interest in applying the social model of public health in her profession.

Jeffery Sobal is a nutritional sociologist and an associate professor in the Division of Nutritional Sciences at Cornell University, where he teaches courses that apply social science concepts, theories, and methods to food, eating, and nutrition. His research interests include the sociology of obesity and body weight, the food and nutrition system, and the food choice process. His recent work on body weight focuses on the relationship between marriage and weight and the construction of body weight as a social problem. He co-edited the book *Eating Agendas: Food and Nutrition as Social Problems* with Donna Maurer in 1995.

Alan Warde is Professor of Sociology at Lancaster University (in the United Kingdom). He has research interests in the areas of politics, work, cities, social change, and, particularly at present, consumption. His recent books include *Consumption, Food and Taste: Culinary Antinomies and Commodity Culture* and *Consumption Matters*, edited with S. Edgell and K. Hetherington, who are also his co-authors on a number of articles and an upcoming book, provisionally titled *Eating Out: A Sociological Analysis*.

William C. Whit is author of *Food and Society: A Sociological Approach*. He is a co-founder of the Association for the Study of Food and Society and the editor of its newsletter. He is Associate Professor of Sociology at Grand Valley State University in Allendale, Michigan.

Deidre Wicks is a senior lecturer in the Department of Sociology and Anthropology at the University of Newcastle. She is also an Investigator in the Australian Longitudinal Study into Women's Health (ALSWH) at the Research Institute for Gender and Health, University of Newcastle. She has published in the areas of nursing and history, and her current interests include work on gender and nursing (the subject of a forthcoming book from Allen & Unwin) and work on the aspirations of a large cohort of young women in the ALSWH.

Lauren Williams is a lecturer in nutrition and dietetics at the University of Newcastle, with tertiary qualifications in science, dietetics, and social science. She is currently undertaking a PhD in the area of public health, investigating women through the menopause transition. Lauren has long held an interest in the social side of nutrition, and since joining the University, this interest has resulted in collaborative research projects with sociologists, the most recent being with John Germov in the area of dieting women. She is an associate investigator with the multidisciplinary team of the Australian Longitudinal Study of Women's Health. Lauren previously worked in the health system, mostly in the area of community and public health nutrition, where she co-wrote the child-care publication *Caring for Children: Food, Nutrition and Fun Activities*.

Acronyms and Abbreviations

ABS — Australian Bureau of Statistics
AGPS — Australian Government Publishing Service
BMI — body mass index
BSE — bovine spongiform encephalopathy
CAC — Codex Alimentarius Commission
CHD — coronary heart disease
COMA — Committee on Medical Aspects (UK)
CSIRO — Commonwealth Scientific and Industrial Research Organisation (Australia)
DES — diethyl stilboestrol
DHSS — Department of Health and Social Security (UK)
EC — European Community
ESRC — Economic and Social Research Council (UK)
FAO — Food and Agriculture Organization (United Nations)
FDA — Food and Drug Administration (USA)
HMSO — Her Majesty's Stationery Office (UK)
MAFF — Ministry of Agriculture, Fisheries and Food (UK)
MRC — Medical Research Council (UK)
NAFTA — North American Free Trade Agreements
NFA — National Food Authority (Australia)
NGO — non-government organisation
NLEA — *Nutrition Labeling and Education Act* (USA)
OST — Office of Science and Technology (UK)
RDA — recommended dietary allowance
RDI — recommended dietary intake
SSHM — Society for the Social History of Medicine (UK)
USFDA — United States Food and Drug Administration

An Appetiser
How to Get the Most out of this Book

We are who we are because we are all things to all people all the time everywhere

Ike Herbert, head of Coca-Cola USA[1]

Food is an important part of a balanced diet

Fran Lebowitz, *Metropolitan Life* (1978)[2]

We lived for days on nothing but food and water

W. C. Fields[3]

This 'Appetiser' is designed to help lecturers and academic readers orient themselves to the format and content of the book, particularly for teaching purposes. The book is designed as a text for a subject on the social aspects of food and nutrition, with definitions of key terms, discussion questions, and extra resources to enhance student learning. This book is also a useful collection of readings for people with a general interest in the sociology of food and nutrition, bringing together many of the key authors in the field and focusing on topics that dominate the literature.

The interdisciplinary nature of studying food and nutrition

The central importance of food in social life means that its study is the province of diverse academic disciplines. In such a field as the study of food and nutrition, there is much that we can learn through interdisciplinary exchange. This book aims to draw together readings from what might be seen as opposing disciplines: sociology and nutrition. Such duality is not commonly found, and it certainly creates unique challenges. Interdisciplinary collaboration is a lengthy and challenging process involving active debate over philosophical assumptions and methodologies, as well as the need to overcome jargon and territorial defences, not to mention the academic structures of universities.

As editors, we have faced the dilemmas of interdisciplinary collaboration in compiling this book. John Germov is a sociologist and Lauren Williams is a dietitian with a

---

1 As quoted in M. Pendergrast 1993, *For God, Country and Coca-Cola: The Unauthorized History of the Great American Soft Drink and the Company that Makes it Mark*, Phoenix, London, p. 398.
2 As quoted in N. Sherrin 1995, *The Oxford Dictionary of Humorous Quotations*, Oxford University Press, Oxford, p. 126.
3 As quoted in Sherrin, p. 123.

science background, and we both work as university academics. Our interdisciplinary collaboration was the result of having to share office accommodation because of a lack of university office space, rather than the product of intellectual foresight. In sharing this space, our office became a daily place of intellectual exploration as we probed the perspectives of sometimes opposing disciplines through discussion and debate. This debate further informed the development of a new sociology subject called 'The Sociology of Food' for both dietetic and sociology students at the University of Newcastle. In establishing the subject, the search for an appropriate textbook led to the genesis of this book. With student learning and interdisciplinary collaboration in mind, we broadened the scope of the book to make it relevant to students across health, nutrition, and social science disciplines.

Part of the value of our collaboration has been the extension of our networks, reflected in the people who have contributed to this book. Most are either sociologists or dietitians who share a common interest in the sociology of food and nutrition. Many of the contributing authors have published widely in the field and are based in the United Kingdom, USA, or Australia. Most chapters provide a review of the literature, while others present empirical findings, particularly where sociological data are scant. This is a reflection of the nascent stages of the development of this field of knowledge.

Our aim in producing this book is to reach a broad readership so that those interested in food, nutrition, and wider issues of consumption and social regulation can discover the relevance of studying the social context of food, with the hope that this will lead to future interdisciplinary collaboration. We encourage readers interested in the social context of food and nutrition—both inside and outside the discipline of sociology—to help break down disciplinary barriers and to facilitate the coalescence of a variety of perspectives through continuing to debate and discuss the issues presented in this book. Despite our enthusiasm for a sociology of food and interdisciplinary collaboration, we do not claim that *A Sociology of Food and Nutrition* provides all the answers for understanding food and eating. The study of food is rightly the province of many disciplines. If the university had placed a geographer in our office, there would no doubt have been more input from that disciplinary field in this text.

We hope that *A Sociology of Food and Nutrition* inspires people from many disciplines to add a sociological perspective to their understanding of why we eat the way we do, and for sociologists to reflect on this relatively 'new' field of study.

Scope of the book

The purpose of this book is to introduce a multidisciplinary readership to sociological enquiries into food, regardless of whether or not they have a sociology background. The first chapter is an introduction for those with little or no sociological background, which can be used both as a 'refresher' for the sociology student and as an insight into the application of sociology to the study of food and nutrition. The book can be used either as part of a formal course of study or as self-directed reading.

In many senses the book is an example of what Wm Alex McIntosh calls 'sociologies of food'—it is not dominated by one thesis or one theory or method, but rather presents a 'potlatch' of topics organised under key sociological themes. We set out to produce a book on food, which remains the main emphasis of the book, yet at times the issues are not limited to food, but extend to nutrition. This is particularly the case in discussing food in relation to health discourses and the body.

Key features and structure of the book

The four parts of the book, outlined in chapter 1, cover topical aspects of food and nutrition from a sociological perspective. Each part has its own introduction, explaining the theme and content of the chapters. Other features of the book include:

- an introductory chapter, which explains the sociological perspective as it is applied to the study of food and nutrition
- a series of questions at the beginning of each chapter designed to grab the reader's interest and to induce a questioning and reflective attitude to the topic
- a brief overview of the topic highlighting the key issues to be discussed
- key terms listed at the front of the chapter, which appear in bold in the text and are defined in a glossary at the end of the book
- a summary of main points highlighting the sociological perspective for each chapter
- discussion questions and further reading lists designed for both teachers and students
- an appendix of key Web resources, books, journals, relevant videos, and associations
- a *Social Appetite* website designed to supplement the book and link the reader to Web resources and to provide regular updates of information after publication. This page also provides readers with an opportunity to give feedback on the book.
- teaching suggestions are also available from the *Social Appetite* website

One final morsel

As you 'consume' the various chapters of this book, we trust you will discover, as indeed we have, that *A Sociology of Food and Nutrition* can be a satisfying guide to the study of food and nutrition. While this book represents an academic enquiry into food, we would like to acknowledge the passion, delight, and hedonism with which food is associated, and for that reason the book is embellished with excerpts from food literature. In both its social and biological connotations, food is the essence of life. The following excerpt by Marcel Proust encapsulates the central role of food as part of *la dolce vita*.

Transcending food

She sent for one of those squat, plump little cakes called 'petites madeleines', which look as though they had been moulded in the fluted valve of a scallop shell. And soon, mechanically, dispirited after a dreary day with the prospect of a depressing morrow, I raised to my lips a spoonful of the tea in which I had soaked a morsel of the cake. No sooner had the warm liquid mixed with the crumbs touched my palate than a shiver ran through me and I stopped, intent upon the extraordinary thing that was happening to me. An exquisite pleasure had invaded my senses, something isolated, detached, with no suggestion of its origin. And at once the vicissitudes of life had become indifferent to me, its disasters innocuous, its brevity illusory—this new sensation having had the effect, which love has, of filling me with a precious essence; or rather this essence was not in me, it *was* me. I had ceased now to feel mediocre, contingent, mortal. Whence could it have come to me, this all-powerful joy? I sensed that it was connected with the taste of the tea and the cake, but that it infinitely transcended those savours, could not, indeed, be of the same nature. Where did it come from? What did it mean? How could I seize and apprehend it?

Marcel Proust[4]

Bon appetit!

John Germov and Lauren Williams
The University of Newcastle, Australia

Suggestions, comments, and feedback

We are very interested in receiving feedback on the book and suggestions for future editions, especially on the relevance of this book to various audiences. You can write to the publisher or visit *The Social Appetite* Web page at <http://www.newcastle.edu.au/department/so/socialappetite.htm>

---

4   M. Proust 1957 (1913), *Swann's Way*, trans. C. K. Scott Moncrieff, Penguin Books, Harmondsworth, in association with Chatto & Windus, as quoted in J. Smith 1997, *Hungry for You: From Cannibalism to Seduction—A Book of Food*, Vintage, London, pp. 342–3.

1

Introducing the Social Appetite: *Why Do We Need a Sociology of Food and Nutrition?*

John Germov and Lauren Williams

Overview

- *Why do we eat the way we do?*

- *What is a sociological perspective, and how does it help us to understand why we eat the way we do?*

- *How does this book contribute to the sociological perspective on food and nutrition?*

This chapter has two main aims. First, we provide a brief overview of the sociological perspective as it is applied to the study of food by introducing the concept of the social appetite. Second, we provide an overview of the themes discussed in this book, highlighting the social context in which food is produced and consumed.

Key terms

agency
McDonaldisation
rationalisation
self-rationalisation
social appetite
social control
social differentiation
social structure
sociological imagination
structure–agency debate

Introduction: food as the nexus of culture and nature

As Joan Smith (1997, p. 334) eloquently puts it:

> food is like sex in its power to stimulate imagination and memory as well as those senses—
> taste, smell, sight … The most powerful writing about food rarely addresses the qualities of
> a particular dish or meal alone; it almost always contains elements of nostalgia for other
> times, places and companions, and of anticipation of future pleasures.

While hunger is a biological drive, there is more to food and eating than the satisfaction of physiological needs. There are also 'social drives' that affect how food is produced and consumed. Food is not only essential to survival; it is also one of the great
pleasures of life and the focal point around which many social occasions and leisure
events are organised. The sociological perspective allows us to conceptualise the social
patterning of food production and consumption in terms of a **social appetite**.[1]

Sociologists look for patterns in human behaviour and assess the extent to which these
patterns are the product of the social environment. By studying social patterns, sociologists seek to uncover the links between social organisation and individual behaviour. The
link between the 'individual' and the 'social' is significant in the social patterning of food
consumption, as observed by L. L. Birch, J. O. Fisher, and K. Grimm-Thomas:

> While we all begin life consuming the same milk diet, by early childhood, children of differ-
> ent cultural groups are consuming diets that are composed of completely different foods,
> [sometimes] sharing no foods in common. This observation points to the essential role of early
> experience and the social and cultural content of eating in shaping food habits (1996, p. 162).

Therefore, despite similar physiological needs in humans, food habits are not universal,
and significant sociocultural variations exist, from the sacred cow in India, to kosher-
eating among the orthodox Jewish community, to the inclusion of animals such as
dogs, horses, and kangaroos on menus in some countries while they serve as pets in
another. Some cultures prohibit alcohol-consumption, while others drink it to excess;
some cultures deem certain foods inappropriate for women, and many have gendered
patterns of food consumption. As Claude Fischler (1988) notes, food is a bridge
between nature and culture, where food habits are learnt through culturally determined notions of what constitutes appropriate and inappropriate foods, and through
cultural methods of preparation and consumption, irrespective of the nutritional value
of these foods and methods (see Falk 1994).

A sociology of food and nutrition concentrates on the myriad sociocultural, political, economic, and philosophical factors that influence the foods we choose, when we
eat, how we eat, and why we eat the way we do. However, the sociological perspective
does not tell the whole story, which is rounded out by many other disciplines, including anthropology, history, economics, geography, psychology, public health, and social

---

1   This concept was first introduced in Germov 1998.

nutrition (including the study of food habits, food ideology, or 'foodways'). Many of these other areas, however, have already been well investigated, while the literature that takes a sociological approach—focusing on explaining the social patterns that underlie food choice—is relatively new, as noted by Stephen Mennell in the Foreword to this book (see Appendix 1 for a list of recent sociological publications).

Understanding the sociological perspective on food: a brief overview

Before we can fully understand how sociology can contribute to the study of food, we need to further investigate the sociological perspective (with which some readers may already be familiar). This section provides a brief overview of the sociological perspective as it is applied to food.

In brief, sociology examines how society is organised, how it influences our lives, and how social change occurs. It investigates social relationships that range from the interpersonal and small-group level to levels of public policy and global developments. Sociology critiques explanations that reduce complex social phenomena to biological, psychological, or individual causes. A sociological explanation of food habits examines the role played by the underlying social environment in which food is produced and consumed. This does not mean that individual choice and personal taste play no role. Rather, because social patterns of food consumption exist, a sociological explanation is helpful in understanding why we eat the way we do. If food choice were totally based on individual or natural preferences for certain tastes, few people would persevere with foods such as coffee or beer, which are bitter on first tasting. These foods are said to be an 'acquired taste', and we 'acquire' them through repetition that is socially rather than biologically driven.

Charles Wright Mills coined the term '**sociological imagination**' to describe the way that sociological analysis is performed, defining the sociological imagination as 'a quality of mind that seems most dramatically to promise an understanding of the intimate realities of ourselves in connection with larger social realities' (1959, p. 15). Interpreting the world with a sociological imagination involves establishing a link between personal issues and social factors; that is, being able to see that the experience of individuals may have a social basis. Therefore, when individuals share similar experiences, a social pattern emerges that implies that such experiences have a common, social foundation. Box 1.1 (on p. 4) provides some everyday examples of the relevance of a sociological imagination to understanding the social appetite.

To help operationalise the concept of the sociological imagination, Evan Willis (1995) outlines a four-part model: historical, cultural, structural, and critical. When these four interrelated features of a sociological imagination are applied to a topic under study, they form the basis of sociological analysis. Figure 1.1 is a useful template to keep in mind when you want to apply a sociological perspective to any issue—simply imagine superimposing the template over the topic you are investigating. For example, a sociological analysis of food choices by people living on a Pacific island could examine:

Box 1.1   Imagining the social context of food

Food is central to social life and it is perhaps this centrality that has resulted in potent symbolism and connections with key social events, reflected in well-known books and films. The film *Eat, Drink, Man, Woman* shows the importance of food to family life and personal identity. *Babette's Feast* contrasts a pious lifestyle of moral austerity with the sensuality and carnality of food as a feast of sight, texture, taste and smell—a spiritual experience of worldly pleasure. *The Wedding Banquet* deals with food as the basis for social meaning in the form of food rituals. Linda Jaivin's book *Eat Me* mixes the sexuality of erotica with the sensuality of food. In many ways, food fiction portrays the key aspects of the social context of food, often counter-poised between social pressures of hedonism and discipline. For example, imagine what you would eat in the following social situations:

- a birthday celebration
- a wedding banquet
- a wake
- a religious famine or feast
- an occasion when you might exercise virtue and restraint in eating
- an occasion when you crave 'naughty but nice' food, your favourite food or comfort food.

To what extent does the food choice reflect the occasion? How?

- historical factors: to understand the influence of traditions on food choice
- cultural factors: cultural values can determine food taboos and define what is edible
- structural factors: how government regulations and the nature of the economy 'structure' the production, distribution, and consumption of food
- critical factors: agricultural production methods may create significant environmental damage—what are the alternatives to the status quo?

Applying the sociological imagination template can challenge your own views and assumptions about the world, since such 'sociological vision' involves constant critical

Figure 1.1 The sociological imagination template

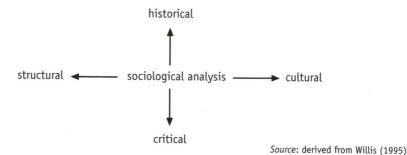

Source: derived from Willis (1995)

reflection. By tapping into your curiosity and employing a healthy dose of scepticism, you quickly come to realise that no subject is off-limits for the sociological gaze. Therefore, it is always worth considering:

* Why are things as they are?
* Who benefits?
* What alternatives exist, or how could things be different or improved?

Such questions are especially pertinent to the issues discussed throughout this book. To develop your own sociological imagination, you can apply such questions to the exercise in Box 1.2. By imagining the sociological template, the social context of food can be examined in terms of an interplay of historical, cultural, structural, and critical factors.

Box 1.2   Developing your sociological imagination

Think of the influences that have shaped the way you eat, your likes and dislikes, by imagining a social occasion where you eat in a particular way (for example on Christmas Day). Apply the sociological imagination template to explain the significance of the food and/or occasion you have chosen, noting for each factor the influences over your food consumption:
* **Historical:** when did you first eat that way?
* **Cultural:** with whom and why?
* **Structural:** in what setting?
* **Critical:** why has or hasn't it changed?
What conclusions can you draw from this analysis?

It is important to note, however, that the sociological template necessarily simplifies the actual process of sociological analysis. In practice, there can be considerable overlap between the four factors, and so they are not as distinctly identifiable as is implied by Figure 1.1. For example, it can be difficult clearly to differentiate historical factors from cultural factors, or structural factors from cultural factors, as they can be interdependent. Cultural values are often intricately intertwined with historical events and may also be the product of, or at least be reinforced by, certain structural factors. Nevertheless, the sociological imagination template is a useful reminder that the four factors—historical, cultural, structural, and critical—are essential elements of sociological analysis.

Food consumption and the structure–agency debate

As Pat Crotty states in chapter 8, a key sociological question is whether food habits are 'matters of life chances or life choices'. In other words, to what extent are the foods we eat the result of the social shaping of food choice compared with individual preference? This represents a key question in any sociological study, and is often referred to as the

structure–agency debate. The term '**social structure**' refers to recurring patterns of social interaction by which people are related to each other through social institutions and social groups. For example:

- the type of economy we have influences the type of agricultural system adopted (with its consequent environmental implications, as discussed in chapter 3)
- the increase in immigration, transport, communication, and multinational companies has influenced the eating patterns of many countries
- changing social values have increased the prominence of social groups with distinct eating patterns, such as vegetarians (see chapter 6).

In this sense we are very much products of our society. However, as self-conscious beings, we have the ability to participate in and change the society into which we are born. The term '**agency**' refers to the potential for individuals independently to exercise choice and influence over their social world and in their daily lives. While we are born into a world that is not of our making and must learn the 'social rules' to survive and prosper, we are not simply automatons responding to some preordained social program. Human agency produces the scope for difference, diversity, and change.

Exploring the social appetite: an overview of the structure of the book

Alan Warde (1997) suggests that four general social trends can be identified that help to explain current influences on food consumption: individual diversity, niche specialisation, collective distinction, and standardisation. We have modified Warde's schema and instead use a three-fold model based on the issues reflected in the chapters of this book, and acknowledge a great debt to Warde in our formulation. Like many classificatory schemes, however, we do not propose that the three trends we identify below are an exhaustive or static depiction, nor do we dispute that there may be grey areas and overlap between them. Nonetheless, we believe these to be the dominant trends in the social appetite in late twentieth-century advanced capitalist societies. The three social trends are **McDonaldisation**, **social differentiation** and **self-rationalisation**. These three trends are briefly discussed below to provide an overview of the book's content and are used as general themes under which the chapters in this book are organised. Further details about how the trends are investigated through the chapters of this book are given at the beginning of each part, and a conceptual synthesis is offered in chapter 17.

McDonaldisation

In *The McDonaldization of Society*, George Ritzer (1993, 1996) expands upon Max Weber's concept of **rationalisation** by using the term 'McDonaldisation' as a modern metaphor for the extension of bureaucratic rationality throughout social life. McDonaldisation is defined as '*the process by which the principles of the fast-food restaurant are coming to dominate more and more sectors of American society as well as the rest of the world*' (1996, p. 1, original emphasis). The McDonaldisation of food refers to a trend towards the standardisation of food production and consumption based on the extension of bureaucratic procedures exemplified by McDonald's restaurants. McDonald's clones have appeared in every food sphere in recent years, increasing the availability and consumption of convenience and take-away food, which has had an impact on the nutritional intake of the population and has changed the social relations of eating and meal preparation at both local and global levels. Stephen Mennell (1996, p. 322, original emphasis) refers to this trend as '*diminishing contrasts and increasing varieties*' in discussing the increasing mass production and distribution of food. The McDonald's restaurant is an example of the trend towards standardised and homogenised modes of food production, which effectively limit the variety of food choices available to the public. This part of the book focuses on the structural issues of food policy and politics, such as world hunger, the environmental implications of food production, and a number of public policy issues to do with food regulation.

Social differentiation

Seemingly at odds with the trend towards the McDonaldisation of food, people in Western societies are presented with a large number of consumption choices to cater for a diversity of lifestyles. Individuals can construct their self-identity based on particular consumption patterns, particularly the food they choose to eat. Social differentiation can be viewed as an alternative influence on people's food habits compared with McDonaldisation, in that neither is exhaustive and the trends coexist (see Figure 17.1 in chapter 17). So, as well as a trend to the homogenisation of food habits, there are diverse food consumption patterns emerging based on the creation of social distinction and self-identity through particular food choices and social-group membership (see Warde 1997; Beardsworth & Keil 1997). The diversification of food consumption clearly serves material interests, but the greater variety of food products and food discourses from which individuals can choose means that food choices are a method by which people can create forms of social differentiation. Despite a recent trend towards social diversity, Pierre Bourdieu (1984) points out that traditional modes of social distinction based on class persist to this day. Therefore, we envisage the social-differentiation trend as incorporating food choice influenced by various forms of social-group membership, whether based on traditional social cleavages or new social movements. The theme of this part is an examination of the relationship between social groups, food consumption, and identity formation, with chapters on vegetarianism, eating out, culture and ethnicity, class, and ageing. The chapters explore how food choices can be used as 'markers' of social differentiation and group membership, and can play a part in the construction of social identity.

Self-rationalisation

The concept of self-rationalisation draws on Michel Foucault's (1979) ideas of surveillance as a form of **social control** and particularly refers to discourses that attempt rationally to manage and regulate the human body. The rationalisation of bodies is not only the result of external social pressures, but is also internalised and reproduced by individuals. Self-rationalisation is a parallel trend to McDonaldisation, but focuses on the micro-social sphere, where analysis of the social construction of nutrition advice and 'ideal bodies' exposes eating as a social and political act. The pleasures of eating now coexist with feelings of guilt. While food companies encourage us to succumb to hedonistic temptations, health authorities proclaim nutritional recommendations that may promote eating as an instrumental act of health maintenance. The social-control overtones of such an approach are clearly evident in the 'lipo-phobic' (fear of fat) health advice given by health authorities. Changing advice from health authorities over the decades and the simplification of scientific findings into media slogans, mixed with the contra-marketing efforts of food companies, have served to create confusion over health promoting food choices. Current health and nutrition discourses illustrate mixed reactions to nutrition messages, leading to some becoming disciplined adherents to the new health propaganda, but also to a counter discourse from those who are increasingly sceptical of health messages. This part concerns discourses related to eating and the disciplining of the body in the context of nutrition and health discourses on obesity, gender, dieting, pregnancy, infant feeding, and the family.

Preliminary conclusions

Sociologists are interested in the study of the relationship between society and the individual—between structure and agency—by investigating how human behaviour is both shaped by, and shapes, society. While the structure of society influences who we are, how we think, and what we do, we also influence the social structure, as is evident in the considerable social changes that have occurred throughout history. The three social trends in food production and consumption discussed above reflect the structure–agency debate. That is, they reflect an ongoing debate over the extent to which the social appetite—the social patterns of food consumption—are shaped by the structure of society or are actively shaped by the actions of members of society. We have included a fourth part in this book, which deals with future directions for the study of the social context of food and nutrition. Chapter 16 deals with 'The Nation's Diet' program in the United Kingdom. This program is an example of significant funding dedicated to social research about food and eating to guide public policy, and as such, it provides a model for future directions. The concluding chapter explicates the main themes discussed in the book and proposes a theoretical synthesis as a foundation upon which we can understand and further explore the social appetite.

Summary of main points

- A sociological perspective challenges individualistic accounts of people's eating habits that assume that personal likes and dislikes primarily govern food choice.

- The 'social appetite' refers to the social context in which food is produced and consumed, and thus influences our food choice.
- Sociology examines how society works, how it influences our lives, and how social change occurs. It adopts a critical stance by asking: Why are things as they are? Who benefits? What are the alternatives to the status quo?
- Evan Willis suggests that the sociological imagination or thinking sociologically is best put into practice by addressing four interrelated factors of any social phenomena: historical, cultural, structural, and critical factors.
- We propose three dominant social trends of food production and consumption: McDonaldisation, social differentiation, and self-rationalisation.
- An understanding of the social structure enables us to examine the way that the social environment influences the way we behave—particularly the way we eat. The structure–agency debate makes us aware of the interplay between human agency and social structure.

Discussion questions

1 Give some examples of how food choice is not simply a matter of personal taste, but can reflect regional, national, and global influences.
2 What does the term 'social appetite' mean?
3 Consider the social meanings and messages given by the examples of the social context of food in Box 1.1.
4 Apply the sociological imagination template to a particular food issue of your choice and discuss, as in Box 1.2.

Further reading

Short introductory sociology texts

Lemert, C. 1997, *Social Things: An Introduction to the Sociological Life*, Rowman & Littlefield, Lanham.
Ruggiero, V. R. 1996, *A Guide to Sociological Thinking*, Sage, Thousand Oaks, Calif.
Willis, E. 1995, *The Sociological Quest*, 2nd edn, Allen & Unwin, Sydney.

Sociology of food texts: some starting points

Beardsworth, A. & Keil, T. 1997, *Sociology on the Menu*, Routledge, London.
Bell, D. & Valentine, G. 1997, *Consuming Geographies: You Are Where You Eat*, Routledge, London.
Crotty, P. 1995, *Good Nutrition? Fact and Fashion in Dietary Advice*, Allen & Unwin, Sydney.
Maurer, D. & Sobal, J. (eds) 1995, *Eating Agendas: Food and Nutrition as Social Problems*, Aldine de Gruyter, New York.
McIntosh, Wm A. 1996, *Sociologies of Food and Nutrition*, Plenum Publishing, New York.
Mennell, S. 1996, *All Manners of Food*, 2nd edn, Illini, Chicago.
Mennell, S., Murcott, A., & van Otterloo, A. H. 1992, *The Sociology of Food: Eating, Diet and Culture*, Sage, London.

Murcott, A. (ed.) 1998, *'The Nation's Diet': The Social Science of Food Choice*, Longman, London.
Ritzer, G. 1996, *The McDonaldization of Society*, revised edn, Pine Forge Press, New York.
Warde, A. 1997, *Consumption, Food and Taste*, Sage, London.
Whit, W. C. 1995, *Food and Society: A Sociological Approach*, General Hall, New York.

References

Beardsworth, A. & Keil, T. 1997, *Sociology on the Menu*, Routledge, London.
Birch, L. L., Fisher, J. O., & Grimm-Thomas, K. 1996, 'The Development of Children's Eating Habits', in H. L. Meiselman & H. J. H. MacFie (eds), *Food Choice Acceptance and Consumption*, Blackie Academic and Professional, London.
Bourdieu, P. 1984 (1979), *Distinction: A Social Critique of the Judgement of Taste*, Routledge & Kegan Paul, London.
Falk, P. 1994, *The Consuming Body*, Sage, London.
Fischler, C. 1988, 'Food, Self and Identity', *Social Science Information*, vol. 27, no. 2, pp. 275–92.
Foucault, M. 1979, *Discipline and Punish: The Birth of the Prison*, Penguin Books, Harmondsworth.
Germov, J. 1998, 'Whetting the Appetite: A Taste of the Sociology of Food and Nutrition', *Annual Review of Health Social Sciences*, vol. 7, pp. 35–46.
—— (ed.), 1999, *Second Opinion: An Introduction to Health Sociology*, revised edn, Oxford University Press, Melbourne.
Lupton, D. 1996, *Food, the Body and the Self*, Sage, London.
Mennell, S. 1996, *All Manners of Food*, 2nd edn, Illini, Chicago.
Mills, C. W. 1959, *The Sociological Imagination*, Oxford University Press, New York.
Ritzer, G. 1993, *The McDonaldization of Society*, Pine Forge Press, New York.
—— 1996, *The McDonaldization of Society*, revised edn, Pine Forge Press, New York.
Smith, J. 1997, *Hungry for You: From Cannibalism to Seduction—A Book of Food*, Vintage, London.
Warde, A. 1997, *Consumption, Food and Taste*, Sage, London.
Willis, E. 1995, *The Sociological Quest*, 2nd edn, Allen & Unwin, Sydney.

Part 1

McDonaldisation: Standardising Food Production and Consumption

People often feed the hungry so that nothing may disturb their own enjoyment of a good meal.

Somerset Maugham, *A Writer's Notebook* (1949)

'Please, sir, I want some more.'

Charles Dickens, *Oliver Twist* (1838)

The chapters of this section are organised under the theme of McDonaldisation. As explained in chapter 1, this term refers to standardising and homogenising influences on food production and consumption. The topics covered range from global issues such as world hunger and environmental consequences to societal-level issues of food public policy and regulation.

It may be hard to accept that something as seemingly innocuous as choosing certain foods can have political or even global consequences. Yet food is an area that brings the best and worst of politics into play, with the subsequent formation of policy at national and international levels. As the chapters in this section show, the food that ends up on our dinner plates is a commodity. The pursuit of profit has implications for food production and distribution, since food is an essential commodity—people must literally eat to live—it therefore has fundamental economic and political value.

In developed countries, food is consumed on such a regular basis that its abundance is taken for granted by most, the exception being those in poverty. The unequal distribution of food is played out on a global scale, and for a large proportion of the world's population, hunger is a way of life, with acute periods of starvation occurring in times of famine or political unrest. In chapter 2, William Whit discusses the causes of world hunger and illustrates how control of food production and international food politics perpetuates global inequity in food consumption. In chapter 3, Terry Leahy continues this discussion in relation to the negative environmental impact of food production techniques as an outcome of the combined social forces of standardisation and capitalism. He argues that the sustainability of the environment for future generations remains a significant issue in relation to current mass-production-based agricultural and industrial food practices.

In chapter 4, Mark Lawrence and John Germov discuss one of the newest controversies surrounding food: the emergence of food products that produce specified health benefits, and which often involve the use of genetic modification. Such 'designer foods', known also as 'functional foods', raise a variety of social issues, including ecological and health side effects, consumer rights issues, and particularly the role of government food regulation in the face of powerful transnational corporations. The issue of designer foods concerns the increasing standardisation and regulation of food production and consumption, but questions remain about who actually benefits from this process.

In chapter 5, John Duff examines the role of government regulation in the form of dietary guidelines, which have become common in Western countries. His analysis exposes the individualistic assumptions and corporate interests that often have an impact on the good intentions of government authorities and health professionals in attempting to regulate the production and consumption of food.

McDonaldisation is a global phenomenon and represents an extension of Max Weber's prediction of the increasing rationalisation of social life. McDonald's is a prototype organisation that is able, through rigid methods of managerial and technical control, to achieve the ultimate rationalised form of food production: no matter where in the world you come across a McDonald's restaurant, you can be assured of the same look, same service, same products, and same tastes. Not only are there now many other food chains based on the same rationalised formula, but as George Ritzer reflects below, there are also fewer and fewer places where you can avoid the McDonald's experience.

The McDonaldisation of the world

There, in the heart of Moscow, stood the new McDonald's. Muscovites are attracted to it in droves for a variety of reasons, not the least of which is the fact that it is *the* symbol of the rationalization of America and its coveted market economy. The rationality of McDonald's stands in stark contrast to the irrationalities of the remnants of communism. Long lines and long waits (so much for fast food) are common, but one sunny Saturday in May the line stretched as far as the eye could see. In fact, teenagers were offering, in exchange for a few rubles, to get you a 'Beeg Meck' in no more than 10 or 15 minutes. Russians are in a headlong rush toward McDonaldization, seemingly oblivious to its potential problems.

Source: George Ritzer 1993, *The McDonaldization of Society*, Pine Forge Press, Thousand Oaks, Calif., pp. xii–xiii.

2

World Hunger

William C. Whit

Overview

- *How did the world come to tolerate hunger in the midst of plenty?*

- *How widespread is hunger? What causes it?*

- *How can it be cured? Will it ever be?*

This chapter examines a number of different perspectives that attempt to explain world hunger. It documents the extent of hunger and then provides a typology of conservative, liberal, and Western neo-Marxist analyses and proposed solutions. While conservatives express qualified satisfaction with present arrangements, liberals propose reforms that work within present world socioeconomic systems. Only neo-Marxists propose real structural change that would actually result in a right to food for every human.

Key terms

capitalism
cultural relativism
conservatism
ethnocentric
liberalism
materialist
multinational oligopolies
neo-Marxist
socialism

Introduction

Most people believe that there is just not enough food to go around. Yet:

> the world is producing, each day, two pounds of grain, or more than 3000 calories for every man, woman and child on earth ... 3000 calories is about what the average American consumes. And this estimate ... does not include the many other staples such as beans, potatoes, cassava, range-fed meat, much less fresh fruits and vegetables. Thus, on a global scale, the idea that there is not enough food to go around just doesn't hold up (Food and Agriculture Organization, as quoted in Lappe & Collins 1977, p. 13).

What is more:

> Forty years ago the Nazis killed six million people. At the Nuremberg trials those responsible claimed they could not personally be blamed, that it was the 'system', that the decisions were made higher up. This was not accepted: they were condemned. Today it is a question of perhaps 20 million dying *every year*. These deaths from starvation are also the result of a system of deliberate policies. What can we say of those, in government, business or international agencies, who operate this system, which results in these deaths? (Buchanan 1982, p. 113).

The facts

Amid a variety of attempts to define hunger, the following definition probably best suits our purposes: hunger is 'inadequacy of dietary intake relative to the kind and quantity of food required for growth, activity, and maintenance of good health' (Millman & Wikates 1990, p. 3). Most importantly, hunger is generally involuntary and usually chronic.

There is some variation in the levels of hunger. According to Sara Millman (1991), 20 per cent of the world's population (1053 million people) are receiving insufficient food energy to be able to do any work at all. Nine per cent of the world's population (477 million people) receive 'insufficient energy for the normal growth of children; minimal activity of adults' (1991, p. 8). Referring to hunger as 'food insecurity', T. Phillips and D. Taylor cite 1986 World Bank estimates that 'in 1980 between 340 and 730 million people suffered from undernourishment' (1990, p. 62). Regionally, 'about two-thirds live in Asia and 20% in sub-Saharan Africa' (Philips & Taylor 1990, p. 62). In the context of world population growth, Nevin Scrimshaw (1990, p. 353) notes that 'in the world today, more people suffer from malnutrition than ever before'.

In addition to depriving people of energy to work, malnutrition causes specific nutritional deficiencies. Before the twentieth century, these usually took the form of:

- beriberi—a lack of B vitamins (often the result of eating white, rather than brown, rice)
- scurvy—vitamin C deficiency (often resulting from a failure to consume enough fresh fruits)

- pellagra—a niacin deficiency (often the result of eating a diet based on corn and sorghum)
- Rickets—lack of exposure to adequate sunlight in order to convert ergosterol in skin to active vitamin D.

(Scrimshaw 1990)

But today's hunger-induced vitamin deficiencies often have other effects. Generally, malnourished or food-deprived people:

- give birth to infants who are underweight, often resulting in stunted growth (24 million infants, representing 16 per cent of the world's infants)
- are underweight for their age (168 million children, representing 31 per cent of the world's children under 5 years) (Chen 1990, p. 9)
- suffer from iodine deficiency (210 million people, representing 4 per cent of the world's population). Most are Asian. R. Chen writes that '190 million suffered from goiter, the enlargement of their thyroid glands (endemic goiter), which may be accompanied by reduced mental function, lethargy, and inbred fetal and infant mortality' (1990, p. 11). This also decreases resistance to infections.
- suffer from iron deficiency (700 million people, representing 13 per cent of the world's population). Nevin Scrimshaw (1990, p. 359) estimates that one-third of the population of developing countries are affected, resulting in lowered learning ability, work performance, and resistance to infection.
- suffer from vitamin A deficiency. Often coming in the aftermath of pervasive diarrhoea in the developing world, vitamin A deficiency causes partial or total blindness, and increases the 'risk of respiratory infection and the incidence of complications from measles' (Chen 1990, p. 11).

The most extreme cases of hunger involve protein or calorie malnutrition (also known as 'protein-energy malnutrition') and usually affect small children:

> *kwashiokor* is the ... name used to describe the disease that occurs when a child is displaced from the breast by another baby. [It involves] moderate to severe growth failures and muscles that are poorly developed and lack tone ... resulting in a large pot belly and swollen legs and face. The child has profound apathy and general misery; he or she whimpers but does not cry or scream (Bryant et al. 1985, pp. 289–90).

Marasmus is a condition resulting from lack of calories. It involves extreme growth failure and generally occurs in the child's first year. The child looks extremely emaciated.

If, as Francis Moore Lappe and Joseph Collins claim, there is enough food for everyone, how does hunger persist? We must understand that, as Millman writes, 'the history of hunger is embedded in the history of plenty' (1991, p. 3). The overriding issue in relation to contemporary hunger is that adequate nutrition can be derived from grains, but 40 per cent of the grain grown in the world is fed to livestock to produce high-priced meat (*The Politics of Food* 1987). In an international **capitalist** system, food goes

Box 2.1 Breast-feeding

No one disputes the superior health benefits of mothers' milk over cows' milk. As Sara Millman of Brown University's Alan Shaw Feinstein World Hunger Program writes: 'Breast-feeding nourishes very young children, minimizes the exposure to environmental contaminants, provides some defense against infection and contributes to a relatively favorable pattern of birth spacing that in turn can have an important positive effect on the health of both your children and their siblings' (1991, p. 91).

In unsanitary and very low-income conditions, breast milk provides a child with many immunities through antibodies from the mother. And it prevents the diarrhoea that is almost universal in the developing world. This malady kills many babies by preventing the absorption of nutrients from food. Unfortunately, the **multinational oligopolies** have sought a new market for infant formula in the developing world. They employ radio and billboards. They make sure that samples of infant formula are dispensed in hospitals. And in 1977 Nestlé Corporation was employing 4000–5000 'mothercraft advisors in nurse-like uniform' (Lappe & Collins 1977, p. 315). They were often given salaries and commissions.

This advertising has combined with the use of infant formula by many middle-class and working mothers to make it a status symbol of Western life. Just as eating at McDonald's is a status symbol for the USA's urban poor, so feeding one's baby on Western infant formula has become one mark of status in the developing world. Unfortunately, living conditions on a low income make infant formula a cause of death. If not used, a mother's natural milk dries up, necessitating the continued use of formula milk, and the cost of formula may consume up to half a poor family's food budget. Because of the expense, uneducated families may dilute the formula with water to make it go farther. This situation soon leads to serious malnutrition and death. While infant formula instructions advise strict sterility, this is often not possible with polluted water supplies and limited cooking facilities. In addition, many of the developing world's poor are illiterate. Because they cannot read, they cannot follow the directions. And even if they could, they often lack the education to understand the importance of a germ-free environment. In this context, infant formula becomes 'nutricidal'.

In 1974 the British group War on Want began an international campaign against Nestlé with its pamphlet *Nestlé Kills Babies* (Lappe & Collins 1977, p. 311). The worldwide boycott of Nestlé forced the corporation to curtail this kind of infanticide. But recently Nestlé has started marketing formula in the developing world again, and the boycott has been reinstituted.

to those who can afford to pay for it. Often they are the fast-food customers in the developed world. Only the few remaining socialist societies seek to provide food as a fundamental right. With the increasing commodification of food in these societies, hunger may become a problem once again.

Conservative analyses and prescriptions

In *Food, Poverty, and Power*, Anne Buchanan (1982) reproduces a cartoon that reads: 'Starvation Is God's Way of Punishing Those Who Have Little or No Faith in Capitalism'. **Conservative** analysts of world hunger have generally seen a (Judaeo-)Christian form of divine providence in the suffering of the poor: 'The poor ye shall always have with you'—(Matthew 26: 11). This is an **ethnocentric** position that generally justifies the suffering from hunger on some combination of theological, value-based, or demographic grounds.

Garrett Hardin (1978) provided the classic demographic justification for doing nothing. His argument rests on an analogy between the Earth and a lifeboat. Each has a limited carrying capacity. Overloading causes catastrophe for all. Therefore, those of us (in the developed world) who now control 'lifeboat Earth' should not permit alleviation of hunger. To do so would create too many people (overloading the lifeboat) and decreasing the quality of the lives we now live. This argument relies on ethical assumptions that the present world system is 'right' and that we in the West, as the world's dominating force, have a responsibility to keep the 'lifeboat' from overloading with other (minority) races and classes.

Demographically, Hardin implores us to 'guard against boarding parties' (1978, p. 75), which could take the form of much higher reproductive rates in developing countries. He is informed by Thomas Malthus's 1798 work 'Essays on the Principle of Population', which took the position that, at the then current rate of growth, population would soon outstrip food production. According to Malthus, food production grows arithmetically while population grows geometrically. In this context, Garrett Hardin argues *against* a world food bank, which would create a means of sustaining people who might otherwise perish from 'natural' causes. He detects the profit motive of private business in the USA's food aid efforts. In addition, he identifies a desire for cheap labour as the motive in liberal demands for increased immigration quotas (1978, p. 79).

The second major conservative argument *for* the continuation of hunger and malnutrition is one that subverts the **cultural relativism** upon which liberal social scientists tend to pride themselves. Consequently, conservatives maintain that an unprejudiced attitude would see us respect the peasant values of the developing world rather than imposing our values on them. And, they argue, those peasant values are one source of hunger and malnutrition.

Hardin believes that the issue of hunger is one of 'slovenly rulers' and incompetent governments that do not plan for lean years. In *Famine in Peasant Societies*, Ronald Seavoy continues this values-based argument. He characterises the peasant mentality as 'survivalist'. Peasants work only to subsist (not to grow rich) and to allow for indolence. In fact, 'peasants will not be motivated by commercial social values until political power is used to destroy the communal institutions that protect the subsistence compromise' (1986, p. 378).

Claire Cassidy (1982) proposes a similar value- or culture-grounded argument in her analysis of the weaning customs of non-industrialised society that may 'potentiate' malnutrition. In the context of her general (liberal) concern for the hungry and malnourished, she shows that many peasant customs (such as early weaning or a preference for large families) have a latent function of 'potentiating' malnutrition, while their manifest function is to socialise and display love for children. Cassidy also echoes Hardin's argument when she demonstrates that malnutrition serves to limit population growth and eliminate those biological organisms that are not strong enough to endure the malnutrition and hardships caused by certain societies' inadequate food supplies. She writes: 'the experience of malnutrition in early childhood may also be adaptive in the sense that it biases developmental plasticity toward the hunger-resistant' (1982, p. 333). She refers to this process (echoing Edward Banfield in *The Unheavenly City* 1974) as 'benign neglect'.

While Hardin truly is a conservative, Cassidy justifies her excursion into conservative territory by her interest in providing more successful nutrition programs. She argues that if nutritionists understand the role of values in developing societies, they can structure really effective programs for alleviating hunger. While Seavoy and Cassidy rightly explore the role of values in 'traditional' societies, they both fail to come to terms with the aetiology of values and the manner in which they change.

'Value longevity' has been the traditional conservative explanation of most social customs. Banfield argues that the values of the lower class inhibit self-improvement. And those values are passed down through the 'culture of poverty' in North America. Values such as 'a taste for excitement,' 'immediate gratification', and 'timelessness' will go on forever among the poor. Therefore, one should do nothing. From a liberal **materialist** perspective, values are *responses* to material situations. The fact that people in 'traditional' societies hold many values in common reflects a collective response to the common conditions of pre-commercial horticultural or agrarian society.

Having large families is a good example. Ronald Seavoy argues that 'large families are desired in peasant societies because child labor allows parents to enjoy indolence' (1986, p. 20). Leisure (values) motivate high birth rates. In contrast, materialists argue that high birth rates function in poor societies as a system of social security. By having a large number of (especially male) children, parents increase the chances of being adequately supported in old age. Demographers speak of the 'fertility transition'. About 40 years after a country 'develops', the birth rate generally drops. From a materialist point of view, there is a new material reality to which to adapt. Developed societies generally have social-security systems that fulfil the function of large families. In addition, developed societies are often predominantly urban. Children—who are positively functional for an agrarian society—(they can do many farming tasks)—are dysfunctional and an economic burden in the city.

Drawing on traditional sociology, we can use the notion of 'cultural lag' (William Ogburn) to explain the values aspect of this transition. Because values are an adaptive response, they change slowly. Generally, one's personal values are formed mostly by the onset of adulthood. These values form the basis of adult personality. But when material conditions change (a social-security system is implemented, or immigrants come to a different society, for instance), the second generation is generally the locus of a *change* in values. Having grown up with a social security-system and in an urban environment, it makes more adaptive 'sense' to have (and to value) a small family.

As for Banfield's analysis of the 'culture of poverty', how does one explain the continuing tendency of some people in the developed world to have large families? First, many poor families in the West are still rural. Extra hands are still needed on farms. And among the urban poor, welfare payments alone provide such a limited retirement income that there remains some belief that a large family will be of benefit in old age. In fact, low-income families are more mutually supporting than middle-class families (again, out of material necessity—more support is needed).

In summary, conservatives such as Hardin (1978) generally support hunger as useful in a potentially overpopulated world. They justify their position on the grounds of protecting the existing élite and of the defective value systems of the malnourished and hungry. They 'blame the victims' of poverty and malnutrition. The conservative solution to world hunger is to allow it to continue. While thinking of themselves as personally compassionate, conservatives support institutional indifference and benign neglect of the problems of the poor, hungry, and malnourished. Their prescription for social change is to have none—even at the cost of 20 million lives a year.

Liberal analyses and prescriptions

Liberals traditionally lean towards technological manipulation and political 'reforms'. Perhaps the best known sociologists who view technology as the key to human evolution are Gerhard and Jean Lenski (1982). They analyse human development from the perspective of food-growing technologies. They identify four categories of food production technology: hunting and gathering, horticultural, agrarian, and industrial.

In the area of hunger, Esther Boserup provides the technological explanation. Blending demography with technologies of food production, she argues that 'population growth itself stimulates agricultural innovation and leads to production increases that more than keep up with population' (Crossgrove et al. 1990, p. 224).

The technology of food production is the key. Instead of being a contained 'lifeboat', the lifeboat (the world's resources) may now be expanded as a result of a technological fix. The 'Green Revolution' and biotechnology (as well as some birth-control) are the current technological focuses of liberal hopes to solve world hunger. Like conservatives, liberals assume the essential goodness of the world economic system. But, unlike conservatives, they feel that with a bit of technological tinkering and policy reform, the world can alleviate food shortages.

The most important policy innovation with regard to hunger alleviation is United States Public Law 480. Passing the United States Congress in 1954, PL 480 reflects a foreign policy to disburse (surplus) food throughout the hungry world. It appeared to be the perfect liberal humanitarian gesture by the USA towards the world's hungry. But the motives for 'doing good' are often mixed, and this policy also provided a solution to some economic problems resulting from surplus food in the USA. In the Great Depression, the USA dumped, burned, and ploughed under surplus food rather than distribute it within a depressed market, which would have undermined the profits of existing business people. With PL 480, this food could be disbursed abroad and, at the same time, profit United States producers. As Dan Morgan writes:

> PL 480 was advertised as an aid program for foreign countries, but above all it provided assistance to American farmers and the grain trade. Foreign governments received authorization from the US government to purchase, with American loans, certain quantities of American farm commodities and foreigners handled the actual transactions, contracting with private exporters to obtain the goods. But payment for these goods actually went straight from the US Treasury to commercial banks in the United States and then to the private exporters. The foreign governments had the obligation to repay the loans, but the terms provided grace periods and long maturities (1980, pp. 147–8).

Implicit in virtually all the aid schemes of the USA, and often of the United Nations, is the assumption that world capitalism is the best system. Imperfections must only be reformed in order to improve the efficiency of the whole system. Nevertheless, there are important criticisms of this approach. Most of these centre on the political nature of choosing aid recipients and the ineffectiveness of the aid in actually improving hunger.

Probably every country regards the fostering of political loyalty and support as a side benefit of providing aid. With PL 480, 'the chief allocations for political reasons [go] to countries considered strategically important' (Kutzner 1990, p. 31). Lappe and Collins criticise United States aid programs for focusing disproportionately on politically loyal countries and having little to do with poverty. For instance, 'Out of 70 odd governments receiving almost $34 billion in US bilateral economic assistance in the first half of the 1980's, just 10 countries got over half the assistance … Israel and Egypt together got almost one-third' (1986, p. 105). Often this aid is dispensed to the most politically repressive dictatorships: 'While El Salvador ranks third among per capita recipients of US economic aid, its government defends the economic structures that have made Salvadorians among the five hungriest peoples in Latin America' (Lappe & Collins 1986, p. 107).

Similarly, food is used as a weapon. The withholding of aid is threatened or implemented when countries institute policies that run counter to United States 'development' objectives. Allende's Chile and Sandinistan Nicaragua were but two countries that constructed social systems to feed their poor and develop the means of feeding them in the future. The USA cut off aid to both of them.

A second major criticism of United States (and international) food aid is that it is ineffectively administered. Again, it rests on the assumption of the fundamental unchangeability of the capitalist market system. Only reforms that maintain profitability as a criterion of eligibility for aid are acceptable. Aid often does not get to the people deserving of it. In many developing countries, villages are controlled by local men (and very few women) of power. In one example cited by Lappe and Collins:

> Thanks to a bribe to a technician, an irrigation pump earmarked for a cooperative of poor farmers in Bangladesh winds up belonging to the village's richest landowner: he graciously allows his neighbors water from the new well in exchange for a third of their harvests. And ' … the landowner can now buy an imported tractor, eliminating desperately needed jobs for the village's landless families' (1986, p. 111).

Another area of ineffectiveness is the manner in which food aid can underprice local producers, driving them out of business. It can discourage local entrepreneurial and productive activity. It is essentially a 'dole' on which people can become dependent. It relieves the local government of responsibility for providing the structural changes that would actually make the country self-sufficient in terms of food production (Lappe &Collins 1986). And since much aid is in the form of loans, these countries often have to orient their agricultural production towards export crops.

Third, United States food aid either may be inappropriate or may function to change local food tastes, causing a move away from indigenous sources of nutrients. Because the USA has often used wheat, there is now some demand for wheat as evidence of Westernisation. In Africa, wheat grows poorly. As a result, the demand for imported wheat grows while many African countries cannot provide their populations with enough basic nutrients and have no foreign exchange with which to purchase wheat.

Until fairly recently, dried milk (of which the USA has a surplus) was often shipped to the African continent as food aid. The endemic lactose intolerance of most Africans (and many Asians) was not recognised. Because these people lack the enzyme lactase to break down the lactose, they suffered upset stomachs and diarrhoea from the milk. Often the milk went unused or served as a whitewash.

India provides the best known example of the liberal reformist approach to eliminating hunger. Its focus has been on population limitation and technological improvements in food production. Twenty years ago, liberal American social scientists were advocating birth-control as the solution to the Indian hunger problem. There were just too many people. At that time, many schemes were devised to provide incentives for Indians to limit births through birth-control and sterilisation. Radios and other 'prizes' were given out in villages as rewards. Not much attention was paid to the violation of human rights by coercive sterilisation programs.

Another area of liberal reform in India has been the attempt to increase food production. India provides one of the best examples of success in scientific agriculture. The 'Green Revolution' or genetic inbreeding of high-yielding varieties (HYV) after 1965 doubled India's grain production. However, these grains were grown only in specific regions: the Punjab, Haryana, and western Uttar Pradesh. The gains were made in wheat production more than in rice, and they failed to increase the yield of jowar and bajra, the staple foods of the Indian poor (Hinrichs 1988). The petrochemicals they used were an additional source of environmental degradation.

Furthermore, because of India's skewed income distribution and lack of a national feeding program, 'nearly half the population lacks the income necessary to buy a nutritious diet' (Lappe & Collins 1986, p. 50). In precisely the area in which the Green Revolution has been successful, the land-ownership structure prevents the two-thirds of the population who are poor from being adequately fed (Lappe & Collins 1986, p. 50).

In much of the developing world, when a surplus is generated, the owners sell it to the highest bidder. This often means that the owners of the grain export it, even in periods of extensive famine. If the poor do not have the funds to purchase the grain, it is of no use to them in a capitalist system. For this reason, many liberal attempts at hunger alleviation call for entitlement programs. These programs are based on the premise that everyone should be entitled to such necessities as air, water, and food. The problem is to accomplish this without intruding on the profit motive in a basically capitalist system. These programs often provide public jobs, which can then supply the cash to buy food. India has taken this approach. As long as the jobs are in the public sector, they do not compete with private profits.

Even in the mixed economy that existed under the Sandinistan government in Nicaragua, ration coupons provided only for basic goods (for example, rice, oil, and salt), leaving the production and sale of more luxurious and varied food commodities in private hands. As Jean Dreze and Amartya Sen write: 'Entitlement protection will almost always call for mixed systems, involving the use of different instruments to provide direct or indirect support to all vulnerable groups. The provision of employment—perhaps with cash wages—combined with unconditional relief for the 'unemployable' is likely to be one of the more effective options in many circumstances' (1989, p. 121).

Liberal analysts have taken the initiative in hunger relief for a long time. Yet hunger persists. Because of their commitment to a world capitalist system (however 'reformed') and their usual optimism, they are perpetually proposing new reform 'fixes'. One recent reform was proposed by the previous chief economist at the United States Agency for International Development, John Mellor. Now a professor at Cornell University, Mellor calls for a massive public-works program (US$15 billion per year) and US$5 billion per year for feeding programs. He asks that the World Bank and World Food Program join to spearhead this effort (Mellor 1990, pp. 499–500). He wants serious money to be spent on rural infrastructures that would allow 'development' and 'modernisation' to occur. Should that happen, countries could begin to become self-sufficient in relation to food. On the other hand, Mellor recognises the utopian nature of his scheme. He writes: 'the politics of foreign aid and national allocations have determined much of the present allocational pattern and it seems unreasonable to expect major changes to occur in the future' (1990, p. 507).

In sum, liberal analyses and plans abound. Most are well intentioned. Yet their track record, as demonstrated by the country in which they have been the most thoroughly applied—India—is short of middling. Without changing the economic system that has previously created, and continues to create, hunger conditions, there is little real hope that hunger will end. Only in countries where there is a different economic and political system has hunger been eradicated.

Western neo-Marxist political economic analyses and prescriptions

By way of introduction, it should be made clear that a Western **neo-Marxist** analysis of the world hunger problem is not an analysis from the perspective of the former Soviet Union or Eastern Bloc. It has very little to do with the 'state capitalist' or 'coordinator' societies that existed in Eastern Europe before the current movement towards capitalism.

Instead, a modern Western neo-Marxist analysis participates in the intellectual tradition that has variously also been called 'critical sociology', 'dialectical, materialist, political economy', 'world systems theory', or '"radical" analysis'. All relate to an intellectual position from which one looks at the political structure in relation to the economy before one looks at societal norms, ideas, values, and ideologies. This perspective assumes that the more important aspects of the social system are to be found in the qualitative analysis of the economy and the manner in which politics and ideology generally flow from it.

Western Marxists have usually been critical of the authoritarian and anti-democratic practices of many supposedly 'socialist' regimes, such as the former Soviet Union. At the same time, it is only in countries that have claimed to be socialist that we have seen a serious attempt to create economic structures that depart from the contemporary norm of global capitalism.

In the developing world, it is only in these socialist countries that effective attempts have been made to alleviate the problem of hunger. Politically, these countries range from the autocratic, one-party dictatorship of China through to the innovative, freely elected communist-party government in the state of Kerala in India. While Western Marxists may be critical of the political character of some of these states, they also see their success in solving the problem of hunger as an effect of the economic structures that socialist countries have instituted.

From this perspective, the economic system is composed of two parts: ownership patterns and technology. In the world capitalist system, the basic ownership pattern is that of private capitalist élites owning most of the productive apparatus in the world. Workers (including farm workers) sell their labour power to them in one form or another. The profit that accumulates in this process flows predominantly to the élites of both the developed Northern hemisphere and the developing Southern hemisphere. Both élites have similar interests in extracting surplus value from workers—regardless of the costs to the countries or their environments.

In this world system, capitalist oligopolies own and control most of the significant productive apparatus that relates to food. These technologies involve land, farming machinery, farm chemicals, seed, and knowledge. These oligopolies also produce research on future profitable technologies of food production that is biased towards their interests. Political economists approach food shortages from a historical perspective in which the problem of food poverty and hunger is rooted in colonialism. Most indigenous peoples knew how to produce enough food for themselves. The groups that did not perished.

The eighteenth century saw new capitalists encircle the globe. Great Britain, France, and Spain staked out claims to a large part of the world's land. Although this process was often ideologically justified in terms of bringing Christianity and Western civilisation to the 'heathen', it actually brought mountainous profits to the entrepreneurs who invested in it. Some critics of colonialism are fond of saying that the missionaries brought the Bible to the new lands. When they were through, the 'natives' had the Bible and the missionaries had the land.

This political-economy perspective characterises the government (or State) as generally bowing to the demands of its leading (socioeconomic) class—that is, the capitalists. The capitalist classes provide the funds to finance the election of people who will represent their interests and who will goad their governments into providing legitimacy and protection for their foreign ventures. These 'democracies' were designed to appear democratic, but in fact they act predominantly in the interests of the capitalist classes.

In what is now the developing world, the plantation pattern often dominated. For instance, sugar became the principal product imported into Great Britain from the British Caribbean. It both enriched the capitalist class and impoverished the diet of the British industrial working class (Mintz 1985; Whit 1995, ch.3). Government-sanctioned slavery created much of the early capital of the imperial European powers by means of the triangular trade in sugar and slaves.

The nineteenth century brought many struggles for political independence throughout the developing world. These subsistence economies had already been reorganised as plantations, and they did not return to subsistence economic production. Instead, the pattern of ownership switched from colonialism to neo-colonialism. Instead of having British administrators (as in India), local governments ruled in name while private foreign companies employing local élites dominated the economies, especially the agricultural sector.

Instead of producing food for the local populations, imperial nations often employed local administrators to produce export crops. Tea (in India) and sugar (in the Caribbean) continued to be sent back to the imperial countries for processing. Thus developed a division of labour that characterise relations between the developed and the developing world to this day. Raw materials (which have lower profits) come from the developing world. The developed world imports raw materials and processes them. It is in the latter processes that the greater share of profit is to be found.

Andre Gunder Frank (1969) termed this process 'the development of underdevelopment', whereby the developed world essentially inhibits indigenous development and keeps the developing world producing raw materials for export. In those instances where food crops are processed locally, foreign stockholders generally own the processing companies so that profits are repatriated to the capitalist élites of the developed world.

The new development in the twentieth century has been the growth of transnational world oligopolies in food: 'Companies such as Cargill, Continental Grain (both American) and Bunge (Argentina), Dreyfus (France) and Andre-Garnac (Switzerland) have an almost total monopoly on the US grain trade' (Bennett & George 1987, p. 177).

It is important to recognise a pervasive pattern in the developed world's treatment of colonial and subsistence food production patterns. This pattern is analysed most extensively in the publications of the Institute for Food Development Policy, formerly headed by Frances Moore Lappe and Joseph Collins. Their 1977 book *Food First* traces the development of this pattern in country after country throughout the developing world. We shall refer to this analysis as the 'Lappe-Collins paradigm'.

According to this paradigm, multinational oligopolistic corporations enter a developing country in search of what all capitalists seek: high profits. Because most of the developing world is not highly industrial, the choice area of profit-generation is the agricultural sector. Whereas, before the oligopolists' entry, peasants may have been successfully producing the subsistence crops that they had always eaten, the newcomers now gain control over the land on which this production has taken place. In the best of cases, they buy it. But sometimes they simply employ local thugs to murder or move the owners (*The Politics of Food* 1987). Regardless, the company gains control of the land. Because the world market is their target, they decide to grow whatever agricultural commodity will sell the most profitably on the world market. It may be flowers for Europe, coffee for North America, or bananas, strawberries, sugar, vegetable oils, or oranges.

A most important need in the developed world is grain to feed cows. The beef of the developing world is a major part of the United States fast-food industry (Heller 1985). Because land in the developing world comes relatively cheap, there is little ecological concern. Although it is true of capitalist agriculture generally that it has tended to ruin the land (Whit 1995, ch.8), in the developing world the land has been even more exploited. In Costa Rica, a leading exporter of beef to the USA, land is overgrazed and therefore environmentally ruined. As a result, many administrators and local owners are cutting down rain forests to convert them to grazing land. Rain forests contain a large number of potential medical substances that have yet to be researched. R. W. Franke and B. H. Chasin report that one-quarter of Central American rain forests have been destroyed and only half a million of several million plant species have been saved: 'The relationship between ecological destruction and food production is ... direct and close. Whenever an environment is degraded, deprived of its basic resources—or even one of the key resources—the environment becomes part of the world food crisis, and the people who live there become its victims' (Franke & Chasin 1980, p. 4).

The lot of the original farmers is even more discouraging. Whereas a country may have previously had a stable rural labouring population, now they are displaced. Of those who choose to stay on the land, some are usually hired back to work for the corporation that now owns it. Because they no longer produce their own food, they must purchase food they previously produced. This practice often gets them further into debt. It is reminiscent of the system of debt peonage in the USA after the formal demise of slavery. Both the displaced and the remaining agricultural workers end up hungry. Displaced workers flee to the city as beggars, prostitutes, and thieves. Those workers who are employed by the new large-scale, capitalist farming enterprises usually make only subsistence wages, often not enough to even feed their families. And, if the international market decreases the value of their agricultural product, they become landless wanderers. This also happens when the soil is depleted from the use of farming technologies that are only geared to short-term profit.

The Lappe-Collins paradigm takes a variety of forms throughout the developing world. Different crops require different soil conditions. Sometimes the political structure is controlled to provide protection for capitalism (as in Chile after Allende, and in Nicaragua after the Sandinistas, for instance). Sometimes there is a need for more labour-intensive agriculture. But, as Lappe and Collins documented (1977), it applies as a paradigm in almost every country in the developing world.

In this context, food aid and financial aid are viewed somewhat more cynically. Unlike the liberal position, which understands aid as potentially helpful, Western neo-Marxist analysts are suspicious of Western aid. They note the political and economic debts that come with aid. And they note the manner in which such institutions as the World Bank generally sponsor agricultural endeavours that fit the Lappe-Collins paradigm of cash crops for export. This usually breeds dependency, poverty, and hunger in developing countries.

Modern Western neo-Marxist prescriptions vary. But generally they focus on food, security, and empowerment. They want people to be able, with the aid of appropriate, environmentally safe technology, to grow food for sustenance. They want to stop ecological destruction, especially of rain forests and areas adjacent to deserts. They want to develop local industry to process their own agricultural produce. If cash crops are produced and sold on the world market, western neo-Marxists want the profit to be used for the development of the country growing the crops, rather than shipped to the developed world or used by developing élites for luxuries.

Environmental concerns

Serious questions have been raised about the manner in which alleviating hunger may degrade the environment. Judged in absolute terms, pollution affects the developing world. But the question is: By what standard should one judge countries in the process of developing? From this perspective, the capitalist industrialised world is hardly blameless (see chapter 3). Pollution of early Western industrial cities is infamous. And today, as P. Idemudia and S. Kole write:

> Western populations (which make up only 16 percent of the world's population and 24 percent of its land) consume approximately 80 percent of the world's resources. In fact, the aver-

age North American consumes more energy commuting to work than the average African uses in an entire year. Furthermore, it is estimated that Western countries are responsible for producing over 75 percent of the world's environmental pollution (1994, p. 108).

Additionally, indigenous ('undeveloped') people were generally self-sufficient with regard to food without significant destruction of their environment. In fact, before the invention and use of petroleum-based fertilisers, pesticides, and herbicides, most food was organically grown. Traditional peoples were experts at maximising yield through intercropping, crop rotation, and labour-intensive planting, weeding, and harvesting. Fertiliser was organic and did not, for the most part, pollute.

V. Smil (1993) raises questions about environmental degradation resulting from development in China. There is no doubt that the Chinese use of soft coal and chemical fertilisers causes pollution. But these uses are layered on top of the self-sustaining agricultural practices of traditional Chinese agriculture. Such widespread practices as using (minimally processed) human excrement ('night soil') as fertiliser both recycle and decrease pollution. And the Chinese commitment to labour-intensive agriculture means that hand planting, weeding, and harvesting consumes significantly less inanimate energy sources. Box 2.2 discusses the situation in Cuba.

Relating to the environmental issue is the progress of the Asian newly industrialising countries: Taiwan, South Korea, Singapore, and Hong Kong. Their relatively recent development resulted from a combination of heavy United States subsidies as well as very active government involvement (such as in Japan) in the economic sphere—much like **socialism**. However, with recent United States demands that it be allowed to dump its surplus rice onto these markets, there are problems with food self-sufficiency.

Environmentally this State-directed, capitalist model has also had bad effects. In Taiwan, virgin and broadleaf forests are sacrificed, to be replaced by fast-growing conifers (Bello & Rosenfeld 1990, p. 195). Today, 'Taiwan is among the top users of chemical fertilizers per square inch in the world' (Bello & Rosenfeld 1990, p. 198). These heavy fertiliser applications contribute to 'soil acidification, zinc loss, and decline in soil fertility. Fertilizer overuse is a major contributor to water pollution … [and] has devastating

---

Box 2.2 Cuba

Cuba is an interesting example. Pushed into alliance with Eastern Europe by the USA, Cubans grew sugar and tobacco as part of the socialist division of labour. They used their petroleum subsidy to apply heavy coats of fertiliser and pesticides. However, with the demise of the socialist bloc and its petroleum subsidy, Cuba has embarked upon a combination of high biotechnology and traditional, labour-intensive ecological farming. Power for ploughing is predominantly derived from animals. Weeding is labour-intensive. And Cuban society recycles just about everything, from glass bottles to all paper products.

effects on surface waters ... [and] groundwater, which is the source of drinking water for many Taiwanese' (Bello & Rosenfeld 1990, p. 198).

This environmental destruction characterises many other countries following a capitalist path to development. In various forms, the Lappe-Collins paradigm details an orientation towards 'mining' rather than preserving the soil. Transnational companies can then move on to other soil, leaving the first decimated of nutrients and full of poisonous pollutants. It is undoubtedly true that all development seems to involve some environmental damage. Therefore, one should not focus on socialist developmental paths to the exclusion of other equally or more polluting countries.

Hunger amid plenty: the developed world

Fundamental to the discussion of hunger in the advanced, industrialised world is the distinction between destitution and poverty (or 'absolute' and 'relative' poverty). Destitution (absolute poverty) describes the lack of the basic necessities for life. Poverty is a relative concept. It refers to a situation in which a minimum of food is available. The food may not be of adequate quality or quantity compared with the norms of the society in which this poverty exists. And the social-psychological context of acquiring food may entail unacceptable rituals of degradation. 'Poverty' refers to inequality. Relative to what is normal, people in poverty have significantly less. What is new in contemporary societies is that today's poverty occurs in the context of a society that actually *could* provide adequate food for all.

Furthermore, poverty can serve certain functions for those in society who are not poor. The poor do menial jobs, buy damaged and outdated goods, are scape-goated as deviants, and provide jobs for a cadre of social workers (Gans 1972, pp. 22–5). From a more theoretical position, capitalist owners and stockholders have always benefited from what Marx termed the 'reserve army of the unemployed'. Having people in need of jobs forces people already in jobs to accept their lower wages. It makes their jobs less secure. Therefore, in spite of their rhetoric, governments of capitalist countries have generally been willing to tolerate a good deal of unemployment.

Parallelling my three positions on world hunger—conservative, liberal, and neo-Marxist—there are three comparable positions relating to domestic hunger in the capitalist industrialised world. The conservative position is characterised by the denial of real poverty and homelessness. Early in the Great Depression, the governments of the most developed countries tried to solve the new poverty through private efforts. Soup kitchens and private, voluntary charity were common to that era. Poor conditions were characterised as private troubles rather than public issues. Presently, according to G. Riches:

> the state has responded to the problem of hunger by denying its existence, by neglecting its legislated and public responsibilities, by framing the issue of welfare costs in terms of fraud and abuse and by 'blaming the victim.' [The state's position] ... is publicly to deny the hunger its policies are creating and to do whatever they can to depoliticize it as an issue. Unfortunately they are frequently aided in this process by the voluntary community (1997b, pp. 170–2).

From a liberal perspective, a fundamental dilemma exists between mobilising volunteers for direct feeding efforts and applying political pressure to change an advanced, industrial, capitalist system in a manner that would create institutional resources to actually solve domestic hunger and poverty. The Great Depression provided the first real challenge to the myth that all people who are able to work hard can earn enough to adequately feed themselves and their families. And, from a liberal perspective, the occasional anomaly of hunger should be approached in the context of not undermining the fundamental motivational structures of capitalist industrialism. Therefore, soup kitchens and breadlines sponsored by churches and private, voluntary welfare organisations provided the first defence against increasing (relative) poverty and hunger.

But ultimately, with 25 per cent unemployment in the USA, the national government began the process of constructing a social safety net. The 'New Deal' in the USA involved projects in which the government became the employer of last resort. Income from public service jobs (Public Law 320) allowed the purchase of food without undermining the profitability of the capitalist market. The food stamp program followed. After a 'rediscovery' of poverty and hunger in the 1960s, the USA has settled into a recent pattern that has eliminated parts of the social security network while maintaining the illusion that poverty and hunger (and homelessness) are not fundamental dynamics of the existing social system.

Contemporary neo-Marxists note that in the 1980s and 1990s, changes in the advanced capitalist industrial economy involved the automation and de-skilling of many manufacturing jobs, creating what has been termed the 'new American poverty'. As industry automates and de-skills, previously well-paid union workers are pushed into menial service jobs in the secondary labour market without benefits or security. There, with much less income, they constitute the new poor. The fast-food industry is a good example.

In addition, the world economy, aided by the North American Free Trade Agreement (NAFTA), allows manufacturing operations to move to developing countries, where the labour rates are significantly lower. As in the early stages of the Great Depression, food banks and soup kitchens stepped in to aid the domestic hungry. Across the industrialised world, a system of direct feeding (not income maintenance) has been employed. As Riches (1997a) writes: 'The story of hunger in late twentieth century Canada is directly related to the rise of charitable food banks as the primary institution providing emergency food assistance to those in need' (pp. 48–9). By 1991, Canada had 292 food banks, supplying 'over 1200 grocery programs and 580 meal programs in more than 300 communities' (p. 49). And J. Wilson writes: 'I think the future of food banks in Australia is, regrettably, one of continued expansion' (1997, p. 40).

Among Western neo-Marxists, there is a deep ambivalence about the role of voluntary associations in assuaging the social problem of hunger in an advanced, automated capitalist society. In addition to the problems of 'donor fatigue' and insufficient free food, such solutions avoid tackling the issue of the kind of social change that would guarantee citizens a *right to food*. By devoting energy to direct provisioning, food banks and soup kitchens take over functions that had been, and perhaps should be, provided by the State. Riches writes of food banks: 'Far from being an emergency response they have become an institutionalized extension of a failing public welfare system' and 'they are not solving the problem of hunger' (1997b, p. 173). Even more significant are reflections on the food systems of contemporary developed societies. According to Riches, with an international capitalist economy supplying the world's food:

> the real goal is local food security. This necessitates going beyond issues of social security reform and requires developing a comprehensive set of policies, focused on rethinking full employment, supporting green economic renewal, ... developing food self-reliance and understanding food policy as health promotion. It requires participatory, 'bottom-up' development informed by the principles and practices of community development with local food security as the primary objective (Toronto Food Policy Council 1994).

Conclusion

In conclusion, conservatives look on both world hunger and industrialised domestic hunger as natural and, in a sense, good. Like evolution, it weeds out the weak and rewards the strong. If people in the developed world begin with a significant head start, they are not to blame for that.

The liberal position is reformist and well intentioned, as well as self-serving. It wishes that the developed world would become altruistic and contribute enough money and social technology to bring an end to hunger while maintaining the essential viability of world capitalism. But the liberal position overlooks the stake the capitalist transnational corporations have in underdevelopment and dependency. Profit maximisers need hungry and needy people to perform low-paid tasks. And these lower paid workers, like the reserve army of the unemployed, put pressure on better paid workers to work without seriously questioning their own pay scale. Transnational corporations need developing-world land that can be inexpensively farmed ('mined') and where one need not take ecological considerations seriously. And they need the multitude of dictatorial and puppet regimes that the USA supports throughout the world to keep these countries safe for exploitation.

The Western neo-Marxist position is the only one that provides an adequate analysis of word hunger. But its solution would involve some variety of socialist (government-directed) development that guarantees all citizens food before undertaking the accumulation of capital required for development. China, Cuba, Sri Lanka, and the Indian democratic socialist state of Kerala provide a range of examples.

In the developed world, Scandinavia shines. It proves that socialistic orientations can work in this context. As Riches concludes, 'the social democratic Scandinavian welfare states have shown that hunger need not exist' (1997b, p. 178). Even with some degree of socialism, it remains an open question whether rapid economic development can be accomplished without disregarding the environment. If that issue is not solved relatively soon, there may be little future development for anyone.

Summary of main points

- World hunger exists in a world that produces enough food for everyone.
- Though variously defined, hunger can be identified by degrees of undernourishment, including vitamin and mineral deficiencies and protein or calorie malnutrition.
- World hunger has different appearances through different conceptual lenses. Conservatives are inclined to tolerate or even approve of world hunger. Liberals want to reform what they regard as basically sound institutions to ameliorate world hunger. Western neo-Marxists want to change society fundamentally to successfully eliminate world hunger.
- Though newly developing countries affect the environment negatively, their pollution is not even close to what the previously industrialised world produced and continues to produce.
- Be it in developed Scandinavia or developing Cuba, Kerala, and China, socialist priorities have made it possible for all citizens to obtain an adequate diet of basic foodstuffs.

Discussion questions

1 How do conservatives look at world hunger?
2 What are the limits of the liberal reformist view of world hunger?
3 Is it possible to maintain a capitalist economic system and feed the hungry?
4 Is world capitalism the root cause of world hunger?
5 What is the relationship between hunger in the developing world and hunger in the developed world?

Further reading and resources

Danaher, K. (ed.) 1994, *50 Years is Enough: The Case Against the World Bank and the International Monetary Fund*, South End Press, Boston.
Franke, R. W. & Chasis, B. H. 1991, *Karala*, Institute for Food and Development, San Francisco.
Lappe, F. M., Collins, J., & Rosset, P. 1998, *World Hunger: Twelve Myths*, 2nd edn, Grove Press, New York.
McIntosh, W. M. A. 1996, *Sociologies of Food and Nutrition*, Plenum Press, New York.

Journal and website
New Internationalist:<http://www.oneworld.org/ni/>

Video
The Politics of Food 1987 (Yorkshire Television, Leeds, four 52-minute episodes). A critical analysis of world hunger, aid, and development.

References

Banfield, E. C. 1974, *The Unheavenly City Revisited*, Little Brown & Co., Boston.

Bello, W. & Rosenfeld, S. 1990, *Dragons in Distress*, Institute for Food and Policy, San Francisco.

Bennett, J. & George, S. 1987, *The Hunger Machine: The Politics of Food*, Polity Press, London.

Bryant, C., Courtney, A., Markesbery, B., & DeWalt, K. 1985, *The Cultural Feast*, West, New York.

Buchanan, A. 1982, *Food, Poverty, and Power*, Spokesman, Nottingham.

Cassidy, C. 1982, 'Protein-Energy Malnutrition: A Culture Bound Syndrome', *Culture, Medicine and Psychiatry*, vol. 6, pp. 325–48.

Chen, R. 1990, 'The State of Hunger in 1990', *The Hunger Report*, 1–26 June.

Crossgrove, W., Egilman, P. H., & Kasperson, J. 1990, 'Colonialism, International Trade and the Nation State', in L. F. Newman, W. Cosgrove, R. Kates, R. Mattew, & S. Millman (eds), *Hunger in History*, Basil Blackwell, Cambridge.

Dreze, J. & Sen, A. 1989, *Hunger and Public Action*, The Clarendon Press, Oxford.

Frank, A. G. 1969, *Latin America: Underdeveloped or Revolution*, Modern Reader, New York.

Franke, R. W. & Chasin, B. H. 1980, *Seeds and Famine: Ecological Destruction and the Development Dilemma in the West African Sahel*, Universe Books, New York.

Gans, H. 1996 (1972), 'The Positive Functions of Poverty', in G. Massed (ed.), *Readings For Sociology*, W.W. Norton, New York.

Hardin, G. 1978, 'Lifeboat Ethics: The Case Against Helping the Poor', in J. D. Gussow (ed.), *The Feeding Web*, Bull Publishing, Berkeley, Calif.

Heller, P. 1985, *Hamburger I: Macprofit*, video documentary, Icarus Films, New York.

Hinrichs, C. C. 1988, Attaining Food Self Sufficiency: The Contrasting Cases of India and China, paper presented at the Association for the Study of Food and Society Conference, Chevy Chase, Md, 27–29 May.

Idemudia, P. & Kole, S. 1994, 'World Bank Takes Control of UNCED's Environmental Fund', in K. Danaher (ed.), *50 Years is Enough: The Case Against the World Bank and the International Monetary Fund*, South End Press, Boston.

Kutzner, P. (1990) 'World Hunger: What Have We Learned?' *Hunger Notes*, vol. 16, pp. 1–2.

Lappe, F. M. & Collins, J. 1977, *Food First: Beyond the Myth of Scarcity*, Houghton Mifflin, Boston.

—— 1986, *World Hunger: Twelve Myths*, Grove Press, New York.

Lenski, G. & Lenski, J. 1982, *Human Societies*, McGraw-Hill, New York.

Mellor, J. 1990, 'Ending Hunger: An Implementable Program for Self Reliant Growth', in H. Baaker (ed.), *The World Food Crisis*, Canadian Scholars Press, Toronto.

Millman, S. 1991, *The Hunger Report: Update 1991*, Alan Shawn Feinstein World Hunger Program, Providence.

Millman, S. & Wikates, R. 1990, 'Toward Understanding Hunger', in L. Newman, W. Cosgrove, R. Kates, R. Mattew, & S. Millman (eds), *Hunger in History*, Basil Blackwell, Cambridge, pp. 3–8.

Mintz, S. 1985, *Sweetness and Power*, Viking Penguin, New York.

Morgan, D. 1980, *Merchants of Grain*, Penguin Books, New York.

Phillips, T. & Taylor, D. 1990, 'Food Insecurity: Dynamics and Alleviation', in H. Baaker (ed.), *The World Food Crisis*, Canadian Scholars Press, Toronto, pp. 61–96.

The Politics of Food 1987, four 52-minute episodes, Yorkshire Television, Leeds.

Riches, G. 1997a, 'Hunger in Canada: Abandoning the Right to Food', in G. Riches (ed.), *First World Hunger*, Macmillan, London, pp. 46–77.

—— 1997b, 'Hunger, Welfare and Food Security: Emerging Strategies', in G. Riches (ed.), *First World Hunger*, Macmillan, London, pp. 165–78.

Scrimshaw, N. 1990, 'World Nutritional Problems', in L. Newman, W. Cosgrove, R. Kates, R. Mattew, & S. Millman (eds), *Hunger in History*, Basil Blackwell, Cambridge, pp. 353–73.

Seavoy, R. 1986, *Famine in Peasant Societies*, Greenwald Press, New York.

Smil, V. 1993, *China's Environmental Crisis*, M. E. Sharpe, New York.

USDA 1985, *Agricultural Outlook*, Government Printing Office, Washington, DC, December.

Whit, W. 1995, *Food and Society: A Sociological Approach*, General Hall, New York.

Wilson, J. 1997, 'Australia: Lucky Country/Hungry Silence', in G. Riches (ed.), *First World Hunger*, Macmillan, London, pp. 14–35.

3

Food and the Environment

Terry Leahy

Overview

- *In what ways do current agricultural practices damage the environment?*

- *Why does the economic system exacerbate the degradation of the environment?*

- *Is permaculture a viable solution for the creation of an environmentally sustainable system of agriculture?*

Modern agriculture is unsustainable. In developed countries problems are caused by monoculture, ploughing, fertilisers, pesticides, overgrazing, tree-clearing, irrigation, the use of fossil fuels, and packaging. Nevertheless, all these unsustainable farming practices make sense economically. It would be difficult to make an equal amount of profit by farming more sustainably. In developing countries the ecological problems of farming are exacerbated by export agriculture, which produces luxury foods for rich countries. In these countries as well, farming to produce maximum profit is at the expense of the environment. The bad environmental effects of farming can be reduced by State regulation and community action. Ultimately, however, sustainable farming is only possible through a radical restructuring of the global economy. This is because the competitive ownership of farming land in capitalist societies means that profit has to come before environmental considerations. Another factor is that consumers in capitalist society demand cheap luxury food products as compensation for the more unpleasant aspects of working life in a capitalist economy.

Key terms

alienated workers
alternative lifestyle/new age
capitalist/capitalist society
cash crops
colonial period
commodity/commodity production
commodity economy
community farms
community-supported agriculture
competitive private ownership
developed world/developing world
gift economy
global capitalist class
global consuming class
global poor
greenhouse effect
monoculture
niche market
non-government organisations (NGOs)
organic
polyculture
permaculture
subsistence production

Introduction

As we humans of the planet Earth go about producing and consuming our food, we set in train a long list of environmental problems. When I say that these are 'problems', I mean that they are problems for us people or that they are problems for the rest of life on Earth. What we are doing is unsustainable because the environmental damage we are causing reduces the productivity of the land for future agriculture uses, making it harder and harder for us to live well. Further, what we are doing is drastically reducing the opportunities for other forms of life to flourish on our planet. What sociology can offer is the insight that these problems develop as a consequence of specific social structures. It is not 'us' as a mass of individuals, or even 'us' meaning the whole of society, that creates environmental problems. These problems come about as the result of our relationships with each other—relationships of class, economy, work, and power. Very often environmental damage is a totally unintended by-product of these relationships. One of the main points considered in this chapter is that the patterns of food consumption that cause environmental problems are in many ways created by the structures of the **capitalist** economy, both locally and globally.

Environmental problems and food production

It is possible to set out some of the ways in which current practices of food production damage the environment. I will pay most attention to the situation in the affluent **developed world** (see chapter 2 on world hunger for detail on developing countries). The following examples are by no means exhaustive but give us some idea of the scope of the problems.

In the developed countries

The term 'monoculture' is used when a particular area of land is used to produce a single crop. When the farming industry is based on large pieces of land serviced by machinery and cheap fuel, monocultural production is usually more efficient (cheaper), than a system of cropping in which a variety of crops are grown together. However, monocultures have undesirable environmental effects. First, a monocultural crop is the perfect environment for a pest or disease species to develop; it spreads easily and has the potential to destroy all the produce of the farm (Lawrence & Vanclay 1992, p. 53; Watson 1992). To prevent this, toxic pesticides are used. These cause some damage to human health and also kill off microbes, earthworms, insects and animals which can actually aid food production. Wild animals are also poisoned by eating insects toxified by pesticides (Henderson 1990, p. 33; Thomas & Kevan 1993). Pests develop resistance to the pesticides that are being used. The crop may be unable to be grown at all, or even more toxic pesticides could be used (Henderson 1990; Lawrence & Vanclay 1992; Lloyd 1997).

Environmentalists generally recommend the development of a **polyculture**, where a mixed variety of foods are grown together. If pest species do cause a problem, it is then confined to only some crops. The rest flourish. Pests are not easily transmitted between small pockets of the same crop grown in places separated by other plants. If any pesticides are used, they should be **organic** sprays, which are not harmful to most life forms. Furthermore, crops chosen for a particular location should be ones that flourish so successfully that pests cannot spoil the crop (Mollison & Holmgren 1978; Mollison 1988; Watson 1992; Morrow 1993). For example, in Australia we grow cotton as our main plant fibre crop and cause vast amounts of environmental damage spraying the crops to prevent insect damage. Cotton is our main fibre crop because it is very profitable to grow. However hemp, linen, and silk are all natural fibres that can be produced in Australia without the use of toxic chemicals.

Companion planting can deal with pest problems. A specific plant is grown that is a companion to another desired species. This controls the pests of the second species. For example, fennel and borage are herbs that host wasp species that attack caterpillars. They can be grown as companions to vegetable species that suffer from attack by caterpillars. Animals can also be used to control pests. Hens can eat fruit fly larva. Ducks can devour snails (French 1993; Morrow 1993; Mollison 1988).

Often the problem is that we are too fussy about pest infestation in food. Some toxic sprays in Australia are used on fruit to prevent fruit fly. Organic methods of control are labour intensive, but they do work (French 1993). However, they cannot guarantee a crop that is free of fruit fly larva. So such methods may be adequate for the home gardener but fail for the farm produce merchant who supplies supermarkets.

Methods of organic pest control and polycultural production work well in a system of farming in which people grow food for their local neighbourhood and have plenty of time to pick, plant, and maintain plants by hand. For farmers who are saving costs through mass-production **monoculture** and the labour-saving that comes with ploughing and harvesting machinery, the polyculture solution to pest problems seems unrealistic. Monocultures and toxic pesticides make sense in terms of commercial agriculture, as it has been developed to market cheap agricultural produce to anonymous consumers (Lawrence & Vanclay 1992, pp. 52–3). Consumers have little knowledge or experience of the problems caused by the pesticides used to produce their food. The only choices they make to keep this system in operation are to buy the cheapest foods. They reject with horror any foods that show evidence of pest attack.

Ploughing with machinery is a technology that saves on labour costs and suits monocultural production. A central use is the production of carbohydrate crops. Indigenous economies often depended for carbohydrates on a mix of root crops, fruits, and nuts. Modern agriculture produces most carbohydrate through production in ploughed fields—rice, wheat, corn, and potatoes (Gardner 1996). This technology has serious effects on soil quality. The continual turning of soil destroys the micro-organisms that create soil fertility. Ploughed fields are very susceptible to erosion, in which rain washes away topsoil. The constant use of heavy machinery packs the soil down and creates an infertile hard pan (Thomas & Kevan 1993; Gardner 1996). So monocultural production of cereals and potatoes through ploughing is unsustainable. The soil is being removed year by year. For example, in Australia's top wheat-growing areas, 13 tonnes of soil is lost through erosion for every tonne of wheat produced (Lawrence & Vanclay 1992, p. 40). In the early 1980s, farms in the USA were losing an average of 10 tonnes of soil per acre each year. Globally, soil is being lost to erosion at the rate of 5 tonnes per person per year (Trainer 1995, p. 18; see also Watson 1992, p. 21; Gardner 1996).

Commercial agriculture makes considerable use of artificial fertilisers such as super-phosphates. Chemical fertilisers destroy micro-organisms that normally create soil fertility and humus. They are a short-term solution that exacerbates the problems of soil infertility. Furthermore, soluble fertiliser is washed into waterways and causes a problem of nutrient overload. The fertiliser in the water provides nutrient on which algae can grow. The prolif-eration of algae uses up oxygen in the water, and so other forms of organic life, such as water-weeds, fishes, and insects, all die. The algae can themselves be poisonous. In Australia we have had years in which the whole of the Darling River was polluted with blue-green algae, poisonous to stock, fish, wild animals, and human populations (Lawrence & Vanclay 1992; Thomas & Kevan 1993; Vanclay & Lawrence 1995; Gardner 1996).

Artificial fertilisers are used for two reasons. The first is to force the maximum pro-ductivity out of any given piece of land in a given year, whatever the long-term effects. The second is that they are cheaper than the organic farming methods of enhancing soil fertility. Methods such as crop rotation, growing living mulch and slashing it, the use of animal manure, planting of tree legumes, or earthworks to increase the water retention of soils all create soil fertility. But they are expensive in terms of labour or machinery and may require the resting of fields from production (Lawrence & Vanclay 1992; Thomas & Kevan 1993). As Frank Vanclay and Geoffrey Lawrence also point out, alternative approaches all involve a considerable investment in skills and knowledge, which is itself expensive (Vanclay & Lawrence 1995; Campbell 1996).

Another cause of nutrient overload is manure being washed into waterways by con-centrations of stock close to the water. This problem is severe where animals are kept in feedlots. The use of feedlots is becoming increasingly common with the increasing demand in the Asian and American markets for beef that is 'marbled' with streaks of fat. This effect can only be produced by feeding cattle with grain in feedlots (Vanclay & Lawrence 1995). There is a separation between markets of consumers, who merely pre-fer a particular food product, entrepreneurs, who supply and promote this product, and farmers, who operate at the site of the ecological damage.

Large animals grown for meat generally cause environmental problems. Overgrazing is a common response to the pressure to produce profits in any given year, although, over time, it reduces productivity (Watson 1992; Brown 1990). Too many sheep or cat-tle pack the soil down hard, destroying soil aeration and killing soil micro-organisms, leaving a hard crust that grows little fodder. Rain water does not readily penetrate the crust, leading to further loss of soil fertility. The overgrazed, exposed soil easily washes away. These problems are rampant in Australian grazing lands but also in other coun-tries such as the USA. They are less prevalent in Europe, where heavy rainfall and deep soils maintain good soil quality despite centuries of grazing (Thomas & Kevan 1993;

Crosby 1986). Ultimately all grazing is parasitic, relying on the humus built up in a previous epoch when the land was forested with trees. Overgrazing, tree removal, and ploughing for cereals by the imperial civilisations of the Ancient World have already led to the desertification of vast areas of the Mediterranean, Africa, and the Middle East. Australia and the Americas are following close behind since the expansion of European farming practices into these continents (Crosby 1986).

Salinity is a common environmental problem resulting from today's farming practices. For example, in Australia 800 000 hectares of agricultural land is affected by salinity, and this area is growing constantly (Watson 1992, p. 19). Salinity problems are linked to irrigation and land clearing. With irrigation, a constant supply of water into dry soils causes the water table to rise. Moisture under the soil rises closer and closer to the surface. Salts that have been trapped in the dry soils are dissolved and rise to the surface. The result is a salt pan, which inhibits the growth of plants. This effect is extremely hard to reverse. The irrigated area becomes a useless desert (Lawrence & Vanclay 1992; Thomas & Kevan 1993). In Australia 1.5 million hectares of land is irrigated, most of it unsustainably (Watson 1992, p. 21).

Where land has been cleared, a similar problem arises. Higher areas of land are known as up-take areas. Water falling on these higher areas is taken into the soil and travels down the slope. Here it causes the water table to rise, bringing salt to the surface. This salty area of low ground becomes poisonous to most plant life. Before clearing, this salinisation process was prevented by deep-rooted tree species. These trees made use of water falling on the higher ground, bringing it up from their roots, releasing it as vapour into the air, and storing it in their foliage. So clearing higher ground for pasture or cereal crops is unsustainable. The effect is to reduce the area in which useful plants can be grown (Lawrence & Vanclay 1992).

There is a commercial angle to these issues. Irrigated land is very profitable for a short period before problems of salinity develop. Clearing higher slopes for pasture or cereal crops is also profitable, as it increases the area that can be farmed—in the short run. Once salinity develops, it is expensive to reverse the process. Up-take areas have to be replanted with deep-rooted trees or perennial shrubs (plants that live for a number of years). The cost of planting and fencing off so that animals do not destroy the young seedlings is considerable. The low areas affected by salting also have to be fenced off and planted out with species that will take up water and can tolerate the salty conditions (Watson 1992, p. 20; Meredith 1995).

Ecological problems are not confined to the paddock. Ploughs and harvesters use fossil fuels (such as oil, gas, and coal). The transport and storage of food also uses fossil fuels, which in the long term are a scarce and irreplaceable resource. Moreover, all use of fossil fuels contributes to the **greenhouse effect** (Thomas & Kevan 1993). Today, many more calories of energy are used to produce fertilisers, to run farm machinery, and to transport and store food than are present in the food itself. In traditional rice cultivation, 1 calorie of human energy produces 20 calories of food energy. In corn production in the USA today, 1 calorie of energy (mostly from fossil fuels) is used to produce 1 calorie of corn, and 20 calories of energy produces 1 calorie of food energy in beef (Bennett & George 1987, p. 34).

The most ecologically sensible way to distribute food is to produce almost all food in the local neighbourhood and distribute it either as gifts or through bartering or small local shops. That way, food is produced within walking distance and does not have to be stored and refrigerated (Trainer 1995). However, within a system of commercial agriculture, the present far-flung distribution of food makes perfect economic sense. Consumers are encouraged to buy foods produced in different climates and sent over long distances. The average distance that food has travelled to reach the plate of a United States resident is 2000 kilometres (Durning 1991, p. 159). For a large food conglomerate, producing a uniform product and distributing it over a large area is cheaper than local marketing of all the different products that a local area can produce. We end up with the ridiculous situation in which bananas from Coffs Harbour in northern New South Wales are sent 550 kilometres to Sydney to be bought by big food conglomerates and redistributed back to Coffs Harbour to be sold. The only decision made by consumers is that of adding a particular food to their supermarket trolleys if they can afford it. The company has already centralised the production and distribution of all its food products so that pricing is uniform wherever the food is purchased.

Packaging of food also makes sense in economic terms but causes environmental problems. The two factors producing excessive packaging are long-distance transport of food and competition between businesses to attract consumers. Consumers merely choose the most attractive packet on the shelf and develop commercially useful brand loyalties to particular products. In doing this they are part of a system in which unnecessary mountains of plastic, aluminium, and paper products are manufactured and distributed, ending up as a waste problem.

In developing countries

As noted above, issues relevant to the **developing world** are covered in detail in chapter 2. Here I will summarise some of the environmental problems associated with food in developing countries. Peasant and tribal **subsistence production** of food has been replaced by food production for the international market (Bennett & George 1987; Trainer 1994). A wealthy landlord or business class usually monopolises land. On the land used to produce **cash crops** for the international market, environmental problems are similar to the problems caused by commercial agriculture in developed countries— for example, erosion caused by ploughing for monoculture crops, toxic pollution caused by fertilisers, herbicides, and pesticides, soil destruction from overgrazing, and so on. As in developed countries, these problems are caused by competition between businesses to produce the cheapest food products on the international market. An effect of the change-over to cash crops is that former subsistence farmers are often driven off the best land. Ted Trainer estimates that 80 per cent of land in developing countries is owned by 3 per cent of the population (Trainer 1994; p. 17; see also Bennett & George 1987; George 1988; Trainer 1995).

Displaced subsistence farmers either starve, try to find some employment in towns, or remain in rural areas. They may become unemployed and be driven to eke out a subsistence by clearing less productive and previously forested land. The environmental effect is that areas of high biodiversity are destroyed by farming. Often soil erosion or leaching of nutrients makes these effects virtually irreversible (George 1988; Pearce et al. 1990; Fargher & Cadaweng 1990; Boyce 1993; Trainer 1994).

Hunger is a common experience for peasant farmers who are not part of the wealthy landlord èlite. It is estimated that one billion of the world's six billion people do not receive sufficient food (Trainer 1994). One response to this insecurity is for parents to have as many children as possible. They hope that at least some of them will survive to provide for them in old age (Bennett & George 1987). While pre-colonial societies had stable populations, increasing population is the norm in developing countries. Currently, while the rate of population increase has slowed, the world's population is still growing (Woodford 1997).

As a result of these processes, more and more areas where humans have previously had little impact are being destroyed to make way for farming, timber extraction, roads, cities, and mining. It is doubly wrong to blame these problems on the developing world. Increasing population in developing countries is a response to food insecurity— caused by the takeover of land for cash cropping for a global market. Much of the land that is being developed at the expense of wildlife is used to grow luxury crops for wealthy consumers in rich countries. So if there is overpopulation, it is really an overpopulation of rich consumers.

One way of looking at this is to consider how much land is used by wealthy consumers to support their lifestyle and how much of this land is outside their own countries. For example 'a Dutch person's consumption of food, wood, natural fibres, and other products of the soil involves exploitation of five times as much land outside the country as inside' (Durning 1991, p. 156). Africa, which is a country in which famines and droughts often claim lives, actually has more cultivated land per person than the USA, but much of Africa's land is used for export crops (Trainer 1995). During the 1984 drought, Zimbabwe and Kenya imported 65 000 tons of maize to feed their hungry populations. At the same time, Zimbabwe produced a record crop of tobacco, soybeans, and cotton for export, while Kenya produced a huge harvest of asparagus and strawberries (Bennett & George 1987).

Commodities such as rubber, sugar, tea, coffee, and meat are all grown in developing countries—to the detriment of areas in which wild animals and plants were formerly dominant. Sixteen million hectares of coffee, tea, and cocoa are grown for export in developing countries (Trainer 1995). Annually, 200 million pounds of meat is exported to the USA from Central America—mostly grown on land that was recently tropical rainforest (Trainer 1995; see also Barnaby 1988; Pearce et al. 1990; Revkin 1990; Trainer 1994). Tropical timbers are also logged unsustainably. These are all luxury crops; wealthy consumers could do without them. However, the only decision made by these consumers is to purchase an available product from a developing country. The destruction of the environment that has made that decision possible is not a choice made by those consumers.

Solutions to environmental problems in developing countries require time, effort, and money. In a world where wealth is very unevenly distributed, there are few resources left to deal with these problems (Trainer 1985, 1991, 1994, 1995). For those of us in the rich countries, our affluence is bought at the expense of environmental destruction—both in the countries in which we live and in the rest of the world.

Fishing

Overfishing is a problem of current food production. In many parts of the world, fish stocks have plummeted. From Newfoundland to Norway, cod has virtually vanished from the seas. Chile and Peru, which used to harvest huge crops of anchovies, have had to close down this industry. In 1996, thirteen of the world's fifteen leading oceanic fisheries were in decline (Brown 1996; see also Trainer 1994). This overuse of fish stocks is a disaster from the point of view of sustainability and biodiversity. Marine animals are being fished to the point of extinction. Technologies such as drift nets and long lines also imperil marine animals that are not sought for food. Dolphins, turtles, and sharks are caught in drift nets, and albatrosses are hooked on long lines. These problems are caused by the commercialisation of fishing for an international market. Half of all the world's fish catch goes to produce fish meal for farm animals and fish dinners for pets in rich countries (Trainer 1995).

Food and deep ecology

Deep ecology is an ethical perspective that validates the moral claims of other species. In terms of this ethic, current food production is problematic. Many of the practices of animal production are cruel—such as keeping hens and pigs in cages, or cattle in feedlots. The amount of land taken up by humans for farms, industry, or urban space is at the expense of other species on the planet. Humans now make use of almost 40 per cent of the photosynthetic activity on the world's land (Brown 1990). Increasing numbers of species are becoming extinct (Brown 1990; Thomas & Kevan 1993; Brown 1996). Even where species are maintaining their existence, numbers have been reduced to the point where species are unlikely to continue evolving through the free development of new varieties by mutation(Foreman 1991; Watson 1992). The combination of human population level and resource use is costly in terms of biodiversity.

How these problems are related to the economic and political structures of global capitalism

In each of the points covered above I have begun to show how the ecological problems of food production are related to existing economic and political structures. There are three basic classes in today's world. First, there is the **global capitalist class,** which in wealthy countries owns more than 90 per cent of shares in companies. This class

accounts for between about 5 per cent and 10 per cent of the population of these affluent countries. It is about 2 per cent of the global population as a whole (Giddens 1989,
p. 217; Waters & Crook 1990, p. 159). The next class comprises the affluent middle class
of all countries and the relatively affluent working class of the **developed world**.
These people are the **global consuming class**. They make up probably about 20 per
cent of the world's population—one billion people. For example the richest 20 per
cent of the world's people consume an average per capita of gross national product that
is forty-six times higher than the average per capita of gross national product consumed
by the poorest half. This rich 20 per cent consumes 80 per cent of the world's production of natural resources such as steel, rubber, and energy (Trainer 1994, p. 3). Finally,
the rest of the world's population are the **global poor**. A large proportion of these
people—approximately one billion—do not get enough food to maintain an adequate
diet. Each of these three groups have a role in causing the ecological problems of food
production. It is the interaction between these groups that creates the problems.

Before the **colonial period**, most land in developing countries was used for subsistence production, either by peasants or by tribal owners—horticulturalists or hunters
and gatherers. This means that crops were not sold on the market. Food was consumed
by the producer, given to kin and community groups, bartered with other producers, or
sent as tribute to landlords. Now, most land is being used to produce food for the **commodity economy**—that is, food that is sold for cash. Small-scale owners of land have
come to depend on this cash income for their livelihood. Unsustainable farming practices come about because such landowners are in competition with larger companies
and other small farmers to produce as cheaply as possible, and to produce whatever is
most profitable, regardless of whether it is ultimately the best thing to grow to sustain
their land.

Larger owners produce food for a global market. Effectively, much land is controlled
by the global rich and is used for cash crops. These are exported for consumption by
the affluent consumer class, usually located in developed countries. The rich either own
this land outright or control the process of farming and the distribution and marketing
of the produce. For example, multinational companies own 85 per cent of the world's
cocoa production, 90 per cent of tobacco, 85 per cent of tea, 90 per cent of coffee, and
60 per cent of sugar (Bennett & George 1987, p.38; see also Lappe 1975; Trainer 1995).
Ecological problems come about because this land is farmed unsustainably or because
this land has been converted from forests or woodlands to its present use. The transport
and packaging of cash crops exported from developing countries is itself an ecological
problem. For shareholders in the transnational companies that manage this farming,
environmental controls interfere with profits. Shareholders respond to any loss of profitability by moving their shares to another company or by moving their company to
another country.

The subsistence peasantry or tribal people who are displaced by these changes may
move onto marginal land to grow subsistence crops, damaging the ecosystems of land
previously used sustainably to provide forest resources. Some are employed as farm

workers in the cash-crop industry. Often the wages of both urban and rural workers in the developing world are insufficient for subsistence. Wages are supplemented by subsistence agriculture. This additional subsistence agriculture is also putting pressure on local ecologies.

In the developed world, small-scale farming is being replaced by the use of land by large conglomerates. For example, in Australia in 1988, 'five of Australia's top agricultural exporters were Japanese trading houses which sent abroad, in one year, approximately $7 billion of unprocessed food and fibre' (Lawrence & Vanclay 1992, p. 47). At the same time, international competition to provide farm products at the lowest possible prices squeezes small farmers and large companies alike. In developed countries with high wages, the effect is to reduce human labour in farming—through the use of fertilisers, farm machinery, monocultural production, and toxic pesticides. For investors, the spending of company money on a more sustainable mode of farming would merely cause a reduction in the profitability of their shares. Managers know that they cannot afford to take such risks. For small owner-operated farms, the price of environmental repair is too high. Farm income is barely enough to make ends meet. For example, in the 1991/92 financial year, an average farmer in the Murray Darling Basin (on the eastern coast of Australia) only got a net farm income of A$2100 (Lawrence & Vanclay 1992; see also Vanclay & Lawrence 1995).

For a government in the developed world, a serious investment in environmental repair and restructuring of the farm industry could be achieved in one of two ways. First, regulations could force changes on the industry. However, then the profitability of farming would drop as farm owners had to pay to conform to the regulations. There would be a fall in export earnings from the farming sector, and farm products would also cost more on the local market. Both these changes would damage the economy as a whole. Alternatively, tax-payers could fund this restructuring, which seems an unlikely prospect at present. If the high-tax alternative was implemented, the money paid by consumers in higher taxes would be diverted from other industries that supply the consumer goods that tax-payers now buy. There would be a decrease in consumer demand as taxes went up.

Either way, this investment in rural restructuring would be at the expense of the profitability of the economy. It would decrease the amount of farm produce that could be sold on the market or make it more expensive to produce. Drawing on research by Lawrence and Vanclay, I will take the Murray-Darling Basin as an example (Lawrence & Vanclay 1992). The basin produces one third of Australia's farm products. The value of its annual production is about A$10 billion (Lawrence & Vanclay 1992). Most of the basin's products are exported, which means that the area makes a strong contribution to Australia's overseas earnings. Seventy per cent of exports from Australia are bulk agricultural commodities, which shows just how important this sector is to Australia's economy as a whole (Lawrence & Vanclay 1992). For this area alone, essential environmental repair would cost between A$2 billion and A$3 billion (Lawrence & Vanclay 1992). So such repairs would make a large dent in earnings from the farm products of the basin. The environmental problems of the basin are typical of the situation in Australia as a whole and in all developed countries. In no country could essential environmental repairs be carried out without drastic effects on the economy.

Governments are aware of the environmental perils of the present situation. Present agriculture is gradually destroying farm land in developed countries. The eventual result must be disastrous for the farming industry and the economy alike (Lawrence & Vanclay 1992). Caught between these pressures, governments make some effort to support sustainable land use, but it is far from adequate to deal with the problems.

The affluent consumers of the global market play a fundamental role in these problems. Since the middle of the nineteenth century, capitalism has depended on sales of mass-produced consumer goods to the employed populations of industrial countries. With increases in productivity caused by new technologies, the provision of consumer goods to the populations of wealthy countries has steadily increased. Since the Second World War there has been a quantum leap in consumption by ordinary people in the affluent countries.

These consumers buy the food that is the cheapest or that fits their desire for luxury goods. They have little knowledge of the ecological effects of food production. They are reluctant to pay more or to restrict their choices by buying only organic produce, only free range meat, less meat, only food that is locally produced, only food supplied in bulk in reusable jars or in paper bags without labels, and so on.

One approach would be to castigate these consumers for their wasteful consumption and their ignorance of the environmental consequence of their choices. But this moral approach does not look at the reasons why wasteful and ignorant consumption comes to appear necessary and attractive. Affluent consumers are also **alienated workers** (Marx 1978a, 1978b; Cardan 1974; Willis 1990). Using this concept from Marx, I want to indicate that affluent consumers have to get a paid job to live. As employees they have no control of what they produce, no control over who gets the products of their work, and no control over the conditions of their work. So work is perceived as a burden rather than as a creative and sociable pleasure. Historically, the workers in developed countries have used their power as trade unionists and voters. They have forced the employing class to pay them more and more to compensate for the experience of alienated labour. The capitalist class has accepted this increase in consumer spending power. It has provided continually expanding markets to soak up expanding industrial production (Cardan 1974). It is through consumption that affluent workers exercise choice and freedom. It is in their leisure that they express their creative and social capacities.

All this ties into the way that affluent consumers look at food. Expensive, well-packaged, and luxurious food seems the appropriate moral reward for a life of thankless labour. Within the context of a puritanical culture, food is one of the few morally legitimate pleasures (Pont 1997). In fact, the foods that are transported from developing countries—at great cost to the environment—are regarded as the epitome of luxury and morality. Meat and dairy products are seen as an appropriate reward for hard masculine labour and as necessary for healthy growth (see chapter 6); sugar is seen as a sweet pleasure and an apt reward for appropriate femininity; coffee, tea, and chocolate are all stimulating but legitimate drugs, aids to concentration at work or a reward after work. Elaborate and decorative packaging, flawless food products untainted by pest attacks, and a wide range of foods from every place on the globe are seen as rewards that affluent consumers deserve in return for all their hard work.

It is these factors that make it difficult to get consumers to direct their food purchasing habits to environmental ends. Also, these factors make it unlikely that affluent consumers would willingly embrace tough environmental regulation of farming and trade. These regulations would inevitably mean that consumers would pay more for food or have less choice of foods.

It can be argued that urbanisation is a factor that distances urban consumers from the environmental consequences of food production in distant farms and in other countries. It is certainly true that the removal of most affluent consumers from direct experience of farming allows people to forget the environmental impact of food production. However, this urbanisation and separation is itself to be explained in terms of the requirements of the capitalist economy and consumers. It makes sense economically to separate farms from affluent cities so that cheap labour or large machinery can be readily employed. It makes sense culturally for consumers, as alienated workers, to want luxuries from far off as compensation for alienated work. This separation is not a technical imperative of efficient farming. As environmentalists point out, cities could be reorganised to grow their own food locally, and city dwellers could be responsible for this local production (Trainer 1995).

Are there any solutions?

Based on the evidence already presented, there are clearly serious ecological problems in the way that we produce and consume our food. There are no easy solutions to these problems. I have explained the reasons why intervention in agriculture is a difficult option for governments in developed countries. At the same time, pressure to regulate and subsidise agriculture for environmental benefits makes sense in any country. Alternative and more radical strategies are also worth consideration.

Permaculture

Permaculture is an agricultural technology that offers a solution to the ecological problems of current farming practices. The term 'permaculture' was coined by Bill Mollison and David Holmgren to mean a system of permanent agriculture—an agriculture that is sustainable because it shares many features with natural forest systems (Mollison & Holmgren 1978, p. 1; Morrow 1993). There is an emphasis on perennial crops, such as tree crops, to replace food that is now grown through annual cropping. This reduces soil erosion because there is no annual ploughing. To achieve stability by controlling pest and weed infestation, permaculture mixes a variety of species in a polyculture. Instead of large areas set aside for pasture, permaculturists favour the integration of animals into mixed farming through the growth of perennial fodder crops for animals and the integration of small animals into domestic and community gardens. Permaculturists emphasise the use of earthworks, such as terracing, dams, and swales, to retain water, improve soil fertility, and prevent soil erosion. Permaculture requires a lot of manual or machine labour to establish these earthworks, but annual use of machinery for ploughing is avoided. Harvesting crops within a permaculture system is labour-intensive, as machinery cannot be used to gather crops from a diverse polyculture. Permaculturists favour the development of agricultural systems that supply a local community with diverse products. They oppose the large-scale transport of agricultural products (Mollison & Holmgren 1978; Morrow 1993; Trainer 1995).

As a technology, permaculture has many advantages: control of soil erosion, no use of chemical fertilisers or toxic pesticides, and little use of fossil fuels for farm machinery or transport. Socially, however, its application is very dependent on the context. In developed countries, the widespread application of permaculture in commercial farming would cause food prices to rise, as the input of manual labour into agriculture increased and access to food from far-away places decreased. While these changes are likely to be resisted by most consumers, permaculture techniques can nevertheless be introduced into **niche markets** for consumers who are prepared to pay a higher price to save the environment. For instance, Ian Crowley of Moree in New South Wales has begun to produce organically grown beef, grown without the use of pesticides, herbicides, or artificial fertilisers, making use of native grasses for fodder. He markets this under the name 'Warramali Natural Beef' and is able to sell it at a retail price that is A$1 per kilogram more than the price of conventional beef (Lehmann 1997; see also Campbell 1996). Changes could be accelerated if governments were to ban some environmentally degrading farming practices.

Permaculture also plays a key role in developed countries as a part of the development of alternatives to the commodity economy. Permaculture, as a subsistence agriculture for **alternative lifestyle or 'new age'** communities, is widespread in all developed countries (for examples, see Ashforth 1997; Smith 1997; Woodrow 1997). It is also used by suburban residents to supplement food bought on the market with food produced in their own backyards (for example, Armstrong & Griffin 1996). **Community farms** are sometimes established, which make use of paid labour and voluntary work to provide food to members of a food cooperative (McWirter & Payne 1996). All these options use the time and surplus money of affluent consumers. They are attempts to bypass the commercial agriculture system and begin to establish a more ecologically sustainable agriculture. They are also a new use of the creativity and choice that these consumers can exercise in their leisure time.

In developing countries, permaculture is often offered by **non-government organisations (NGOs)** as a development strategy committed to community empowerment. For instance, in Cambodia, Quaker Service Australia and Australian Catholic Relief employed the permaculture educator and designer Rosemary Morrow to set up permaculture instruction in villages in which land was owned by local peasant agriculturists (Morrow 1994; see also Francis 1990; Morrow 1993; CAA 1997; Moore 1997). As indicated earlier, unequal land tenure is a barrier to establishing permaculture in developing countries. Those who need to supplement their diets with subsistence agriculture do not own enough land to grow food. For reasons that have been explained above, agricultural production is often oriented towards cash crops for export, rather than towards local subsistence.

Permaculture is particularly effective where there is government support for locally oriented peasant agriculture—for example, in Vietnam, Cuba, and South Africa (Morrow 1994; Tiller 1994; Morrow 1993; Khumbane 1997). Permaculture is also effective where traditional landowners still have rights to land. Permaculturists encourage local subsistence food production and the conservation of agricultural and forestry resources. Examples are the Solomon Islands and Papua New Guinea (Tutua & Jansen 1994).

New age diets and affluent consumers

Within affluent countries, consumers can use their buying power to favour organic agriculture and the conservation of farming land. A growing minority embrace alternative diets, such as vegetarianism, the macrobiotic diet, fit-for-life diet, or the Stone-Age health diet, not to mention various versions of heart health diets promoted by State institutions (Pritikin 1983; Diamond & Diamond 1985; Michell 1988; Eaton et al. 1989). What these diets have in common is less use of industrially processed foods and packaging. In all these diets, meat and dairy consumption is reduced. These changes benefit the environment. A growing number of consumers also prefer to buy organic foods, grown without the use of artificial fertilisers or toxic pesticides. This preference may reflect people's concerns about health or their concerns about the environment (Henderson 1990).

One of the most interesting manifestations of this trend is the **community-supported agriculture** system, in which a group of consumers become members of a food-growing cooperative. As subscribers, they pay in advance for a box of fruit and vegetables every week. This is grown organically by a local farm developed specifically to service the cooperative. These are usually located in urban areas on unused patches of land owned by local councils or governments. The box of food is more expensive than the mass-produced food available at the supermarket, but is guaranteed to be locally and organically grown (O'Brien 1995; McWirter & Payne 1996).

Another way that affluent consumers can have an impact on the sustainability of agriculture is through financial support for non-government development organisations such as Oxfam, Community Aid Abroad, or World Vision. These organisations frequently promote sustainable agriculture as a means to food security, community empowerment, and environmental protection. As well, by educating people and developing systems of cheap community-controlled credit, NGOs create the financial security likely to produce population stability (Francis 1990; Morrow 1994, 1993; CAA 1997; Moore 1997).

Conclusion: towards the gift economy

In the arguments presented above, I have suggested that capitalist agriculture is extremely likely to cause environmental problems. Though there are many accounts of this connection, I will here trace it to two central features of capitalism (Trainer 1985; Daly & Cobb 1991; Trainer 1991; McLaughlin 1993; Trainer 1994).

The first is **competitive private ownership** of farming land. Owners of land are in competition with each other to secure the biggest possible market share of whatever farm product they are trying to sell. They do this by producing farm goods at the lowest possible price and marketing them successfully. Farms that are less effective in gaining profits lose value, lose investors, and are ultimately sold. Their owners sell to pay back debts or to save some equity from a failing enterprise. Competitive ownership places intense pressures on the environment. In any given year, the pressure is to produce the most output from the farm with the least cost in labour and other purchased inputs. In very many cases, the most effective way to do this is to exploit the land unsustainably.

The second source of environmental problems for agriculture in a capitalist economy is the role of the consumer. For consumers, the purchase of more and more consumer goods seems to be the only adequate compensation for a life of forced labour. They purchase produce of a desired quality at the cheapest price. They do not know about the environmental impacts of the goods that they buy, and they cannot control these impacts. They regard their level of consumption as sacrosanct. They treat any attempt to increase taxes as a kind of theft—putting strict limits on government spending on the environment. Consumers who are also employees fiercely oppose environmental restrictions on farming that may result in job losses.

These problems are intrinsic to the very structure of the capitalist economy. They account for massive resistance to any attempts to control the environmental consequences of agriculture. Within any given country, there is always the threat that business and employment will relocate elsewhere. Nothing short of detailed global regulation could actually prevent the dire environmental effects of this economic structure. But politically, this solution is very unlikely.

So it has been argued that a different economic structure might be better for the environment (see, for example, Goldsmith 1988; Mollison 1988; Daly & Cobb 1991; Trainer 1995). My own view is that these problems are best tackled at their roots. A **gift economy** is one in which there is no money and no wage labour. Instead people produce things for their own consumption or as gifts for other people. An economy like this would be a vast extension of the kinds of voluntary work now done by citizen groups such as Lions' Clubs or Cleanup Australia. It would not be a return to some earlier pre-industrial tribal society (collective traditional ownership by a tribe, clan, or kin group). Clubs and associations would still produce technologically complex goods and services. But these would be produced as gifts, not with the expectation of financial returns. People would be motivated to give by desires for social status and the social pleasure of giving. The standard of living would be the effect of multiple gift networks (Vaneigem 1983; Pefanis 1991; Leahy 1994).

In farming, producers would see no advantage in overusing their land. Instead they would seek to conserve their agricultural and environmental resources, to ensure their ability to live well in the future and to continue to be able to gain status by giving farm produce to others. In a capitalist economy it makes sense for entrepreneurs to market anything that can be sold, regardless of the effect on the environment. It also makes sense for consumers to purchase these goods, since they are already tied into a life of forced labour. These factors cause overproduction and overuse of land and other resources. In a gift economy, people's efforts in production would be tempered by the desire to enjoy a leisured existence and a beautiful and healthy environment. Their own material wealth would depend on the desires of others to give; no amount of productive effort on their part would make the slightest difference.

Creativity and choice, which now only find an outlet in leisure, would be here turned to creating a productive process that was also environmentally benign. In terms of farming, permaculture is the ideal complement to such an economic system. Creating and harvesting a stable polyculture entails an enjoyable appreciation of the bounties of nature as well as a sustainable mode of agricultural production (Mollison & Holmgren 1978).

While this proposal may be seen as a call for a total revolution, I am very aware that few people favour such a drastic option. However, the various measures that I have outlined above—State regulation, permaculture, and alternative diets—may all be seen as ways of bringing elements of the gift economy into today's society. They all represent ways of avoiding the environmental consequences of the market's normal functioning; they can be seen as attempts by consumers to control production. They produce environmentally welcome effects as gifts for the global community. Many of the proposals mentioned above represent attempts by consumers to develop choice, creativity, and power. They aim to go beyond the constraints of forced labour and passive leisure that are the system's usual mode of operation.

Summary of main points

- Modern agriculture is unsustainable.
- In developed countries, problems are caused by monoculture, ploughing, fertilisers, pesticides, overgrazing, tree clearing, irrigation, the use of fossil fuels, and packaging.
- Unsustainable farming practices make economic sense.
- In developing countries, the ecological problems of farming are exacerbated by export agriculture, which produces luxury foods for rich countries.
- The bad environmental effects of farming can be reduced by State regulation and community action. Ultimately, sustainable farming is only possible through a radical restructuring of the global economy.

Discussion questions

1 What are some environmentally damaging agricultural practices?
2 Why does the author argue that these damaging practices make sense economically?
3 What is permaculture and what makes it an environmentally sustainable form of agriculture?
4 How do consumers in developed countries contribute to environmental degradation in developing countries?
5 Why does the author argue that the gift economy would be more compatible with sustainable agriculture than the current economic structure?

Further reading and resources

Books

Mollison, B. 1988, *Permaculture: A Designers' Manual*, Tagari Publications, Tyalgum.

Morrow, R. 1993, *Earth User's Guide to Permaculture*, Kangaroo Press, Sydney.

Trainer, F. E. 1994, *Developed to Death: Rethinking Third World Development*, Green Print, London.

—— 1995, *The Conserver Society: Alternatives for Sustainability*, Zed Books, London.

Vanclay, F. & Lawrence, G. 1995, *The Environmental Imperative: Ecosocial Concerns for Australian Agriculture*, Central Queensland University Press, Rockhampton, Qld.

Journal

Permaculture International Journal: <http://www.nor.com.au/environment/perma/>

Websites

Eco-Village Information Service: <http://www.gaia.org/>

Permaculture International: <http://www.nor.com.au/environment/perma/>

Videos

Global Gardener 1991 (Australian Broadcasting Corporation, 120 minutes). Tony Gailey, Julian Russell, and Bill Mollison talk about permaculture in different parts of the world.

Eat Your Garden (Australia, 56 minutes). A step-by-step guide to small-scale permaculture gardens.

References

Armstrong, J. & Griffin, T. 1996, 'Ageless Gardeners', *Permaculture International Journal*, vol. 59, pp. 41–2.

Ashforth, J. 1997, 'The Living Classroom', *Permaculture International Journal*, No. 63, pp. 12–16.

Barnaby, F. 1988, *The Gaia Peace Atlas: Survival into the Third Millennium*, Pan Books, London.

Bennett, J. & George, S. 1987, *The Hunger Machine: The Politics of Food*, Polity Press, London.

Boyce, J. K. 1993, *The Political Economy of Growth and Impoverishment in the Marcos Era*, Ateneo de Manila University Press, Manila.

Brown, L. 1990, 'The Illusion of Progress', in L. Brown et al., *State of the World 1990: A World Watch Institute Report on Progress toward a Sustainable Society*, Allen & Unwin, Sydney.

—— 1996, 'The Acceleration of History', in L. Brown et al., *State of the World 1996: A World Watch Institute Report on Progress toward a Sustainable Society*, Allen & Unwin, Sydney.

CAA. See Community Aid Abroad.

Campbell, R. 1996, 'Farming in Twelve Dimensions', *Permaculture International Journal*, no. 60, September–November, pp. 16–19.

Cardan, P. 1974, *Modern Capitalism and Revolution*, Solidarity, London.

Community Aid Abroad 1997, 'Enough to Eat', *Horizons*, vol. 5, no. 3, summer, p. 4.

Crosby, A. W. 1986, *Ecological Imperialism: The Biological Expansion of Europe, 900–1900*, Cambridge University Press, Cambridge.

Daly, H. & Cobb, J. B., Jr. 1991, *For the Common Good*, Beacon Press, Boston.

Diamond, H. & Diamond M. 1985, *Fit For Life*, Angus & Robertson, Sydney.

Durning, A. 1991, 'Asking How Much is Enough', in L. Brown et al., *State of the World 1991: A World Watch Institute Report on Progress toward a Sustainable Society*, Allen & Unwin, Sydney.

Eaton, S. B., Shostak, M., & Konner, M. 1989, *The Stone-Age Health Program: Diet and Exercise as Nature Intended*, Angus & Robertson, Sydney.

Fargher, J. & Cadaweng E. 1990, 'Grassland Management for Reforestation in Tropical Uplands', *Permaculture International Journal*, no. 37, pp. 33–4.

Foreman, D. 1991, *Confessions of an Eco-Warrior*, Crown Trade, New York.

Francis, R. 1990 'Progress at Penukonda: Permaculture in South India', *Permaculture International Journal*, no. 37, pp. 31–2.

French, J. 1993, *The Wilderness Garden: Beyond Organic Gardening*, Aird Books, Melbourne.

Gardner, G. 1996, 'Preserving Agricultural Resources', in L. Brown et al., *State of the World 1996: A World Watch Institute Report on Progress toward a Sustainable Society*, Allen & Unwin, Sydney.

George, S. 1988, *A Fate Worse than Debt*, Penguin Books, Harmondsworth.

Giddens A. 1989, *Sociology*, Polity, Cambridge.

Goldsmith, E. 1988, *The Great U-Turn*, Green Books, Hartland, Devon.

Henderson, C. 1990, 'Don't Panic, It's Organic—but Will There Be Enough?', *Chain Reaction*, vol. 60, April, pp. 29–33.

Khumbane, T. 1997, 'In the Hands of the People: Rebuilding Food Security in South Africa', *Permaculture International Journal*, no. 61, December–February, pp. 13–16.

Lappe, F. M. 1975, *Diet for a Small Planet*, Ballantine, New York.

Lawrence, G. & Vanclay, F. 1992 'Agricultural Production and Environmental Degradation in the Murray–Darling Basin', in G. Lawrence, F. Vanclay, & B. Furze, *Agriculture, Environment and Society: Contemporary Issues for Australians*, Macmillan, Melbourne.

Leahy, T. 1994, 'Some Problems of Environmentalist Reformism', *People and Physical Environment Research*, vol. 46, pp. 3–13.

Lehmann, N. 1997, 'Long Black: Return to Grassroots', *Sydney Morning Herald*, 10 June.

Lloyd, A. 1997, 'Surge in Biotech Disease Control', *The Land*, 17 July.

McWirter, K. & Payne, S. 1996, 'Permaculture Farming in the City', *Permaculture International Journal*, vol. 59, pp. 20–3.

Marx, K. 1978a, 'Economic and Philosophic Manuscripts of 1844', in R. C. Tucker (ed.), *The Marx–Engels Reader*, W. W. Norton, New York.

—— 1978b, 'Wage Labour and Capital', in R. C. Tucker, *The Marx–Engels Reader*, W. W. Norton, New York.

McLaughlin, A. 1993, *Regarding Nature: Industrialism and Deep Ecology*, State of New York Press, Albany.

Meredith, P. 1995, 'Landcare: Grassroots Revolution Down on the Farm', *Australian Geographic*, October–December, pp. 66–85.

Michell, K. 1988, *The Practically Macrobiotic Cookbook*, Healing Arts Press, Rochester, Vt.

Mollison, B. 1988, *Permaculture: A Designers' Manual*, Tagair Publications, Tyalgum, NSW.

Mollison, B. & Holmgren, D. 1978, *Permaculture One: A Perennial Agriculture for Human Settlements*, Tagair Publications, Tyalgum, NSW.

Moore, A. 1997, 'Rebuilding the Roots of Life: The Self-Employed Women's Association of India', *Permaculture International Journal*, no. 63, June–August, pp. 20–3.

Morrow, R. 1993, *Earth User's Guide to Permaculture*, Kangaroo Press, Sydney.

—— 1994, 'Minefields and Mandalas', *Permaculture International Journal*, no. 52, pp. 32–3.

O'Brien, N. 1995, 'The West Goes Wild: Perth City Farm', *Permaculture International Journal*, no. 56, pp. 12–14.

Pearce, D., Barbier, E., & Markandya, A. 1990, *Sustainable Development: Economics and Environment in the Third World*, Earthscan, London.

Pefanis, J. 1991, *Heterology and the Postmodern: Bataille, Baudrillard and Lyotard*, Allen & Unwin, Sydney.

Pont, J. J. 1997, Heart Health Promotion in a Respectable Community: An Inside View of the Culture of the Coalfields of Northern New South Wales, PhD thesis, Department of Sociology and Anthropology, University of Newcastle.

Pritikin, N. 1983, *The Pritikin Program for Diet and Exercise*, Bantam, New York.

Revkin, A. 1990, *The Burning Season: The Murder of Chico Mendes and the Fight for the Amazon Rain Forest*, William Collins Sons, London.

Smith, C. 1997, 'Dreams and Dilemmas: The Difficult Art of Living Sustainably', *Permaculture International Journal*, no. 63, June–August, pp. 17–19, 69.

Thomas, V. G. & Kevan, P. G. 1993, 'Basic Principles of Agroecology and Sustainable Agriculture', *Journal of Agricultural and Environmental Ethics*, vol. 6, no. 1, pp. 1–19.

Tiller, A. 1994, 'The New Green Road for Cuba', *Permaculture International Journal*, no. 52, p. 29.

Trainer, F. E. 1985, *Abandon Affluence*, Zed Books, London.

—— 1991, 'A Green Perspective on Inequality', in J. O'Leary & R. Sharp (eds), *Inequality in Australia: Slicing the Cake*, William Heinemann, Melbourne.

—— 1994, *Developed to Death: Rethinking Third World Development*, Green Print, London.

—— 1995, *The Conserver Society: Alternatives for Sustainability*, Zed Books, London.

Tutua, J. & Jansen, T. 1994, *SAPA—The Natural Way of Growing Food for the Solomon Islands*, APACE, University of Technology, Sydney.

Vaneigem, R. 1983, *The Revolution of Everyday Life*, Left Bank Books and Rebel Press, London.

Vanclay, F. & Lawrence, G. 1995, *The Environmental Imperative: Ecosocial Concerns for Australian Agriculture*, Central Queensland University Press, Rockhampton, Qld.

Waters, M. & Crook, R. 1990, *Sociology One: Principles of Sociological Analysis for Australians*, Longman Cheshire, Melbourne.

Watson P. 1992, 'An Ecologically Unsustainable Agriculture', in G. Lawrence, F. Vanclay, & B. Furze, *Agriculture, Environment and Society: Contemporary Issues for Australians*, Macmillan, Melbourne.

Willis, Paul 1990, *Common Culture: Symbolic Work at Play in the Everyday Cultures of the Young*, Westview Press, Boulder.

Woodford, J. 1997, 'What on Earth Has Happened since Rio?', *Sydney Morning Herald*, 21 June.

Woodrow, L. 1997, 'Life Was Meant to Be Easy: Home Gardening with Linda Woodrow', *Permaculture International Journal*, vol. 62, pp. 25–7.

4

Future Food: *The Politics of Functional Foods and Health Claims*

Mark Lawrence and John Germov

Overview

- *What are the costs and benefits for food manufacturers, society, and individuals of functional foods that make health claims?*

- *What has politics got to do with food policy and regulation?*

- *What are the appropriate roles for the public and private sectors in terms of evaluating and monitoring food-related health claims?*

Future eaters will increasingly be faced with a medicalised food supply, with new food products being marketed as health-enhancing or illness-preventing foods—otherwise known as 'functional foods'. This chapter reviews controversies associated with functional foods and health claims, analyses the issues, challenges the assumptions that have emerged, and explores options for moving forward. The functional foods debate provides a valuable case study of public policy in relation to food and health. From a sociological perspective, it reflects a coalescence of the interests of food manufacturers and medical scientists in seeking to exert control over the composition and marketing of food. At a broader political level, the debate takes place within a climate characterised by the globalisation of food trade, a reduction in public-sector spending, and market deregulation. The increasing medicalisation of the food supply is discussed as having significant social implications, of which consumers, health professionals, and government authorities should be aware.

Key terms

active micro-organisms
conservatism
economic liberalism
functional food
health claims
healthism

medical–food–industrial
  complex
medicalisation
phytochemicals
technological
  determinism

Introduction

Consider the following examples:

- Scientists have discovered an anti-plaque agent, which may be introduced into food products to help prevent tooth decay—its first application is to be its use in confectionery.
- So-called 'smart drinks'—with names such as 'Memory Fuel', 'Rise and Shine', and 'Power Maker'—have been marketed as cocktails of antioxidant vitamins, amino acids, and minerals that produce effects ranging from increased memory to working as an anti-ageing elixir.
- In an aggressive public attack, a high-profile representative of a law firm described the United States government's cautious policy on **health claims** as making the war in Bosnia–Herzegovina 'look like child's play'.
- In the near future, scientists claim that 'ingredient X' can be introduced into any food, allowing manufacturers to claim that 'eating a food containing X will lower your chance of cancer'.

For millennia, people have been searching for a miracle food that could make them healthier, enhance performance, or immunise against disease. Hippocrates (460–360 BC) is quoted as saying 'Let your food be your medicine, and your only medicine be your food' (as quoted in Bender & Bender 1997). With the exception of breast milk in the first few months of life, no food in isolation can promote health. The above examples represent attempts by food manufacturers to medicalise the food supply. These new designer foods are referred to by a number of names, such as 'pharmafoods', 'nutraceuticals' or '**functional foods**'. 'Functional foods' is the most common term used in the literature, even though there remains a lack of consensus on a definition and the term is not officially recognised by regulatory agencies. Functional foods are generally described as food products that deliver a health benefit beyond providing nutrients (National Food Authority 1994, 1996; American Dietetic Association 1994). Medical scientists have speculated that the health benefits of functional foods may be conferred by a variety of production and processing techniques, such as:

- fortifying certain food products with specific nutrients
- using **phytochemicals** and **active micro-organisms**
- genetic-engineering techniques.

Designer foods are not new—selective breeding and food fortification have existed for some time and have been subject to stringent government regulation.

However, the increasing sophistication of molecular biology and biotechnology is now enabling scientists to investigate, in considerable detail, the functional characteristics of food and its impact on the human body. Some scientists suggest that the increased genetic knowledge about humans, diseases, and foods, combined with advances in food technology, will make it possible to construct functional foods to prevent and even treat diseases in the individual (Thomas & Earl 1994).

Certain food manufacturers and, to a lesser extent, some medical research scientists are calling on food regulators to permit the use of health claims on food products. Such claims are currently prohibited in most countries. The rationale for this prohibition is the fundamental public health principle that it is the total diet, not individual food products, that determines health. Conventional wisdom acknowledges that there is no such thing as a good or bad food, only good or bad diets. Such health claims are an international issue, with many countries reviewing their food regulation policies. Health claims can be defined as 'any representation that states, suggests or implies that a relationship exists between a food or a nutrient or other substances contained in a food and a disease or health-related condition' (CAC 1995).

At its twenty-fourth session, the Food Labelling Committee of the Codex Alimentarius Commission—the international food standards agency—agreed that health claims would not be included in the consideration of nutrition claims so as not to compromise the progression of the draft guidelines (CAC 1996). With the adoption of the *Draft Guidelines for Use of Nutrition Claims*, Codex has now agreed to circulate *Proposed Draft Recommendations on Health Claims* for comment (CAC 1997). Most countries do not permit the use of health claims, but in recent years several countries, including the USA, Sweden, and Japan, have developed regulatory frameworks permitting certain claims to be made, albeit within strict guidelines.

The existence and promulgation of functional foods will be contingent upon regulatory approval of the use of health claims. Food manufacturers state candidly that if they do not have the ability to promote the potential health benefits of their products to consumers, research and development of functional foods is unlikely to proceed. In the USA, researchers have described health claims as the 'engine that powers' functional food development (Hasler et al. 1995). In this context, functional foods and health claims may be regarded as forming a strategic 'agenda' on the part of some manufacturers to enable a specific form of development of the food supply.

This topic is one of the most complex and controversial facing food regulators, both nationally and internationally. Opponents of functional foods and health claims state that it is the total diet that is important for health, not so-called 'magic bullet' approaches, which enable manufacturers to indulge in marketing hyperbole and essentially blur the distinction between food and drugs, misleading the public and exploiting consumer anxiety. Conversely, proponents of these developments respond that functional foods may reduce health care expenditure and that health claims are a legitimate nutrition education tool, which will help them inform consumers of the health benefits of certain food products.

The conceptual nature of functional foods and the prohibition on health claims in most countries have resulted in a lack of information on which to make decisions. Stakeholders have tended to initiate and frame this public-policy debate around opinions and speculation, relying on the liberal use of 'ifs', 'buts', and 'maybes'. The purpose of this chapter is to place the debate in a firm context, review the current developments, challenge the assumptions that have emerged from the often adversarial debate between different stakeholders, and explore options for moving forward.

The functional foods and health claims debate: promoting or compromising public health?

A variety of interventions are required to promote and protect public health. Generally, these interventions may be categorised into two broad health paradigms:

- the health promotion paradigm, which aims to promote health in populations as a whole
- the medical paradigm, which aims to reduce risk factors and treat disease in individuals.

The most powerful determinants of the health of populations are the social, economic, and cultural circumstances in which people live (Blane et al. 1996). Populations with lower socioeconomic status suffer a disproportionate burden of ill health and disease (see National Health Strategy 1992). Interventions to promote the health of populations need to address the underlying social, economic, and cultural circumstances in which health is created. Such interventions are ecological in scope, preserving the integrity and sustainability of environmental resources—including the food supply—that are essential for health (World Health Organization 1991). By contrast, interventions that aim to prevent disease in individuals by addressing the risk factors associated with disease focus on changing lifestyle behaviours, including dietary behaviour. In this context, food is regarded as a commodity that may be modified to assist the dietary reform process. Selected characteristics of these paradigms in relation to food and health are summarised in Table 4.1 below.

Table 4.1   Selected characteristics of health promotion and medical paradigms

	Health promotion paradigm	Medical paradigm
Scope	population	individuals
Health	a positive resource for living	the absence of disease
Food	a prerequisite for health	a product to help prevent or treat disease
Cause of ill health	Socioeconomic circumstances	an individual's behaviour and biology

Table 4.1 clearly simplifies each paradigm for the purposes of comparing key features and highlighting differences. While both paradigms coexist and can be complementary, in practice the medical paradigm dominates the organisation and delivery of health care. For example, the medical paradigm concentrates on curing individuals once they are sick through individual pathological change. The health promotion paradigm focuses on changing the social environment to prevent individuals from becoming ill. However, the health promotion paradigm is not without its critics, with a number of authors noting the implicit individualism in much health promotion as well, which in practice concentrates on delivering health-education messages aimed at changing individual behaviour (see Richmond 1998; Naidoo 1986; Tesh 1988).

Extrapolating scientific evidence from one paradigm to another can be problematic and may falsely raise expectations. For example, caution is needed in applying the findings of medical research from trials on individuals to generate public health policy intended for the total population. The application of correlations established under controlled experimental settings to the 'real world'—where people consume varied diets and adopt a range of other lifestyle behaviours—can clearly interfere with the variables investigated in an experimental or clinical setting. Box 4.1 provides a salutary lesson regarding the expected positive health outcomes of functional foods. It needs to be emphasised that it is not science per se that is at fault, but rather the misinterpretation and misapplication of scientific investigation that is unintentionally facilitating what Illich describes as the medicalisation of life (Illich 1975).

The concept of functional foods and their complementary health claims are often described in terms of value-added food products, in which sophisticated food technologies are used to produce products in accordance with medical research findings. Such a perspective represents a form of **technological determinism**. It is unreason-

---

Box 4.1   Psyllium: a functional ingredient?

Psyllium is a very rich source of soluble fibre and has been included as an ingredient in a particular breakfast cereal. Feeding trials have indicated that a psyllium-based breakfast cereal reduced cholesterol levels by approximately 9 per cent when consumed as part of a low-fat diet (Anderson et al. 1988; Greenberg et al. 1994). A food manufacturer urged the United States Food and Drug Administration (FDA) to consider the following health claim regarding the relationship between psyllium and coronary heart disease (CHD) (*Food Labeling News*, 23 December 1993, pp. 20–1): 'Low-fat diets that include foods high in soluble fiber from psyllium may help lower blood cholesterol levels, which are among the risk factors for heart disease'.

The questions raised by this scientific data, and by any health claims resulting from it, are:

1 How relevant are the findings to the majority of the population? The feeding trials involved middle-aged men who were hypercholesterolaemic (having high cholesterol levels). Is it appropriate to extrapolate these findings to men who are not hypercholesterolaemic, or to women? Is it desirable to expose children to products that may lower their cholesterol levels?

2 Are there special considerations that need to be taken into account? The studies reported that between three and five serves of the breakfast cereal per day were required to achieve the 9 per cent reduction in cholesterol levels.

Despite these unresolved issues, the FDA approved a health claim in early 1998 that links psyllium with helping to reduce the risk of CHD.

able to expect technological interventions to 'solve' complex social problems. Instead, it is more appropriate to place expectations regarding functional foods and health claims within the context in which they were developed: in relation to the potential impacts on certain individuals.

Scientific substantiation will be essential to the success of functional foods and health claims. Invariably, substantiation is conducted within a medical research setting, in which findings relate to risk factors in individuals, as distinct from measuring the broader public health impact. This analysis places health claims regarding functional foods within a medical paradigm. They may offer individuals increased choice in constructing their diets, or they may be directly beneficial to individuals who are at risk. In the case of psyllium, other studies have concluded that a psyllium-enriched breakfast cereal can be a useful adjunct to the dietary treatment of hypercholesterolaemia (Stoy et al. 1993; Roberts et al. 1994). In this context, a health claim targeted to specific individuals may be warranted; however, it is not clear how a health claim relevant to the population as a whole could be substantiated. Nonetheless, regulatory requirements would need to specify strict criteria for the marketing of a psyllium-enriched product to protect against unnecessary confabulation and to ensure it was directed only to the intended users. Despite the fact that scientific reasoning will be based on research with individuals, food is consumed on a population basis. Food standards regulations are generally oriented to 'protect' public health and safety, as distinct from seeking explicitly to 'promote' public health and safety. Yet the functional foods and health claims agenda presents a novel challenge. There are few precedents upon which an assessment can be based to determine whether it is likely to have any acute public health and safety impacts. The concerns that are raised relate to the general theme of 'medicalising' the food supply—producing food that approximates drugs.

Medicalising food and healthism

Peter Conrad (1992) defines **medicalisation** as a process of adopting medical terminology and treatment for non-medical, social problems. The medical paradigm (identified above) is necessarily individualistic, but in health-education arenas, such individualism merges with an ideology of **economic liberalism** that assumes the only requirement is the delivery of a health-education message—it is then up to individual choice whether a lifestyle change occurs. An alternative approach to an emphasis on individual risk-taking would be to change the social structure that induces 'risk-imposing behaviour' (see Ratcliffe et al. 1984). For example, regulations regarding advertising and minimum production standards for fat content in food—including labelling requirements that removed ambiguity over labels such as 'lite', 'low-fat', and 'cholesterol-free'—could be introduced. Such a population-based public health approach is likely to have a greater impact on individual health than is a sole focus on health education.

The other implicit message of the educative approach—effectively a 'buyer beware' stance—is what Richard Crawford (1980) terms '**healthism**'. Healthism refers to the belief that health attainment and maintenance are primary human values. The key philosophical principle underpinning healthism is self-responsibility. Such a belief is based on an idealised 'health consumer', who consciously responds to health–education messages by modifying individual lifestyle choices, in this case choices relating to food consumption. Such a conceptualisation doesn't account for the manipulation of 'choices', or for obstacles to exercising choice, such as the social inequalities suffered by marginalised groups (especially as functional foods are likely to be marketed as premium, and thus high-priced, goods, restricting access for low socioeconomic groups).

The medicalisation of food involves treating food like a drug with therapeutic properties that are able to prevent disease. Such a view represents a pathologised and reductionist approach to health promotion and food consumption. The likely outcome is that the individual will be blamed for any diet-related illness, since the mode of prevention 'simply' becomes a matter of food consumption choices. A preoccupation with the consumption of individual foods for their hypothetical health benefits ignores the fact that disease-causation is multifactorial and an outcome of wider social influences. Therefore, universal claims of health benefits resulting from consumption of functional foods are meaningless and give a misleading message by overemphasising diet risk factors at the expense of others (for example, smoking and hypertension are also risk factors in heart disease, along with diet).

Functional food claims may distort people's food consumption patterns, privileging foods that carry health claims, decreasing variety in the public's diet, and hence distorting nutritional intake. There are many aspects of the relationship between food and health that remain unknown. It is premature to start predicting the public health impact of novel changes in the composition or structure of the food supply. The reduction of nutritional analysis to single foods or nutrients, and to single outcomes, is problematic, as the introduction of one intervention can create broader and more profound impacts, particularly by distorting nutrient metabolism. For example, the interaction between nutrients may affect their bio-availability, as occurs when excessive calcium intake interferes with iron absorption (Hallberg et al. 1992).

Conventional risk-assessment procedures for novel ingredients and products are generally limited to short time frames and consider the ingredient or product in isolation. Comprehensive information on the broader public health impact of products in combination with other foods and over extended time periods is required—especially consumer research to establish how people react to functional foods (see Norton & Lawrence 1996). Therefore, it is premature to introduce a health intervention without knowing its likely impact on dietary behaviour and nutritional intake.

Will functional foods and health claims inform or mislead consumers?

Information regarding the impact of health claims on consumers' understanding of diet and health is limited to that available from studies that have evaluated the FDA's *Nutrition Labeling and Education Act 1990* (NLEA) in the USA. The final regulations implementing the NLEA were issued in 1993, and this has resulted in extensive changes to food labelling in the USA, including permission being given for manufacturers to use model health claims for those food products that satisfy specified qualifying and disqualifying criteria (US Department of Health and Human Services 1993a, 1993b). For example, one model health claim states that 'Low-fat diets rich in fiber-containing grain products, fruits, and vegetables may reduce the risk of some types of cancer, a disease associated with many factors' (US Department of Health and Human Services 1993a, p. 2542). Preliminary research using focus-group testing indicated that consumers were sceptical of health claims and felt 'bombarded' by diet and health information (Levy 1996). Different wordings and different presentation styles for improving the communication effectiveness of FDA-approved health claims was then trial tested in consumer research conducted by the FDA (Levy et al. 1997). The results of this testing did not support the view that the use of health claims is an effective public health intervention to change people's food choices and achieve healthier diets.

The relationship between food and health is complex, and thus does not lend itself to simple cause-and-effect explanations. Unfortunately, there is often a temptation for 'experts' to overstate or simplify their findings, or for media to take scientifically rigorous research out of context and to distort it. In these circumstances, the precision in conducting the scientific investigation and the intention of accurately informing a lay audience gets subverted. Alan Petersen and Deborah Lupton (1996) argue that medical and epidemiological findings are often oversimplified by the media and health authorities so that tentative conclusions come to be presented to the public as unquestionable 'facts'.

Health claims are not a panacea to promote consumer understanding. The food label is one tool already in place that can complement broader nutrition education initiatives (Lawrence & Cumming 1997). It would be simplistic to assume that providing more information on the label will necessarily help. While some consumers may assiduously read food labels, others are clearly overwhelmed when confronted with the bewildering array of messages, often couched in technical language. As addressed by the NLEA, potential health claims need to be considered as a component of an integrated and comprehensive nutrition-education strategy (Kulakow et al. 1993). It is within this broader educational context that health claims may have a role. Otherwise, the marketing of functional foods will oversimplify the diet–disease link, as illustrated in Box 4.2 below.

The assumptions of economic analysis

A critical component of the decision-making process associated with the passage of the NLEA was the publishing of a regulatory impact analysis in the form of an economic cost and benefits study. In 1993 the FDA estimated that allowing manufacturers to make food-label changes in response to the NLEA—particularly to place nutrient content claims and health claims on product labels—would, over a 20-year period, result in at least 12 600 lives saved and 79 000 life-years saved (US Department of Health and

---

Box 4.2 The Heart Smart Egg: a warning of things to come?

In Australia, the Heart Smart Egg (containing omega-3 fatty acids) was withdrawn from the market as a result of misleading health claims. The Heart Smart Egg was marketed as reducing the risk of arthritis and asthma, and lowering blood pressure. In legal proceedings initiated by the Australian Competition and Consumer Commission, it was argued that the health claims were misleading and unsubstantiated. The manufacturers were unable to substantiate any of their claims and were ordered to change the name of the product, abandon current advertising, stop making health claims, and undertake to correct the misleading information. The example of the Heart Smart Egg serves as a warning sign of the potential misinformation, confabulation, and exaggeration that can surround functional foods.

Human Services 1993b). This analysis represents the distillation of a litany of assumptions, including that consumers will:

- read and understand health claims
- then be motivated to change behaviour
- be able to change behaviour.

This exercise was confined to a medical paradigm, with little attempt made to assess the broader public health impact of the policy change. Instead the analysis uncategorically predicted that consumers' uncertainty and ignorance 'will' decrease and many 'will inadvertently eat a better diet' as a consequence of the NLEA. The FDA's own research (Levy 1996; Levy et al. 1997) is now confounding the critical assumptions central to this costing exercise. The validity of this assumption is questioned by J. Allred (1993), who makes the interesting correlation between the increased consumption of low-fat foods and the increasing weight of the American population—clearly cautioning against the adoption of a simplistic, technical, quick-fix approach to individual and public health problems.

Is there a scientific basis for attempts to change the food supply and its regulation?

An implicit assumption of the functional foods and health claims agenda is that the food supply needs to be 'fixed' on public health grounds. This assumption is itself based on a series of other assumptions, including that:

- the current food supply is in some way deficient
- diets are inadequate
- a 'technological fix' will solve the problem.

An example of this situation is analysed in Box 4.3 below.

Box 4.3   'Fortified cereals—nutritional "must" for kids'

'Fortified cereals—nutritional "must" for kids' was the headline of a food manufacturer's newsletter (*Issue*, 1997, vol. 3, pp. 1–2). This headline accompanied a
summary of an article that presented the findings from a survey of the dietary
habits of schoolchildren in Northern Ireland. According to the article, 'For those
[children in the survey] who did not eat fortified breakfast cereals there was a
greater chance of nutritional deficiency, but this decreased as fortified breakfast
cereal consumption increased'. The headline represents a bold interpretation of
the survey findings. It infers that nutrient fortification is the only 'solution' to the
reported need. Yet, in most developed countries there are few inherent nutrient
deficiencies in the food supply. Dietary problems are embedded in underlying
socioeconomic circumstances. In this context, fortified cereals represent a form
of technological fix that may 'treat' the immediate symptom without addressing
the underlying cause. This sort of solution is non-sustainable, as the cause remains
unaltered and a reliance on ongoing 'treatment' may be created rather than preventing the original source of the problem.

Some stakeholders have criticised current food regulatory policy in relation to health
claims as being both 'old and outdated' in relation to encouraging research and development opportunities and not being able to prevent abuse. However, this regulatory policy
is based on the fundamental scientific principle that it is the total diet, not individual
foods, that determine health outcomes. This principle is as relevant today as it was when
the regulatory policy was first prepared.

Many manufacturers express concern that abuse by the few will damage the credi-
bility of the many, and there is already evidence to support this concern. While the
majority of food manufacturers abide by regulations, research in Australia has identified
a significant level of contravention of the health claims prohibition (Kneale & Truswell
1997). The study of food and drink advertisements found that 7.4 per cent contained
illegal health claims. One example of an illicit health claim was for a margarine product
called Gold'n Canola. It stated that 'Gold'n Canola contains the fats essential for normal growth and development—essential nutrients that can actually help prevent heart
disease, lower cholesterol, even lessen the symptoms of arthritis and possibly asthma'. A
variety of other claims were also reported, including those described as 'well-being
claims'. For example, the fruit juice drink Vibe, which is fortified with vitamin C and
beta-carotene, was promoted with the words: 'Drink Vibe regularly and it will enhance
your health' and 'Drink Vibe regularly and it will lift your well being to a higher level'.

It would appear that the problem is not inherent in the regulatory policy position as
such; rather, there is a need to strengthen enforcement capabilities and to tighten loop-
holes that are fostering misinterpretation of the intent of the policy position. Food

manufacturers are able to take advantage of many opportunities to incorporate nutrition information on their food labels and in advertising. For example, Codex and most countries have regulations permitting the use of nutrient-content claims on food labels to describe the level of a nutrient contained in a food—for example 'low fat' or a 'source' of a particular vitamin (CAC 1996). In addition, food manufacturers are encouraged to use nutrient-function claims, which describe the physiological role of the nutrient in growth, development, and normal functions of the body—for example, 'Contains folic acid: folic acid contributes to the normal growth of the fetus' (CAC 1996). Difficulty arises when it is not clear whether a claim may be an illegal health claim or a legal nutrient-function claim. This is more an issue of the interpretation of the regulation, rather than a flaw in the logic underpinning the regulation, and there is a need for food regulators to clarify permissible nutrient claims.

Consumer groups have asked why the converse of health claims cannot be implemented in parallel with any review of the current prohibition. That is, where the manufacturers of certain food products are permitted to make dietary guideline-type claims—as represented by the model NLEA claims—then there should also be a requirement for manufacturers to include 'disease claims' on their labels where there is evidence that the product may be inconsistent with dietary-guideline recommendations. An example of a disease claim might be: 'this is a high sugar food; high sugar foods eaten frequently cause tooth decay'.

The political dimension: the rise of the medical–food–industrial complex

The functional foods and health claims agenda reflects a coalescence of the interests of food manufacturers and medical scientists in seeking to exert control over the composition and marketing of food. Moreover, certain government agencies appear united with food manufacturers in their support of functional foods (Hindmarsh 1996; Downer 1994). The impetus for their support appears to be the potential economic gain, particularly export dollars, that the pundits predict the development of functional foods will bring.

Together these bodies constitute a new '**medical–food–industrial complex**'.[1] The corporate agenda is for minimal regulation and limited public debate in pursuit of rapid return on capital investment. Certain government bodies are supporting these developments because of the predicted economic benefits, and medical scientists are either captives of the promise of substantial research funding or advocates of the individualistic medical paradigm of public health critiqued above.

---

1   This term has been adapted from the term 'medical–industrial complex' — a term often associated with an article by Arnold S. Relman (1980), but originally coined in 1967 by Robb Burlage, Sander Kelman, Howard Berliner, and Vincente Navarro (Navarro 1998).

The authority of food authorities

The nature of regulatory bodies is that they generally respond to change rather than initiate change themselves. However, the functional foods and health claims agenda is seeking food regulators to establish a regulatory regime that will provide food manufacturers with a secure framework for their product research, development, and marketing. Food regulators are being required to make this assessment largely in the absence of evidence on which to base decisions. This situation provides fertile ground for the public-policy process to become dominated by those stakeholders with the greatest resources and who lobby the most effectively (see Mills 1992). This is considered in Box 4.4.

Box 4.4 Public policy and evidence-based decision-making

In August 1991 the newly established National Food Authority (NFA) chose to review the Australian food standard that regulates the addition of vitamins and minerals to food products. This was a defining political decision for the new agency. The agency chose this issue to demonstrate both its interpretation of the nature and scope of public health in food regulation matters and the need to base such policy decisions on science. Specifically, the NFA based its policy position on the need to protect the nutritional integrity of the food supply. The authority noted that Australia had one of the best food supplies in the world; certainly there are no inherent nutrient deficiencies (ABS 1993). It adopted the Codex Alimetarius Commission's 'General Principles for the Addition of Essential Nutrients to Foods' (National Food Authority 1996). These general principles state that vitamins and minerals should only be added to foods on the basis of restoration of nutrients lost during processing, except for:

• nutritional equivalence of substitute foods
• fortification where there is an identified and proven public health need.

This position was supported by public health practitioners and by the Australian Consumers Association. It was opposed by sections of the food industry and some medical research scientists, who believed it was 'extreme' and would restrict trade opportunities. A truncated and adversarial process then ensued over several years. The political divide associated with this policy position led to challenges to the roles and responsibilities of the NFA.

Ultimately, the political pressure exerted on the NFA resulted in a modified policy position. In marked contrast to the original policy proposal, the revised policy was more aligned to the interests of the food industry and medical research scientists involved in the debate. This outcome raises fundamental questions about the political support provided to this authority to uphold scientific principles in the decision-making process.

This experience described in Box 4.4 now assumes greater significance in the context of the functional foods and health claims agenda. Health claims might be regarded as the extension of the vitamins and minerals debate. Whereas the decision-making associated with Standard A9 (on vitamins and minerals) ceded significant influence to sectors of the food industry in relation to food composition, and established a precedent for the influence of industry groups on food regulation, the outcome of the health claims debate will determine who controls the information environment within which food products are promoted.

These political pressures upon food regulators are not unique to the Australian context. Ron Nixon (1996) provides a detailed description of the FDA's aggressive lobbying and agenda-setting in the USA to effect a compromise in regulatory standards in accordance with corporate interests. He describes the strategy as one of generating as much bluster, noise, and hyperbole as possible in order to stimulate the need for reviewing regulation and then to extract as much compromise as possible—that is, the more extreme the initial ambit claim, the more leeway there is to compromise to a resolution in favour of corporate interests.

A climate of reduced public-sector spending and deregulation

From an economic perspective, the functional foods and health claims agenda represents a critical dilemma for food regulators. Responding to the requests of the private sector and establishing a regulatory framework will potentially generate significant administrative costs and will create a demand for 'protective' services, including nutrition education, monitoring and evaluation, enforcement, and interpretation, all of which will place an economic burden on the public purse.

Within a climate of reduced public-sector expenditure and of deregulation, there appears to be an inherent contradiction in proposing to liberalise a public-policy position on the understanding that sufficient and timely resources will be committed to 'protective' measures. It is likely that private-sector funding will be required to implement the regulations. This option may be attractive to some governments as it may be seen as an opportunity to abrogate responsibility for nutrition education, monitoring, and evaluation, and to shift the funding of such services from the public to the private sector. This is particularly the case in environments with **conservative** governments (influenced by economic liberalism) that promote themselves as 'business friendly'. Yet this raises fundamental questions about whether it is appropriate for public money to be spent on services to complement a policy initiated for private sector's benefit. Alternatively, if there is a reliance on private-sector contribution, who is responsible for public-sector services intended to protect public health and safety? The nature and strength of food regulations are now being reviewed. These reviews are generally operating within a climate of deregulation. For example, the 'Blair Review' in Australia has released its draft report, which had as its first objective, 'while protecting public health and safety, to: reduce the regulatory burden on the food sector, and examine those regulations which restrict competition, impose costs or confer benefits on business' (Food Regulation Review 1998, p. 4).

The reality of changed regulation is that both opportunities and challenges will be created. A differential impact of the regulation on different stakeholders should be anticipated. New players from the pharmaceutical industry may emerge. Food manufacturers with substantial research and development budgets will be better placed than primary producers, including fruit and vegetable producers, to take advantage of regulatory change. The increased investment in research and development anticipated to result from a change in regulation to promote the functional foods and health claims agenda is likely to increase opportunities for medical researchers, although the opportunities for conventional public health practitioners and social scientists are less clear.

Does policy change promote stability or is it the thin end of the wedge?

Does regulation review 'solve' issues, or does it open the door to an ongoing process of change? Being a political process, the review of food regulation policy is subject to a range of lobbying and advocacy. The most vociferous voices often do not necessarily reflect the broad interests of the community. Yet, there is a strong policy temptation to 'oil the squeaky wheel' in order to avoid confrontation. In the case of the functional foods and health claims agenda, there are concerns that this could compromise public health principles. Prohibition provides an unambiguous policy position. As such, it provides clear parameters for all stakeholders to work within. The review of the black-and-white status of prohibition policy inevitably leads to the creation of a grey area. The challenge associated with a revised policy position is that of avoiding uncertainty and excessive resource demands upon regulators and the public purse in relation to interpretation and enforcement procedures. In addition, the effect of any potential functional food regulation will need careful consideration in relation to existing theories of public and private law regarding liability and obligation (Preston & Lawrence 1996). For example, what would be the legal response if a person consumed a product with the expectation of preventing a neural tube defect birth, but then tragically conceived a baby with a neural tube defect?

Many of the concerns of public health practitioners and consumer representatives relate to anxiety that any change to the current public health policy could be the 'thin end of the wedge', leading to the incremental erosion of public health principles and consumer information standards. The United States NLEA experience has been instructive in this regard. Once in place, manufacturers effectively made the NLEA the benchmark in seeking further concessions to increasing flexibility. Concern has been expressed that the food industry has continually pressured the FDA to weaken some of its rules in implementing the Act (Silverglade 1996). For example, there is concern that certain food manufacturers are seeking amendments to previous regulation in order to eliminate the requirement of FDA approval of health claims. This concern was reflected in this response of a community nutritionist to a research interview asking whether health claims should be permitted: 'Allow an advertiser an inch and he'll take three miles' (Kneale & Truswell 1997, p. 22).

Moving forward

The pre-eminent political challenge facing policy-makers as they attempt to move the functional food debate forward is that of reconciling the divergent viewpoints of the different stakeholders involved. The use of 'scenarios' is a useful way to move the debate beyond a stalemate between those for and those against functional foods and health claims. Scenarios are a powerful tool that involve stakeholders working together to construct different outcomes, based on certain common assumptions, in order to consider public-policy decisions. The preferred scenario is identified to provide the consensus outcome to be worked towards. This procedure combines the key strategies of communication, setting clear expectations, and cooperation in planning. The scenario process has been successfully employed in health promotion (Hancock 1997).

The 'best case scenario' would deliver a win–win situation by providing a secure framework within which manufacturers could pursue research and development opportunities while ensuring the protection of public health and safety. Conversely, a 'worst case scenario' may arise from the so-called 'fundamental conflict' of the health claims debate: the difference in ethical standards of the marketing and science communities (Miller 1991). This scenario has been termed 'quick-fix nutrition', characterised by providing marketers with increased leverage for exploitation of dubious messages (Yap et al. 1997). Selected characteristics of these scenarios are summarised in Table 4.2 below.

The general prohibition on health claims common to most countries is firmly based on public health principles. However, there may be a need to accommodate the potential food product developments that are anticipated to result from the application of medical research findings and technological advances. For example, the policy of many governments to encourage folate fortification of staple foods as an intervention to prevent neural tube defects creates a unique opportunity for the functional foods and health claims agenda. These policies are based on the findings of epidemiological trials that showed that an increase in a mother's folate intake during the periconceptional period may help reduce the risk of her giving birth to a baby with a neural tube defect (Medical Research Council 1991; Czeizel & Dudas 1992). There is no clear explanation of the actual biological mechanism that underlies this preventative action, although the folate is likely to be compensating for a congenital defect affecting a biochemical pathway involved in folate metabolism in certain susceptible women (see Box 4.5 below).

Table 4.2 Selected characteristics of potential scenarios relating to functional foods and health claims

Best case (win–win)	Worst case ('quick-fix nutrition')
Promote consumer confidence and understanding of the food supply	Exacerbation of confusion, anxiety, and mistrust of the food supply
Food promoted within the total diet as a resource to promote health	Diet is deconstructed to be viewed as individual foods and nutrients designed to ward off single diseases (defensive eating)
Opportunities for research and development of innovative products	A 'power race' of indiscriminate fortification and claims between manufacturers
Clarification of regulations	Blurring of regulations
Strengthened enforcement	Escalation of regulatory abuse
Increased opportunities for nutrition education, monitoring, and evaluation	Domination of the information environment by a few large stakeholders, with public funds diverted to compensate for distorted messages

---

Box 4.5   Folate fortification: a case for functional foods?

The challenges for policy-makers in translating the epidemiological findings of the relationship between folate and neural tube defects into public health policy are, first, that the genetic condition that predisposes some women to neural tube defect births is not fully understood and cannot be detected and, second, that a significant proportion of pregnancies are unplanned. Consequently, those interventions that may best target individuals—nutrition education and the promotion of folate supplement consumption—may not achieve maximum coverage. By contrast, folate fortification of staple food products can reach all individuals at risk. Essentially a population-wide intervention is being implemented to address a medical condition in specific individuals.

Many governments have effectively sanctioned the development of functional foods by promoting folate fortification for a targeted disease-prevention outcome in individuals. Substantiation of a functional claim on the basis of specific, contextual research has been implicitly condoned within the policy-development process. The use of a health claim to complement this intervention would assist the target individuals by informing them of the benefit of consuming fortified products, would inform other individuals who may wish to avoid such products, and would provide manufacturers with an incentive to implement government policy (where fortification is a voluntary recommendation) and invest in research and development (Lawrence 1997; US Department of Health and

Human Services 1996). This would result in a win–win situation for government and the food manufacturer.

With increased understanding of the folate and neural tube defect relationship and of the dietary habits of target individuals, and with advances in molecular biology, it may be possible to refine the 'dosage' of folate (and other nutrients) in food products and to identify at-risk individuals. In Australia, these developments have resulted in an eighteen-month pilot study of a folate-related health claim, which comes into effect in November 1998 (ANZFA 1998). In this context, folate fortification is setting expectations that certain food products will approximate the actions of therapeutic agents.

To conserve the public health intent of the conventional health claims policy, the general prohibition would need to be maintained, with potential health claims perhaps being permitted as exemptions to this prohibition on a case-by-case basis, providing they could satisfy special scientific substantiation criteria. The elements of a potential regulatory framework to accommodate functional foods and health claims from a public health policy perspective have been proposed elsewhere (Lawrence & Rayner 1998). This framework details the scientific substantiation criteria for potential functional foods and emphasises the integral role of nutrition education, and of monitoring and evaluation, in the implementation of such a policy.

Conclusion

The functional foods and health claims agenda provides a valuable case study of the public-policy process in relation to food and health. How the relationship between food and public health is defined and who is best placed to inform consumers have become the moral questions around which this public policy debate has been framed. At a technical level, the debate concerns the appropriateness of using medical research data, most often derived from trials on individuals, to change public health policy intended for society as a whole. Here the concern is whether food as a form of technological intervention can solve health problems that are essentially socially generated. At a more fundamental level, the agenda is a component of the political economy of food, in which the food supply is being transformed from a public health resource to a valuable commercial commodity within a political climate of deregulation and reducing public-sector spending.

Significant controversy exists regarding the need to change this public policy, the nature and quality of the evidence, who is driving the change, for whose benefit, and what the consequences will be for individuals and society as a whole. The analysis in this chapter has found that there is a lack of both empirical and theoretical evidence to sustain an argument that functional foods and health claims will significantly or equitably promote public health, or that they will reduce health care costs. The medical paradigm within which change is being sought is inadequate to substantially affect health outcomes at a population-wide level. Rather, there may be potential benefits for certain individuals, particularly those with adequate resources and skills to appropriately incorporate potential functional food products into their diets. The most significant, sustainable, and equitable health benefits for the population as a whole will result from those initiatives that focus on the social, economic, and ecological circumstances within which public health is created (see Germov 1998).

The challenge for food regulators will be to provide a secure framework for manufacturers to position their product research, development, and marketing, while upholding the protection of public health and safety. It would be less disingenuous and more constructive to frame the agenda in terms of a commercial and medical paradigm. The rationale for regulatory change would then be that of offering individuals more choice to construct a diet consistent with medical advice and to assist at-risk individuals to reduce risk factors and help prevent disease. This outcome could be achieved by reaffirming the general prohibition on health claims in order to uphold public health principles, while permitting exemptions on a case-by-case basis where products have been scientifically substantiated. This change will be accompanied by the need to secure adequate and timely resources both to manage the implementation and enforcement of the regulation and to conduct complementary nutrition-education, monitoring, and evaluation activities.

Summary of main points

- Functional foods and health claims are complementary initiatives that seek to promote the potential health-enhancing or disease-preventing properties of individual food products. Currently there is no universally accepted definition of functional foods. The conventional analysis of food and health states that it is the total diet that is important for health, and individual products that have a direct health effect are drugs.
- The scientific arguments supporting a potential public health benefit for functional foods are couched in a medical paradigm, in which medical research findings are being used to argue for public health policy decisions.
- The functional foods and health claims agenda is an important component of the corporatisation of food. Policy decisions associated with this agenda will have a significant influence on the composition and labelling of food products. Stakeholders predict that functional foods will be profitable, value-added products.
- The decision-making environment for food-regulation policy is being influenced by the expanding political economy of food. This political framework is characterised by the

desire to take advantage of opportunities emerging from the globalisation of food trade, to pursue deregulation objectives, and to reduce public-sector spending.

- Food is a fundamental public health resource for society. There is a lack of evidence to suggest that potential functional foods and health claims will significantly, sustainably, or equitably promote health or reduce health care costs at a population-wide level. Instead, they may offer potential benefits for some individuals. The most significant, sustainable, and equitable health benefits for the population as a whole will result from those initiatives that focus on the social, economic, and ecological circumstances within which public health is created.

Discussion questions

1 Nutrition education has been described as 'ineffective', 'idealistic', and not appropriate for promoting public health nutrition, while functional foods and health claims are said to be able to modify and enhance the food supply without individuals needing to change their dietary behaviour. What is your opinion?
2 Is it inevitable that the social and cultural agenda of food and health and the economic agenda of food and trade will be in conflict? How might public–policy-makers resolve this dilemma?
3 What are the potential costs and benefits of functional foods and health claims to food manufacturers, society, and individuals?
4 Food regulation is a political process. What does the functional foods and health claims agenda illustrate about the role and influence of different stakeholders on the decision-making associated with this process?
5 If functional foods and health claims were to be permitted, what do you think should be the respective roles of the public and private sectors in relation to food, (for example, in terms of nutrition education, monitoring, and evaluation)?

Further reading and resources

Reading

Gussow, J. D. & Akabas, S. 1993, 'Are We Really Fixing up the Food Supply?', *Journal of the American Dietetic Association*, vol. 93, no. 11, pp. 1300–4.

Cannon, C. 1987, *The Politics of Food*, Century Hutchinson, London.

Turshen, M. 1989, *The Politics of Public Health*, Zed Books, London.

Websites

For the latest information on functional foods and an opportunity to respond to discussion papers, visit the Australia New Zealand Food Authority:
<http://www.health.gov.au/anzfa/>

Other sites of interest:

Institute of Food Science and Technology: <http://www.easynet.co.uk/ifst/>

Public Health Nutrition: <http://www.hbs.deakin.edu.au/nutpub/natspec/>

Public Health Nutrition Information on the Web: <http://weber.u.washington.edu/~larsson/phnutrit/internet/nutrlist.html>

US Food and Nutrition Information Center: <http://www.nal.usda.gov/fnic/>

References

ABS. See Australian Bureau of Statistics.

Allred, J. 1993, 'Lowering Serum Cholesterol: Who Benefits?', *Journal of Nutrition*, no. 123, pp. 1453–9.

American Dietetic Association 1994, *Position Statement of the American Dietetic Association: Phytochemicals and Functional Foods*, American Dietetic Association.

Anderson, J., Zettwoch, N., Feldman, T., Tietyen-Clark, J., Oeltgen, P., & Bishop, C. 1988, 'Cholesterol-Lowering Effects of Psyllium Hydrophilic Mucilloid for Hypercholesterolemic Men', *Archives of Internal Medicine*, no. 148, pp. 292–6.

ANZFA 1998, *ANZFA News: The Monthly Newsletter of the Australian and New Zealand Food Authority*, August, no. 4.

Australian Bureau of Statistics 1993, *Apparent Consumption of Food Stuffs and Nutrients Australia, 1990–91*, Cat. No. 4306.0, ABS, Canberra.

Bender, D. & Bender, A. 1997, *Nutrition: A Reference Handbook*, Oxford University Press, New York.

Blane, D., Brunner, E., & Wilkinson, R. (eds) 1996, *Health and Social Organization: Towards a Health Policy for the Twenty-First Century*, Routledge, New York.

CAC. See Codex Alimentarius Commission.

Codex Alimentarius Commission 1995, *Appendix 1: Draft Guidelines for Use of Health and Nutrition Claims*, Food and Agriculture Organization of the United Nations, World Health Organization, CL 1995/26-FL.

—— 1996, *Report of the Twenty-Fourth Session of the Codex Committee on Food Labelling, Ottawa, Canada, 14–17 May 1996*, Food and Agriculture Organization of the United Nations, World Health Organization, ALINORM 97/22.

—— 1997, *Executive Committee Report*, Food and Agriculture Organization of the United Nations, World Health Organization.

Conrad, P. 1992, 'Medicalization and Social Control', *Annual Review of Sociology*, vol. 18, pp. 209–32.

Crawford, R. 1980, 'Healthism and the Medicalisation of Everyday Life', *International Journal of Health Services*, vol. 10, no. 3, pp. 365–88.

Czeizel, A. & Dudas, I. 1992, *Prevention of the First Occurrence of Neural-Tube Defects by Periconceptional Vitamin Supplementation*, New England Journal of Medicine, vol. 327, pp. 1832–5.

Downer, A. H. 1994, 'Functional Foods: What's in it for the Australian Food Industry', *Food Australia*, vol. 46, no. 9, pp. 414–15.

Food Regulation Review 1998, *Draft Report*, <www.health.gov.au/anzfa/exec.htm> 5 June 1998.

Germov, J. 1998, (ed.), *Second Opinion: An Introduction to Health Sociology*, Oxford University Press, Melbourne.

Greenberg, E., Baron, J., Tosteson, T., Freeman, D., Beck, G., Bond, J., Colacchio, T., Coller, J., Frankl, H., & Haile, R. 1994, 'A Clinical Trial of Antioxidant Vitamins to Prevent Colo-rec-tal Adenoma', *New England Journal of Medicine*, vol. 331, pp. 141–7.

Hallberg, L., Rossander-Hulten, L., Brune, M., & Gleerup, A. 1992, 'Inhibition of Haem-Iron Absorption in Man by Calcium', *British Journal of Nutrition*, vol. 69, pp. 533–40.

Hancock, T. 1997, Health Promotion Futures, workshop of the Fourth International Conference on Health Promotion, Aikenhead Centre, St Vincent's Hospital, Jakarta, 13–14 August.

Hasler, C., Huston, R., & Caudill, E. 1995, 'The Impact of the Nutrition Labeling and Education Act on Functional Foods', in R. Shapiro (ed.), *Nutrition Labeling Handbook*, Marcel Dekker, New York.

Hindmarsh, R. 1996, 'Bio-Policy Translation in the Public Terrain', in G. Lawrence, K. Lyons, & S. Momtaz (eds), *Social Change in Rural Australia*, Rural Social and Economic Research Centre, Queensland.

Illich, I. 1975, *Medical Nemesis*, Penguin Books, New York.

Kneale, C. & Truswell, A. 1997, *Health Claims: An Exploration of the Current Debate in Australia*, The University of Sydney Nutrition Research Foundation, Sydney.

Kulakow, N., Baggett, W., & McNeal, G. 1993, 'Putting the E into NLEA!', *Nutrition Today*, September/October, pp. 37–40.

Lawrence, M. 1997, *Highlight Interview*, Food Australia, vol. 49, no. 3, p. 106.

Lawrence, M. & Cumming, F. 1997, Editorial, *Australian Journal of Nutrition and Dietetics*, vol. 54, no. 1, p. 3.

Lawrence, M. & Rayner, M. 1998, 'Functional Foods and Health Claims: A Public Health Policy Perspective', *Journal of Public Health Nutrition*, vol. 1, no. 2, pp. 75–82.

Levy, A. 1996, 'Summary Report on Health Claims Focus Groups', in *Final Report of the Keystone National Policy Dialogue on Food, Nutrition and Health*, Keystone Center, Denver, Colo. and Washington, DC.

Levy, A., Derby, B., & Roe, B. 1997, *Consumer Impacts of Health Claims: An Experimental Study*, US Food and Drug Administration, Center for Food Safety and Applied Nutrition, Washington, DC.

Medical Research Council Vitamin Research Group 1991, 'Prevention of Neural Tube Defects: Results of the Medical Research Vitamin Study', *Lancet*, no. 338, pp. 131–7.

Miller, S. 1991, 'Health Claims: An Ethical Conflict?', *Food Technology*, vol. 45, May, pp. 130–56.

Mills, M. 1992, *The Politics of Dietary Change*, Dartmouth, London.

Naidoo, J. 1986, 'Limits to Individualism', in S. Rodmell & A. Watt (eds), *The Politics of Health Education: Raising the Issues*, Routledge & Kegan Paul, London.

National Food Authority 1994, *Discussion Paper on Functional Foods*, AGPS, Canberra.

—— 1996, *Review of the Food Standards Code: Concept Paper on Health and Related Claims*, AGPS, Canberra.

National Health Strategy 1992, *Enough to Make You Sick: How Income and Environment Affect Health*, AGPS, Canberra.

Navarro, V. 1998, 'Book Review of *Private Medicine and Public Health: Profits, Politics and Prejudice in the American Health Care Enterprise* by Lawrence D. Weiss', *Contemporary Sociology*, vol. 27, no. 4, pp. 419–20.

Nixon, R. 1996, 'The Corporate Assault on the Food and Drug Administration', *International Journal of Health Services*, vol. 26, no. 3, pp. 561–8.

Norton, J. & Lawrence, G. 1996, 'Consumer Attitudes to Genetically-Engineered Food Products: Focus Group Research in Rockhampton, Queensland', in G. Lawrence, K. Lyons, & S. Momtaz (eds), *Social Change in Rural Australia*, Rural Social and Economic Research Centre, Rockhampton, Qld.

Petersen, A. & Lupton, D. 1996, *The New Public Health: Health and Self in the Age of Risk*, Allen & Unwin, Sydney.

Preston, C. & Lawrence, M. 1996, 'Regulatory and Legal Aspects of Functional Foods: The Australian Perspective', *Nutrition Reviews*, vol. 54, no. 11(supplement), pp. 156–161.

Ratcliffe, J., Wallack, L., Fagnani, F., & Rodwin, V. 1984, 'Perspectives on Prevention: Health Promotion vs Health Protection', in J. deKervasdoue, J. R. Kimberly, & V. G. Rodwin (eds), *The End of an Illusion: The Future of Health Policy in Western Industrialized Nations*, University of California Press, Berkeley.

Relman, A. S. 1980 'The New Medical Industrial Complex', *New England Journal of Medicine*, no. 303, pp. 963–70.

Richmond, K. 1998, 'Health Promotion Dilemmas', in J. Germov (ed.), *Second Opinion: An Introduction to Health Sociology*, Oxford University Press, Melbourne.

Roberts, D., Truswell, A., Bencke, A., Dewar, H., & Farmakalidis, E. 1994, 'The Cholesterol Lowering Effect of a Breakfast Cereal Containing Psyllium Fibre', *Medical Journal of Australia*, no. 161, pp. 660–4.

Silverglade, B. 1996, 'The Nutrition Labeling and Education Act: A Public Health Milestone is Now Under Attack', *Journal of Nutrition Education*, vol. 28, no. 5, pp. 251–3

Stoy, D., LaRosa, J., Brewer, B., Mackey, M., & Meusing, R. 1993, 'Cholesterol Lowering Effects of Ready-to-Eat Cereal Containing Psyllium', *Journal of the American Dietetic Association*, vol. 93, no. 8, pp. 910–12.

Tesh, S. N. 1988, *Hidden Arguments: Political Ideology and Disease Prevention Policy*, Rutgers, New Brunswick, NJ.

Thomas, P. & Earl, R. (eds) 1994, *Opportunities in the Nutrition and Food Sciences: Research Challenges and the Next Generation of Investigators*, National Academy Press, Washington, DC.

US Department of Health and Human Services 1993a, 'Food and Drug Administration, Final Rules to Amend the Food Labeling Regulations', *Federal Register*, vol. 58, no. 3, pp. 2533–620.

—— 1993b, 'Food and Drug Administration, Regulatory Impact Analysis of the Final Rules to Amend the Food Labeling Regulations', *Federal Register*, vol. 58, no. 3, pp. 2927–41.

US Department of Health and Human Services, Food and Drug Administration 1996, 'Food Labeling; Health Claims and Label Statements; Folate and Neural Tube Defects, and Food

Standards: Amendments of Standards of Identity for Enriched Grain Products to Require Addition of Folic Acid, Final Rules', *Federal Register*, vol. 61, no. 44, pp. 8749–807.

Willis, E. 1998, 'The Human Genome Project: A Sociology of Medical Technology', in J. Germov (ed.), *Second Opinion: An Introduction to Health Sociology*, Oxford University Press, Melbourne.

World Health Organization 1991, *The Sundsvall Statement on Supportive Environments for Health*, WHO/HED/92.1.

Yap, M., Petrina, L., & Pritchard, S. 1997, Food and Nutrition, conference working paper, Health Promotion Futures, New Players for a New Era: Leading Health Promotion into the 21st Century, Fourth International Conference on Health Promotion, Aikenhead Centre, St Vincent's Hospital, Jakarta, 13–14 August.

5

Setting the Menu: *Dietary Guidelines, Corporate Interests, and Nutrition Policy*

John Duff

Overview

- *Are dietary guidelines an effective means of influencing food production and consumption?*

- *To what extent do corporate interests work against the public interest in the area of nutrition policy?*

- *What alternative nutrition policies could be pursued?*

Food and nutrition have become central to public health policy because of their potential to improve public health. A common form of nutrition policy in developed countries is the use of dietary guidelines to achieve population-based targets, which nonetheless become used to direct individual decisions about food and diet. This approach to policy, based on rational individualism, fails to account adequately for the systematic impact of food production, processing, and marketing on the food supply. These in turn shape the choices that individuals are able to make. Food corporations take a strong interest in the direction and wording of dietary guidelines. These are a site of ideological contest, with the potential for conflict between corporate interests and public health goals. This chapter illustrates this conflict using the example of Australian nutrition policy. Nutrition policy that focuses on individual decisions while neglecting the food industry and its interests results in only a partial understanding of the problem of nutrition and public health policy.

Key terms

ideological contest
individualism
medical model of diet
'new' public health
rational individualism
structuralism

Introduction: why do people choose the food they do?

Food and nutrition have become central to public health policy because of their potential to improve public health. Current public health policy on food and diet, however, focuses too much on individual choices and too little on the way those choices are structured. The main thrust of public health policy on nutrition in developed countries is to encourage individuals to change the choices that they make about food and diet, while the way their choices are structured remains relatively unexamined. The production and marketing of food are significant examples of structured influences on food choice. While a great deal can be achieved by focusing on individual choices, neglect of the food industry and its interests gives us, at best, a partial understanding of the problem of nutrition and public health policy.

This concern with nutrition policy is part of a more general issue in the social sciences: the question of how we explain social phenomena. Two different, but complementary, approaches are **structuralism** and **individualism**. These complementary aspects of social behaviour are frequently described as structure (the way our society shapes our decisions in everyday life) and agency (the way our everyday decisions shape our society) (Giddens 1984).

Explanations of what people choose to eat, for example, frequently focus on individual behaviour, motivation, preferences, and knowledge. Such explanations fail to account for structured aspects of social life, over which individuals exert no direct control. Marvin Harris (1986), in his *Good to Eat: Riddles of Food and Culture*, demonstrates the influence of culture on our preferences for some foods over others, and on shared notions of what is good to eat and what is repulsive. In similar fashion, Mary Douglas (1982) explains how the symbolism attached to food makes it quite 'natural' to combine foods the way we do, and quite bizarre to break these rules (for example, serving ice-cream with roast beef). This chapter will examine a different structural influence on food choices: that of food production and marketing. An understanding of structure helps us appreciate that the question 'Why do individuals choose to eat the way they do?' is much more complex than it seems at first.

The problem

There are two reasons that food and nutrition have become central to current public health policy, with its strong focus on prevention in Australia as in many other developed countries. The first is that diet-related causes account for more deaths in affluent industrialised countries than do any other cause (Lester 1994). The second is that the cost-effectiveness of nutrition programs makes them a very attractive preventative strategy in public health. Compared with the cost of building health care facilities and staffing them, or increasing the literacy of a population, the benefits of public health policy directed to nutrition education and promotion seem greatly to outweigh the cost.

Australia provides a good case study of the interaction between public health policy and nutrition-related deaths. Its population has had inexpensive meat and dairy products in abundance, and over the twentieth century has become increasingly sedentary in its habits. From the 1930s to the 1960s, there was a steady rise in the rate of deaths from cardiovascular causes. From the 1960s to the present, Australia has seen a steady reduction of the death rate attributable to coronary heart disease (Russell & Dobson 1994; Lester 1994, p. 225). This reduction in the rate of deaths from heart disease in Australia is an example of what a public health program that encourages dietary changes can achieve. Twenty years of promoting diet and exercise regimes conducive to better health appear to have been effective, and to have offered a model worthy of emulation.

Health promotion programs encouraging changes to lifestyle seem to be effective in reducing diet-related causes of death. The four leading causes of death in 1990 for Australians from 55 to 75 years of age were cancer, ischaemic heart disease (that is, related to an obstruction of the blood supply to the heart), cerebrovascular disease, and obstructive airways disease (Castles 1992, pp. 92–3). In 1921 diseases of the circulatory system caused 22 per cent of all deaths in Australia, with cancers adding another 10 per cent (Australian Institute of Health and Welfare 1994, p. 5). By 1965, however, these causes together accounted for 75 per cent of all deaths. These are the 'diseases of affluence', and diet is implicated in their cause.

The concern of public health policy advisers with reducing the costs of preventable deaths is evident in most reports on diet-related diseases. A report by the Nutrition Taskforce, established by the Australian government to investigate diet-related diseases, emphasised 'the enormous costs to the Australian community, both in economic terms and in terms of human suffering' (English 1987, p. 48). Using extrapolations from 1977 United States figures, they estimated potential savings in Australia in 1984/85 of around A$5 billion in the cost of health care. A 1989/90 estimate of the cost of cardiovascular disease alone puts direct medical costs at A$2 billion, with another A$1.25 billion in indirect costs, such as sick leave and earnings foregone (Commonwealth Department of Human Services and Health 1994, p. 41).

With the costs of diet-related diseases in mind, public health policy aims to promote better nutrition and more exercise to bring about a dramatic reduction of illness and death. Policy-makers have established baseline information about rates of death, particularly from cardiovascular causes. Specific targets have been set for a reduction both in death rates and in associated risk factors (Commonwealth Department of Human Services and Health 1994). Baseline data for 1992 in Australia, for example, reveal that around 50 per cent of men and women have an 'ideal' body mass index (BMI) of between 20 and 25. A target of 60 per cent has been set for the year 2000. Strategies to achieve this target include reducing the average consumption of fat as a proportion of total energy in the food supply from 34 per cent to 32 per cent, and the proportion of adults not engaged in regular physical activity from 36 per cent to 25 per cent. Public health policy promises to make a real difference by promoting healthy lifestyles.

The nutrition goal of 'new' public health

It is easy to see that the problem of cardiovascular diseases is a worthwhile target for public health policy. If such policy is effective, the health of the population should improve, and the social and economic costs of ill health should diminish. There are problems, however, in understanding precisely how people make decisions about food and diet, and why there are group differences in food patterns. Consequently, there are problems in understanding how policy can most effectively influence those decisions. Influences on food choices are diverse. They include: the culture of food preferences in different social groups; varying ability to pay for food; the priority food assumes in the lives of people in diverse situations; the convenience factor; differences in knowledge about food and diet, and so on. Research responding to the aims of the **'new' public health** movement is trying to address this lack of understanding.

'New' public health measures are directed not only to health issues in a narrow sense, but also to broader social, political, and economic conditions that produce differences in health among different groups. Research explaining these differences in terms of individual characteristics will lead to policies that attempt to remedy individuals' 'ignorance', or the 'low priority' they give to health. Such policies are typically top-down, relying on education programs to change lifestyle, or on regimes of supplementary professional assistance to disadvantaged groups. Advantaged individuals are likely to have the resources to benefit most from these programs, which, as a result, may do little to diminish health inequalities. Policy that emphasises individual choices but ignores the social circumstances that presents different groups with different choices must, in the final analysis, be regarded as imperfect policy (Donahue &McGuire 1995).

Rational individualism: dietary guidelines as nutrition policy

Researchers and policy-makers can call on two distinct paradigms when explaining the way we make food choices. The first is **rational individualism**, which emphasises the voluntary aspect of choices, and the second is a form of structuralism that emphasises the way that food production, processing, and marketing shapes the choices open to us.

Rational individualism is most evident in the use of expert advice to guide individual decisions about food. Nutrition scientists' advice on nutrition and diet presumes an idealised consumer of food who applies the technical rationality of nutrition science to the body, in order to maximise health. Bryan Turner (1992) wrote of modern dietetics as 'science of diet expressed, in practice, as a medical regimen' that subjects the body to disciplined government and regulation. Those who do not follow the 'medical regimen' then appear as if they are not acting in their own best health interests—that is, not acting rationally. The beginnings of nutrition policy in industrialised countries can be found in the development of dietary guidelines to help individuals make rational choices based on sound knowledge.

In 1979 the Australian Department of Health formalised this approach with the publication of 'A Food and Nutrition Policy' (Langsford 1979). The policy consisted of broad dietary goals, which were soon followed by more specific prescriptions about diet (Commonwealth Department of Health 1981). Nutrition education became the favoured vehicle of implementation. The information was biomedical with few links to the culture of food and eating, or to the political economic structure of food production and marketing.

The centre-piece of Australia's first 'food and nutrition policy' is a list of eight policy goals, and is similar to those introduced in countries such as the USA, the United Kingdom, and elsewhere at about the same time (United States Congress 1977; Turner & Gray 1982; Pinstrup-Andersen 1993; Milio 1990). The goals aim to change the 'poor eating habits', identified through epidemiological studies as the source of much illness and avoidable death (Langsford 1979, p. 100). The eight dietary goals, and the corresponding guidelines that were issued two years later (Commonwealth Department of Health 1981), are set out in Table 5.1.

Table 5.1 Australian dietary goals and guidelines

Dietary goals	Dietary guidelines
Increase breastfeeding.	Promote breastfeeding.
Provide nutrition education on a balanced diet for all Australians.	Choose a nutritious diet from a variety of foods.
Reduce the incidence of obesity.	Control your weight.
Decrease total fat consumption.	Avoid eating too much fat.
Decrease refined sugar consumption.	Avoid eating too much sugar.
Increase consumption of complex carbohydrate and dietary fibre ie. wholegrain cereals, vegetables and fruits.	Eat more bread and cereals (preferably wholegrain) and vegetables and fruit.
Decrease consumption of alcohol.	Limit alcohol intake.
Decrease consumption of salt.	Use less salt.

Sources: Langsford 1979; Commonwealth Department of Health 1981

The individualistic orientation in which the distribution of health and illness is explained in the 1979 policy could hardly be more clear (Langsford 1979, p. 103):

> The individual must accept responsibility for life-style decisions, which affect both his [*sic*] nutritional and health status. Nutritional health is not a gift or a right. It has to be earned chiefly by sensible habits of food selection, exercise and rest. The consumer has the responsibility to become informed on nutritional matters and to fit that knowledge into practice when selecting both foods to include in his diet and their quantity.

These guidelines for adults have been revised (NHMRC 1992) and a set developed for children and adolescents, with particular advice about physical activity, fats, alcohol, calcium, and iron (NHMRC 1997).

Recommended dietary intakes (RDIs)

Vital adjuncts to the dietary guidelines are tables of food composition and recommended dietary intakes (RDIs). Food-composition tables provide information on 'micronutrients' (vitamins and minerals), as well as on 'macronutrients' (protein, fat, carbohydrate, and alcohol) and energy (Lester 1994, p. 72). The tables are compiled to provide information on the levels of these nutrients that can be monitored in the diet of particular populations:

> Using these tables it should be possible to:
> (a) obtain an approximation of the nutrient content of daily or weekly dietary intakes;
> (b) select many combinations of foods which would provide a varied and adequate diet.
>
> (Corden & Thomas 1971, p. 7)

Nutritionists (for example, Sumner et al. 1983) point out that rational planning for micronutrients becomes difficult because of changes produced by processing, storing, and cooking. The complexity of the information required to take all these contingencies into account makes the tables of limited practical value. The 1971 edition of the tables primarily lists the basic foods from which meals in households are made. There is limited reference to snack foods, and almost none to the 'fast-foods' that have since proliferated. A major revision in 1989 (Cashel et al. 1989) pointed out the limitations of the previous tables. These included: the use of food values from other countries where different foods are known by similar names; the effects of different agricultural practices in different countries; and the omission of fast-foods where food values can differ with brands. The new tables have given priority to providing information about foods that are of concern to consumers and health professionals, especially foods from take-away outlets. A simplified version has been published for community use and includes brand-name fast-foods; it is also available through several computer dietary analysis packages (English & Lewis 1991).

RDIs, which had their origins in the crude calculations of the nineteenth-century 'dietaries' for prisons and hospitals, make highly specific recommendations for dietary intake of a huge array of food components. An Australian table of recommended dietary allowances was first compiled in 1954 (Palmer 1982, p. 157). In 1981 the Australian National Health and Medical Research Council (NHMRC) Nutrition Committee recommended a revision of the tables, which are now under constant review. Expert panels (see, for example, Rutishauser 1982; Wood 1985) have established upper and lower limits for listed nutrients on the basis of laboratory and epidemiological analyses.

The food composition tables and the RDIs provide the backbone of rational regulation of diets. The problem confronting health professionals and policy-makers is to ensure that people are guided by this formal knowledge of nutritionists, and to ensure compliance with dietary guidelines. Consumers also receive information from other sources, ranging from alternative health workers to industry advertising. Not only does the model of the ideal rational food consumer pay little attention to other influences on eating, but it also gives the knowledge of nutrition science a privileged status, as a typical study of nutrition knowledge shows: 'This survey has shown that many high school students … leave school with insufficient knowledge to put into perspective the variety of information on food and nutrition presented by the health professions, the media and the food industry' (Crawford & Selwood 1983, p. 33).

It is in the interest of food producers to provide information about their products, and to do so in a form that is consistent with RDIs, since they can use the status of science to enhance their marketing. To regulate claims made for foods, nutrition information must be supplied in an approved form on food labels, unless producers or marketers choose to make no claim at all (Lester 1994, p. 122). Food producers adopt the strategy of counteracting negative attitudes to processed foods by presenting them in a good light. This can be done in two ways. The first is to assure consumers that each food item is of a high quality. This may require showing that the food meets all legislated requirements. The second is to show that the food has a place in an 'approved' diet. This is done by relating it to the RDIs; the connection between the food producers and the RDIs of the health professionals gives the appearance of an endorsement.

RDIs are designed to guide nutrition advisory programs. They provide the benchmark against which a given population's consumption of food constituents is measured. In some cases, the dietary advice may be to increase some food factor up to the lower limits of the RDI, while in other cases it may be to reduce it to an upper limit (Darnton-Hill & English 1990). A consideration of salt in the Australian diet demonstrates the limitations of rational strategies designed to help individuals regulate the amount that they consume.

An example: salt in the diet

Common salt has two components: sodium and chloride. The RDIs recommend an upper limit to sodium intake because of health risks associated with high intake. The discretionary consumption of salt (sodium chloride) in the diet (that is, salt added by individuals in cooking and eating meals) accounts for only a minor portion of total sodium consumption. This is because most sodium in the present-day diet occurs naturally in food or is added during processing. United States figures show that discretionary use of sodium accounts for between 10 per cent and 40 per cent of total sodium use (Bullock 1982), although others put the figure nearer 6 per cent for Australia (Crawford & Baghurst 1990, p. 103). Someone who eats common foods such as bread or breakfast cereals would have to adopt a sophisticated information-gathering and processing regime to regulate sodium intake. Where constituents such as salt or sugar are added to resolve the technical problems of large-scale food production, individuals' rational decisions about what to eat come into direct conflict with the rational decisions of producers about the production process. Large-volume, high-speed bread production, for example, has depended on using higher levels of salt than is required in small bakeries (Brown 1983, p. 128). As a result, individuals who eat a lot of bread to increase their consumption of complex carbohydrates, would necessarily consume larger amounts of sodium than they may otherwise choose to do.

The official RDI reference paper for sodium steps delicately around this issue. The reference paper on sodium (Bullock 1982) pointed out that discretionary use of salt accounted for most of the differences between individuals, because of the background levels attributable to bread and other manufactured foods. Although the average sodium consumption in Australia was, at the time, substantially above the RDI level, the paper concludes that 'it is not considered practical to recommend an intake which would require major changes in the usual diet. It is considered that the recommended range of intake should be one which can be achieved by elimination of intake of discretionary sodium without appreciable alteration in the consumption of staple foodstuffs' (Bullock 1982, p. 184).

The focus on discretionary sodium leads to two conclusions. The first is that as discretionary use diminishes, sodium consumption becomes increasingly invisible and cannot easily be monitored by individuals. For this reason dietary surveys to estimate sodium consumption are increasingly unreliable. This may account for conflicting accounts of sodium-intake levels. Two studies that relied on people answering questions about how much salt they ate provided a figure towards the lower end of the RDI range for sodium, while one smaller study, which measured sodium levels in urine, produced a figure 60 per cent above the upper limit of the RDI (Lester 1994, p. 170). People were aware of the salt they had chosen to eat, but were less aware of the salt they had not chosen to eat.

The second conclusion is that nutrition researchers regard structured determinants of sodium intake, especially food production and processing, to be less easily managed than individual consumer decisions. Consequently, high sodium intake is represented, and acted on, as a failure of personal control over diet. The provision of information on food labels about sodium levels in processed foods completes the shift of the onus onto individuals.

The structure of food production, processing, and marketing

Public health strategies regarding nutrition are based largely on the **medical model of diet**, requiring individual consumers to comply voluntarily with dietary advice. The impact of those strategies is, however, weakened by the effect of industrialised agriculture and food production on dietary patterns in the developed economies of the West.

Michael Symons (1993, p. 9), who has done much to explain the development of the 'industrialised' cuisine, regards the changes in eating as being a direct consequence of the commercialisation of food. He identifies three main phases of 'industrial cuisine'. The first saw the flow of capital into enclosures in the United Kingdom and into colonial plantations from the eighteenth century, with the colonisation of Australia being part of that development. The second phase, from the late nineteenth century, involved the flow of capital into food preservation and retailing with the establishment of familiar food brand names. The third phase has seen the concentration of capital in global food companies, which lessen national differences and often grow, process, prepare, and serve whole, brand-named meals. Food technology dedicated to improving profitability 'commands the entire technical battery of growing, preserving, processing, distribution and cooking' (Symons 1993, p. 11), and displaces local food cultures. Geoffrey Lawrence (1987), in his analysis of recent changes in Australian agriculture, shows in more detail how the technical demands of capital-intensive feedlotting of cattle and pigs, of factory production of chickens, or of potato production for chains such as McDonald's changes the nature of food available for consumption. The growing global uniformity of food 'choice' supports the view that food choice follows, rather than shapes, the technologies of food.

Harvey Levenstein (1988) analysed the transformative power of the food industry in *Revolution at the Table*, an account of changes in American food and eating over the past century. In the nineteenth century, Levenstein argues, smaller producers found themselves competing against new processing technologies introduced by more highly capitalised companies. Companies such as Heinz took the view that their substantial investment in new technologies was threatened by the public's distrust of processed foods brought about by smaller operators. The small companies were accused of using inconsistent raw materials or dangerous additives to keep costs down. The large manufacturers led the movement to involve the State in defining and policing food standards to counteract public distrust of processed foods.

The success of large-scale agriculture, processing, and marketing depended not only on a carefully nurtured trust in manufactured food, but also on changes in traditional eating habits. The technical demands of large-scale production and the need for consumption patterns to change as food technology changes have been major forces in the transformation of diet over the past 200 years. Stuart Ewen (1976, p. 64) is sceptical of an explanation that simply sees dietary change as being a result of labour-saving solutions to meals. Ewen shows how home production of food by many American migrant groups was targeted by mass producers in search of disciplined mass markets. He records the efforts of American advertisers, often using patriotism, to persuade European migrants to abandon home production in favour of American manufactured goods. Levenstein (1988, pp. 42–3) supports Ewen's analysis: 'Because of the rise of the giant food processing industries, by 1914 the United States was on the verge of becoming a country in which traditional rules no longer held … The great changes in business organisation would play a major role in dictating what Americans would consume'.

At a broader level, and covering a longer period, Sidney Mintz (1986) makes the same point by exploring the symbiotic development of sugar, tea, and cocoa in European cuisine as a result of the colonisation of the New World. The increasing scale and capital intensification of agriculture has continued to transform national diets by changing the food supply itself. Developments such as genetic engineering, 'designer' low-fat meat, or the falling cost of foods once restricted to the wealthy offer the prospect of increasing choice. The important point is that the choice may be a product not so much of consumer pressure as it is of the production process.

In *The McDonaldisation of Society*, George Ritzer (1993) analyses the fast-food chain as the most highly developed example of the industrialised cuisine, showing how the demands for efficiency in fast-food franchises effectively reduce, rather than extend, choice. Taken as a whole, fast-food may provide a wide choice, but generally not in any one 'outlet', and with limited choices about how the food is cooked. The manipulation of the culture of food and eating, where marketing illusions are more important than the food they seek to promote, is driven increasingly by the need to maintain profitability, and less by consideration of local customs. The restriction of food choices by the streamlined production processes, and the use of oil and salt to maintain appearance and taste throughout the production process, alter what constitutes a meal, how it is eaten, and what proportions of different ingredients are combined in the whole.

Industrialised food has so come to dominate the way we eat that Ritzer feels compelled to make a striking suggestion about McDonaldisation. 'At least once a week', he writes, 'pass up a lunch at McDonald's and frequent a local greasy spoon. For dinner, again at least once a week ... cook a meal from scratch' (1993, p. 184). Colin Binns, the then Chairperson of the Australian NHMRC Nutrition Committee, tells us why this might be a difficult task. Writing of his shopping experience while visiting the 'McDonaldised' USA, he says:

> A stroll down the aisles of our local supermarket in Boston reveals a bewildering array of health claims, all on lavishly packaged, processed food products. The leaders in the claims appear to be any foods which contain even a sprinkling of oat bran, although recent research has shown that enthusiasm to have been a little premature. The fresh fruit and vegetables cringe in the back corner, unpromoted, unloved and probably unprofitable. 'Plain rice? Sure, we stock it. It's usually over there'. But we didn't mean the precooked 'instant' rice, and it took us three trips to buy one of our staple foods. Without a car and therefore without a choice where to shop, one gains a new perspective on purchasing food (Binns 1990, p. 58).

Any analysis of food habits and food choice that neglects the transformation brought about by the globalised food industry not only of diets, but even of what constitutes a meal, and concentrates on 'individual choice' is far from complete.

Corporate interests and nutrition policy

The food industry is vulnerable to charges that it contributes to mortality and morbidity by actively seeking to increase consumption of the foods on which profits depend, regardless of the nutritional consequences. The lengthy libel suit brought by McDonald's in the United Kingdom shows how sensitive food companies are on this issue (McLibel 1997). The companies have no wish to be seen as responsible for excess food consumption, or for promoting profitable diets before healthy ones. The fragmentation of diet into constituent nutrients, which is a consequence of the institutionalised use of tables of food composition and RDIs, makes the broader structures of food production more difficult to see, and makes it easier for food companies to project an image of being 'good' public health citizens. They present themselves as providing an ever increasing range of pure food items, leaving individuals, guided by health workers, to accept the responsibility for assembling the constituents into diets suited to their needs.

Good diets, according to this line of reasoning, have two requirements: information about the constituents of different foods, and the knowledge to assemble them according to sound dietary principles. Constituents can be regulated by the State, but diets remain the responsibility of individuals. The constant change in foods brought about by developments in agriculture and food technology means that anyone intent on regulating the amount of any nutrient in their diet must be forever taking in and acting on new information.

The Commonwealth Department of Health (1981) considered models in other countries when developing the Australian dietary guidelines. The United States Department of Agriculture, which has responsibility for providing dietary advice to the public, first established dietary guidelines in 1917 (Nestle 1993, p. 484). Foods were grouped as a guide to meeting all nutritional needs, while encouraging the consumption of United States farm products. Not surprisingly, the guidelines enjoyed the support of the primary producers. In 1977 the United States Department of Agriculture issued the first of a new generation of guidelines, *Dietary Goals for the United States*, as a public health response to the chronic illnesses attributed to overconsumption (United States Congress 1977; Nestle 1993). These guidelines, unlike the earlier ones, encouraged a reduction in the consumption of some farm products that contributed to dietary fat, particularly meat, eggs, and dairy products. Marion Nestle, in her analysis of the debate over the United States guidelines, follows the recommendation about meat through successive publications to 1990. Changes of wording between editions resulted from negotiations between conflicting interests. Nestle's analysis shows the influence of commercial interests on dietary guidelines.

In the first edition of the United States *Dietary Goals* in 1977, the statement 'decrease consumption of meat' provoked an immediate demand from meat interests that the word 'decrease' be removed. Over successive revisions, the guideline was transformed into an encouragement to eat meat. A second edition the same year stated 'Choose meats … which will reduce saturated fat intake', which in the 1980 revision became 'Choose lean meat'. Nestle reports that early in the Reagan administration the human nutrition research unit in the United States Department of Agriculture, which had done much of the developmental work for the *Dietary Goals*, was disbanded. In 1990 the statement became 'have two or three servings of meat … with a daily total of about 6 ounces' (Nestle 1993, p. 491).

Similar changes took place in the Australian guidelines, when the words 'avoid too much' in the 1981 guidelines became 'choose a diet low in' in a review by the NHMRC (1992). There is little direct evidence that this change of wording to the dietary guideline in Australia was brought about by lobbying from producer interests. However, the changes closely parallel those in the USA.

In 1987 the Nutrition Taskforce of the Australian Better Health Commission recommended a review of the guidelines that had been in use since 1981, noting the support of the representative of the Food Council of Australia for the review (English 1987, p. 66). The review of the guidelines was published by the NHMRC in 1992. For the first time, the guidelines were set out in order of importance (see Table 5.2). The breast-feeding guideline is placed last because of the relatively small number of people to whom it applies at any one time (NHMRC 1992, p. x).

Table 5.2   Dietary guidelines, 1981 and 1992

Dietary guidelines (1981)	Revised dietary guidelines (1992)
Promote breastfeeding.	Enjoy a wide variety of nutritious foods.
Choose a nutritious diet from a variety of foods.	Eat plenty of breads and cereals (preferably wholegrain), vegetables (including legumes) and fruits.
Control your weight.	Eat a diet low in fat, and in particular, low in saturated fat.
Avoid eating too much fat.	Maintain a healthy body weight by balancing physical activity and food intake.
Avoid eating too much sugar.	If you drink alcohol, limit your intake.
Eat more bread and cereals (preferably wholegrain) and vegetables and fruit.	Eat only a moderate amount of sugars and food containing added sugars.
Limit alcohol intake.	Choose low fat foods and use salt sparingly.
Use less salt.	Encourage and support breastfeeding.

Sources: Commonwealth Department of Health 1981; NHMRC 1992

The words 'avoid', 'less', and 'too much' disappeared from the guidelines in the 1992 revision. There are several explanations for this. The first is the reliance of Australian nutritionists on the United States policy statements as a 'resource'. To the extent that this is the case (and the 1992 review does cite United States and other policies), lobbying by agricultural and food interests in the USA extends its influence to other countries such as Australia. The second is the attempt to overcome the negative approach of the original guidelines, which look like a list of 'bad' foods. Representatives of the food industry spoke against the negativity of the 1981 guidelines. Their argument (Cartwright 1991, p. 310) is that the food industry uses the 'Dietary Guidelines for Australians' for product development, and negative statements are not helpful in this respect. Nutritionists were in general agreement with the shift from negative to positive statements. They believe an association with negative messages can diminish their efforts when compared with the positive messages received from advertising and from popular food journalism.

Conclusion

At the time that food producers were reacting so strongly to the Australian dietary guidelines, few people had heard of these guidelines (M. Lawrence 1987, p. 57). How, then, is the strong concern over the wording of nutrition policy to be explained? Nutrition policy is a site of **ideological contest** that tests out the proposition that the interests of food producers are compatible with the interests of public health nutrition.

The ideological contest is evident in the defensive position of food producers, who are sensitive about being depicted as hostile to public health goals.

The conflict over the wording of the policy or guidelines reflects the document's strategic importance for increasing food sales. As discussed by Mark Lawrence and John Germov in chapter 4, nutritionists have expressed concern about a form of 'public education' used by both public health agencies and food producers that deflects attention from the whole diet onto foods about which a particular claim can be made. Sindall and others (1994) refer to a 'nutrition power race', in which producers fortify foods so as to be able to make a positive claim about vitamins or minerals, or modify production so a food can be represented, in terms matching the guidelines, as 'low fat' or 'low salt'.

The conflict between public health and corporate interests is evident in the attempt to regulate advertising, and particularly television advertising, directed at children as part of a food and nutrition policy. About a third of the advertising budget of the top 100 advertisers in Australia in 1993 was spent on food and drink advertising. The figures include A\$45 million for McDonald's, A\$36 million for Kelloggs, A\$30 million for Pepsico, A\$12 million for the Australian Meat and Livestock Corporation, and A\$11.5 million for the Australian Dairy Corporation (Sindall et al. 1994, p. 159). An earlier study documented the concentration of television advertising for children on precisely the foods already well overrepresented in children's diets (Morton 1990). The 'Dietary Guidelines for Children and Adolescents' provide information to show that a third to a half of the fat intake for boys and girls aged 10–15 years comes from heavily advertised snack foods (NHMRC 1997). Successive attempts to build regulation of this advertising into policy have been unsuccessful (NHMRC 1981, 1989).

The guidelines produced in the 1970s in Australia and the USA were a first response to diet-related morbidity and mortality. Their intent, however modest, was to alter patterns of food consumption at the population level. The increase in fruit, vegetables, and cereals recommended by the guidelines implied a reduction in the consumption of processed, or 'value-added', foods for which brand names could be established and maintained. Likewise, the recommended decrease in the consumption of fatty foods was in conflict with the interests of meat producers and processors, while the recommended decrease in fats, sugar, and salt were a challenge to many food processes in which they were essential or cost-effective components.

While the intent of the guidelines was to bring about real changes in eating patterns, and by implication to the food supply, the means of implementation was primarily at the level of knowledge—that is, by nutrition education programs. Food producers have been able to affect this policy strategy in two significant ways. The first is by placing an ideological emphasis on individual choice, which steers the public health debate away from the question of the food supply itself. The second is the high degree of control exercised by food producers over the shape of the food supply. Taken together, these mean that policy focusing on individual choices does too little to address the structure of food production and marketing that shapes these choices.

Summary of main points

- Diet-related causes account for more deaths in industrialised countries than does any other cause.
- 'New' public health policy has the goal of reducing the rate of avoidable deaths by preventative measures that pay attention to the social and economic conditions that cause ill health.
- Nutrition policy has relied on dietary guidelines, which assume an idealised consumer making rational decisions based on scientific information. Those who do not make the 'right' decisions are represented as failing to act in their own best interests.
- The way in which the production, processing, and marketing of food is structured has a substantial influence on the choices available to us.
- Nutrition policy that does not take the structure of food production, processing, and marketing into account is not an adequate basis for 'new' public health strategies.

Discussion questions

1 Why does nutrition policy rely so heavily on dietary guidelines? Are dietary guidelines equally useful to more affluent and less affluent segments of the population?
2 In what ways does the production, processing, and marketing of food (including its cost) affect the choices adults and children make about food?
3 Does labelling of food make it easier for us to make rational choices about diet?
4 Less affluent groups generally experience higher rates of diet-related illness and death. What might be some of the reasons for this?
5 Large food companies are sometimes accused of being responsible for people eating too much of the foods that are bad for their health. Can such accusations be justified, given that individuals choose what they eat?

Further resources

Reading

Harris, M. 1986, *Good to Eat: Riddles of Food and Culture*, Simon & Schuster, New York.

Levenstein, H. 1988, *Revolution at the Table: The Transformation of the American Diet*, Oxford University Press, New York.

Milio, N. 1990, *Nutrition Policy for Food-Rich Countries: A Strategic Analysis*, Johns Hopkins University Press, Baltimore.

Ritzer, G. 1993, *The McDonaldization of Society: An Investigation into the Changing Character of Contemporary Social Life*, Pine Forge Press, New York.

Santich, B. 1995, *What the Doctors Ordered: 150 Years of Dietary Advice in Australia*, Hyland House, Melbourne.

Symons, M. 1993, *The Shared Table: Ideas for an Australian Cuisine*, AGPS, Canberra.

Relevant journals

Australian and New Zealand Journal of Public Health

Australian Journal of Nutrition and Dietetics

Food Policy Review

Health Promotion International

International Journal of Health Services

International Journal of Sociology of Agriculture and Food

Journal of the American Dietetic Association

Milbank Quarterly: A Journal of Public Health and Health Care Policy

Social Science and Medicine

Sociology of Health and Illness

Websites and discussion lists

DNH-PILOT is a discussion group on the Diet, Nutrition and Health project in the European Community. Topics are sociology, food science and technology, agricultural economics, and psychology: <http://www.santel.lu/SANTEL/maillists/dnh-pilot.html>

The Food and Agriculture Organization (FAO) of the United Nations has a site on Food and Nutrition: <http://www.fao.org/WAICENT/faoinfo/economic/esn/Nutri.HTM>

The FAO also has a site on the Codex Alimentarius. The Codex negotiates common food standards among the 162 member countries:
<http://www.fao.org/waicent/faoinfo/economic/esn/codex/default.htm>

Hardin MD is a medical site with a page dedicated to Internet resources in the field of nutrition: <http://www.lib.uiowa.edu/hardin/md/nutr.html>

The International Union of Nutrition Sciences provides a page with links to nutrition guidelines in different countries, and to books, monographs, reports, and theses:
<http://www.monash.edu.au/iuns/>

McSpotlight is a site that grew up around the year-long libel case brought by McDonald's in the United Kingdom against two activists who distributed pamphlets accusing McDonald's of being bad for public health and the environment: <http://www.McSpotlight.org/>

United States Food and Drug Administration (USFDA), Center for Food Safety and Applied Nutrition. The USFDA is influential in its evaluations of food safety:
<http://vm.cfsan.fda.gov/list.html>

References

Australian Institute of Health and Welfare 1994, *Australia's Health 1994: The Fourth Biennial Health Report of the Australian Institute of Health and Welfare*, AGPS, Canberra.

Binns, C. 1990, 'A letter from America', *Australian Journal of Nutrition and Dietetics*, vol. 47, no. 2, p. 58.

Brown, U. 1983, 'Take Another Slice or Two', *Journal of Food and Nutrition*, vol. 40, no. 3, pp. 118–20, 128.

Bullock, J. 1982, 'Sodium (Na)', *Journal of Food and Nutrition*, vol. 39, no. 4, pp. 181–6.

Cartwright, I. 1991, 'How to Develop a Corporate Nutrition Policy', *Food Australia*, vol. 43, no. 7, pp. 308–10.

Cashel, C., English, R., & Lewis, J. 1989, *Composition of Foods, Australia*, AGPS, Canberra.

Castles, I. 1992, *Social Indicators, Number 5, 1992*, ABS, Canberra.

Commonwealth Department of Health 1981, 'Dietary Guidelines for Australians', *Journal of Food and Nutrition*, vol. 38, no. 3, pp. 111–19.

Commonwealth Department of Human Services and Health 1994, *Better Health Outcomes for Australians: National Goals, Targets and Strategies for Better Health Outcomes into the Next Century*, AGPS, Canberra.

Corden, M. & Thomas, S. 1971, *Simplified Food Composition Tables: Composition of Selected Raw and Processed Foods Expressed in Common Household Portions*, AGPS, Canberra.

Crawford, D. & Baghurst, K. 1990, 'Diet and Health: A National Survey of Beliefs, Behaviours and Barriers to Change in the Community', *Australian Journal of Nutrition and Dietetics*, vol. 47, no. 4, pp. 97–106.

Crawford, M. & Selwood, T. 1983, 'The Nutritional Knowledge of Melbourne High School Students', *Journal of Food and Nutrition*, vol. 40, no. 1, pp. 25–34.

Darnton-Hill, I. & English, R. 1990, 'Nutrition in Australia: Deficiencies, Excesses and Current Policies', *Australian Journal of Nutrition and Dietetics*, vol. 47, no. 2, pp. 34–41.

Donahue, J. & McGuire, M. 1995, 'The Political Economy of Responsibility in Health and Illness', *Social Science and Medicine*, vol. 4, no. 1, pp. 47–53.

Douglas, M. 1982, 'Food as a System of Communication', in M. Douglas (ed.), *In the Active Voice*, Routledge & Kegan Paul, London, pp. 82–104.

English, R. 1987, *Towards Better Nutrition for Australians: Report of Nutrition Taskforce of the Better Health Commission*, AGPS, Canberra.

English, R. & Lewis, J. 1991, *Food for Health: A Guide to Good Nutrition with Nutrient Values for 650 Australian Foods*, AGPS, Canberra.

Ewen, S. 1976, *Captains of Consciousness*, McGraw-Hill, New York.

Giddens, A. 1984, *The Constitution of Society*, Polity Press, Cambridge.

Harris, M. 1986, *Good to Eat: Riddles of Food and Culture*, Simon & Schuster, New York.

Langsford, W. 1979, 'A Food and Nutrition Policy', *Food and Nutrition Notes and Reviews*, vol. 36, no. 3, pp. 100–3.

Lawrence, G. 1987, *Capitalism and the Countryside: The Rural Crisis in Australia*, Pluto Press, Sydney.

Lawrence, M. 1987, 'Making Healthier Choices Easier Choices—The Victorian Food and Nutrition Project', *Journal of Food and Nutrition*, vol. 44, no. 2, pp. 57–9.

Lester, I. 1994, *Australia's Food and Nutrition: A Report of the Australian Institute of Health and Welfare in Collaboration with the NHMRC Expert Panel on National Food and Nutrition Monitoring and Surveillance Strategy*, AGPS, Canberra.

Levenstein, H. 1988, *Revolution at the Table: The Transformation of the American Diet*, Oxford University Press, New York.

McLibel 1997, 'Quotes from Dave Morris Following the Judgment in the McLibel Trial 21st June 1997', <http://www.McSpotlight.org/>.

Milio, N. 1990, *Nutrition Policy for Food-Rich Countries: A Strategic Analysis*, Johns Hopkins University Press, Baltimore.

Mintz, S. 1986, *Sweetness and Power: The Place of Sugar in Modern History*, Penguin Books, New York.

Morton, H. 1990, 'Television Food Advertising: A Challenge for the New Public Health in Australia', *Community Health Studies*, vol. 14, no. 2, pp. 153–61.

National Health and Medical Research Council 1981, 'Report of the Working Party on Television Advertising of Foods Directed to Children', *Report of 92nd Session, Canberra, October 1981*, AGPS, Canberra, pp. 223–99.

—— 1989, *Implementing the Dietary Guidelines for Australians: Report of the Subcommittee on Nutrition Education*, AGPS, Canberra.

—— 1992, *Dietary Guidelines for Australians*, AGPS, Canberra.

—— 1997, *Dietary Guidelines for Children and Adolescents*, AGPS, Canberra.

Nestle, M. 1993, 'Food Lobbies, the Food Pyramid, and US Nutrition Policy', *International Journal of Health Services*, vol. 23, no. 3, pp. 483–96.

NHMRC. See National Health and Medical Research Council.

Palmer, N. 1982, 'Recommended Dietary Intakes for Use in Australia', *Journal of Food and Nutrition*, vol. 39, no. 4, pp. 157–8.

Pinstrup-Andersen, P. 1993, 'Household Behavior and Government Preferences: Compatibility or Conflicts in Efforts to Achieve Goals of Nutrition Programs', in P. Pinstrup-Andersen (ed.), *The Political Economy of Food and Nutrition Policies*, published for the International Food Policy Research Institute, The Johns Hopkins University Press, Baltimore, pp. 116–30.

Ritzer, G. 1993, *The McDonaldization of Society: An Investigation into the Changing Character of Contemporary Social Life*, Pine Forge Press, New York.

Russell, M. & Dobson, A. 1994, 'Age-Specific Mortality from Cardiovascular Disease and Other Causes, 1969 to 1990', *Australian Journal of Public Health*, vol. 18, no. 2, pp. 160–4.

Rutishauser, I. 1982, 'Vitamin B-6', *Journal of Food and Nutrition*, vol. 39, no. 4, pp. 158–67.

Sindall, A., Wright, J., & O'Dea, K. 1994, 'Food Production, Human Nutrition and the Impact of Health Messages: A Public Health Perspective', *Proceedings of the Nutrition Society of Australia*, no. 18, pp. 156–66.

Sumner, J., Eu, S., & Dhillon, A. 1983, 'Ascorbic Acid Retention in Foods', *Journal of Food and Nutrition*, vol. 40, no. 1, pp. 43–8.

Symons, M. 1993, *The Shared Table: Ideas for an Australian Cuisine*, AGPS, Canberra.

Turner, B. 1992, 'The Government of the Body: Medical Regimens and the Rationalization of Diet', in B. Turner, *Regulating Bodies: Essays in Medical Sociology*, Routledge, London, pp. 177–95.

Turner, M. & Gray, J. (eds) 1982, *Implementation of Dietary Guidelines: Obstacles and Opportunities*, British Nutrition Foundation, London.

United States Congress 1977, *Eating in America: Dietary Goals for the United States: Report of the Select Committee on Nutrition and Human Needs, US Senate*, MIT Press, Cambridge, Mass.

Wood, B. 1985, 'Thiamin', *Journal of Food and Nutrition*, vol. 41, no. 3, pp. 110–18.

Part 2

Social Differentiation: *Food Consumption and Identity*

Like cannibalism, a matter of taste

G. K. Chesterton

Beulah, peel me a grape

Mae West, *I'm No Angel* (1933 film)

Social differentiation refers to the emergence of diverse food consumption patterns in developed societies. In some cases, it is an attempt to redress the McDonaldisation process—for example, the growing concern for animal welfare, reflected in the debate over battery versus free-range chickens and eggs. A trend towards social diversity is not simply the product of individual preference, but is tied to the creation of social distinction and self-identity through particular food choices and social group membership. Social differentiation is a concept that we use to represent the nexus of structure and agency in influencing food choices. The adage that 'you are what you eat'—originally intended as a nutrition slogan to encourage healthy eating—gains symbolic validity through particular food choices and food habits, in which a food or eating experience imbued with a certain status or image becomes associated with the individual consumer. For example, people can seek to differentiate themselves from others or, alternatively, convey their membership of a particular social group through their food consumption (among other things). Ordering a vegetarian meal, eating a meat pie, dining at a trendy café, or eating an exotic cuisine may be used and interpreted as social 'markers' of the individual's social status and group membership.

The food choices individuals make do not occur in a social vacuum and can be imbued with specific social meaning and significance. For example, food is often defined as 'good or bad, masculine or feminine, powerful or weak, alive or dead, healthy or non-healthy, a comfort or punishment, sophisticated or gauche, a sin or virtue, animal or vegetable, raw or cooked, self or other' (D. Lupton 1996, *Food, the Body and the Self*, Sage, London, pp. 1–2). These couplets illustrate the social meanings, classifications, and emotions that we attach to the food we eat, which thus serve to define who we are. However, social patterns in food consumption are not static, and as self-conscious individuals, we have scope to choose from a variety of products and associated discourses of food symbolism. Therefore, the theme of social differentiation reflects this nexus of social and individual agency—that is, the interplay between social and individual factors that produce particular patterns in food consumption.

In chapter 6, Deidre Wicks discusses the growing numbers of people who describe themselves as vegetarian. She argues that vegetarianism can be seen as both a way of defining the self and as a social movement, based on ethical considerations about animal rights and the environmental and health implications of producing and consuming animals. Alan Warde and Lydia Martens note in chapter 7 that 'eating is considered quintessentially a domestic activity', with repercussions for the eating-out industry that they explore. Nonetheless, they find an increasing trend towards eating out across all social groups, although there are still distinct differences in the food choices and food venues preferred by various social groups. For example, Pat Crotty in chapter 8 argues that, while class differences persist in food consumption, these differences have 'diminished without disappearing altogether', and the differences that do exist have no significant nutritional consequences. Therefore, according to Crotty, concern about the 'poor diets of the poor' tends to reflect class prejudices based on social distinction, rather than an objective assessment of nutritional inequalities.

Joanne Ikeda observes in chapter 9 that no culture promotes eating in solitude. While food consumption is a personal experience, it often occurs during some form of social gathering and thus acts as a bridge between culture and individuality—a feature Ikeda discusses in her chapter on food and nutrition in culturally diverse societies. Wm Alex McIntosh and Karen Kubena, in chapter 10, discuss the social impact of ageing on food consumption and, in turn, on self-identity and social interaction as a further example of social differentiation.

The following excerpt from Laura Esquivel's *Like Water for Chocolate* is a good example of the sensuous nature of food as an expression of self-identity. Tita, the main character, is able to infuse her emotional state into the foods she prepares, communicating her desires with interesting effects.

Quail in Rose Petal Sauce

12 roses, preferably red, 12 chestnuts, 2 teaspoons butter, 2 teaspoons cornflower, 2 drops attar of roses, 2 tablespoons anise, 2 tablespoons honey, 2 cloves garlic, 6 quail, 1 pitaya.

Everyone was a little tense as they sat down at the table, but that's as far as it went until the quail were served. It wasn't enough he'd made his wife jealous earlier, for when Pedro tasted his first mouthful, he couldn't help closing his eyes in voluptuous delight and exclaiming, 'It's a dish for the gods!' Mama Elena knew the quail was exquisite; none the less, Pedro's remark did not sit well with her, and she replied, 'It's too salty.' Rosaura, saying she was feeling sick and getting nauseous, barely took three bites. But something strange was happening to Gertrudis.

On her the food seemed to act as an aphrodisiac; she began to feel an intense heat pulsing through her limbs ... something strange was happening to her. She turned to Tita for help, but Tita wasn't there, even though her body was sitting up quite properly in her chair; there wasn't the slightest sign of life in her eyes. It was as if a strange alchemical process had dissolved her entire being in the rose petal sauce, in the tender flesh of the quails, in the wine, in every one of the meal's aromas. That was the way she entered Pedro's body, hot, voluptuous, totally sensuous.

With that meal it seemed they had discovered a new system of communication, in which Tita was the transmitter, Pedro the receiver, and poor Gertrudis the medium, the conducting body through which the singular sexual message was passed.

Pedro didn't offer any resistance. He let Tita penetrate to the farthest corners of his being, and all the while they couldn't take their eyes off each other ...

It truly is a delicious dish. The roses give it an extremely delicate flavour.

Source: Laura Esquivel 1989, *Like Water for Chocolate*, Black Swan, London, pp. 48–9.

6

Humans, Food, and Other Animals: *The Vegetarian Option*

Deidre Wicks

Overview

- *Why are large numbers of people voluntarily removing meat from their diets?*

- *What are some of the ideologies that operate to separate 'meat' from the living animal from which it came?*

- *Can concepts derived from sociology enhance our understanding of vegetarianism?*

This chapter overviews and reviews the recent sociological literature on vegetarianism. The focus is on the voluntary rejection of meat, which is explored in relation to philosophy and ethics, ecology, aesthetics, and health. The chapter examines the concept of 'life politics' developed by Anthony Giddens, discusses its usefulness for understanding vegetarianism in the late modern period, and concludes by examining the contradictory forces at work that are influencing the survival and possible growth of vegetarianism into the future.

Key terms

anti-vivisection
biological determinism
socially constructed
unproblematised

Introduction

Eating is a highly personal act. At the same time, for most people, it is a social act. When we eat, how we eat, and, more particularly, what we eat are, for those of us not experiencing genuine scarcity, decisions that are driven by complex motives. While these motives include the 'natural' or the biological—such as hunger—they also include social factors, such as taste, manners, expectations, and obligations. In this way, the act of eating becomes imbued with social meaning. The connections between nature, culture, eating, and the meaning of food become even more complex when we examine the choice to include certain foods, such as meat, in the diet, or to exclude them. For this very reason, such an examination ought to hold great interest for students of human behaviour and of social movements and social change.

For the purposes of this chapter, we can divide those who do not eat meat into two categories. First, there are those who are forced to exclude meat from their diet. These include those who are compelled to take this course of action for either economic or environmental reasons, or a combination of both. Second, there are those who voluntarily exclude meat. This group can themselves be divided into those who exclude meat for religious reasons and those who do so for a variety of other reasons, such as philosophical and ethical, political, or health motives. It is this latter group that we will be primarily concerned with in this chapter, not because they are the most important, but because they hold the most interest sociologically. These people are at the nexus of the natural and the social, the private and the public. In what follows, I will examine the key issues that underlie the decision of a growing number of people to forgo voluntarily a nourishing and pleasure-giving food. I will then attempt to interpret these decisions within a framework of recent sociological theory.

Vegetarianism and the social sciences

It is interesting to note that, despite the potential for rich social observation and analysis, there has been little research and writing on vegetarianism from the perspective of the social sciences, although as we shall see, there have recently been some very useful exceptions. Why this long period of neglect within a discipline that is always on the 'look out' for new areas of social analysis? It can partly be explained by the social sciences' more general neglect of the whole area of food consumption (Murcott 1983). This in itself is interesting and relates to the more specific reasons for the neglect (or avoidance) of the subject of vegetarianism by social scientists. It is fair to say that sociologists are uncomfortable and suspicious of theoretically focusing on 'the natural' or 'the biological' for analysis of social issues, social patterns of behaviour, or social change. There are good reasons for this. In a very real sense, sociology is constructed around opposition to the notion that the social can be reduced to our biological origins and destiny (**biological determinism**). Over several decades, sociological analyses have successfully challenged biologically determinist accounts and rationalisations of inequality in the areas of class, gender, and ethnicity. Clearly these challenges have been confined neither to the pages of books nor to debates within universities, but have had profound effects on social attitudes and social policy worldwide.

Yet while behaviour and attitudes concerning discrimination based on class, gender, and ethnicity are regarded as **'socially constructed'** and therefore socially amenable to change, the issue of what we eat—and therefore our relationship with other living creatures—has remained strangely **unproblematised** and therefore implicitly regarded as natural. Put another way, it seems that *homo constructivist* and *homo disciplinis* become *homo naturalis* when it comes to eating meat. When searching for reasons for this blind spot in social analysis, it is impossible to ignore the bedrock of Judaeo-Christian teachings, which conveniently mesh with a sociological view of humans as having distinct and unique characteristics that mark them out as superior to all other living creatures. In so doing, sociologists have reinforced the tendency to deny the animal in humans as well as the social in animals (Noske 1989). Social scientists have, on the whole, been content to leave the study of animals to the natural scientists and to criticise their subject–object approach only if it is applied to humans (Noske 1989, p. 83).

It must also be said that a study of vegetarianism frequently leads to the breakdown of the fragile edifice of denial and mystification involved in eating animals. Perhaps for many social scientists the possibility that academic research will prompt fundamental personal (in this case dietary) change is an unwelcome and uncomfortable prospect and is therefore best avoided. Whatever the reasons for the past neglect, social scientists are now turning their attentions to the area of food in general and diet choice in particular for research and analysis.

Historical overview

While vegetarianism is a relatively modern phenomenon, it is informed and underpinned by a collection of rich and varied historical antecedents. Alan Beardsworth and Teresa Keil (1997) provide a useful account of the historical and cultural background of meat-rejection, as does Colin Spencer (1995). Suffice to say that one of the earliest coherent philosophies of meat rejection was put forward by the Greek philosopher and mathematician Pythagoras (born approximately 580 BC). The Pythagorean doctrine was based on the belief of the transmigration of souls, which implied a kindred relationship and a common fate for all living creatures. It also embodied what would now be called environmental or ecological concerns (Beardsworth & Keil 1997, p. 220). This theme, concerning the connection and relatedness of all creatures (including humans) has surfaced many times throughout the history of Western thought and has been a constant in many Eastern religions as well as the belief systems of many indigenous peoples. It is encapsulated in the words of Della Porta: 'When one part suffers, the rest also suffer with it' (as quoted in Merchant 1980, p. 104).

Another historical theme that has emerged at various times and places has been concerned with the connection between the rejection of meat and the health of individuals and societies. In Italy in 1558, in England in the seventeenth century, and in Germany, the USA, and the United Kingdom in the nineteenth century, various theorists have posited the connection between vegetarianism and a long and healthy life (Spencer 1995, p. 274). In the 1830s in the USA, a Presbyterian preacher named Sylvester Graham (of Graham Cracker fame, makers of a wholemeal biscuit) preached that vegetarianism was the natural diet and that meat was probably not included in the food of the 'first family and the first generations of mankind' (as quoted in Fieldhouse 1995, p. 155). These theories were enhanced by the 'conversion' of prominent individuals, such as the co-founder of Methodism, John Wesley, and literary figures such as Percy Bysshe Shelley, Leo Tolstoy, and George Bernard Shaw. Spencer (1995) makes the important point that, as well as the emphasis on health, the vegetarian movement has historically maintained long-standing links with movements such as ethical socialism, animal rights, **anti-vivisection**, and pacifism. Links with other, kindred social movements are still apparent within modern vegetarianism.

What is a vegetarian?

Before studying the extent of modern vegetarianism and the reasons for its voluntary adoption, we must first be clear on what we mean by vegetarianism, which is a surprisingly 'broader church' than is commonly thought. Technically speaking, a vegetarian is a person who eats no flesh. There are further subcategories, such as lacto-vegetarians and ovo-vegetarians, who eat no flesh but who eat some of the products of animals—in this case milk and eggs. A vegan, on the other hand, not only refuses flesh, but also abstains from eating (and sometimes wearing) all animal products. Vegans argue that animal products cannot be separated from animal mistreatment. They point, for instance, to the connection between eating eggs and the keeping of hens in 'battery' cages and between drinking milk and the breeding and slaughter of 'veal' calves, which are necessary to keep dairy cows in milk (Singer 1975, p. 179–80; Maurer 1995, p. 153). For this reason, many vegans also refuse to wear or use products based on animal material—for example, soap, wool, and leather. They make the point that it would be incongruent to be entertained by a vegetarian on a leather lounge. Other variations are vegetarians who will eat free-range eggs but refuse milk, and others who will eat fish but refuse the flesh of other animals.

A fascinating recent study from the United Kingdom indicates that there are even more complex permutations to a vegetarian diet and a vegetarian identity. In her study based on fieldwork in south-east London, Anna Willetts found that the terms 'vegetarian' and 'vegan' covered a varied set of dietary practices, including the ingestion of fish and sometimes chicken and other meat (1997, p. 115). While some vegetarians presented meat-eating as a momentary 'lapse' (as in not refusing a lovingly cooked meat-based casserole at a dinner party), others developed a more fluid definition, as with the woman who said 'I'm often vegetarian apart from the fact that I buy chicken now ... I do like chicken curries' (Willetts 1997, p. 117). On the other hand, another woman stated that she didn't think of herself as a vegetarian, even though she abstained from meat and fish because she did wear leather shoes and ate dairy products. Both of these statements, and others of similar ilk, do, however, reveal a consciousness of a vegetarian identity and a conscious effort to remove or reduce animal matter from the diet.

How many are there?

Notwithstanding problems of definition, there have been several attempts to calculate the extent of vegetarianism across a number of countries. Beardsworth and Keil (1997) make the point that the data available for countries such as the United Kingdom and the USA are sparse and fragmentary. On the basis of conflicting surveys, they estimate the proportion of self-defined vegetarians in the United Kingdom to be between 4 and 6 per cent and conclude that this proportion is steadily rising. Spencer (1995, p. 338) has calculated that the number of people who avoid red meat in the United Kingdom has increased from around 2.2 million in 1984 to 8.2 million in 1991, which is 16 per cent of the population. He notes that, 'Historically, of course, in the West, this is the greatest number of vegetarians ever to exist within a meat eating society who are not part of any one idealistic or religious group, who have abstained from meat for a variety of different reasons, though they broadly share the same view of society itself' (1995, p. 338). In the USA, the proportion of self-defined vegetarians falls between 3 and 7 per cent (Beardsworth & Keil 1997, p. 225). This does not necessarily mean that all these individuals refrain from eating exactly the same food. It does mean that a very large and ever increasing number of people have adopted a vegetarian identity and make a conscious effort to remove animal products from their diet, or at least to restrict them.

The Australian situation appears to be similar. A national survey involving 1100 respondents aged 13 years and over was conducted by the advertising agency Young & Rubicam in 1993. This survey (which was adjusted for gender and class) indicated that 5 per cent of respondents identified themselves as vegetarian, with another 2 per cent 'mainly vegetarian' and a further 8 per cent 'partly vegetarian' (Young & Rubicam 1993). The most recent National Nutrition Survey (McLennan & Podger 1997) has produced similar results. In this case, 14 000 respondents were asked to self-report on their type of diet. In the category 'Special Diet', respondents were given the options of: 'vegetarian', 'weight-reduction', 'diabetic', 'fat-modified', and 'other(s)'. The highest numbers of self-reported vegetarians occurred in the 19–24 years category, with males at 4.3 per cent and females at 6.2 per cent. More generally, there were 3.7 per cent of males and 4.9 per cent of females aged 19 years and over who classified themselves as vegetarian. It is, however, important to note that a further 10.3 per cent of males and 11.8 per cent of females over 19 years placed their diets in the non-specific 'other(s)' category of 'special diet'. As there were no categories for 'partly vegetarian' or 'vegan', it is reasonable to assume that some of these diets were included in the category of 'other(s)' and so the numbers for different types and degrees of vegetarian diets may well be underreported. Certainly the categories in both surveys can be criticised for being wide and inexact. Yet these figures, like those for the United Kingdom and the USA, point to the fact that vegetarianism in the West is no longer the territory of a few 'cranks' but has become something approaching a mass movement, with millions of adherents worldwide.

Why become vegetarian?

There are many reasons why people stop eating meat. There are the rational 'head' reasons, based perhaps on the procedures involved in meat production, and there are the 'gut' reasons, such as the sudden, sickening realisation that a piece of meat about to be cooked is actually part of an animal's muscle, which is bleeding onto the plate. This sort of realisation occurs when there is a breakdown in the edifice of denial and avoidance concerning the meat on the plate and the cow or pig from which it came. This occurs despite the best efforts of advertisers and meat organisations to disguise the various cuts and combinations of animal parts as 'chops' and 'sausages' and 'schnitzel' and various other euphemisms. Not infrequently, the gut reaction comes first and is followed by further reading and exploration, which reveal the rational and persuasive facts with which most people feel more comfortable when pressed for an explanation. The gut reactions are individual and private, and are only uncovered through qualitative research, such as that undertaken by Beardsworth and Keil (1992). Much more of this type of research needs to be done. There are, however, many intellectual reasons for voluntary abstinence from meat, and I will deal with these in the next section.

Philosophical approaches to animal rights

The decision to stop eating meat is inevitably tied up with questions such as: Who am I? Why am I here? What is my place in relation to others on the planet? These questions go straight to the heart of issues concerning 'human nature' (Cowen 1994). These are the important, difficult questions that organised religion and secular philosophy have attempted to answer since the beginning of human time. For those of us with a Judaeo-Christian heritage, they are tied up with interpretations from the Old Testament concerning the place of humans in relation to other species. The pivotal passage comes from Genesis, where we are told:

> And God blessed them, and God said unto them, Be fruitful, and multiply, and replenish the earth, and subdue it; and have dominion over the fish of the sea, and over the fowl of the air, and over every living thing that moveth upon the earth (Gen. 1:24–8).

The Jewish and Christian religions have, on the whole, chosen to interpret 'dominion' as the right to have power over, to control, and to use all other species for the benefit of the human species. These religious traditions are so pervasive in the West that they constitute the bedrock of morality for the majority of people, including those who do not ostensibly adhere to organised religions. We are, on the whole, brought up to believe that eating meat is not wrong or, more commonly, that we are not even required to question whether it is right or wrong. This is not to say that individuals and sects of Jews and Christians have not questioned the morality of the killing and eating of animals, but they have usually been treated as outsiders at best and, at worst, as heretics (Singer 1975; Spencer 1995). These individuals and sects have often come to another interpretation of 'dominion', one that emphasises the responsibilities of care and nurture that inhere to humans in relation to other species on the planet. This inter-pretation has had a profound influence on the animal rights movement, as well as on the environmental and ecological movements more generally.

There have also been attempts to develop philosophies of animal rights within sec-ular traditions. Probably the best known is 'animal liberation', a philosophy and a social and political movement most notably championed by the Australian philosopher Peter Singer. In his book *Animal Liberation* (1975), Singer details the shocking litany of mis-treatment inflicted on animals through animal experimentation and meat production and slaughter, particularly those associated with modern, intensive farming methods. This book was one of the first public exposes of, for instance, the fact that battery hens spend their entire lives in cages no larger than the area of an A4 page, that the lights in the battery sheds are left on over a 24-hour period so that their bodies are tricked into producing two eggs instead of one, that sows are immobilised by iron bars during the weeks following the birth of their piglets so that they can feed but cannot turn to nuz-zle their young, and that these naturally intelligent, curious, ruminating animals are kept in tiny, cement-floored stalls, which are too small for the sow even to turn around, let alone exercise in any way. Perhaps even more shocking were Singer's exposes con-cerning modern veal-production methods. He detailed the way that tiny day-old calves are removed from their mothers and housed in tiny, dark wooden 'crates', where they live, immobilised, for the next 13–15 weeks. Singer comments:

> Of all the forms of intensive farming now practised, the quality veal industry ranks as the most morally repugnant, comparable only with barbarities like the force-feeding of geese through a funnel that produces the deformed livers made into pate de foie gras. The essence of veal raising is the feeding of a high-protein food—which should be used to reduce mal-nutrition in poorer parts of the world—to confined, anaemic calves in a manner that will produce a tender, pale-coloured flesh that will be served to gourmets in expensive restau-rants (Singer 1975, p. 127).

The calves are deliberately made anaemic so that the colour of their flesh remains a desirable pale colour for the pleasure of the consumer. Other miseries experienced by these calves are detailed in Singer's book and make sobering reading for lovers of veal scaloppine. While 'crating' is widespread in Europe and the USA, it is not yet a signifi-cant part of Australian veal production; however, there are constant pressures on all sec-tors of Australian farming to become more intensive and 'productive'.

Singer bases his critique on the utilitarian philosophy developed by Jeremy Ben-tham in the eighteenth century. Bentham held that the ability of non-human species to experience happiness and their interest in avoiding pain had 'been neglected by the insensibility of the ancient jurists' to the extent that animals were used merely as 'things' (as quoted in Tester 1991, p. 96). Singer has taken up this philosophy and argued that the capacity of animals to experience suffering and pleasure implies that they have their own interests that ought not to be violated. This in turn means that they are not beyond the realm of moral and ethical consideration. Singer argues that to inflict suffering on animals, which includes killing them for food, is a form of 'speciesism' that parallels racism and sexism within human relationships. Thus utilitarian principles demand the adoption of a vegetarian diet (Singer 1975).

Other philosophers, such as Mary Midgley (1979), also reject the view that animals lay outside moral consideration and therefore can be 'used' for whatever purposes the human species cares to develop. For Midgley, the key to the human–animal relationship is to recognise that we humans are culture-building animals and that 'nature and culture are not opposites at all' (1979, p. 29). If humans are indeed animals, then we need to recognise our entwined kinship as well as our differences. She argues that all animals should be seen as morally relevant subjects, regardless of their species. In a positive vein, she contends that, historically, the boundaries of moral consideration have been continually advancing, and that they can and must now breach the 'species barrier' (1983).

Some other philosophers, who agree with the underlying approach of Singer and Midgley, nevertheless have reservations about using utilitarian concepts to discuss animal rights and animal liberation. T. Regan (1984), for example, emphasises the *inherent value* in animals (not the value we humans may choose to attribute to them) and so emphasises the way that this inherent value demands our *respect*. S. R. L. Clark (1984), on the other hand, points to the responsibility of *stewardship*, which entails the rejection of all forms of exploitation, while Barbara Noske (1989) argues for an end to the objectification of animals and for the undertaking of a quest for their '*resubjectification*'. For all of these authors and their many followers, the idea of killing and eating other animals becomes, upon close examination, a morally repugnant option. Such examination therefore provides an important rationale for becoming a vegetarian.

Ecological and environmental reasons

Many vegetarians make the decision to remove meat from their diet because of the adverse impact of meat production on the environment. The facts are persuasive. Meat production is an inefficient and energy-intensive process, especially when intensive farming methods are involved. Grain, which could be used to feed people, is instead fed to cattle, pigs, and fowls, and in the process of converting grain to meat, a large amount of food energy is wasted. There are two dimensions to the environmental consequences of this process. These entail the effects on both human and non-human life forms. In terms of human consequences, it is clear that the high meat consumption within affluent countries has an adverse impact on people in developing countries. This is illustrated by the fact that the European Union is the largest buyer of animal feed in the world, and 60 per cent of this imported grain comes from developing countries. These countries grow the cereals as cash crops (for desperately needed foreign exchange) when they could grow crops for food, which would halt malnutrition among their own people (Spencer 1995, p. 341).

Spencer (1995) makes the crucial point that if the world's population is to be fed adequately, then a more efficient way of producing protein must be adopted. He states:

> A large percentage of the protein fed to cattle (94%), pigs (88%) and poultry (83%) is lost, mostly in their dung. The world's cattle alone consume a quantity of food equal to the calorific needs of 8.7 billion people, which is nearly double the population of the planet now. To halve the number of livestock reared would dramatically alleviate world hunger (Spencer 1995, p. 341).

Writing recently in the *Guardian Weekly*, Tim Radford makes a similar point when he points out that 'Cattle are especially wasteful—it takes 790 kg of plant protein to turn into 50 kg of beef protein. But all animals are expensive. In 1979, the United States fed 145 million tons of grains and soybeans to livestock and got back only 21 million tons in meat, poultry and eggs (Radford 1996).

Jeremy Rifkin (1993) has researched in great detail both the human and non-human consequences of beef production. He argues that if the United States land mass that is currently used for growing feed for livestock was converted to growing grain for human consumption, 400 million more people around the world could be fed. World-wide, cattle occupy a quarter of the world's land mass and consume enough grain to feed hundreds of millions of people. While these figures are staggering, it is important to note the crucial point made by Beardsworth and Keil (1997) that this argument does not address crucial issues of the distribution of wealth and income. Those who experience malnutrition and starvation tend to be the poor, who are without the resources to produce or buy the food they need for themselves and their families. These structural constraints, with their political and economic roots, are as significant as the increase in the global pool of grain that would result from increased vegetarian consumption patterns (Beardsworth & Keil 1997, p. 231). Any realistic action to reduce world hunger would need to take account of both these dynamics.

Rifkin describes beef as an inefficient food. It requires 5455 litres of water to produce one 250-gram boneless steak in California. In United States feedlots (where cattle are kept in small holding areas for their entire lives and fed solely on grain and processed food), this intensive feeding results in a ten-fold loss of energy. *In fact, it takes 8–10 kilograms of grain to produce 1 kilogram of meat.* Rifkin claims that cattle production is destroying Central American rain forests and United States range lands, and is polluting lakes and waterways. The problem of waste is even more dramatic in countries with small acreage and highly developed farming, such as the Netherlands. Dutch farms produce 94 million tonnes of manure every year, the problem being that their soil can only absorb 50 million tonnes (Spencer 1995, p. 331).

Even a country with a vast land mass such as Australia is now experiencing serious problems with animal waste run-off. A recent report by the New South Wales Department of Land and Water Conservation, titled *Window on Water: The State of Water in NSW*, stated that up to 300 bore sites across New South Wales were found to be badly polluted. It found that ground-water supplies used by 250 000 people for drinking contained dangerously high levels of nitrates. Among other health effects, these high levels threaten the lives of small children, making them susceptible to a condition that results in reduced oxygen-carrying capacity of the blood. The rise in pollution is attributed to run-off and leakages from piggeries, animal feedlots, dairies, and septic and sewerage systems. The report also found that the quality of New South Wales rivers and storage dams was rapidly declining (*Sun–Herald*, 17 August 1997).

The relationship between meat production and environmental degradation can be seen with pristine clarity when we focus on hamburger production. Hamburger chains such as McDonald's make billions of dollars worldwide each year through manipulative and aggressive marketing. This marketing successfully presents their hamburgers as an integral and fun-filled part of today's busy lifestyles. The reality is that the production and consumption of these hamburgers is having a catastrophic effect on the surviving rainforests of the planet. It has been calculated that, after rainforest clearing for cattle grazing, the cost of a hamburger produced in the first year is approximately half a tonne of mature forest, since such forest naturally supports about 800 000 kilograms of plants and animals per hectare. This same area under pasture will yield around 1600 hamburgers. This means that the *real* price of a hamburger is not an amazing $1.99, but anything up to 9 square metres of rich, highly diversified, and irreplaceable rainforest (Spencer 1995, p. 331). It is for these and other compelling reasons that many individuals active in ecological and environmental movements are also vegetarians.

Aesthetic reasons

Delicacy and a heightened sense of beauty and ugliness may also prompt the refusal of meat. Norbert Elias (1978) has interpreted vegetarianism as a logical development in the 'civilizing process', which entails a strong and conscious effort to remove the distasteful from the sight of society. This process has resulted in activities such as urination, vomiting, and defecation being removed from the public sphere and located in the private sphere. In relation to meat-eating, it has entailed the removal of the obvious signs of the living and dead animal from public view. Where once a whole carcass would be carved at table, it is now likely to be hidden from view, with the diner being presented with a dainty portion of meat often surrounded and hidden by vegetables and salad. In the same way, from the 1960s onwards, butchers carved the animal carcass at the back of the shop and began to remove pigs' and calves' heads from the window. There was a discernible move towards buying meat cut, sealed, and packaged and a shift towards buying it in a supermarket rather than from the more confronting (and more honest) butcher's shop (Spencer 1995, p. 327).

Elias (1978) goes on to suggest that the rejection of meat altogether is the next logical step on this civilising curve. Those who are repulsed by the sight and taste of meat have a 'threshold of repugnance' that is lower than that of twentieth-century civilised standards in general. He argues that, while vegetarians may be considered deviant by their contemporaries, they are in fact at the vanguard of a larger social movement of the type that has produced social change in the past. These sentiments are echoed in the statement of an interviewee in Willetts' study, a teacher who commented on the large number of his students who were vegetarian: 'I have a prediction that in about a hundred years eating meat will be seen as something you don't mention, something obscene. It might not be outlawed, but you'd have to go to special restaurants to eat it' (as quoted in Willetts 1997, p. 125). Then again, George Bernard Shaw said something similar over one hundred years ago when he made the statement: 'A hundred years hence a cultivated man [*sic*] will no more dream of eating flesh or smoking than he now does of living, as Pepys' contemporaries did, in a house with a cesspool under it' (as quoted in Smith 1997). Clearly the civilising process moves in fits and starts, and is obviously capable of getting stalled at times. The fact that it does get stalled begs the question: is the period of late modernity more conducive to this type of social change than, say, the late Victorian period? This is an interesting and important issue, and one that we shall revisit in the final section of the chapter.

Health reasons for becoming vegetarian

For many individuals and families, the decision to become vegetarian is based on health considerations. In a recent Gallop survey in the United Kingdom, adults gave the main reason for becoming vegetarian as health (76 per cent), although other reasons (animal welfare) followed closely (cited in Spencer 1995, p. 338). A positive motivation may be the desire to reduce saturated fat intake and introduce more fibre into the diet. A more negative motivation may be tied up with fears of contamination or what Beardsworth and Keil have called an idiom of 'endangerment' (1997, p. 230). Fears about contamination revolve around issues concerning contamination from additives (chemicals and hormones) as well as those concerned with bacterial contamination.

There is evidence to indicate that both of these motivations are valid. In terms of the positive motivation to improve health, there are at least two major studies worth noting. The 'China Study' began in 1983 and its results were published in 1990. It involved a survey of 6500 Chinese, who contributed 367 facts about their diet. In general terms, the study found that the fewer animal products eaten, the lower the incidence of disease and death (Berriman 1996, p. 54). More specifically, the study found that in those regions of China where meat consumption has begun to increase, it has been closely followed by an increase in the diseases of affluence, such as cardiovascular disease (sometimes fifty times the rate for a more traditional Chinese diet), cancer, and diabetes (Spencer 1995, p. 339). The larger 'Oxford Study' confirms these findings. In this study of 11 000 people, half were maintained on their traditional meat-based diet, while the other half consumed either vegetarian or near vegetarian diets. It was found that the latter group had nearly 40 per cent less cancer, 30 per cent less heart disease, and were 20 per cent less likely to die up to the age of 80 years. These figures were adjusted for factors such as smoking and alcohol consumption (Berriman 1996, p. 54).

Public fears over contamination of meat have grown as more information concerning practices associated with intense 'factory farming' have filtered into public awareness. These practices have included the use of antibiotics and growth hormones, which hasten the fattening process for animals. One of the most infamous growth promoters was DES (diethyl stilboestrol), which was banned in 1981 after it was found that some small children in Italy had developed sexual features after eating commercial baby food made from veal. Residues of DES were found in the food after large amounts had been injected into the calves' rumps (where it remained in the meat) instead of their ears. There has also been concern about the overreliance on antibiotics, which are necessary when animals are reared in overcrowded conditions. Residues have been found in the organs of animals as a result of this practice, which has been actively encouraged by pharmaceutical companies. Bacterial resistance to antibiotics is now worldwide, and there is concern that this use of antibiotics is adding to the problem (Spencer 1995, p. 223).

These concerns pale, however, in the light of recent scares over bacterial contamination of meat. Through the 1980s there were several major salmonella outbreaks in the United Kingdom that had their origins in animal products. It has been estimated that 10 000 Britons suffer from food poisoning each week, while 100 people die from it each year. More than 95 per cent of these cases originate in animal or poultry products (Spencer 1995, p. 335). A recent example occurred in 1996, when an *E Coli* outbreak that originated in a butcher's shop in Scotland killed twenty people who consumed the meat from this long-established 'family butcher'. Professor Pennington, Professor of Bacteriology at Aberdeen University, who led the inquiry into the *E Coli* outbreak, stated that the British government was failing to implement the safety measures that were needed to curb an 'outrageous food poisoning crisis'. He went on to say that 'Food poisoning in the UK has now reached unacceptable levels. A million cases a year is outrageous' (*Guardian Weekly*, 18 January 1998). His warning came hard on the heels of another warning from the British Medical Association that the public should treat all raw meat as infected, a claim dismissed by the Meat and Livestock Commission as 'scaremongering' (*Guardian Weekly*, 18 January 1998). In Australia in 1995 and 1996, there were several serious outbreaks of food poisoning, including one in South Australia that resulted in the death of a young child. The source was traced to a smallgoods factory that produced 'salami' (in reality fermented, uncooked meat) that was infected with a strain of *E Coli*.

The major food scare and scandal of the 1990s has concerned bovine spongiform encephalopathy (BSE) or 'mad cow' disease. This disease causes the development of holes in the cow's brain and is exactly the same symptom that affects sheep suffering from scrapie. While it has not been proven, most experts now concede that it was the feeding of feedlot cows with the scrapie-infected sheep meat that caused the disease to occur in cattle (Berriman 1996, p. 47). It is now feared that this disease can manifest itself in humans who have consumed infected meat, as the brain-destroying Creutzfeld-Jakob disease (CJD). While millions of cattle have been destroyed in the United Kingdom, there are fears that the disease may still be present, undetected, in some stock. In December 1997, a new report offered evidence that BSE had been detected in the bone marrow of farm animals. As a result, the government was forced to pass extraordinary legislation, which made it illegal to sell any meat in the United Kingdom that still adheres to bone. This includes such staples as leg of lamb, T-bone steak, rib-steaks, and oxtail (*Guardian Weekly*, 14 December 1997).

As the facts emerged, ordinary people in many countries became disgusted to learn that recycled waste from intensive farming—the excreta, feathers, soiled straw, and remains of dead birds and animals—were being pasteurised and processed into pellets and fed to domestic and farm animals, including the naturally herbivorous cow (Spencer 1995, p. 335). While this scare has been focused on the United Kingdom, it is important to note that until recently many intensively reared animals in Australia were fed a diet that included between 4 per cent and 10 per cent animal protein, most commonly a rendering of bone, fat, and blood. Not unrelated to this practice was the outbreak of botulism, which occurred in two cattle feedlots in Queensland in 1990 after chicken litter, including carcases, were used in the feed (a practice now banned) (Berriman 1996, p. 47).

The image of an endless recycling of infected animal matter, which is able to infect humans, is a powerful reminder of the 'danger' of meat-eating in the late modern era. According to Spencer (1995, p. 336), there can be little doubt that the image of, and increasing knowledge about, the realities of factory farming has increased the numbers of vegetarians. In the United Kingdom throughout 1990, 28 000 people per week were converted to giving up meat. Among these 'voluntary abstainers', the class composition of vegetarianism was also changing. Research undertaken in 1988 and 1990 showed that the converts were from the lower middle classes and lower income groups. No longer just a movement of middle-class radicals, converts are growing across the class structure, with the numbers of converts thinnest among the top-income groups (Spencer 1995, p. 337). At the same time, the gender balance remains strongly in favour of women. In the United Kingdom, the 1995 Realeat Survey indicated that women were showing twice the rate of vegetarianism as men (cited in Beardsworth and Keil 1997, p. 224). Australian data (such as they are) support this. A 1993 Australian study of 11 000 individuals also found that the majority of vegetarians were women (17 per cent of women and 12 per cent of men described themselves as some sort of vegetarian ('partly vegetarian', 'mainly vegetarian', 'lacto-ovo vegetarian', 'lacto vegetarian', 'vegan'), (Young & Rubicam 1993). More gender-conscious research needs to be undertaken to explore the reasons for the propensity of women to convert to vegetarianism.

Understanding the shift away from meat

While there may be any number of rational and other reasons available for individuals to consider becoming vegetarian, historians and sociologists alike know well that logic and rationality does not a social movement make. There are times in history when whole groups *en masse* begin to embrace an attitude and forms of behaviour that are significantly different from what has been considered the social norm. One social theorist who is interested in this phenomenon is Anthony Giddens, whose recent work has explored changes in the ways that people think and act in their daily lives within the period that he calls 'high' or 'late modernism' (the late twentieth century). This work also has some useful insights and concepts for understanding the emergence of vegetarianism in the late modern age (Giddens 1991). In particular, Giddens is interested in the emergence of what he calls 'life politics', which is a politics of lifestyle in the sense that it involves a politics of life decisions or life choices (1991, p. 215). The decisions that are involved in life politics concern those questions that philosophical thought has always been concerned with: Who am I? What am I here for? How should I live? In the deepest sense, the decisions involved in life politics affect self-identity itself (1991, p. 215). Giddens, however, sees this as a reflexive process, one in which self-identity is constructed out of the debates and contestations that derive from the dynamic between the ongoing formation of identity and the changing context of external life circumstances.

Before making connections between life politics and the growth of vegetarianism, it is important to grasp another concept that is related to the idea of life politics. Giddens argues that in order for people to be in a position to make life choices, they must have attained a certain level of autonomy of action (1991, p. 214). This makes sense. People are only able to make choices when they are in a material and political position to make them. Giddens goes on to argue that the ability to make such choices is unique to the period of high modernity and it is built on the political orientations and achievements of the modern period—orientations in which *emancipatory politics* were of central concern. Giddens defines emancipatory politics as 'a generic outlook concerned above all with liberating individuals and groups from constraints which adversely affect their life chances' (1991, p. 210). He goes on to say that emancipatory politics is concerned to reduce or eliminate *exploitation, inequality, and oppression*. In all cases, the objective is either to 'release under-privileged groups from their unhappy condition, or to eliminate the relative differences between them' (1991, p. 211). The aim of liberating people from exploitation is predicated on the adoption of moral values, and indeed these values are often expressed within a framework of justice, ('social justice', for example). It is possible, then, according to Giddens, to see emancipatory politics as a politics concerned with the conditions that liberate us in order to make choices. So, while emancipatory politics is a politics of *life chances*, life politics is a politics of *choice* (1991, p. 214).

It is possible to see the adoption of a vegetarian diet as a choice that is part of the life politics of late modernity. It is also possible to regard it as a choice that involves the application and extension of the emancipatory politics of the modern period *beyond the human species*. In the modern period, the concepts of oppression and emancipation extended to apply to all humans, regardless of race or gender. It may be that the conditions of late modernity are conducive to the extension of the concept of emancipation to the animal world. This, of course, is precisely what philosophers such as Singer (1975) have been attempting to achieve. What Giddens shows is that this attempt can be seen in a social and political context as part of a great social movement—in fact, a 'remoralising' of social life. This gives us a sociological framework for understanding the growing awareness of animal rights and the voluntary adoption, by growing numbers of people, of a meatless diet for reasons connected with animal welfare. If Giddens is correct when he states that 'the concerns of life politics presage future changes of a far-reaching sort: essentially, the development of forms of social order "on the other side" of modernity itself', then it may well be that the growing numbers of voluntary vegetarians are indicative of a real change in social attitudes and behaviour towards animals (Giddens 1991, p. 214).

The future?

While Giddens provides us with a theoretical framework for understanding the emergence of life politics—which, I suggest, includes for many the choice to abstain from meat—it by no means enables us to predict the future of vegetarianism as a social movement in Western developed countries. While the data are too fragmentary to generate any predictive certainty (Beardsworth & Keil 1997, p. 240), there are, as we have seen, indications that voluntary vegetarianism is on the increase. It is also true to say, however, that late modernity produces contradictory pressures on individuals and groups. On the one hand, late modernity has produced a level of personal autonomy for many in the developed world, particularly the educated middle class. Yet, on the other hand, for many of these same people, late modernity has also provided more rushed and busy lives with little time for the promised leisure and pleasure. At the same time, this period has seen the development of huge disparities in wealth between different populations both within and between countries. In this environment, life choices may become pragmatic, based more on expediency and survival than on principle. It may be that a remoralising of social life and a heightened sensitivity to personal and political issues results in an 'I should but ... ' attitude, with associated guilt and neurosis becoming a defining feature of the construction of the self in late modernity.

This became visible recently with the huge amount of public angst expressed over two pigs who escaped from a slaughterhouse in Malmesbury in England and ran away. The English public *en masse* supported the pigs and demanded that they be allowed to live out their lives in peace. Nevertheless, there was no indication that sales of bacon were affected in the slightest. Once again, it seems, people were able to separate those two particular adventurous and cute pigs from the other pigs who face slaughter each day of the week to provide bacon for a 'real' English breakfast. The ideology that separates meat from the living animal is powerful and pervasive, and operates subtly and silently to reinforce the status quo. Animal rights groups will need to develop strategies that result in good media coverage if this powerful ideology is to be exposed.

At a more pragmatic level, much may depend on the ready availability of healthy, cheap, vegetarian convenience food from take-aways and supermarkets. Much may also depend on 'cultural exchanges' between vegetarians and non-vegetarians. Ask any vegetarian and you will be told that vegetarians are constantly accosted by (especially women) meat-eaters who say, 'I would love to eat less meat but I don't know what to cook. Can you give me some recipes?' It is not enough to direct these questioners towards the appropriate cookbooks. They are looking for some personal contact and for some kind of reassurance that their lives will not be turned upside down if they remove or greatly reduce meat from their diet. A recent attempt to achieve this goal can be found in the recent Australian release of the annual *Gourmet Vegetarian* magazine. This magazine is not directed at the overtly health-conscious or 'hippie' section of the market, but rather to the taste- and trend-conscious 'foodie' section of the population. This and other like publications are clearly an attempt to widen the appeal of vegetarian food and to remove its 'crank' and wholesome image.

At a less individual and personal level, social, economic, and environmental pressures regarding meat consumption are also contradictory. On the one hand, United States hamburger chains such as McDonald's continue to grow and penetrate new markets in the developed and developing world (including India, where 'mutton burgers' are sold instead of beef). Companies such as McDonald's develop clever marketing strategies (such as easy, cheap staff-run birthday parties for children) that have the effect of developing a taste for their bland, mass-produced food. When you look at the exponential growth of McDonald's, it is hard to envisage a successful challenge to their hamburger hegemony. Yet the company is facing a profit squeeze in its major markets as the customer base levels off. David Leonhardt (1998) has argued that McDonald's has lost some of its relevance to United States culture, with the result that domestic sales have climbed only 18 per cent since 1989, while operating profits (at 2 per cent) have not even kept pace with inflation. In addition, there are compelling arguments (as we have seen) regarding the environmental limitations of meat production. In a recent article titled 'Why Meat Will Soon Be Off the Menu', Radford concludes his argument with these facts:

> Right now the US diet is made up of 31 per cent animal products. With even a 1.1 per cent annual population growth rate, the number of mouths to feed in the US will double by 2050. Right now, each American has 1.8 acres of cropland to feed him or her—and provide $155 worth of food exports each year. By 2050, each American will have to live off 0.6 acres per capita. The US diet by then will be 85% vegetarian (Radford 1996).

It is clear that the transition to the new millennium will be marked by economic pressures towards increased productivity and an expanded market share for meat-based products. This strategy must inevitably entail a continuation and expansion of intensive farming methods. At the same time, the growth of ecological and animal rights movements, and the move towards a 'remoralising' of private and public life, will mean that these economic strategies will come under great pressure from social movements within the political arena. I said at the beginning of the chapter that vegetarianism was at the nexus of the natural and the social. It is now apparent that the issues of meat-eating and vegetarianism are also positioned at the nexus of economic 'rationalism', globalisation, and a politics based on personal ethics and ecological awareness. As well as having an ancient and multicultural historical heritage, vegetarianism can now be seen to represent one of the key moral and political issues of the late modern period.

Summary of main points

*   Vegetarianism is not just a movement of the twentieth century, but is one with an ancient history encompassing many different cultures.
*   Definitions of what constitutes a vegetarian vary widely.
*   There is evidence that indicates that the numbers of voluntary vegetarians is increasing worldwide.
*   The main reasons for the adoption of a vegetarian diet can be categorised as: philosophical or ethical, ecological or environmental, aesthetic, and health consciousness.
*   Recent theoretical contributions towards a theory of late modernism may assist our understanding of voluntary meat-rejection in this period.

Discussion questions

1   What might be some reasons for the long period of neglect of meat-eating and vegetarianism within sociology?
2   What has aesthetics to do with diet in general, and with the rejection of meat in particular?
3   Discuss some of the ethical and philosophical reasons put forward to support a vegetarian diet.
4   Discuss some of the health and/or environmental reasons put forward to support a vegetarian diet.
5   Relate the ideas of Giddens concerning life politics and emancipatory politics to the issue of meat-rejection.

Further reading

Beardsworth, A. & Keil, T. 1997, *Sociology on the Menu*, Routledge, New York.

Giddens, A. 1991, *Modernity and Self-Identity*, Polity Press, Cambridge.

Singer, P. 1975, *Animal Liberation: A New Ethics for Our Treatment of Animals*, Avon, New York.

Spencer, C. 1995, *The Heretic's Feast*, University of New England, Hanover, NH.

Tester, K. 1991, *Animals and Society*, Routledge, London.

References

Beardsworth, A. & Keil, T. 1992, 'The Vegetarian Option: Varieties, Conversions, Motives and Careers', *The Sociological Review*, vol. 40, pp. 253–93.

—— 1997, *Sociology on the Menu*, Routledge, New York.

Berriman, M. 1996, 'Mad Cow Disease, the Watergate of the Meat Industry', *New Vegetarian and Natural Health*, winter edition, pp. 47–8.

Clark, S. R. L. 1984, *The Moral Status of Animals*, London University Press, London.

Cowen, H. 1994, *The Human Nature Debate*, Pluto Press, London.

Elias, N. 1978, *The Civilizing Process*, Basil Blackwell, Oxford.

Fieldhouse, P. 1995, *Food and Nutrition: Customs and Culture*, Croom Helm, Kent.

Giddens, A. 1991, *Modernity and Self-Identity*, Polity Press, Cambridge.

Leonhardt, D. 1998, 'Trouble Underneath the Arches', *Australian Financial Review*, 9 March.

Maurer, D. 1995, 'Meat as a Social Problem: Rhetorical Strategies in the Contemporary Vegetarian Literature', in D. Maurer & J. Sobal (eds), *Eating Agendas: Food and Nutrition as Social Problems*, Aldine de Gruyter, New York.

McLennan, W. & Podger, A. 1997, *National Nutrition Survey Selected Highlights Australia 1995, Australian Bureau of Statistics*, Department of Health and Family Services, Canberra.

Merchant, C. 1980, *The Death of Nature*, Wildwood House, London.

Midgley, M. 1979, *Beast and Man: The Roots of Human Nature*, Harvester, Hassocks, UK.

—— 1983, *Animals and Why They Matter*, Penguin Books, Melbourne.

Murcott, A. (ed.) 1983, *The Sociology of Food and Eating*, Gower, Aldershot.

Noske, B. 1989, *Humans and Other Animals*, Pluto Press, London.

Radford, T. 1996, 'Why Meat Will Soon Be Off the Menu', *Guardian Weekly*, 28 April.

Regan, T. 1984, *The Case for Animal Rights*, Routledge & Kegan Paul, London.

Rifkin J. 1993, *Beyond Beef: The Rise and Fall of the Cattle Culture*, Plume, New York.

Singer, P. 1975, *Animal Liberation: A New Ethics for Our Treatment of Animals*, Avon, New York.

Smith, J. 1997, *Hungry For You*, Vintage, London.

Spencer, C. 1995, *The Heretic's Feast,* University Press of New England, Hanover.

Tester, K. 1991, *Animals and Society*, Routledge, London.

Willetts, A. 1997, 'Bacon Sandwiches Got the Better of Me': Meat-Eating and Vegetarianism in South-East London', in P. Caplan (ed.), *Food, Health and Identity*, Routledge, London.

Young & Rubicam 1993, *Australian Vegetarian Diets*, Young and Rubicam, Sydney.

7

Eating Out: *Reflections on the Experience of Consumers in England*

Alan Warde and Lydia Martens

Overview

- *Why is the incidence of eating out on the increase?*

- *Should the expansion of eating out be welcomed?*

- *Why do some people eat out more than others?*

This chapter offers an introductory sociological analysis of the eating of meals away from home, a subject that has been neglected in academic studies of food consumption. The chapter draws on an empirical study undertaken in England to describe the parameters of the practice. The chapter opens with a discussion of what might be meant by the term 'eating out'. It then examines the growth of eating out and explores the significance of the increasing number of commercial establishments selling prepared meals. Differential rates of access to eating out among different categories of person are also discussed. The final substantive section discusses evidence about the nature of the experience of dining out, of the relationships between customers and staff, and the levels of satisfaction reported by consumers.

Key terms

ethnography
post-Fordism
social class

Introduction: what is eating out?

As Roy Wood (1992, p. 3) ruefully observes, dining out is 'a much neglected topic and one that is often regarded as trivial'. This is partly because social sciences have traditionally been more concerned with the sources of misery and suffering than of enjoyment and pleasure. Furthermore, eating is considered quintessentially a domestic activity; symbolically it is identified with home, the domestic kitchen, and the family table. Hence most of our limited sociological information concerns the domestic preparation and consumption of food. Yet the amount of food eaten away from home is considerable in most developed societies—more so in some, like the USA, and less in others. The concomitant decline of domestic provision has fuelled speculation about the demise of family meals—a prospect usually viewed with regret because of the emotional, moral, and culinary virtues typically attributed to domestic cookery. The buying of meals already prepared (whether as take-away food or as eaten in a commercial establishment specialising in such provision), though a means of relief from domestic drudgery and from time pressure, is still greeted with ambivalence.

Food and its consumption can be examined at different levels, in terms of nutrients, ingredients, dishes, meals, and cuisines. Each level poses different kinds of analytic problems and arouses different kinds of popular concern. Hitherto, most scholarly attention has been focused on nutrients and ingredients. Work on whole dishes has been primarily practical, being the basis of training in cooking, whether domestic or professional. By comparison, there has been very little work on meals, which is the most clearly sociological topic, since meals presume forms of social ordering, rules of personal behaviour, and associated social obligations to, and bonds with, those with whom meals are shared (see Douglas 1975; Wood 1995; Marshall 1995). It is not accidental that the 'proper meal' has been at the core of sociological analyses of the practices of eating (see Murcott 1983; Charles & Kerr 1988).

Measuring the extent to which the habit of eating out is eroding the domestic mode of provision depends very much on how it is defined. Yet definition is difficult. On the face of it, 'eating out' is the taking of food in some location other than one's own place of residence. In that sense, there are a great many eating-out events: eating a packet of crisps or fish and chips in the street, eating a sandwich in the office, attending a barbecue at a friend's house, and enjoying an elaborate dinner in a restaurant would all count as eating out, while returning home with a take-away pizza or a made-up dish from the supermarket would not (see Figure 7.1).

There are many different sorts of places outside the home where currently people may sit down and eat a meal. Some of these are commercial establishments that specialise entirely in the provision of food. Thus we have, among others, cafés, restaurants, steak-houses, diners, brasseries, bistros, pizzerias, kebab-houses, grill rooms, coffee bars, tea shops, ice-cream parlours, food courts, snack bars, refreshment rooms, transport cafés and service stations, buffets, and canteens. There are also commercial places that are not entirely, or even primarily, devoted to food provision, but that also provide food,

Figure 7.1 Eating events: at home and away

such as the tavern, the pub, the wine bar, the hotel, the boarding house, and the motel. In addition, there are places that are not solely commercial, such as the canteens, dining halls, and refectories of institutions such as factories, hospitals, schools, universities, prisons, and the armed forces, where the food provided is subsidised or free. There are places that are often commercial but not permanently fixed, such as mobile cafés, or catering tents at weddings, race meetings, or carnivals. And, of course, one can eat out at someone else's home, in their kitchen, dining room, living room, or banqueting hall, depending upon the nature of your friends or family. The social, symbolic, and practical significance of these very different alternatives makes the analysis of eating out potentially very complex. Some of these alternatives, particularly the non-commercial ones, remain almost entirely unexamined sociologically.

The lack of general scholarly or official interest in the topic means that it is difficult to describe and analyse the processes. While there are obviously substantial cross-national differences in eating-out behaviour, there are insufficient sources to which to refer, and it would be folly to pretend to offer adequate generalisation about how practices are changing on the global scale. There has been gross neglect of eating out from the point of view of consumers, and it was in this context that we mounted an empirical study of the topic. As it happened, government agencies began to make some attempt to collect data at about the same time. The 1994 National Food Survey (United Kingdom), which had entirely ignored eating away from home for over 50 years, reported on outline patterns. In addition, the distinction between the snack, the meal out, and the take-away was incorporated in British national statistical categories for the first time in 1994 when the Family Spending survey recorded the pattern of current food expenditure (see Table 7.1).

Table 7.1 British household expenditure per week—in total, on food, and on food not from household stock—1994–95

Type of expenditure	Average amount spent per week per household (£)	Percentage of food expenditure	Percentage of all expenditure
All expenditure	283.58	–	100.0
Food expenditure	50.43	100.0	17.8
Expenditure on food not from household stock	13.64	27.1	4.8
Restaurant and café meals	6.74	13.4	2.4
Take-away meals at mealtime	2.06	4.1	0.7
Other take-away food and snack food	3.07	6.1	1.1
State school meals and meals at work	1.77	3.5	0.6

Source: Adapted from Department of Employment 1996

Previously, official household spending statistics had merely reported expenditure on meals eaten outside the home and had consigned much of the rest to a miscellaneous category. Nevertheless these surveys offer only sketchy accounts of the cost and the nutritional value of food eaten away from home. As a result, this chapter refers extensively to the findings of a study undertaken by the authors in England in the mid-1990s.[1] Unfortunately, the extent to which its findings apply to other countries is impossible to estimate.

Our study attempted both to identify statistical patterns and to explore the collective meanings associated with eating out. Initially it involved interviews with thirty-three principal food providers in diverse circumstances living in or around Preston, a medium-sized city in north-west England. The interviews were of a semi-structured type and lasted between one and two hours. Discussion was wide-ranging, covering aspects of eating at home and eating out. The key topics were:

- routines of preparing and eating food at home
- perceptions of change
- sources of food information
- definition, frequency, and reasons for eating out
- discussion of the last three meals eaten away from home.

The interviewees were people from diverse backgrounds, contacted through informal means (mostly volunteers from community groups, associations, and clubs). The interview transcripts informed the development of a structured survey instrument, which contained almost entirely closed questions, and which was administered by a commercial market research company and took about half an hour to complete. A total of

---

1   We are grateful to the Economic and Social Research Council for funding this study. It is part of the ESRC research program 'The Nation's Diet: The Social Science of Food Choice'.

1001 people were surveyed in three English cities: London, Bristol, and Preston. A quota sample matched respondents to the overall population of diverse local areas (wards) by age, sex, class, and ethnic group. The survey was undertaken in April 1995, and questions were asked about frequency of eating out, types of outlet visited, attitudes to eating out, and the nature of the most recent meal eaten away from home. The answers to these questions have been analysed to explore social variations in eating out by class, income, age, gender, education, place of residence, and so forth. We use the term 'interviewee' to refer to the people involved at the qualitative stage, and the term 'respondent' to apply to those contacted in the survey.

Interviewees were asked what they meant by the term 'eating out'. Lay definitions revealed five prominent themes. The first is spatial, entailing a journey from home, to an establishment specialising in food provision, primarily, if not solely, for the purpose of eating. That is to say, eating out was socio-spatially defined. The second theme was that it was expected that money would be exchanged; eating out is associated with commercial-sector service provision. Third, eating out is associated with consuming a substantial meal, rather than a snack; unless certain types of food were available and a set of food rituals were enacted, then the activity would not be deemed eating out. Fourth, eating out was a special activity, to be defined in contra-distinction to routine and regular behaviour. Finally, eating out meant the temporary suspension of domestic obligations to provide food for other household members (for further elaboration, see Martens & Warde 1997). One interesting aspect of these popular definitions was the association of eating out with an appropriate form of a *meal*.

For most interviewees, the quintessential eating-out event involved going to a restaurant or a pub where one could sit down with others for a reasonable period of time, eat a substantial meal rather than a snack, often with more than one course, and where eating would be the main purpose of the event. Hence it might seem that the restaurant meal emphasises, perhaps even more than its domestic counterpart, two key aspects of the proper meal: its content and its mannered rituals. Indeed, it may be that the closest approximation of the structure of a proper meal is now provided by a restaurant.

In the rest of this chapter we first examine the development of the catering trades; we then explore issues of access to eating out, and finally consider some aspects of the experience of eating out.

The growth of provision

Historical accounts of food provision tend to concentrate either on overall levels of consumption within societies that are affected by poverty and hunger, or with particular foodstuffs, like sugar or tea. For the United Kingdom, John Burnett (1989) gives a comprehensive overview of changing behaviour since the industrial revolution, showing how differences of class and region influenced types of diet and overall standards of nutrition. There are useful short sections on changing patterns of eating out, but only a small proportion of a large book is devoted to meals away from home.

There is no satisfactory historical account of the catering industry or restaurants. General histories of eating in the USA, like those of Harvey Levenstein (1988, 1993), make more reference to eating out, which has played a more prominent role in national food habits. And the USA is markedly better served with studies of the history and geography of the spread of establishments of different types (see Pillsbury 1990; Zelinsky 1985). However, the literature is sparse, and summaries of the development of the practice of eating out are thinly sketched by social scientific sources (see Mennell 1985; Wood 1995; Beardsworth & Keil 1997).

Most historical accounts of the development of commercial meal provision have concentrated on trends in frequency of travel, reasoning that being more than a certain distance from home necessitates eating out (Medlik 1972). There was a network of inns in England, offering sustenance, entertainment, and accommodation, at least as far back as the fifteenth century, and there travellers ate (Medlik 1972; Heal 1990). Commuting to work, increasingly common from the late nineteenth century, and the popularisation of vacations, in the first half of the twentieth century, by the same logic further fuelled the expansion of catering services. In these cases, however, the growth of eating out was associated with, and secondary to, the pursuit of other activities. This is also true of the main institutional locations for eating meals out. Factories, offices, hospitals, and schools all provide on-site refreshment in a canteen or refectory (for a clientele restricted by criteria of membership that transcend the ability to pay). As T. Chivers (1973, p. 641) notes, this sector of provision developed only after the First World War but is now considerable and apparently a lucrative market for an increasing number of private contract catering businesses. From the point of view of consumers, however, use of such outlets is rarely considered to be eating out. Rather, these are places where it is convenient or unavoidable to eat, and though providing the pleasure of relief from hunger, they would never be conceived as eating out.

Until very recently eating out was a comparatively restricted and infrequent activity, and the idea of doing so, for its own sake as a type of 'entertainment', is a recent one. In England, paying to dine out for pleasure (by preference, in situations where a domestic alternative was available), rather than out of necessity, began at the end of the eighteenth century, in the private gentleman's club (Chivers 1973, p. 643). From the late nineteenth century, large hotels had dining rooms open to non-residents, where elaborate meals could be eaten, and the specialised restaurant dates from the same period. The emergence of specialised places to eat out, particularly where there was a choice of food rather than a limited menu, was essentially a commercial innovation of the twentieth century. It is this kind of dining that people primarily associate with the idea of eating out. This is not to say that eating away from home out of necessity has declined; probably the opposite is true. But the last hundred years have been characterised by the gradual transformation of eating out into a popular leisure activity. Burnett (1989, p. 318) records that 'in a recent survey of leisure activities, going out for a meal or entertaining friends to a meal at home were rated as the most popular occupations after watching television'. Eating out has become popular entertainment.

The increased importance of commercial provision is indicated by the changing proportion of food expenditure devoted to meals eaten away from home. Table 7.2 shows changes in household expenditure on eating out since 1959. This table shows that eating out has accounted for a steadily increasing proportion of the household expenditure on food, rising from 10 per cent around 1960 to 21 per cent in 1993. This indicates a major shift in the ways that households provide for themselves. Clearly, expenditure is shifting out of the retail sector, which sells food for (further) preparation at home, into the commercial delivery of fully prepared meals. John Dawson's (1995) analysis of the monetary value of receipts to the catering industry in 1985 was £9.9 billion, exactly one-third the value of receipts to the retail food sector.

Table 7.2 British household expenditure per week—in total, on food, and on food not from household stock—1959–93

Year	Total expenditure (£)	Food expenditure		Eating out		
		£	% of total	£	% of food	% of total
1959–61	16.40	5.04	31.0	.50	9.8	3.0
1970	28.57	7.35	25.7	1.00	13.6	3.5
1980	102.55	23.52	22.9	3.95	16.8	3.9
1990	247.16	44.81	18.1	9.42	21.0	3.8
1993	276.68	49.98	18.1	10.43	20.9	3.8

Source: Adapted from Department of Employment, (various years)

Provision has become increasingly complex, a function both of producers' search for profitable commercial opportunities and of the changing social circumstances of potential consumers. Probably the most striking features of the changing nature of production are the increase in the scale of the industry and the differentiation of the types of establishment. Expansion has occurred alongside increasing specialisation of the establishments providing prepared foods. Types of commercial establishment vary in character with respect to a number of criteria: the putative requirements of their main clientele, the elaborateness of cooking, the ostensible pedigree of the cuisine, the nature of the service, and whether alcohol is for sale (see Martens & Warde 1998). The potential range of ways of combining these elements (self-service pizza for the rapid lunch, formal oriental banquets requiring sustained concentration, or a casual evening meal as adjunct to drinking in a pub, for example) create much opportunity for innovation, novelty, difference, and brand distinctiveness, which thematise particular meal experiences. Commentators on eating out, particularly market researchers and food journalists, alight excitedly on new trends and fashions. Among the most recent trends gaining publicity in the United Kingdom, with both commercial and aesthetic consequences, are:

- the emergence of food halls in shopping centres (Payne & Payne 1993)
- the introduction of other entertainment into restaurants (Crang 1994)

- a proliferation of specialisation in the provision of more exotic and authentic ethnic cuisines (Warde 1998)
- growing distinctions between the establishments whose principal function is providing meals: the restaurant and its generic types, the brasserie, the bistro, and the café.

On the face of it, variety and options have increased. Such tendencies might lend support to general theories of **post–Fordism**, the idea that provision becomes increasingly differentiated and flexible to satisfy customers who are more discerning, more concerned with the aesthetic aspects of lifestyle, more likely to demand items tailored to their individual preferences. However, the trends are not so simple.

Counter-trends operate. Capital concentration continues to create chains of outlets, often franchised, which provide a standardised product using industrial production techniques redolent of the car assembly plant. In 1998 McDonald's reputedly had 23 000 restaurants around the world dedicated to providing a virtually uniform meal experience. A large segment of the catering industry is oriented towards producing nothing more than acceptable nourishment to people with an immediate need to eat. Many independent outlets use the same suppliers of the same pre-prepared foods, which are simply reconstituted at the retail site. The accelerating routinisation of new fashion—transmuting the exotic into the mundane within a few years, as successful innovations are rapidly copied and the dedicated seekers of novelty are satisfied—again flattens the sense of variety. Thus it is not without grounds that Wood (1994a, 1995), for example, complained about the tendency towards the standardisation and indifferent quality of meals out in the United Kingdom. Ultimately, the availability of dozens of different pizza toppings or a hundred alternative flavours of ice-cream might warrant celebration of unprecedented and extensive choice, or it might simply prompt the observation that all are merely variants of pizza and ice-cream. Whichever, it is clear that the catering industry offers many examples both of mass production and consumption, and of specialisation and differentiation.

Access

Increasing consumption of food away from home is a function not only of the search by capital for new sources of profit but also of the new requirements of consumers. No one has yet written a persuasive account of the relative importance of the different factors influencing the expansion of the practice of dining out. A multi-causal explanation of increasing consumption would consider, among other factors, perceptions of 'time famine'; the normalisation of consumer culture and the consumer attitude; limited employment opportunities for immigrant settlers; the changing social status of women and the levels of married women's participation in the workforce; greater travel and daily spatial mobility; intense attention paid to food by the mass media; and increasing affluence among the population.

It is generally argued that food consumption exhibits a long-term trend towards equalisation (Burnett 1989; Mennell 1985; but see the qualifications of Warde 1997).

Eating out is not an exception. Until at least the 1950s in the United Kingdom, eating elaborate meals out was mostly restricted to the urban middle class, and was disproportionately a male activity. It has now become a much more common and popular activity, although the extent to which access is still socially unequal should not be underestimated. Nor should it be assumed that it is simply inequalities of income that determine the frequency or quality of eating out. Our survey gives an estimate of the distribution of the practice among different social groups in the mid-1990s.

Excluding holidays and eating at the workplace, the respondents to the survey ate a main meal on commercial premises about once every three weeks on average (in a pub, restaurant, café or similar establishment). Twenty-one per cent ate out at least once a week, and 7 per cent claimed never to eat out. Mean frequency of eating at someone else's home was about the same, but a much larger proportion of people (20 per cent) never did so. Some groups of people were likely to eat out more frequently than others. Eating out frequently was associated primarily with having high household income, being highly educated, being younger, being a student, having no children in the household, being unmarried, or not living with a partner. The inquiries of the National Food Survey (MAFF 1995, 1996) also indicate that income, age, region, and household composition affect how often people eat out.

The mean frequency of eating out was highest in London. The evidence suggests that there are some systematic differences in patterns of eating out between the capital and the two provincial cities. Greater frequency of commercial eating out, opportunities seized to eat more variously, longer distances travelled, and the patterns of companionship (eating out is characterised by markedly less involvement of kin) all suggest a distinctive metropolitan mode of consumption. To a large extent, however, the metropolitan mode is a function of the distinctive social composition of its population.

Casual observation suggests that different types of venue attract different social groups. For instance, the French government's anxiety about the demise of its culinary traditions is partly generated by the knowledge that young people are increasingly frequenting the fast-food outlets of international and national corporate chains (Fantasia 1995). The social and symbolic significance of eating out is more evident when eating out is analysed in relation to the use of different types of venue.

Sociologists have often commented on the way that social status is registered by means of consumption. Pierre Bourdieu (1984), the most influential modern sociologist of consumption, argues that styles of consumption are more than just means of using up resources. He argues that display of goods is part of a system of reputation, wherein judgments about suitability, expressed as definitions of good taste, result in members of different **social classes** systematically picking some items in preference to others. Some tastes are more prestigious than others. Our survey threw up evidence of statistical association between people sharing similar socio-demographic characteristics and behavioural patterns, demonstrating social differentiation in this field and giving some basis for inferring the existence of a cultural hierarchy. Respondents were asked to recall which kinds of restaurants they had used in the last twelve months. Most types of venue are, to some degree, socially differentiated in their custom, being used dispro-portionately by customers with higher incomes and with longer hours in employment. There is also almost always some statistically significant association with age, education, and income. This was particularly pronounced with respect to 'ethnic' restaurants.

Wide availability of meals provided commercially by establishments specialising in a particular ethnic cuisine is a relatively recent development and is still far from evenly dispersed across the United Kingdom. A considerable proportion of people in our sur-vey avoided ethnic restaurants altogether: 48 per cent had not eaten in any such estab-lishment in the last twelve months. In addition, 27 per cent of respondents never eat ethnic take-away meals, even though they are even more widely accessible. Many fac-tors are associated with the propensity to try 'ethnic' food, but some factors particularly suggest that the field of ethnic cuisine carries a certain level of cultural distinction. A constructed scale recording the number of different types of ethnic restaurant visited in the last year exhibited measures of association greater than for other forms of eating out. There is more pronounced involvement among those with higher income, those living in London, the better educated, and professional, managerial, and intermediate white-collar workers. There was also a strong correlation between the social class of the respondent's father at age of 16 years and the use of ethnic restaurants. This might sug-gest that social distinction is being maintained in at least one corner of the immense field of food provision. Social class still matters (see also Warde & Tomlinson 1995).

The survey also suggested that members of England's ethnic minorities were dis-tinctive in their behaviour. They were particularly likely never to eat out: whereas only 5 per cent of White people never ate out, 17 per cent of ethnic minority respondents never did. In addition, minority respondents generally avoided particular kinds of venues, most notably pubs and pub restaurants, hotels, and steak-houses.

Gender differences were less pronounced. Although it remains problematic for women to eat alone in restaurants (Mazurkiewicz 1983), when in company they eat out as frequently, and more or less in the same places, as do men. Some differences were apparent. Women eat somewhat different foods, preferring main courses of chicken and fish rather than red meat. They exert less control over decisions about whether and where to eat out when they do so solely in the company of their male partners. Their reasons for wanting to eat out differ (see Martens 1997). In addition, the National Food Survey demonstrates that men eat greater quantities of food than do women. But, over-all, gender differences were muted, suggesting that this was one realm where women participate on increasingly equal terms.

The experience of eating out

A book by M. Campbell-Smith, *Marketing the Meal Experience* (1967), is often credited with institutionalising the marketing insight that there are many factors that influence customer satisfaction with commercially provided meals. The restaurant should be not only a provider of food, but also a site of a theatre performance, in which the atmosphere, appeal to sensual perception, and the nature of service are all key elements. A text for the aspiring restaurateur, it concentrates on aspects over which an owner might exercise control. The degree of power exercised by the provider is one issue of dispute in studies of dining out, highlighted particularly by the (partly philosophical) critique of the practice by Joanne Finkelstein.

Finkelstein's *Dining Out* (1989), one of very few books devoted to the subject, argues counter-intuitively that 'the practice of dining out is ... a rich source of incivility'. Although she devotes the first half of the book to a history of the restaurant, the behaviours involved in eating out, and a classification of different types of venue, her purpose is primarily to expose the superficiality and lack of self-reflection that she believes characterise individuals in modern societies. Her central thesis is that restaurants are organised in such a way that dining out does not require the 'engagement' of customers in the creation of their own environment of sociality. Thus the decor, service, and atmosphere are designed in such a way as to relieve customers of the 'responsibility to shape sociality', and this 'weakens our participation in the social arena' (Finkelstein 1989, p. 5). Dining out encourages us to imitate the behaviour of other people in the restaurant, without there being any need 'for thought or self-scrutiny', thus constituting a 'constraint on our moral development' (Finkelstein 1989, p. 5). The regimes of commercial establishments are planned in a way that encourages simulated, rather than genuine, engagement (Finkelstein 1989, p. 52). Conventional behaviour in restaurants amounts to accepting an 'obligation to give a performance in accord with the normative demands of the circumstances' (Finkelstein 1989, p. 53). It is never quite clear whether Finkelstein is objecting to people being manipulated by owners with a view to profit or to the shallowness of customers who fail to appreciate the proper purpose of sociality. But the former is certainly possible, since the interaction between staff and customer can be seen as a struggle for power and respect.

The one area of the catering trade relatively well documented by sociological enquiry is the process of service delivery. Studies of the labour process are comparatively well developed, with a little research on chefs and commercial cooking (see Fine 1995; Gabriel 1988; Chivers 1973) and a considerable amount on service delivery. **Ethnography**, observation, and interviews have been effectively used to map the variety of work activities in different kinds of establishment that have developed over the years. W. H. Whyte (1948), G. Mars and M. Nicod (1984), and Y. Gabriel (1988) all examine the work of waiters in traditional restaurant settings. P. Crang (1994), Gabriel (1988), and M. Sosteric (1996) offer insights into the experience of waiting in less formal settings, including pubs and theme restaurants, since the 1980s. In addition, work in fast-food places has been the subject of intense scrutiny as an exemplar of alienated, routinised, Fordist work in the service industries (see Leidner 1993; Reiter 1991). Such literature tells us something about the orientations and experiences of the workers, but it is only tangentially concerned with the impact that such work has upon consumers.

The literature on waiters, waitresses, and the delivery of meals in restaurants tends to suggest that customers can be manipulated and, if desired, humiliated by staff (see

Whyte 1948; Mars & Nicod 1984; Leidner 1993). But this does not seem to have been a common experience of our interviewees. They sometimes recall and complain about poor, slow, or incompetent service, but not much about manipulation. There is little evidence that customers are intimidated by waiting staff, and this might be in part because eating out has become a much more informal activity than it once was. Not only is there a wide variety of establishments with different levels of formality, but the staff themselves are increasingly less likely to be full-time professionals with sufficient social gravitas to manipulate their clients. The existence of appropriate codes of conduct in restaurants are, however, acknowledged. There is potential for embarrassment, as some of our interviewees observed, and there may, therefore, be some support for C. Wouters's (1986) claim that informalisation simultaneously requires greater self-discipline as part of the civilising process. Certainly, with one exception, interviewees seemed concerned that they should always behave appropriately, including being suitably quiet, fittingly dressed, physically restrained, and so forth. There are codes of conduct that constrain people, and as Finkelstein (1989) observes, they are functions of the restaurant regime. But the codes seem to be largely self-imposed and self-policed, scarcely evidence of a particular agent exercising power. One important mechanism in avoiding embarrassment is, as we have shown, that people simply avoid places that they consider too formal. There is a process of self-selection in operation, and it is governed by people's wish to avoid feeling 'uncomfortable'.

Stephen Mennell (1985) claims that restaurant and domestic kitchens are tending to converge, both in terms of their equipment and the kind of food they might deliver. Wood (1994b) concurs with respect to the twentieth-century development of hotels, which have become increasingly like homes, evidenced by the provision of tea- and coffee-making 'facilities', a television for private use, a drinks cabinet, a private bathroom, and so on. However, he denies that this is pronounced with respect to eating out (Wood 1994a). Our evidence is ambivalent. Insofar as interviewees see eating out as special and a 'treat', and where a significant proportion aim to eat food they would not have at home, Wood is vindicated. On the other hand, our interviewees often defined good standards of service in restaurants in terms of friendliness and homeliness, suggesting that they expect and welcome a convergence of the commercial and the domestic.

The aspect of Finkelstein's argument that is most inconsistent with our evidence, a matter that is also ignored by Campbell-Smith, is the role of companions and their apparently autonomous capacity to make the experience of eating out an enjoyable one. The second key dimension of the experience of eating out is the relationship among diners. There are two sorts of relationship: that among those at the same table who are companions in a party, and that between different parties. Attitudes towards other parties—strangers, in effect—are mixed. There is generally little inter-party interaction, suggesting that the restaurant is a form of 'quasi-public space' (see Martens & Warde 1997). The pleasures that are derived from being in a public space where one can watch and be observed should not be underrated. But nor should one ignore the possibility that such situations may also be irksome or onerous. There was a marginal preference among our respondents for eating in the homes of friends rather than in commercial establishments because the event was completely restricted to family, friends, and acquaintances. It is probably more distressing to have uncongenial companions than poor service or bad food.

What little analytical literature there is on eating out tends to be highly critical of the nature and quality of meals eaten out. Restaurants are condemned variously for the quality of the food from a gastronomic point of view (Driver 1983), for the standardisation accompanying mass-production techniques (Wood 1994a), and for offering oppressively unauthentic contexts for social interaction (Finkelstein 1989). There are many other reasons why many people might be negative about their eating-out experiences. There is evidence of widespread ambivalence about food in general. Thus Deborah Lupton (1996) reports that some interviewees showed a breathtaking enjoyment of food, while others had very little interest in it, viewing it simply as a necessity of survival. Similarly, K. Purcell (1992) found that a significant proportion of her Oxford sample considered food to be nothing more than a biological necessity: food is merely fuel. In addition, there is widespread current concern about being overweight, which in extreme circumstances manifests itself in serious eating disorders, suggesting that occasions that require more eating may be unattractive to some people. Furthermore, concern is often expressed that many British foodstuffs are potentially damaging to health. There is considerable suspicion of the food production system, which might make eating in restaurants—where one is ignorant of the sources and qualities of the raw ingredients—seem particularly risky. Then again, English food has not traditionally had a reputation for excellence—rather the contrary. Yet, despite all these drawbacks, which are potential sources of discontent, people register overwhelmingly high levels of satisfaction.

In light of this, one remarkable feature of the survey of English urban populations was the great sense of pleasure and satisfaction that people claim to derive from eating out. As Figure 7.2 shows, 47 per cent of people agreed strongly with the proposition 'I *always* enjoy myself when I eat out', and a further 35 per cent registered agreement. Only 7 per cent disagreed. Moreover, when asked 'How much did you enjoy the overall occasion when you *last* ate out?', 82 per cent said that they liked it a lot, and a further 14 per cent said that they liked it a little (see Figure 7.3). We also asked about the extent to which people liked the various elements of that meal experience. Again, an overwhelming majority of respondents were very pleased with almost every aspect of the occasion. Aspects of sociability were the most likely to be pleasing, with over 95 per cent of people saying that they liked the company and the conversation. But 94 per cent said they liked the food, 87 per cent the service, and the same proportion thought they had received value for money. The least appreciated feature was decor, but even then more than four out of five people said that they liked it (see Table 7.3).

In the absence of any other data with which to compare this expressed level of satisfaction, it is possible only to speculate about why customers are apparently so satisfied.

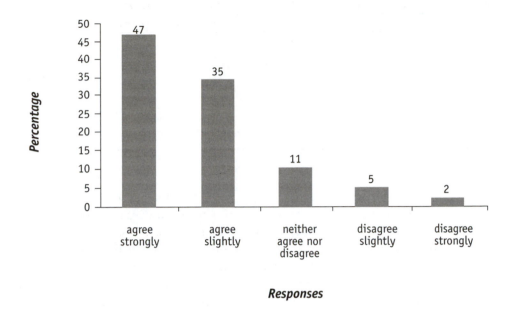

Figure 7.2 Responses to the statement 'I always enjoy myself when I eat out'

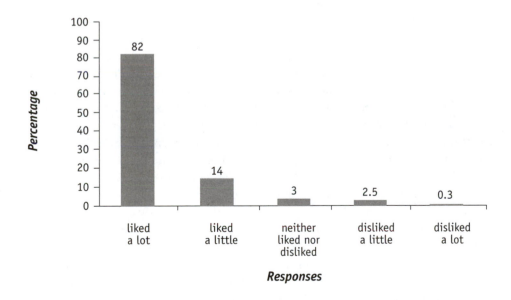

Figure 7.3 Responses to the question 'How much did you enjoy the overall occasion when you last ate out?'

Table 7.3   Percentage of respondents who liked various aspects of their last eating-out experience

Aspect	Percentage of respondents who liked the aspect
Food	93.6
Company	96.7
Décor	81.2
Service	87.2
Conversation	95.8
Atmosphere	90.7
Value for money	87.2
Overall, the total occasion	95.3

One reason is that people insulate themselves from the possibility of an uncongenial experience by revisiting the same restaurants. In response to questions about the last eating-out experience, 62 per cent said that they had been to that same venue before. Among these, over 99 per cent said they enjoyed themselves overall. However, there are more fundamental reasons, and they are associated with the very definition of eating out and with the several types of gratification involved. Traditional sensual pleasures are involved. If eating out involves a substantial meal, then the physical transformation from discomfort to comfort that A. Hirschman (1982) identifies as a reliable and regular source of pleasure will be achieved. Although occasionally diners may feel that they have not eaten sufficiently—and the size of portions was a matter frequently referred to in discussions with interviewees about restaurant meals—in most instances (and even sometimes when not totally satisfied), a pleasure-giving physical sensation will be achieved. The absence of toil is another universal feature of eating out, and one that is also a predictable basis for gratification. This is not to say that work is never a source of gratification—far from it. However, the welcome release from routine practical activity and from the social responsibility of preparing food is another likely source of gratification. On this topic, responses to the question 'Would you like to eat out more often?' found significantly more affirmative replies among women. Relaxed interaction and conversation with friendly companions is an opportunity furnished by eating out. That this occurs as a special occasion, especially when there is cause for celebration, is likely to heighten the degree of pleasure obtained. So too is the potentiality for new and varied food. Most restaurants will offer some opportunity for experimentation in eating, whether this amounts to offering ingredients or dishes previously unknown to the customer, elaborate presentation that would be absent from daily domestic meals, or merely the variety that arises from the techniques of a different cook. Reflection on such matters may give rise to complex comparison and evaluation of the merits of particular foods or venues. The range of gratification is thus considerable, and it is perhaps not surprising that, on balance, most meals are at least satisfactory. If the food is considered expensive and the service poor, one may be compensated by the company and by no longer being hungry. The worst-case scenario, where the food is inedible and the company unbearable, is likely to occur very infrequently.

Conclusion

There has been little research on eating out, a practice that is absorbing an increasing proportion of food expenditure in societies such as the United Kingdom. People often eat out because there is no acceptable and convenient alternative, although recent decades have also seen dining out emerge as a form of popular amusement. The number and range of available commercial venues has increased enormously in recent years, offering different foods and regimes of service. Yet, the domestic mode of provision is still overwhelmingly the most important source of food, and the communal mode—the entertaining of family and friends at home—remains comparatively strong. Nonetheless, the opportunity to eat out is not equally distributed across the population, and there is evidence that preferences for different venues are associated with education, income, class, ethnicity, age, and gender. The experience of eating out, though occasionally disappointing, is reported generally as a source of very considerable pleasure and satisfaction.

Summary of main points

- The limited research on eating out belies the fact that it has become a very significant element of the food habits of Western populations. It often occurs because any alternative is unacceptably inconvenient. But recent decades have also seen its emergence as a form of popular amusement.
- The number and range of available commercial venues has increased enormously in recent years, offering different foods and regimes of service. However, they are far from having replaced the domestic mode of provision, which remains overwhelmingly the most important source of food. It is also clear that the communal mode—the entertaining of family and friends at home—remains comparatively strong in this field.
- The opportunity to eat out is not equally distributed across the population, and there is evidence that preference for different venues is associated with education, income, class, ethnicity, age, and gender.
- Much of what is interesting sociologically about the practice is the nature of the social interaction when a predominantly private activity—eating—occurs in public situations. This can be a source of embarrassment and distress, but is mostly not so. With many venues becoming increasingly informal, potential customers can usually select a place that accords with their threshold tolerance for formality.
- The many kinds of gratification offered by eating out, in particular that of companionship, renders the experience generally highly satisfactory.

Discussion questions

1 Why would an activity such as eating out interest a sociologist?
2 How would you account for the rising incidence of eating out in contemporary England? Do you think that these reasons are equally applicable to other countries?

3   Do you agree with Finkelstein that eating out is 'a rich source of incivility'?
4   Should the expansion of eating out be welcomed?
5   Why do some people eat out more than others?

Further reading

Beardsworth, A. & Keil, T. 1997, 'Eating out', in A. Beardsworth & T. Keil, *Sociology on the Menu: An Invitation to the Study of Food and Society,* Routledge, London, ch. 5.
Finkelstein, J. 1989, *Dining Out: A Sociology of Modern Manners*, Polity, Cambridge.
Mennell, S. 1985, *All Manners of Food: Eating and Taste in England and France from the Middle Ages to the Present*, Blackwell, Oxford.
Warde, A. & Martens, L. 1999 (forthcoming), *Eating Out: A Sociological Analysis*, Cambridge University Press, Cambridge.
Wood, R. 1995, 'Dining Out', in R. Wood, *The Sociology of the Meal,* Edinburgh University Press, Edinburgh, ch. 3.

References

Beardsworth, A. & Keil, T. 1997, *Sociology on the Menu: An Invitation to the Study of Food and Society*, Routledge, London.
Bourdieu, P. 1984, *Distinction: A Social Critique of the Judgement of Taste*, Routledge & Kegan Paul, London.
Burnett, J. 1989, *Plenty and Want: A Social History of Food from 1815 to the Present Day*, 3rd edn, Routledge, London.
Campbell-Smith, M. 1967, *Marketing the Meal Experience: A Fundamental Approach*, University of Surrey, Guildford.
Charles, N. & Kerr, M. 1988, *Women, Food and Families*, Manchester University Press, Manchester.
Chivers, T. 1973, 'The Proletarianisation of a Service Worker', *Sociological Review*, vol. 21, pp. 633–56.
Crang, P. 1994, 'It's Showtime: On the Workplace Geographies of Display in a Restaurant in Southeast England', *Environment and Planning D: Society and Space*, vol. 12, pp. 675–704
Dawson, J. 1995, 'Food Retailing and the Consumer', in D. Marshall (ed.), *Food Choice and the Consumer*, Blackie, London, pp. 77–104.
Department of Employment 1996, *Family Expenditure Survey*, HMSO, London.
—— (various years), *Family Expenditure Survey*, HMSO, London.
Douglas, M. 1975, 'Deciphering a Meal', *Daedalus*, vol. 101, no. 1, pp. 61–81.
Driver, C. 1983, *The British at Table, 1940–80*, Chatto & Windus, London.
Fantasia, R. 1995, 'Fast Food in France', *Theory and Society*, vol. 24, pp. 201–43.
Fine, G. 1995, 'Wittgenstein's Kitchen: Sharing Meaning in Restaurant Work', *Theory and Society*, vol. 24, pp. 245–69.
Finkelstein, J. 1989, *Dining Out: A Sociology of Modern Manners*, Polity, Cambridge.
Gabriel, Y. 1988, *Working Lives in Catering*, Routledge, London.
Heal, F. 1990, *Hospitality in Early Modern England*, The Clarendon Press, Oxford.

Hirschman, A. 1982, *Shifting Involvements: Private Interest and Public Action*, Princeton University Press, Princeton, NJ.

Leidner, R. 1993, *Fast Food, Fast Talk: Service Work and the Rationalisation of Everyday Life*, University of California Press, Berkeley, Calif.

Levenstein, H. 1988, *Revolution at the Table: The Transformation of the American Diet*, Oxford University Press, Oxford.

—— 1993, *The Paradox of Plenty: A Social History of Eating in Modern America*, Oxford University Press, Oxford.

Lupton, D. 1996, *Food, the Body and the Self*, Sage, London.

MAFF. See Ministry of Agriculture, Fisheries and Food, National Food Survey Committee.

Mars, G. & Nicod, M. 1984, *The World of Waiters*, Allen & Unwin, London.

Marshall, D. (ed.) 1995, *Food Choice and the Consumer*, Blackie, London.

Martens, L. 1997, 'Gender and the Eating Out Experience', *British Food Journal*, vol. 99, no. 1, pp. 20–6.

Martens, L. & Warde, A. 1997, 'Urban Pleasure? On the Meaning of Eating Out in a Northern City', in P. Caplan (ed.) *Food, Identity and Health*, Routledge, London, pp. 131–50.

—— 1998, 'Food Choice: A Sociological Approach', in A. Murcott (ed.), *The Nation's Diet*, Longman, London.

Mazurkiewicz, R. 1983, 'Gender and Social Consumption', *Services Industries Journal*, vol. 3, no. 1, pp. 49–62.

Medlik, S. 1972, *Profile of the Hotel and Catering Industry*, Heinemann, London.

Mennell, S. 1985, *All Manners of Food: Eating and Taste in England and France from the Middle Ages to the Present*, Blackwell, Oxford.

Ministry of Agriculture, Fisheries and Food, National Food Survey Committee (various years), *Household Food Consumption and Expenditure*, HMSO, London.

—— 1995, *National Food Survey, 1994*, HMSO, London.

—— 1996, *National Food Survey, 1995*, HMSO, London.

Murcott, A. 1983, 'Cooking and the Cooked: A Note on the Domestic Preparation of Meals', in A. Murcott (ed.), *The Sociology of Food and Eating*, Gower, Aldershot.

Payne, M. & Payne, B. 1993, *Eating Out in the UK: Market Structure, Consumer Attitudes and Prospects for the 1990s*, Economist Intelligence Unit Special Report no. 2169, Economist Intelligence Unit and Business International, London.

Pillsbury, R. 1990, *From Boarding House to Bistro: The American Restaurant Then and Now*, Unwin Hyman, London.

Purcell, K. 1992, 'Women's Employment and the Management of Food in Households', *Food and Beverage Europe*, Routledge, London.

Reiter, E. 1991, *Making Fast Food: From the Frying Pan into the Fryer*, McGill & Queen's University Press, Montreal.

Sosteric, M. 1996, 'Subjectivity in the Labour Process: A Case Study on the Restaurant Industry', *Work Employment and Society*, vol. 10, no. 2, pp. 297–318.

Warde, A. 1997, *Consumption, Food and Taste: Culinary Antinomies and Commodity Culture*, Sage, London.

—— 1998, 'Eating Globally: Cultural Flows and the Spread of Ethnic Restaurants', in D. Kalb, M. R. van der Land, B. Staring, B. van Steenbergen, & N. Wilterdink (eds), *Globalization, Inequality and Difference: Consequences of Transnational Flows*, Routledge, London.

Warde, A. & Martens, L. 1999 (forthcoming), *Eating Out: A Sociological Analysis*, Cambridge University Press, Cambridge.

Warde, A. & Tomlinson, M. 1995, 'Taste among the British Middle Classes, 1968–88', in T. Butler & M. Savage (eds), *Social Change and the Middle Classes*, UCL Press, London, pp. 241–56.

Whyte, W. H. 1948, *Human Relations in the Restaurant Industry*, McGraw-Hill, New York.

Wood, R. 1990, 'Sociology, Gender, Food Consumption and the Hospitality Industry', *British Food Journal*, vol. 92, no. 6, pp. 3–5.

Wood, R. 1992, 'Dining Out in the Urban Context', *British Food Journal*, vol. 94, no. 9, pp. 3–5.

—— 1994a, 'Dining Out on Sociological Neglect', *British Food Journal*, vol. 96, no. 10, pp. 10–14.

—— 1994b, 'Hotel Culture and Social Control', *Annals of Tourism Research*, vol. 21, no. 1, pp. 65–80.

—— 1995, *The Sociology of the Meal*, Edinburgh University Press, Edinburgh.

Wouters, C. 1986, 'Formalization and Informalization: Changing Tension Balances in Civilising Processes', *Theory Culture & Society*, vol. 3, pp. 1–18.

Zelinsky, W. 1985, 'The Roving Palate: North America's Ethnic Restaurant Cuisines', *Geoforum*, vol. 16, no. 1, pp. 51–72.

8

Food and Class

Pat Crotty

Overview

- *Are there class-based differences in food choice?*

- *Are these class differences diminishing?*

- *What are the underlying implications of equating low social class with poor food choices?*

Food is one of the most basic necessities of life. Its inequitable distribution on the basis of some form of social stratification is perhaps as old as human organisation. In recent times in industrialised countries, concern about nutrition and health has rekindled interest in differences in food consumption. In the recent past, differences in nutritional intake and food choice between lower and higher socioeconomic strata have probably diminished. Nevertheless there continues an active discourse that, to a greater or lesser extent, blames health problems in low-income groups on poor diet. Two areas of growing interest are, first, the important distinction that can be made between 'food choice' and 'diet', and the possibility of the existence of class differences in food choice independent of income. Nutritional science alone is not enough to help explain the concern among nutrition experts about the diet of low-income population groups. Ideas drawn from the work of Pierre Bourdieu link food choice with the concepts of life chances and life choices, and with the creation of 'health lifestyles'. The possibility that a distinction is created through criticism of the food choices of people on low incomes also needs to be examined.

Key terms

cultural capital
dichotomous view
*Dietary Guidelines for
   Australians*
food insufficiency

health lifestyle
life chances
life choices
'modern' foods
'traditional' foods

Introduction

Studies that have examined differences in the diets of socioeconomic groups in developed countries suggest that socioeconomic differences in both diet and food choice have diminished without disappearing altogether (Prattala et al. 1992; Nelson 1993; Popkin et al. 1996; Dobson et al. 1997b). Those differences that continue have been considered by some to be minor contributors to differential disease rates (for example, Smith & Baghurst 1992 for Australia; Murphy & Bayer 1997 for the USA). Others have seen diet as a major contributor (for example, James et al. 1997 for the United Kingdom). In reference to current nutrition guidelines, the diets of higher socioeconomic groups more closely approximate recommendations. However, the proportion of diets achieving these standards are small in all socioeconomic groups. In addition, there may be greater diversity in food choice between socioeconomic groups than in nutrient intake. Foods that are eaten in greater quantities by higher socioeconomic groups include fruit and some vegetables, cheese, and fruit juices. Lower socioeconomic groups most commonly eat more of foods such as butter, potatoes, and bread. The former may be seen as **'modern' foods** and the latter as **'traditional' foods** (Roos et al. 1996).

Regardless of what is currently in the literature, the diet of lower socioeconomic groups is commonly viewed as uniformly 'unhealthy'. Recommendations are frequently made for the improvement of diet in low-income groups so that it more closely approximates that of the higher social classes, which are often assumed to be uniformly 'healthier'. The food choices and diets of the affluent may thus become an inappropriate surrogate standard for 'healthy eating' by low-income groups. Class differences in diet can be seen in a number of ways: as differences in nutrition or in food choice, or as symbolic consumption. The ability to distinguish between these is important, particularly for those conducting nutrition programs that encourage dietary change.

Social, as distinct from health, studies have found a range of demographic factors, other than income or head of household's occupation, to be useful in explaining differences in consumption at the household level. The presence of children and the age of people in the household are examples of such factors. Nevertheless, **food insufficiency** remains a source of concern in developed societies, particularly because of its association with homelessness, unemployment, the young—including students and sole parents—and older people.

One major area of difficulty is the terminology used to signify socially stratified groups in the literature discussed here. In general, the terms used by the authors of studies have been maintained, but generally terms are used interchangeably to mean segments of society who have more or less access to material and **cultural capital**.

Food and class: conceptualising difference

In 'The Measure of My Powers', M. F. K. Fisher depicts in a typically delicious, entrancing, and observant way, the character of Ora, a cook in her childhood household:

Grandmother hated her. I don't know any real reasons, of course, after such a long time, but I think it was because Ora was not like the friendly stupid hired girls she thought were proper for middle-class kitchens. And then Ora did things to 'plain good food' that made it exciting and new and delightful, which in my poor grandmother's stern asceticism [*sic*] meant that Ora was wrong (Fisher 1976, p. 360).

This short quote includes within it a rich diversity of social concepts connecting food to class. Ora was not unintelligent and servile like 'good' cooks in middle-class households should be, and she did not cook and serve 'good plain food', presumably of the type she should have been preparing in her own home. Fisher sums up her grandmother's attitude to food as 'Take what God has created and eat it humbly and without sinful pleasure'—a dictum defied by Ora's culinary practices (Fisher 1976, p. 361).

In the older woman's eyes, at least the lower classes and children should have a sober and controlled approach to the gifts of the table. This example is drawn from the early decades of this century and expresses views of the relationship between class and food that were entirely consistent with the views of nutrition scientists of the day. While this may have reflected a widely held view of proper behaviour for all classes, it was especially unacceptable for the poor to eat in a way that implied anything other than pious abstemiousness. Both nutritionists and home economists of the day linked scientific thinking with Christian morality and an emphasis on getting good nutritional value for money.

Wilbur O. Atwater (1844–1907), a pioneering nutritionist in the USA, believed people who lived on high-carbohydrate but low-protein diets in India, China, northern Italy, and parts of Germany, Ireland, and the USA were not only ill nourished, but also suffered 'physically, intellectually and morally thereby'. Conversely, he believed that other national groups, such as the Scots, 'while subsisting largely upon [such] frugal but rational diets, are well nourished, physically strong, and distinguished for their intellectual and moral force' (Atwater 1888, p. 442). While Atwater's assessment of the consequences of inadequate diets in strictly nutritional terms compares well with modern interpretations of deficient diets, the moralistic and prejudicial overtones would be unacceptable today as part of a scientific understanding of nutritional problems. Or would they?

In January 1997 the *Australian* newspaper ran an article with the headline 'Fast-Food Fashion Fuels Nutritional Underclass' (Meade 1997, p. 7). Quoting, and no doubt interpreting, 'leading dietitians, the Commonwealth Scientific and Industrial Research Organisation (CSIRO), Division of Human Nutrition, and the Australian Institute of Health and Welfare', the article made a number of points about meals purchased out of the home in Australia. Principally, wealthier and better educated people make better nutritional choices by purchasing 'nutritionally dense' take-aways, such as Indian, Thai, and Japanese food, while lower socioeconomic status people choose McDonald's, Kentucky Fried Chicken, pizzas, and hot chips, which are high in fat and low in nutritional value. As a consequence of the social trend towards purchasing more meals away from home, the article stated that fast-foods were growing in popularity and thus creating a 'nutritional underclass' with distinct eating patterns.

Such stories about the problematic food choices and diet of lower socioeconomic groups are not uncommon in the media in developed countries. It is easier with the hindsight of history to identify the association of upper-class prejudices with lower–social-class food behaviour. It is not so easy to do so in one's own time, and as a consequence, it is particularly important to be vigilant. The rest of this discussion seeks to clarify three types of association between class and food that are often not made explicit in technical and popular discussions similar to the historical and contemporary examples quoted above—that is, differences in:

- nutrition
- food choice
- symbolic consumption.

The exploration of these differences raises questions about the extent to which modern nutritional science has helped us separate the facts of nutrition from the prejudices of privilege. In the best tradition of enlightenment, has nutritional science been liberating in this context?

While making these three distinctions may serve the purpose of this discussion, it should be remembered that in reality these associations coexist. Objectively, lower income households may consume more meat pies, but the behaviour also itself carries consonant symbolic content. In television commercials, those eating pies and tomato sauce with their hands are more likely to be overall-wearing workmen than executive women. Showing executive women eating such foods in the same manner would carry a powerful and widely understood message in affronting taken-for-granted ideas about what kinds of people eat certain foods, and how they eat them.

Distinguishing terms: nutrition, food choice, and symbolic consumption

First some clarification. One may arrive at a health-sustaining dietary pattern by many routes. Differences in food choice do not necessarily lead to problematic differences in nutrition. In addition, it is important to separate, as the Food and Agriculture Organization of the United Nations (FAO) does, the idea of food inadequacy from that of undernutrition. A low-income family may indeed be well nourished in a nutritional sense, but may nevertheless experience painful deprivation through lack of access to highly valued foods, the preferred amount of food, or consistent amounts of food. None of these problems will necessarily end in poor nutrition measured against nutrient intake norms, although they increase the likelihood that this will occur. Similarly, choosing 'nutritionally undesirable' foods in the context of an overall healthy dietary pattern is inconsequential.

Dietary patterns consistent with health can be as diverse as those characteristic of subsistence farmers, nomadic herdsmen, or youth from deepest suburbia. However, any food pattern that fails over time—either on the quantity criterion (too much or too little) or in terms of variety, or worse, on both—can have serious consequences because it does not provide the nutrients and energy needed for health, for work, and possibly, in the longer term, for life. This section is concerned with this possibility in the context of social inequality.

Differences in nutrition

Global issues in food inequity

Restrictions of space here mean that life-threatening nutritional inadequacy, such as that common among the disadvantaged in many areas of the world, cannot be treated in detail (see chapter 2). However, the Sixth FAO World Food Survey (FAO 1996) shows that, in the triennium 1990–92, the developing world, which constitutes 76 per cent of the world's population, had access to 71 per cent of the world's dietary energy supply, but only 66 per cent of its protein, and 57 per cent of its fat supply. In this period, the average person in the developed world consumed a third more energy than the average person in the developing world.

FAO has a number of different methods for assessing inequality in relation to food access and consumption, and although food inadequacy cannot be equated with undernutrition, one in five people in the developing world are living with food inadequacy. Chronic, everyday food inadequacy and undernutrition lead to suffering, disease, and death on a scale rarely experienced by industrialised countries outside wartime devastation.

Developed countries and food inequity

While there is probably always concern at some level in developed societies about those who have 'poor diets', there are times when interest is rekindled by particular circumstances. Wartime is one such instance, and concern usually centres around the impact of poor diets on the health of young males and their fitness to serve in the armed forces. Additionally, in this context, food shortages and the capacity of the domestic workforce to support agricultural and industrial production may be a focus for government action. More recently, concern about poor diets in developed countries has focused on the relationship of diet to heart disease. Because of the demonstrated higher rates of chronic disease, especially coronary heart disease, among low-income groups, interest in the diets of these groups has increased. This interest usually takes the form of discussion about the diets in lower social strata conforming less well to government nutrition advice for lowering risk of chronic disease. Research into social stratification and diet has been stimulated, and fat consumption has received particular attention because of its association with heart disease. Commonly when 'mean' levels of nutrients in the diets of lower socioeconomic groups are compared with those of higher socioeconomic groups, a greater proportion of total dietary energy for the lower socioeconomic group comes from fat. Unfavourable comparisons are usually made with reference to the 'average' diet or to the diets of the more affluent or better educated segments of society.

Differences in food choice

Food insufficiency and socioeconomic status

Dietary intake that is related to chronic disease is by no means the only concern, however. A more general concern about **food insufficiency** has also been part of recent interest. Kathy Radimer and her colleagues have worked at developing measures that are able to assess the prevalence of food insufficiency in populations. Radimer's work in the USA has described in some detail the various aspects of the experience of hunger, including food-supply depletion and constant worry about this, the monotony of the food supply, and the experience of unbalanced or 'not proper' eating (Radimer et al. 1997). In a recent report of data collected in a health survey of more than 10 000 households in Queensland, Australia, the prevalence of food insufficiency at the household level was shown to be close to 10 per cent. People were asked in a telephone interview 'In the last 12 months, were there times that your household ran out of food and there wasn't money to buy any more food?' In this study, the unemployed and the young are shown to be particularly vulnerable.

In a study by Gavin Turrell, again in Queensland, a group of recipients in a welfare service who were younger and more likely to be unemployed than other study participants had food practices that differed markedly from other groups in the community, including those on low incomes. In Turrell's study, those in the low-income category who were not attending a welfare agency reported practising particular dietary behaviours at similar rates to those in higher income categories (Turrell 1996). This is consonant with other Australian data, which show the diets of low-income sole parents in receipt of welfare payments but not attending a welfare agency to be similar to more affluent Australians (Crotty et al. 1992). This introduces the likelihood, discussed by Turrell, that groups needing the services of welfare agencies are underrepresented in nutrition studies, and this may mask some important dietary differences between higher and lower socioeconomic groups (Turrell & Najman 1995).

In summary, it seems that, in Australia at least, there may be cause to differentiate between a general low-income category and specific sub-groups within that category when discussing differences in food behaviour and diet. There is likely to be a group of particularly disadvantaged people who are young and unemployed, and who may also be in a parenting role. Students too are possibly at risk for food insufficiency. Food insufficiency is probably a higher priority problem for these groups. However, this group should be viewed, at least in terms of diet, as distinctly different from generalised categories such as 'low-income' or 'low socioeconomic' groups in Australia.

The relationship between food choice and nutrition

In countries such as Australia, the nexus between 'undesirable food choices' and 'poor nutrition' is usually assumed and is strongly associated with lower social status groups. These groups are most frequently categorised by income but often also by occupational category or educational attainment. However, there are some pieces of evidence that further caution against generalising about such a broad category. Work by the Division of Human Nutrition at CSIRO in Adelaide, South Australia, has shown that when the diets of those categorised by occupational prestige are assessed for conformation to the *Dietary Guidelines for Australians* (NHMRC 1993), diets in the upper groups are more frequently closer to the guidelines; there is considerable overlap between the diets of high and low groups, and the differences between the groups may not be great (Smith & Baghurst 1992). For an Adelaide-based Australian population, there were small differences in nutrient intake between the top and bottom quintiles stratified by occupational prestige. Almost twice the number of diets in the upper occupational-prestige group complied with Australian targets for fat consumption compared with the lowest; however, the difference was between 19 per cent of complying diets in the highest status group and 9 per cent in the lowest. Therefore, conformation to the recommendations in the dietary guidelines is unlikely in any category.

Gavin Turrell and Jake Najman have recently shown that if the detailed composition of low-income groups is not clarified, important information is disguised. In this study, dietary practices (for example buying low-fat milk) rather than dietary intake were examined (Turrell 1996; Turrell & Najman 1995). Comparing a population sample stratified by income and a sample of clients from a welfare centre, the study shows clearly that the low-income group was very similar to those in the higher income categories in terms of reported dietary practices, while the welfare service clients were very different from all income groups. Using a score (out of twenty) based on individuals reporting the frequency of choosing 'recommended' foods, the mean scores for high-income, medium-income, low-income, and welfare-service groups were 10.4, 9.9, 9.8, and 5.3 respectively (Turrell 1996). Apart from being much younger and more likely to be female, unemployed, and sole parents, those in the welfare-services group were least likely to claim that they adopted recommended food practices such as choosing low-fat and wholemeal varieties of foods. Keeping in mind the particularly disadvantaged, these Australian data are not really a good foundation upon which to base a **dichotomous view** of high- and low-income groups in relation to food behaviours or nutrient intake when measured against the 'healthy diet' and recommended behaviours. Recent data from other countries are supportive of this phenomenon.

Ritva Prattala's conclusions in summarising data for the Nordic countries are that social class differences in diets have diminished since the 1970s and that lower social class diets follow those of the upper social classes, with a 5–10 year time lag (Prattala 1995; Prattala et al. 1992). Eva Roos and others (1996) investigated who in Finland followed the Finnish national dietary guidelines. They found that there were no substantial differences in nutrient intake on the basis of educational or income levels, although there were some differences in vitamin C and carotenoids in favour of the higher status groups. There were, however, interesting differences in foods chosen. In a creative discussion of their results, Roos and colleagues (1996) designate those foods that Finns are consuming in increasing amounts (fruit juices, vegetables and fruit, cheeses, and candies) as 'modern' foods, and designate those for which consumption is falling (milk, potatoes, bread, and butter) as 'traditional' foods. By labelling the foods, in contemporary nutritional terms, as 'healthy' or 'unhealthy', they demonstrate that traditional healthy foods such as potatoes and bread have higher consumption in lower socioeconomic groups and 'modern' healthy foods are consumed in greater amounts by higher status groups. 'Unhealthy modern' foods, such as cheese and candies, and 'unhealthy traditional' foods, such as butter, follow the same pattern. Food choices at all income levels are likely to have both good and bad points when measured against dietary recommendations and, in the end, may add up to nutrient intakes that are not very different.

In Australia, those foods for which consumption is increasing reflect these trends with some variations. Foods for which there is good evidence of increasing consumption include fresh fruit, vegetables, and breakfast foods; those that are decreasing include butter, margarine, sugar, and alcohol. Consumption of bread and eggs may be decreasing, and milk consumption may be increasing, but the data are inconsistent (Dobson et al. 1997a). This introduces the notion of desirable and undesirable aspects of both high–and low–socioeconomic-status eating patterns, something usually not recognised in health promotion campaigns or media stories.

Differences in symbolic consumption

Social stratification and food choice

The Second World War seems to have had a homogenising influence on food choice in at least two ways. In terms of the exchange of foods between cultures, European foods were carried to other countries through both the experience of national armies and post-war migration. Also, early in the century in the United Kingdom, enormous differences had existed between the diets of the poor and of affluent sectors of society, so that the poorest 10 per cent of the British population 'barely subsisted' on a diet of tea, butter, potatoes, and a small amount of meat in addition to the staple bread (Nelson 1993). However, food rationing during and after the Second World War changed both poor and affluent diets, resulting in considerably fewer differences in food choices between classes (Hollingsworth 1985). Gail Braybon and Penny Summerfield's (1987) account of women of all classes during the war gives some idea of the way in which, through the rationing system, a more equitable distribution of the available, severely reduced, food supply was achieved. This period is sometimes seen as a time when dietary restrictions made affluent diets 'healthier' and contributed to lower rates of some diseases, such as diabetes. However, it is at least as plausible that the diets of the poorest sections of the population were improved by wartime organisation of the food supply, ensuring what was available was distributed with reasonable equity. While those with more resources always had more options, the homogenising influence on diets across classes was considerable.

Nevertheless, even while there has been an evening out of disparities between socioeconomic groups in terms of food choices and diets, differences persist. A lively and interesting discussion has developed about the reasons for different food choices, even where there seems to be equitable access to a wide variety of foods and no difference in income. Are there class-based differences in food choice that are independent of income?

Social stratification, food, and symbolic boundaries

Mark Tomlinson and Alan Warde (Tomlinson & Warde 1993; Tomlinson 1994) have used data from the Family Expenditure Survey of 1968 and 1988, both involving 7000 English households. They note that most interest in the literature on food and class is of the type already discussed—that is, where nutritional problems are linked with 'poverty and ignorance'—which they believe obscures symbolic differences in food choice. Within this data set, households belonging to four different classes (by occupational group), but with the same level of disposable income per household head per week, were identified. There were important differences in the food-purchasing patterns of the classes. The higher class groups spent more per head per week on food, on eating out in restaurants, on take-aways, and on 'street food'. The 'manual' group spent more than all other groups on food eaten at work. In these studies, the 'modern' foods were fruit juices, wine, cereal, and fresh vegetables and fruit (see chapter 7).

Some clues to factors other than 'class' that may help explain food choice by household are offered by market researchers (Gerhardy et al. 1995). In examining what variables may be used to differentiate households according to food consumption, a limited number of foods were studied through two-week food diaries that were kept for 102 households in Newcastle upon Tyne (United Kingdom). Household social class was not a good discriminator, and other discriminators, such as the presence of children or the educational level of the main food preparer, were more useful. The researchers note that paying attention to household composition, especially the presence of children, is more informative, particularly for foods consumed at breakfast and lunch. Other explanatory factors are demonstrated in a study by Margaret Wichelow and Tony Prevost (1996), which examined the diets of a random sample of some 9000 British adults through a food-frequency questionnaire collected for the 1984–85 Health and Lifestyle Survey. They did not look at nutritional adequacy or diet, but using thirty-nine foods, they discerned four dietary patterns, which explained much about how different groups—defined demographically, geographically, and by lifestyle factors—consume 'patterns' of food. The different patterns were defined as a:

1 low-fat, high fruit and vegetable pattern
2 high-carbohydrate pattern consistent with a traditional meal structure of meat and vegetables as well as another course
3 high-fat pattern
4 high refined carbohydrate pattern.

Keeping in mind that these patterns were not discussed in terms other than food choices, there are a large range of associations reported, such as which groups are more likely to consume which dietary pattern. Pattern one, for example, was favoured more by the middle-aged, rather than by the very young or old, and was strongly associated with socioeconomic status and the south-east region of England. However, of particular interest is the researchers' statement that demographic factors alone explain a high proportion of the variation in the low-fat, high fruit and vegetable pattern and the high-fat pattern. How might we explain, then, the relative importance of behavioural lifestyle factors (beliefs and practices) in determining dietary patterns as compared with where one lives or at what stage of the life cycle one is (either personally in terms of age or by stage of family formation)? This introduces the sociologist's question of whether 'lifestyle' is most influenced by **life chances** or **life choices.**

Food and class distinction

Simon Williams (1995) has attempted to develop a link with the work of Pierre Bourdieu in order to build some bridges between social theory and the sociology of health and illness, and so clarify the connections between class, health, and lifestyle. The relative importance of 'life chances' and 'life choices' has been a feature of interest to a number of social theorists. Williams notes that the relative importance of behaviours and lifestyles, compared with wider socioeconomic determinants of health, is still debated and that the interrelationship between the two is complex. For example, a belief that one is not able to control one's health may be engendered by frequent illness experiences, a more likely occurrence for lower socioeconomic groups. In other words, personal experiences and living and working conditions shape beliefs about health and illness. Thus, life chances are present in life choices.

In the modern world, the creation of personal and group **health lifestyles** (as distinct from 'healthy' lifestyles) is an important social practice. In addition to these insights, Bourdieu provides a theoretical explanation of why a dichotomous approach to quality of diet and socioeconomic status lingers on, even in the face of contrary evidence. Those who have more cultural capital—that is, those groups in society who are better able to create notions of 'good taste'—legitimate the forms of consumption to which they have more access. They are able to define their bodies, their lifestyles, and, in this case, their preferred food choices as superior, worthy of respect, and 'classier' (Williams 1995). Thus, Indian take-away is better than take-away hamburgers and, what is more, is chosen by better educated and better paid people.

Is a nutritional underclass likely to result from low-income people buying McDonald's? Not really. According to figures released by the Australian Bureau of Statistics from the 1993–94 Household Expenditure Survey (ABS 1996), households in the highest 20 per cent of the income distribution spend on average nearly A$38 per week on meals in restaurants, hotels, and clubs. Households in the lowest 20 per cent of income, on the other hand, spend on average less than A$6.50 in this category. In round figures, in terms of the total amount spent on meals eaten out of the home, including take-away food and lunch money, A$60 is spent by the highest 20 per cent, compared with A$11by the lowest 20 per cent. This points to the rather unhappy possibility that nutritionists and others are 'doing class' or 'doing distinction' when they adopt a 'dichotomous approach' to social status and food choice.

The creation of distinctions reflects a desire within groups to concentrate themselves and separate themselves from others. Such distinctions are not only 'cultural'; they are also political (Lamont & Fournier 1992). What will happen when the lower social classes catch up with the consumption of 'modern' foods, such as fruit juice, cheese, and fresh fruit and vegetables, and forsake 'traditional' foods, such as potatoes and butter? Prattala, quoting Swedish data, suggests that when class differences level off, 'Instead of the differences in the use of single foods social classes are likely to differ in the way they talk about food, set their tables and combine their foods into dishes and meals. Without any changes in nutrient content a snail becomes an escargot!' (Prattala 1995, p. 20). And maybe hot chips and *pommes frites* will be seen as equivalent. The more important question is, of course, whether health differentials will also be subject to this 'catch up'.

Food then is perhaps one of the most accessible sites for 'boundary work' and can be used to signify class and style. But it can also be used to dominate—common, inexpensive take-aways are undesirable, while Mediterranean cuisine becomes healthy. There is still plenty of room in discussing food choice, nutrition, and socioeconomic status to give due recognition to the behavioural, social, and cultural complexities of this important area.

Conclusion

The available literature for developed countries suggests that differences in food choice and nutrient intake on the basis of socioeconomic status, however they are measured, have diminished without disappearing altogether. To what extent these differences explain health differentials, and therefore determine the potential value of dietary change programs directed at the poor, is more controversial. The contemporary tendency to dichotomous thinking about food choice, diet, and class needs to be reviewed. At the same time, there is cause to be increasingly concerned about a sub-group within the 'low-income' category who seem to be quite distinct and particularly disadvantaged.

Summary of main points

- In developed countries, there is mounting evidence to suggest that differentials in food choice and diet between lower and higher socioeconomic groups are diminishing and that those that persist are not great.
- The common criticisms of the diets and food choices of people on low incomes is often ill informed.
- There are sub-groups within low socioeconomic strata in developed societies who consume foods and have diets very different from other groups. This pattern is probably associated particularly with unemployment, reliance on welfare services other than pensions, youth, and old age.

- There may be differences in food choice that are class-related rather than income-depen-dent. Other demographic factors—such as region, age, and the presence of children in the household—may go a good way towards explaining food choices.
- The urge to create distinction helps to explain oversimplified interpretations of the links between food choice, health, and socioeconomic status, given that available data suggest more complex relationships.

Discussion questions

1 Give two examples of 'modern' foods and two of 'traditional' foods in your society.
2 What factors might make 'traditional' and 'modern' foods socially specific, culturally spe-cific, or international?
3 How might health lifestyle, life chances, and life choices converge to produce healthy food choices and diets in low-income households?
4 One of the major differences in expenditure on food between low-income and high-income households in Australia is the amount of money spent on food eaten away from home. Discuss.
5 People who use the services of welfare agencies are probably the most at risk of limited food choices, insufficient food, and nutritionally inadequate diets. What groups in soci-ety may be represented in this category?

Further reading

Kempson, E. 1996, *Life on a Low Income*, Joseph Rowntree Foundation, York.
Kohler, B. M., Feichtinger, E., Barlosius, E., & Dowler, E. (eds) 1997, *Poverty and Food in Welfare Societies*, Edition Sigma, Berlin.
Warde, A. 1997, *Consumption, Food and Taste: Culinary Antinomies and Commodity Culture*, Sage, London.

References

ABS. See Australian Bureau of Statistics.
Atwater, W. O. 1888, 'Pecuniary Economy of Food: The Chemistry of Food and Nutrition, V', *Century Illustrated Monthly Magazine*, vol. 35, no. 3, pp. 437–46.
Australian Bureau of Statistics 1996, *Household Expenditure Survey, 1993–94*, Cat. no. 6531, ABS, Canberra.
Braybon, G. & Summerfield, P. 1987, *Out of the Cage: Women's Experiences in Two World Wars*, Pandora, London.
Crotty, P. A., Rutishauser, I. H. E., & Cahill, M. 1992, 'Food in Low-Income Families', *Australian Journal of Public Health*, vol. 16, no. 2, pp. 168–74.
Dobson, A., Porteous, J., McElduff, P., & Alexander, H. 1997a, 'Dietary Trends: Estimates from Food Supply and Survey Data', *European Journal of Clinical Nutrition*, vol. 51, pp. 193–8.

—— 1997b, 'Whose Diet Has Changed?', *Australian and New Zealand Journal of Public Health*, vol. 21, no. 2, pp. 147–54.

FAO. See Food and Agricultural Organization.

Fisher, M. F. K. 1976, 'The Measure of My Powers', in *The Art of Eating*, Vintage Books, New York.

Food and Agricultural Organization 1996, *The Sixth World Food Survey*, FAO, Rome.

Gerhardy, H., Hutchins, R. K., & Marshall, D. W. 1995, 'Socio-economic Criteria and Food Choice across Meals', *British Food Journal*, vol. 97, no. 10, pp. 24–8.

Hollingsworth, D. 1985, 'Rationing and Economic Constraints on Food Consumption in Britain since the Second World War', in D. J. Oddy & D. S. Miller (eds), *Diet and Health in Modern Britain*, Croom Helm, London, pp. 255–73.

James, W. P. T., Nelson, M., Ralph, A., & Leather, S. 1997, 'The Contribution of Nutrition to Inequalities in Health', *British Medical Journal*, vol. 314, pp. 1545–9.

Lamont, M. & Fournier, M. (eds) 1992, *Cultivating Differences: Symbolic Boundaries and the Making of Inequality*, University of Chicago Press, Chicago.

Meade, A. 1997, 'Fast-Food Fashion Fuels Nutritional Underclass', *The Weekend Australian*, 25–26 January.

Murphy, S. & Bayer, O. 1997, 'Evaluating Dietary Quality among Low-Income Groups in the United States', in B. M. Kohler, E. Feichtinger, E. Barlosius, & E. Dowler (eds), *Poverty and Food in Welfare Societies*, Edition Sigma, Berlin, pp. 113–23.

National Health and Medical Research Council 1993, *Dietary Guidelines for Australians*, AGPS, Canberra.

Nelson, M., 1993, 'Social-Class Trends in British Diet, 1860–1980', in C. Geissler & D. Oddy (eds), *Food, Diet and Economic Change Past and Present*, Leicester University Press, Leicester, pp. 101–20.

NHMRC. See National Health and Medical Research Council.

Popkin, B. M., Siega-Riz, A. M., & Haines, P. 1996, 'A Comparison of Dietary Trends among Racial and Socioeconomic Groups in the United States', *New England Journal of Medicine*, vol. 335, pp. 716–20.

Prättälä, R. 1995, 'Social Class and Food in the Nordic Countries', in E. Feichtinger & B. M. Köhler (eds), *Current Research into Eating Practices: Contributions of Social Sciences*, AGEV Publication Series, vol. 10, Supplement to *Ernährungs-Umschau*, vol. 42, pp. 16–20.

Prättälä, R., Berg, M.-A., & Puska, P. 1992, 'Diminishing or Increasing Contrasts? Social Class Variation in Finnish Food Consumption Patterns, 1979–1990', *European Journal of Clinical Nutrition*, vol. 46, pp. 279–87.

Radimer, K., Allsopp, R., Harvey, P. W. J., Firman, D. W., & Watson, E. K. 1997, 'Food Insufficiency in Queensland', *Australian and New Zealand Journal of Public Health*, vol. 21, no. 3, pp. 303–10.

Roos, E., Prattala, R., Lahelma, E., Kleemola, P., & Pietinen, P. 1996, 'Modern and Healthy? Socioeconomic Differences in the Quality of Diet', *European Journal of Clinical Nutrition*, vol. 50, pp. 753–60.

Smith, A. M. & Baghurst, K. I. 1992, 'Public Health Implications of Dietary Differences between Social Status and Occupational Category Groups', *Journal of Epidemiology and Community Health*, vol. 46, pp. 409–16.

Tomlinson, M. 1994, 'Do Distinct Class Preferences for Foods Exist? An Analysis of Class-Based Tastes', *British Food Journal*, vol. 96, no. 7, pp. 11–17.

Tomlinson, M. & Warde, A. 1993, 'Social Class and Change in Eating Habits', *British Food Journal*, vol. 95, no. 1, pp. 3–10.

Turrell, G. 1996, 'Structural, Material and Economic Influences on the Food Purchasing Choices of Socioeconomic Groups', *Australian and New Zealand Journal of Public Health*, vol. 20, no. 6, pp. 611–17.

Turrell, G. & Najman, J. M. 1995, 'Collecting Food-Related Data from Low Socioeconomic Groups: How Adequate Are our Current Research Designs?', *Australian Journal of Public Health*, vol. 19, no. 4, pp. 410–16.

Whichelow, M. J. & Prevost, A. T. 1996, 'Dietary Patterns and their Associations with Demographic, Lifestyle and Health Variables in a Random Sample of British Adults', *British Journal of Nutrition*, vol. 76, pp. 17–30.

Williams, S. J. 1995, 'Theorising Class, Health and Lifestyles: Can Bourdieu Help Us?', *Sociology of Health and Illness*, vol. 17, pp. 577–604.

9

Culture, Food, and Nutrition in Increasingly Culturally Diverse Societies

Joanne P. Ikeda

Overview

- *How does food facilitate social well-being in all cultures, whether Westernised or traditional?*

- *What are some of the barriers health professionals trained in biomedicine face in dealing with persons from traditional cultures?*

- *What are the potential benefits of adopting a holistic approach to health in culturally diverse societies?*

This chapter describes the issues related to food habits and health that arise when large numbers of people from traditional cultures immigrate to countries where biomedical health values and beliefs dominate. In the past, the unstated assumption was that cultural differences would disappear as a result of assimilation of these populations into the mainstream. However, today most ethnic minorities are committed to sustaining their cultural identity and are reluctant to change their values, beliefs, and practices. As a result, health professionals are challenged to become more cross-culturally sensitive and competent. They are also beginning to reflect on their narrow approach to health, which emphasises physical well-being over other aspects of well-being.

Key terms

biomedicine
culture
cross-cultural
  competency
cultural sensitivity
ethnocentric
family commensality
feeding relationship

food security
foodways
psychological well-being
spiritual well-being
shaman

Cultural views of food and health

In Western **culture**, health professionals are trained to view food as a source of nutrients, which provide energy, regulate body processes, and furnish essential compounds needed for growth and maintenance of the human body. The assumption is that people will purposely choose foods that contribute to their long-term physical well-being by reducing their risk of chronic disease. There is little doubt that a diet compatible with human biological needs is essential to the survival of the species. However, anthropologists and sociologists have identified many non-biological influences on food choices and food behaviour. When Maslow's hierarchy of needs is applied to food habits, eating for survival evolves into eating to satisfy needs for security, then for belongingness, then for self-esteem, and finally, for self-actualisation (Lowenberg 1970, p. 32).

Members of traditional cultures have difficulty relating to the Western **biomedical** bias, according to which food selection should be based on the physical needs of the body. In these cultures, there is a much greater degree of integration between spiritual beliefs and health beliefs. For example, healers or **shamans** in traditional cultures have been described as physician-priests (Muecke 1983, p. 835). They generally conceptualise well-being as the attainment of harmony and balance in body, mind, and spirit (Bodeker 1996, p. 280) (see Box 9.1).

In these cultures, an imbalance in these forces can cause disease. Treating the disease means bringing the forces back into balance and harmony. In Chinese, South-East Asian, Filipino, and Hispanic cultures, this can be accomplished through avoiding some foods and consuming others. Some foods are considered yang or 'hot', while others are considered yin or 'cold'. If an illness is considered yang (hot), then the patient needs to consume yin (cold) foods and vice versa.

The categorisation of foods as hot or cold is not necessarily consistent between or within cultures. The best way health professionals can deal with this is to ask if the

---

Box 9.1   Healers in non-Western cultures

In Mexican-American communities, healers are known as *curanderos* or *curanderas*; in Hmong communities they are *neng*; Vietnamese have *thay thuoc*; Koreans have *mansin*; Native Americans have medicine men. These traditional healers are quite knowledgable about treatment remedies as well as spiritual healing ceremonies specific to their culture. Chinese, Vietnamese, Cambodians, and Laotians refer to the two opposite forces of yang and yin. Yang is masculine and is represented by light, heat, or dryness. Yin is feminine and represents darkness, cold, and wetness. Some Filipinos and Mexican-Americans also believe that health represents a state of equilibrium between hot and cold, wet and dry. Many Native Americans consider wellness to be harmony in body, mind, and spirit.

patient is avoiding or favouring any particular foods in order to treat this condition. For the most part, these practices have little effect on overall nutritional status unless they are prolonged and exclude broad categories of food.

There are other practices that affect the balance of hot and cold, including bathing, washing one's head, and keeping oneself wrapped in blankets. Herbal remedies are also used to help restore balance. Chinese and South-East Asians may use acupuncture, coining, cupping, pinching, and moxibustion for this purpose. These practices may be implemented or avoided depending on whether the illness is viewed as 'hot' or 'cold'.

The concept of health in traditional cultures—the achievement of harmony and balance in body, mind, and spirit—initially appears to be very similar to the Western definition of health, which is 'a state of complete physical, mental, and social well-being, and not merely the absence of disease or infirmity' (World Health Organization 1946, as quoted in *Mosby* 1994, p. 835). However, in the field of biomedicine, physical well-being has been overemphasised, with token attention given to social, mental, and **spiritual well-being** (Engel 1977, p. 129). There are indications that this may be changing. According to Gerard Bodeker, the molecular approach to human biology and treatment of disease is being called into question by new findings from mind/body medicine and environmental health that support a more holistic view of human health. This view is more consistent with concepts underlying traditional systems of health and human potential (Micozzi 1996, p. 289). If this is so, health professionals will need to move beyond their limited view of the potential value and impact of food and nutrition programs. Instead of confining their expectations to improving clinical parameters of health such as weight, blood pressure, and serum glucose and lipid levels, they should anticipate the impact their efforts will have on many aspects of well-being.

Food and social relationships within cultures

Food is used to build and maintain social relationships in all cultures. Paul Rozin points out that the basic tasks of growing, harvesting, processing, and preparing food almost always involve the efforts of multiple individuals working together. In traditional cultures, the family, and even groups of families comprising a village, cooperate to insure that their most basic need for food is met. The consumption of food is a social occasion, with family members and/or villagers gathered together for the purpose of eating. There is no culture that promotes solitary eating. Food is an extremely valuable social instrument for humans because it promotes social interaction (Rozin 1996, p. 244).

The offering of food by one person or group to another is generally viewed as a sign of friendship. The acceptance of food indicates a willingness to establish or strengthen a bond. Failing to offer food refreshment or refusing to partake when it is offered may be viewed as an indication of an unwillingness to establish or maintain a relationship. As George Foster and B. G. Anderson point out, we do not share food with our enemies. On the rare occasion when we do, it is well understood that antagonisms are to be laid aside, at least temporarily. Meals are seldom viewed as an appropriate milieu for discord

(Foster & Anderson 1978, p. 268). In fact, it is usually the opposite: mealtimes are viewed as occasions for sharing and bonding, and most people believe that a pleasant atmosphere is desirable.

Vanessa Clendenen and her colleagues believe the most powerful of factors affecting food intake is social influence. They found that when people dine with others, a social facilitation of eating occurs; subjects in her study ate substantially more, almost doubling intake, when they ate in pairs or in groups of four than when they ate alone (Clendenen et al. 1994, p. 10). Thus an individual's consumption is modified by the mere presence of another person.

One of the few nutrition programs that has actually documented its effect on improving the social and **psychological well-being** of participants is the senior nutrition program authorised by the United States *Older Americans Act 1972*. Masako Ishii-Kuntz has found that adults benefit psychologically from close personal relationships, and quality of social interaction is positively related to psychological well-being across all stages of adulthood (Ishii-Kuntz 1990, p. 36). Older persons are particularly susceptible to social isolation and loneliness. Loneliness may be defined as 'a feeling and realization of a lack of meaningful contacts with others and a lack or loss of companionship' (Berg et al. 1981, p. 342). Roxanne Smith, Larry Mullins, and their colleagues documented reduced social isolation in older people participating in a senior citizen nutrition and activities program (Smith et al. 1994, p. 21; Mullins et al. 1993, pp. 37, 342).

Some nutritionists and dietitians will be resistant to the idea that programs such as the senior nutrition programs should do more than improve dietary intake and nutritional status, and reduce the risk of chronic disease. However, others will feel enlightened and liberated by the realisation that their impact is not limited to physical aspects of well-being but can benefit the absolute health of people. It is hoped that there will be more effort put into documenting these benefits.

Health professionals rarely acknowledge the role that food plays in building and maintaining social relationships, and yet food is commonly used to establish and strengthen friendships and family relationships in Western culture. People often welcome new neighbours with gifts of food. They hold sit-down dinners for 'special guests'. Office workers bring food to be shared at work breaks. 'Pot-luck dinner' describes a meal where all participants bring food to share with each other. Refreshments are served at 'tea time' or 'coffee break' at conventions, symposia, and meetings of all types; this is considered conducive to establishing mutually beneficial relationships with others, a process popularly known as 'networking'.

Strong sentiment becomes attached to favourite dishes and foods that are traditionally served at celebrations (Bryant et al. 1985, p. 151). These foods are symbolic of the loving ties that bond family members, and the serving of these foods at other times is used to symbolise that these bonds are permanent. Extended families gather at events such as weddings, funerals, and holidays to share food and maintain kinships. The food served at these gatherings often serves as a reminder of the cultural heritage shared by family members. Many Chinese-American families continue to hold 'red egg and ginger parties' for newborn children who are fourth- and fifth-generation Americans. Californian Native American families still gather for pow-wows, where traditional dishes made from acorns as well as 'Indian tacos' are enjoyed by an open fire. *Issei, Nisei, Sansei*, and *Yonsei*—that is, second-, third-, fourth-, and fifth-generation members of the Japanese-American community—gather annually in San Francisco just before the New Year to pound hot, steamed glutinous rice into *mochi* to be shared by all. Asian-American students at colleges and universities throughout the USA take time off to head home to celebrate 'Chinese New Year' with their families, who are busy preparing traditional New Year's food. African-American families gather at Grandma's or Auntie's for a Sunday dinner that may include fried chicken, greens, cornbread, or sweet potato pie.

Thirty years ago, the USA was described as a great 'melting pot', with the implication that immigrant groups were expected to gradually lose their cultural identity and take on the attitudes, beliefs, and values of mainstream American culture—mainstream American culture being that of White, middle-class citizens. But two major historical events altered the popular idea of the USA as a 'melting pot'. First, a sizeable minority population asserted their desire and their right to retain and take pride in their cultural identity and heritage as part of the Civil Rights Movement. At the same time, the USA experienced a second great wave of immigration, but instead of coming from the United Kingdom, Ireland, Scandinavia, and Europe, the majority of newcomers came from Mexico, Central and South America, China, and South-East Asia. Thus the United States population became much more culturally and racially diverse over a fairly short period of time. This has led to increased acceptance of the concept of the USA as a 'mosaic' of diversity, with various groups committed to retaining their sense of cultural identity and community.

The health implications of cultural diversity

Cultural influences on **foodways** are receiving more and more attention as migration has increased the ethnic and cultural diversity of Western society to include more people from traditional cultures (Sanjur 1995; Kittler & Sucher 1997). Health professionals are attempting to learn about the foodways of people from a variety of backgrounds so that they can design relevant and sensitive nutrition education programs for them (Ikeda 1996, p. 1). It is generally acknowledged that 'one size fits all' programs tend not to be effective with minority populations, as members of these groups view these programs as being targeted to the dominant mainstream culture and find little advice that is applicable to them.

These programs are usually designed from a 'culture-bound' point of view by persons who have little experience with cultures other than their own. When confronted with different values, customs, and behaviours, culture-bound individuals tend to assume that their own values, customs, and behaviours are admirable, sensible, and right. They lack **cultural sensitivity** in that they do not have the ability to view the world from another person's point of view without making any judgment about the values, assumptions, and beliefs that structure that person's behaviour.

Many health professionals have come to realise that they need to acquire new knowledge and skills in order to become **cross-culturally competent**—that is, to work with people from different cultures in an effective way. Most dietitians and nutritionists know that dietary needs can be met in a variety of ways, and usually promote retention of traditional food habits when economically feasible. They also recognise that recent immigrants are being exposed to many new and unfamiliar foods and food preparation practices, and need assistance in deciding if and how to incorporate these foods into their diets. The challenge is to help new immigrants adapt to a changed food supply and exposure to Western food habits without sacrificing foodways integral to their cultural identity.

Health professionals need to consider how their advice on food choice, preparation, and intake is going to affect a person's ability to maintain social relationships and cultural identity. People may be unwilling to omit certain foods from their diet because it means sacrificing the social benefits associated with these foods. They may not be anxious to adopt new versions of favourite recipes, despite the fact that the new versions may be healthier, if traditional preparation methods symbolise cultural origins or family ties that need to be maintained. They may be reluctant to adopt dietary changes because this may place a burden on other family members and they may feel guilty about imposing their needs on the family.

The challenge for health professionals is to help patients change their diets in ways in which the sociocultural function of food remains intact. If health professionals are cognisant of the role that food plays in helping people retain their sense of cultural identity, they are much more apt to propose a variety of options for improving diet. They will encourage clients to evaluate proposed changes in terms of their potential for successful adoption. Most importantly, they will promote open communication that invites clients to identify barriers to change so that these can be considered when determining a course of action.

The role of food in helping to establish positive relationships among individuals and family members needs to be exploited. Food offerings between family members are symbols of love and affection. The father who patiently spoons food into the mouth of the toddler is nurturing not only the child's physical well-being, but also the social and emotional development of the child. A mother breast-feeding an infant is testimony to the intimacy of the loving relationship between mother and child (see Box 9.2).

Even though fathers do not breast-feed, they are often involved in decisions about infant feeding. Among Mexican-Americans, the father's being Hispanic was negatively associated with breast-feeding (Balcazar et al. 1995, p. 74). It is important for health professionals to recognise the influence that the male head of traditional households has on all aspects of family life. It is appropriate to include him in counselling sessions in which changes in diet and/or lifestyle are recommended since he may have the final word as to whether the changes are to be implemented.

Family and cultural diversity

Some years ago, Donald Allen and his colleagues (1970) used a Family Commensality Score to test his hypothesis that family relationships and nutritional factors affect stu-

---

Box 9.2   Breast-feeding and cultural diversity

Physicians agree that breast-feeding is the ideal way to feed an infant; however, breast-feeding rates vary tremendously among cultural groups in the USA. Native Americans generally have some of the highest rates of breast-feeding, while South-East Asians have low rates. Why have some traditional cultures retained this practice while others have essentially abandoned it?

A number of researchers have investigated the reasons why South-East Asian women, who breast-fed in their homeland, are no longer doing so in the USA (Tuttle & Dewey 1994, p. 282; Rassin et al. 1994, p. 132). They found that these women viewed bottle-feeding as convenient; the idea that others could help feed the baby was appealing to them. They thought it was the way most American women fed their babies since it was the only infant-feeding method they had actually observed American women using, with breast-feeding in America almost always done in privacy. They concluded that it must be the best way to feed a baby. This notion was reinforced by the fact that most American infants appeared larger than South-East Asian babies. These women also associated breast-feeding with the thinness of infants in their homeland, and the death of some of these infants (see chapter 2).

In order to promote breast-feeding in this population, health professionals will need to deal with these perceptions. C. R. Tuttle and K. G. Dewey found that the single most important predictor of intention to breast-feed among South-East Asians was being advised to breast-feed in prenatal visits (Tuttle & Dewey 1994, p. 282). This was also found to be the case with Mexican-American and non-Hispanic White women (Balcazar et al. 1995, p. 74). Yet a national random survey of physicians in the USA found that they were ill prepared to counsel breast-feeding mothers (Freed et al. 1995, p. 472).

---

dent performance and aspirations. He found that **family commensality**—as measured by questions about meals eaten together by the whole family, attractiveness and quality of the food, appetite of the student, and which family member did the cooking—was the factor most fully correlated to intrafamily and performance factors. Family commensality had significant positive effects on students' academic performance, academic goals, personal problems, money problems, perceptions of levels of family love, and family role performance. Increases in family commensality were also associated with increases in food likes, improvement of dietary adequacy, and more positive perceptions of health (Allen et al. 1970, p. 333).

Family mealtime has provided an important opportunity for family members to share news of the day's events, express feelings, and listen to one another. With respect to nutrition, children learn rules of cuisine primarily by observation and experiences at family mealtimes (Hertzler &Vaughan 1979, p. 23; Birch 1990, pp. 129–30). This includes what is and what is not considered edible, as well as the appropriateness and value of consuming foods in different contexts and combinations. Vietnamese children learn that dog is acceptable as food, while Australian children learn that dogs are pets, not food. Japanese children learn that it is acceptable to pick up one's soup bowl and drink from it, whereas American children are told that this is impolite. More than half the world's children learn to use chopsticks as their primary eating utensil. Hmong and Vietnamese children dip their food in fish sauce, a condiment most American children have never tasted. Mexican children become accustomed to hot salsas that would be resolutely rejected by children from other cultures. American children know that peanut butter and jelly is a desirable sandwich filling, whereas most Asian children have never heard of a peanut butter and jelly sandwich. These are just a few examples of how food is culturally defined.

Typically health professionals have provided parents and child-care givers with nutrition information on what to feed children. Pamphlets on this topic generally feature the basic food groups, and the number and appropriate portion sizes of servings from each group. Advice on handling child-feeding problems was limited and was based on common sense, intuition, and experience. Emerging research on parent–child interactions involving food and eating has provided a foundation for conceptualising and promoting the establishment of a healthy **feeding relationship** between parent and child. According to Elleyn Satter (1987) there are many benefits of establishing a healthy feeding relationship between parent and child. An appropriate feeding relationship supports a child's developmental tasks and helps the child to develop positive self-esteem. It helps the child to learn to discriminate between feeding cues and respond appropriately to them. It enhances the child's ability to consume a nutritionally adequate diet and to regulate the quantity of food consumed. Satter believes that the feeding relationship is characteristic of the overall parent-child relationship and that distortions that show up in feeding are likely to appear in other parent–child interactions.

Support for the promotion of a positive feeding relationship has come from extensive research conducted by Leann Birch and others (Birch 1990; Birch & Fisher 1994). According to Birch, her research shows that children can be given substantial control over food intake, especially the quantity of food consumed. Infants are born with the ability to self-regulate energy intake. This ability persists into the preschool years unless parents or care givers attempt to control children's eating by imposing contingencies and coercive practices. Birch feels that parents can promote healthy self-control of eating by offering repeated opportunities to sample healthful foods in non-coercive, positive contexts, so that through associative learning processes some of the foods offered will become preferred and accepted (Birch 1996, pp. 2–5). Based on Birch's research, Satter calls for a division of responsibility in the feeding relationship, with parents assuming responsibility for providing a variety of nutrient-dense foods at regular meal and snack times, and children determining whether or not to eat and how much to eat (Satter 1987, p. 14).

Nutritionists and dietitians have made a special effort to help parents establish a positive feeding relationship with their children. They are basing their advice to parents on these recent research findings. However, there is a need to document the effectiveness of these efforts. Is there an improvement in the feeding relationship as a result of this new trend in counselling parents? One concern about Birch's research is that most of it has been carried out with mainstream middle-class families. Do her findings apply to low-income children who may experience hunger regularly, or to children from minority groups where parenting practices are quite different from those of the mainstream population?

Anthropologist Katherine Dettwyler has described tremendous cultural variability with respect to the amount of control care givers exert over food consumption in infants and children around the world (Dettwyler 1989, p. 679). This ranges from cultures that sanction maximum control by care givers to those that allow the almost complete autonomy of infants. She raises a number of interesting questions about the effect these 'styles' of feeding have on nutritional status as well as how children develop life-long attitudes towards hunger, satiety, food, and eating. She points out that parent–child power relationships are usually established around the control of food consumption. Parental authority, and children's obedience to and respect for their parents are major values within many traditional cultures. It may be difficult for these families to accept the concept that infants and children are capable of internal self-regulation of food intake and should be allowed to eat as much or as little of nutrient-dense foods as they want for meals and snacks. Some parents will be tempted to exert control over quantities of foods consumed by encouraging eating or by limiting consumption. Explaining that children have an innate ability to self-regulate energy intake, and emphasising that parents are responsible for the quality of foods served, may help to mediate this tendency.

It is also important to make sure that parents do not misinterpret this division of responsibility to mean that children should be given whatever they want, whenever they want. This is certainly not what Birch and others are advocating. Although foods with low nutrient density—such as chips, confectionery, biscuits, cakes, and the like—should not become 'forbidden fruits', these foods should be given infrequently as occasional adjuncts to nutritious meals and snacks.

The immigrant experience

Immigrants from developing countries who migrate to developed nations often have little experience with the idea that some foods are more nutrient dense than others. In their homeland, 'junk food' did not exist. My colleagues and I have introduced the notion of 'any day foods', 'some day foods', and 'not many day' foods to the Hmong living in California in order to introduce them to the concept of nutrient density and the idea of limiting consumption of foods of low nutrient density (Ikeda et al. 1991a; Ikeda et al. 1991b).

Susan Crockett and Laura Sims have identified dramatic changes in lifestyle and the environment that have brought about significant alterations in children's eating patterns and food choices. Many of the sociocultural and demographic factors that characterise the United States population today have combined to affect what children eat, where children eat, and with whom they eat. Decisions that used to be made by parents are now increasingly in the domain of care givers and peers (Crockett &Sims 1995, p. 235). The days are long gone when most children shared home-cooked meals around the family dinner table. This is because mothers, who were once the primary teachers of sound eating practices for their children, now face stiff competition from the media and child-care providers. Government, education, public communications, and business professionals must understand the reality and complexity of our changed societal eating environment and adjust programs accordingly.

In the state of Oregon, Dairy Council Nutritionists have been so concerned about the decline in family meals that they have started a campaign, 'Resetting the Family Table', to publicise the importance of family members sharing meals as often as possible (Evers 1995, p. 1). They want to acknowledge the important contribution family meals make not only to nutritional well-being, but also to family strength and unity. Their campaign has been targeted at mainstream families.

Surveys in the USA and elsewhere do show a decline in the number of meals that families eat together (MacKenzie 1993, p. 99). However, Audrey Gillespie found that the vast majority of families with young children surveyed in upstate New York ate the evening meal together most of the time, and my colleagues and I reported similar findings after surveying Native American families in California (Gillespie & Achterberg 1989, p. 509; Ikeda et al. 1998, p. 25). Traditional communities tend to maintain a slower paced lifestyle, in which days are not regularly scheduled with activities and family meals are an integral part of the daily routine. With respect to Gillespie's findings in mainstream families, parents may feel that family meals are less important as children get older.

In light of the fact that as many as 11.6 million children under the age of 13 years are enrolled in child-care programs outside of the home, some attempt needs to be made to extend research on child feeding to child-care providers. Marcia Nahikian-Nelms measured the nutrition knowledge and attitudes of child-care providers and observed their behaviour as they interacted with children at mealtimes (Nahikian-Nelms 1997, p. 505). She found that although care givers believed that they positively influenced children's eating habits, they demonstrated poor nutrition knowledge and exhibited behaviours at mealtimes that were inconsistent with their beliefs and with expert recommendations. They often did not sit and eat with the children; they did not model behaviours they wanted to instil; and they often attempted to influence the amount of food consumed in inappropriate ways. There is little doubt that these programs are introducing children from immigrant families to a wide variety of foods that are unfamiliar to their families. Acknowledgment of this and attempts to measure its impact appear to be non-existent. In most schools, the provision of school meals has an almost mechanical quality and is done as efficiently as possible in order to conserve time and expense. Although some school food-service directors have attempted to include some 'ethnic' foods on the menu, entrees generally consist of more widely popular items, such as pizza and spaghetti.

Food, culture, and psychological well-being

A good deal is known about the relationship of food and mental health. Mental health has been defined as a 'relative state of mind in which a person who is healthy is able to cope with and adjust to the recurrent stress of everyday living in an acceptable way' (*Mosby* 1994, p. 10). Carol Ryff has argued for a broader definition with respect to psychological well-being. Using the points of convergence within the literatures of developmental psychology, clinical psychology, and mental health, she found that the key dimensions of psychological well-being were self-acceptance, positive relationships with other people, autonomy, environmental mastery, purpose in life, and personal growth:

> Taken together, these six dimensions encompass a breadth of wellness that includes positive evaluations of one's self and one's life, a sense of continued growth and development as a person, the belief that life is purposeful and meaningful, the possession of good relationships with other people, the capacity to manage one's life and the surrounding world effectively, and a sense of self-determination (Ryff 1995, p. 99).

It was noted earlier that the most basic need of humans is to survive, and that in order to survive, people must eat food. Food deprivation has a dramatic negative effect on all elements of well-being, especially psychological aspects, as identified in the classic study on human starvation that was carried out in 1945 by Ancel Keys and his colleagues at the University of Minnesota (see Box 9.3).

Numerous studies in developing countries have confirmed the devastating effect that starvation and hunger have had on the physical, social, and mental well-being of millions of children and adults (Lewis 1992; see also chapter 2). In developed countries, social-welfare systems and special nutrition programs have been established to prevent these problems. However, these systems have not totally eradicated the problem of hunger in the USA. Nutritionists are very concerned about growing hunger and homelessness in the USA, and **food security** has become a public-policy issue that is receiving a great deal of attention from them (Nestle & Guttmacher 1992). Much of this stems from the concern that there may be a resurgence of general malnutrition, as well as from evidence of specific nutrient deficiencies among the poor. In recent years, United States politicians have decided that illegal and even legal immigrants are ineligible for the benefits of these nutrition programs. This step has alienated members of minority communities, who view this as racial discrimination.

At the same time that people are going hungry because of a lack of food resources, self-imposed semi-starvation among women for the purpose of achieving a thin body has become commonplace in many Western societies (see chapter 12). This process, better known as dieting, is an attempt, either successful or unsuccessful, to restrict calorie

---

Box 9.3 The 1945 food-deprivation study

Results of the 1945 study are documented in two volumes, published as *The Biology of Human Starvation* (Keys et al. 1950). In chapter 38, there is an extensive description of the changes that took place in male subjects as they became semi-starved. These changes included:

- striking changes in physical appearance
- marked reduction in strength and endurance
- constant craving for food
- strong tendency towards introversion
- almost no social interaction during eating, with subjects giving total attention to food and its consumption
- preoccupation with thoughts of food, with food becoming the principal topic of conversation, reading, and day-dreams
- emotional instability, with transitory and sometimes protracted periods of depression
- heightened irritability
- neglect of personal appearance and grooming
- diminution of the sex drive
- compulsion to overeat or eat constantly once food restrictions were lifted

---

intake with the intention of losing or maintaining weight, or altering body image (Polivy 1996). Janet Polivy points out that the consequences of food deprivation are extraordinarily similar in animals and in human beings. It does not matter if the food restriction for human beings is involuntary (that is, controlled by external forces) or is a voluntary choice to restrain one's eating either for the benefit of science (as in the starvation study by Keys et al.) or for personal goals (such as those of dieters or patients with eating disorders). Persons who are food deprived exhibit a variety of cognitive, emotional, and behavioural changes. Almost all of these changes have negative consequences.

Health professionals have, for the most part, minimised the adverse affects that constant dieting has on health. They continue to advise individuals to lower their energy intake in order to achieve and maintain a 'healthy weight' (National Task Force on Prevention and Treatment of Obesity 1994). Less than 2 per cent of those who attempt to do so actually accomplish this goal, primarily because obesity is the result of powerful biochemical defects in the systems responsible for the control of body weight (Schwartz & Seeley 1997, p. 54). Finally, there is little evidence that weight loss would actually benefit the obese (Lee & Paffenbarger 1996, p. 116; see also chapter 11). None of this has dampened enthusiasm among health professionals for 'treating' obesity by recommending restriction of food intake. The situation has become even more serious with evidence that dieting and a 'fear of fat' is damaging all aspects of well-being in children and adolescents (Berg 1997).

This emphasis on thinness is confusing to new immigrants to the USA, many of whom are from developing countries that value fatness as a symbol of wealth and well-being. A study of Mexican–American women showed that mothers of obese children selected a chubby baby as the ideal baby significantly more often than mothers of non-obese children (Alexander et al. 1991, p. 53). Indeed, in remote areas of Mexico, where medical treatment may not be readily available, fatter infants have a better chance of surviving diseases and food scarcity than do thinner infants. Recently immigrated Mexican–American men may take pride in having fat wives and children as evidence of their ability to provide for their families.

Although mainstream American women may be highly dissatisfied with their weight, this is not the case among immigrant women. When 209 Hmong women living in California were asked about their weight, 60 per cent said that they were 'just right', 25 per cent thought they were 'too thin', and only 15 per cent said they were 'too fat' (Ikeda et al. 1991a, p. 171). Another minority group in the USA, African Americans, are much more tolerant of obesity than Caucasian women. Sheila Parker and her colleagues found African American females to be more flexible than their White counterparts in their concepts of beauty. They also tended to de-emphasise external beauty as a prerequisite for popularity. African American girls were more apt to be supportive of each other with respect to 'looking good', as opposed to White girls, who were apt to be envious and competitive with respect to appearance. White girls tended to view appearance as the most critical factor in becoming popular (Parker et al. 1995, p. 103).

A number of nutritionists are advocating a new approach to weight management, called the 'non-dieting, size acceptance' approach to health promotion for large people, in the hope of diminishing the adverse effects of rampant body dissatisfaction among girls and women (Berg 1992, p. 85; see also chapter 12).

Emotions and food

Bernard Lyman has examined the relationship between food and emotions. He says that food:

> is a symbol calling forth diverse associations that carry with them patterns of emotions, attitudes, ideas, and beliefs, characterized by an overall aura of pleasantness or unpleasantness. This air of pleasantness or unpleasantness, in conjunction with specific associations, is particularly important in establishing moods and outlooks. Thus, the food is a symbol-stimulus for pleasant or unpleasant associations and for the moods or sense of well-being which they engender (Lyman 1989, p. 157).

Interestingly, research on food preferences and choices has been carried out from a totally different perspective. Scientists have examined how physiological responses to food in terms of taste and satiety have influenced food preferences (Capaldi 1990). They have also begun to look at how physiological mechanisms might be influencing preferences for specific macronutrients, and how mood state may be affected by macronutrient consumption (Wurtman &Wurtman 1995). But could it be that psychological factors play a more critical role than physiological factors in influencing food preferences and choices? Lyman's work has raised important questions: Do people prefer to eat certain foods because these foods make them feel good? And do they avoid other foods because of unpleasant associations with these foods? Are these associations specific to the individual and his or her unique life experiences? Do these associations play a much greater role with respect to food preferences and choices than factors currently under investigation? The answers to these questions would help nutritionists better understand the factors influencing food selection.

Spirituality and healing within mainstream and traditional cultures

Traditional cultures have long recognised the importance of spiritual beliefs within the healing encounter. They have created complex ceremonies and rituals to alleviate anxiety and cultivate the expectancy of healing. Treatments used by shamans are always linked to the cause of the illness. If the body is out of balance, then balance must be restored. If the soul has been lost, then it must be found. If a taboo has been broken, penance is due. If an object has entered the body, it must be removed. Western health professionals have difficulty accepting the notion that conditions such as soul loss or spirit possession actually exist. However, members of traditional cultures may believe that these conditions exist and are the cause of their illness. G. Galanti points out that 'Whether these etiologies are the true causes of the disease is irrelevant. A patient who believes he or she is ill because of soul loss will not be cured by any amount of antibiotics. The mind is very powerful, as the placebo effect demonstrates. The patient's beliefs, as well as the body, must be treated' (Galanti 1991, p. 102).

To maximise the chances that the patient will be cured, traditional healing should occur simultaneously with biomedical treatment. Interestingly, most shamans do not object to families seeking Western medical treatment while using traditional treatment, and some even encourage it, since the two are not considered incompatible. Although there are a limited number of studies regarding the use of traditional and modern health services by refugees and immigrants, those that have been done indicate that medical care and traditional care are apt to be used simultaneously (Gilman et al. 1992, p. 310). Western-trained health professionals, who often resist the use of traditional medicine, can take some solace in the fact that patients tend not to abandon biomedical treatment when using traditional medicine.

David Aldridge has addressed spirituality as a viable idea in modern medical practice. He believes that issues of abandonment, suffering, loss of hope, and meaning of life, as well as the transitions from living to dying are essentially spiritual, not solely physiological, psychological, or social (Aldridge 1993, p. 4). Spiritual well-being has been described as having three dimensions: the need for meaning, purpose, and fulfilment in life; the hope or will to live; belief and faith in self, others, and a supreme being (Ross 1995).

Steven Hawks believes that spirituality is a vital component of human wellness, and that there may be ways in which health practitioners can enhance spirituality (Hawks et al. 1995, p. 371). After conducting an extensive literature search of the ERIC, PSY-CHLIT, and MEDLINE databases, he concluded that imagery, meditation, and group support activities have the potential to address components of spirituality, including meaning and purpose in life, self-awareness, and connectedness with self, others, and a larger reality. He found evidence of a relationship between spiritual health and positive changes in health behaviours such as communication, diet, activity, and treatment compliance. There was also documentation of improved outcomes with respect to heart disease reversal and cancer survival rates.

Interestingly there has been very little attempt in the biomedical literature to examine the potential relationship between spirituality and the 'placebo effect'. The placebo effect can be defined as any therapeutic practice that has no clear clinical or physiological aspect, but that in practice brings about an observable change in a patient's condition (Brody 1985). Placebo effects have been found with drugs, medical treatments, surgery, biofeedback, psychotherapy, and diagnostic tests (Turner et al. 1994). Judith Turner and others (1994) found that individuals do not consistently demonstrate placebo responses across placebo administrations. However, patients' positive expectations of treatment increases responsiveness to treatment. Turner also points out that a provider's warmth, friendliness, interest, empathy, and positive attitude towards the patient and towards the treatment are associated with positive effects of placebos as well as of active treatments. Turner admits that confusion and uncertainty exists among physicians and other health professionals about placebo effects. There is a general failure to appreciate the interaction of body processes with past experiences, anticipated events, and immediate environmental influence. These factors are inextricably intertwined, and may never be unravelled by biomedical research.

Neil Adams believes that Western practitioners no longer see science and spirituality as diametrically opposed or as mutually exclusive, and that barriers to their integration are being overcome (Adams 1995, p. 201). If Gerard Bodeker (1996) is correct, in the next century there will be greater acceptance of the body's ability to heal itself, and much greater effort will be focused on maximising this effect. As mentioned earlier, traditional healers have long recognised the importance of creating an environment that promotes the expectancy and anticipation of healing. They have learned to maximise the body's ability to heal itself, and have unquestioningly accepted this ability without the need to understand the intricacies of how this happens.

Conclusion

The immigration of large numbers of peoples from developing nations has resulted in societies that are increasingly culturally pluralistic in the USA, United Kingdom, Australia, and Canada. Foodways, health beliefs, and practices that are representative of traditional cultures in developing countries are quite different from those that characterise

Western society. Health professionals in Western societies are challenged to become less **ethnocentric** and more understanding, accepting, and respectful of the values, assumptions, and beliefs shared by members of traditional cultures. The process of becoming more cross-culturally sensitive, competent, and knowledgable may influence Western-trained health professionals to become more open to holistic approaches to health that encompass total well-being.

Summary of main points

- Because of the immigration of large numbers of peoples from developing countries, cultural diversity is increasing in countries such as Australia, the USA, and Canada.
- People from developing countries are apt to practise traditional forms of medicine that are more holistic with respect to the concept of health.
- Health professionals, trained in biomedicine, feel an increasing need to become cross-culturally competent since they are working with patients from very diverse cultures.
- Health professionals need to understand and accept the values, assumptions, beliefs, and practices of people who are members of other cultures in order to help these people.
- Health professionals are beginning to reconsider the narrow approach to health that promotes physical well-being over other aspects of well-being.

Discussion questions

1 What are the similarities and differences with respect to the concept of health in biomedicine and in traditional medicine?
2 How does food facilitate social and psychological well-being in all cultures, whether Westernised or traditional?
3 What are some of the barriers that health professionals trained in biomedicine have to overcome in order to effectively treat people who are from traditional cultures?
4 Are there potential benefits to the adoption of a more holistic approach to health by Western health professionals?
5 Can health professionals trained in biomedicine accept the positive benefits of the placebo effect while being unable to explain the biomedical basis for these effects?

Further reading

Capaldi, E. D. (ed.) 1996, *Why We Eat What We Eat*, American Psychological Association, Washington, DC.

Kittler, P. G. & Sucher, K. 1997, *Food and Culture in America*, revised edn, Van Nostrand Reinhold, New York.

Micozzi, M. S. 1996, *Fundamentals of Complementary and Alternative Medicine*, Churchill Livingstone, New York.

Polivy, J. 1996, 'Psychological Consequences of Food Restriction', *Journal of the American Dietetic Association*, vol. 96, no. 6, pp. 589–92.

Turner, J., Deyo, R., Loeser, J., Von Korff, M., & Fordyce, W. 1994, 'The Importance of Placebo Effects in Pain Treatment and Research', *Journal of the American Medical Association*, vol. 271, no. 20, pp. 1609–14.

References

Adams, N. 1995, 'Spirituality, Science, and Therapy', *Australian and New Zealand Journal of Family Therapy*, vol. 16, no. 4, pp.201–8.

Aldridge, D. 1993, 'Is There Evidence for Spiritual Healing?', *Advances*, vol. 9, no. 4, pp. 4–21.

Alexander, M. A., Sherman, J. B., & Clark, L. 1991, 'Obesity in Mexican-American Preschool Children—A Population Group at Risk', *Public Health Nursing*, vol. 8, no. 1, pp.53–8.

Allen, D. E., Patterson, Z. J., & Warren, G. L. 1970, 'Nutrition, Family Commensality, and Academic Performance among High School Youth', *Journal of Home Economics*, vol. 62, no. 5, pp. 333–7.

Balcazar, H., Trier, C. M., & Cobas, J. A. 1995, 'What Predicts Breastfeeding Intention in Mexican-American and Non-Hispanic White Women? Evidence from a National Survey', *Birth*, vol. 22, no. 2, pp.74–80.

Berg, A., Mellstrom, D., Person, G., Swanborg, A. 1981, 'Loneliness in the Swedish Aged', *Journal of Gerontology*, vol. 36, pp. 342–9.

Berg, F. M. 1992, 'Nondiet Movement Gains Strength', *Obesity and Health*, vol. 6, no. 5, pp. 85–90.

—— 1997, *Afraid to Eat: Children and Teens in Weight Crisis*, Healthy Weight Publishing Network, Hettinger, N. Dak.

Birch, L. L. 1990, 'The Control of Food Intake by Young Children', in E. Capaldi (ed.), *Taste, Experience, and Feeding*, American Psychological Association, Washington, DC.

—— 1996, 'Food Acceptance Patterns: Children Learn What They Live', *Pediatric Basics*, no. 75, pp. 2–5.

Birch, L. L. & Fisher, J. A. 1994, 'Appetite and Eating Behavior in Children', *Pediatric Nutrition*, vol. 42, no. 4, pp. 931–52.

Bodeker, G. C. 1996, 'Global Health Traditions, Fundamentals of Complementary and Alternative Medicine', in M. S. Micozzi (ed.), *Fundamentals of Complementary and Alternative Medicine*, Churchill Livingstone, New York.

Brody, H. 1985, 'Placebo Effect: An Examination of Grunbaum's Definition', in L. White, B. Tursdky, & G. E. Schwartz (eds), *Placebo Theory, Research, and Mechanisms*, Guilford Press, New York.

Bryant, C. A., Courtney, A., Markesbery, B. A., & DeWalt, K. 1985, *The Cultural Feast: An Introduction to Food and Society*, West Publishing Co., St Paul.

Capaldi, E. D. (ed.) 1996, *Why We Eat What We Eat*, American Psychological Association, Washington, DC.

Clendenen, V. I., Herman, P. C., & Polivy, J. 1994, 'Social Facilitation of Eating among Friends and Strangers', *Appetite*, vol. 23, pp. 1–13.

Crockett, S. J. & Sims, L. 1995, 'Environmental Influences on Children's Eating', *Journal of Nutrition Education*, vol. 27, no. 5, pp. 235–49.

Dettwyler, K. A. 1989, 'Styles of Infant Feeding: Parental/Caretaker Control of Food Consumption in Young Children', *Research Reports: American Anthropologist*, vol. 91, pp. 696–703.

Engel G. 1977, 'The Need for a New Medical Model Challenge for Biomedicine', *Science*, vol. 196, no. 42, pp.129–36.

Evers, C. 1995, 'Bringing Back Mealtime', *Healthy Kids Magazine*, December/January, pp. 64–5.

Foster, G. & Anderson, B. G. 1978, *Medical Anthropology*, John Wiley & Sons, New York.

Freed, G. L., Clark, S. J., Sorenson, J., Lohr, J. A., Cefalo, R., & Curtis, P. 1995, 'National Assessment of Physicians' Breast-Feeding Knowledge, Attitudes, Training, and Experience', *Journal of the American Medical Association*, vol. 273, no. 6, pp. 472–6.

Galanti, G. 1991, *Caring for Patients from Different Cultures: Case Studies from American Hospitals*, University of Pennsylvania Press, Philadelphia.

Gillespie, A. & Achterberg, C. 1989, 'Comparison of Family Interaction Patterns Related to Food and Nutrition', *Journal of the American Dietetic Association*, vol. 89, pp. 509–12.

Gilman, S.C., Justice, J., Sawpharn, K., & Charles, G. 1992, 'Cross-Cultural Medicine: Use of Traditional and Modern Health Services by Laotian Refugees', *Western Journal of Medicine*, vol. 157, pp. 310–15.

Hawks, S. 1995, 'Review of Spiritual Health: Definition, Role, and Intervention Strategies in Health Promotion', *American Journal of Health Promotion*, vol. 9, no. 5, pp. 371–8.

Hertzler, A. A. & Vaughan, E. C. 1979, 'The Relationship of Family Structure and Interaction to Nutrition', *Journal of the American Dietetic Association*, vol. 74, no. 1, pp. 23–7.

Ikeda, J. P. 1996, 'Nutrition Education in a Culturally Pluralistic Society', *Networking News*, no. 17, pp. 1, 5–7.

Ikeda, J. P., Ceja, R. C., Glass, R. S., Harwood, J. O., Lucke, K. A., & Sutherlin, J. M. 1991a, 'Food Habits of the Hmong Living in Central California', *Journal of Nutrition Education*, vol. 23, no. 4, pp. 168–74.

Ikeda, J. P., Chan, S., Harwood, J. O., Lucke, K. A., & Sutherlin, J. M. 1991b, 'Nutrition Education for the Hmong', Great Educational Material, *Journal of Nutrition Education*, vol. 23, no. 4, p. 198.

Ikeda, J. P., Murphy, S., Mitchell, R. A., Flynn, N., Mason, I. J., Lizer, A., Pike, B., & Lamp, C. 1998 (in press), 'Foodways and Dietary Quality of Rural California Indian Homemakers', *Journal of the American Dietetic Association*.

Ishii-Kuntz, M. 1990, 'Social Interaction and Psychological Well-Being: Comparison across Stages of Adulthood', *International Journal of Aging and Human Development*, vol. 30, no. 1, pp. 15–36.

Keys, A., Brozek, J., Henschel, A., Mickelson, O., & Taylor, H. L. 1950, *The Biology of Human Starvation*, The University Of Minnesota Press, Minneapolis.

Kittler, P. G. & Sucher, K. 1997, *Food and Culture in America*, revised edn, Van Nostrand Reinhold, New York.

Lee, M. & Paffenbarger, R. S. 1996, 'Is Weight Loss Hazardous?', *Nutrition Reviews*, vol. 54, no. 4 (supplement), pp. 116–124.

Lewis, S. 1992, 'Food Security, Environment, Poverty, and the World's Children', *Journal of Nutrition Education*, vol. 24, no.1 (supplement), pp. 3–11.

Lowenberg, M. E. 1970, 'Socio-Cultural Basis of Food Habits', *Food Technology*, vol. 24, no. 8, pp. 27–32.

Lyman, B. 1989, *More Than A Matter of Taste. A Psychology of Food*, Van Nostrand Reinhold, New York.

MacKenzie, M. 1993, 'Is the Family Meal Disappearing?', *The Journal of Gastronomy*, vol. 7, no. 1, pp. 99–104.

Micozzi, M. S. 1996, *Fundamentals of Complementary and Alternative Medicine*, Churchill Livingstone, New York.

Mosby's Medical Nursing and Allied Health Dictionary 1994, 4th edn, Mosby, St Louis.

Muecke, M. A. 1983, 'Caring for Southeast Asian Refugee Patients in the USA', *American Journal of Public Health*, vol. 174, no. 7, pp. 431.

Mullins, L. C., Cook C., Mushel M., & Machin G. 1993, 'A Comparative Examination of the Characteristics of Participants of a Senior Citizens Nutrition and Activities Program', *Activities, Adaptation and Aging*, vol. 17, no. 3, pp. 15–37.

Nahikian-Nelms, M. 1997, 'Influential Factors of Caregiver Behavior at Mealtime: A Study of 24 Child-Care Programs', *Journal of the American Dietetic Association*, vol. 97, no. 5, pp. 505–9.

National Task Force on Prevention and Treatment of Obesity 1994 'Towards Prevention of Obesity: Research Directions', *Obesity Research*, vol. 2, no. 6, pp. 571–84.

Nestle, M. & Guttmacher S. 1992, 'Hunger in the United States: Rationale, Methods, and Policy Implications of State Hunger Surveys', *Journal of Nutrition Education*, vol. 24, no. 1 (supplement), pp. 18–22.

Parker, S., Nichter, M., Nichter, M., Vuckovic N., Sims C., & Ritenbaugh C. 1995, 'Body Image and Weight Concerns among African American and White Adolescent Females: Differences that Make a Difference', *Human Organization*, vol. 54, no. 2, pp.103–13.

Polivy, J. 1996, 'Psychological Consequences of Food Restriction', *Journal of the American Dietetic Association*, vol. 96, no. 6, pp. 589–92.

Rassin, D. K., Richardson, C. J., Baranowski, T., Nadar, P. R., Guenther, N., Bee, D. E., & Brown, J. P. 1994, 'Incidence of Breast-Feeding in a Low Socioeconomic Group of Mothers in the United States: Ethnic Patterns', *Pediatrics*, vol. 73, pp. 132–7.

Ross, L. 1995, 'The Spiritual Dimension: Its Importance to Patients' Health, Well-Being and Quality of Life and Its Implications for Nursing Practice', *International Journal of Nursing Studies*, vol. 32, no. 5, pp. 457–68.

Rozin, P. 1996, 'Sociocultural Influences on Human Food Selection', in E. Capaldi (ed.), *Why We Eat What We Eat*, American Psychological Association, Washington, DC.

Ryff, C. 1995 'Psychological Well-Being in Adult Life', *Current Directions in Psychological Science*, vol. 4, no. 4, pp. 99–104.

Sanjur, D. 1995, *Hispanic Foodways, Nutrition and Health*, Simon & Schuster, Massachusetts.

Satter, E. 1987, *How To Get Your Kid To Eat ... But Not Too Much*, Bull Publishing Company, Palo Alto, Calif.

Schwartz, M. W. & Seeley, R. J. 1997, 'The New Biology of Body Weight Regulation', *Journal of the American Dietetic Association*, vol. 97, no. 1, pp. 54–8.

Smith, R., Mullins L. C., Mushel M., & Roorda, J. 1994, 'An Examination of Demographic, Socio-Cultural, and Health Differences between Congregate and Home Diners in a Senior Nutrition Program', *Journal of Nutrition for the Elderly*, vol. 14, no. 1, pp. 1–21.

Turner, J., Deyo, R., Loeser, J., Von Korff, M., & Fordyce, W. 1994, 'The Importance of Placebo Effects in Pain Treatment and Research', *Journal of the American Medical Association*, vol. 271, no. 20, pp. 1609–14.

Tuttle, C. R. & Dewy, K. G. 1994, 'Determinants of Infant Feeding Choices among Southeast Asian Immigrants in Northern California', *Journal of the American Dietetic Association*, vol. 94, no.2, pp.282–6.

Wurtman, R. & Wurtman, J. J. 1995, 'Brain Serotonin, Carbohydrate-Cravings, Obesity, and Depression', *Obesity Research*, vol. 3, no. 4 (supplement), pp. 477–80.

10

Food and Ageing

Wm Alex McIntosh and Karen S. Kubena

Overview

- *Why are older people at risk of hunger and poor nutrition?*
- *What role does social isolation and stress play in older people's nutrition?*
- *How do social relationships reduce the risk of hunger and poor nutrition among older people?*

Older people are considered a group at high risk of food insecurity, hunger, and poor nutrition. They are particularly vulnerable because they tend to have fewer socioeconomic resources, as well as being more prone to isolation, disability, and stress. These problems tend to be even more prevalent among older people who are members of ethnic minorities. In addition, many countries, including the USA, have reduced funding for food-assistance programs such as food stamps and congregate meals. Private charities have been unable to compensate for these cutbacks. Many older people, however, are able to compensate for their lack of resources and physical isolation through their social networks. Older people who live alone may find mealtime companionship among their friends and neighbours. In addition, relatives and neighbours provide many disabled older people with shopping and cooking assistance.

Key terms

ageism
activities of daily living
disabilities
life chance
nutritional risk
role
social isolation
social network

social support
socioeconomic status (SES)
status

Introduction

Older people are an important group for sociological study for a number of reasons. First, older people represent one of the fastest growing segments of the populations of most developed countries. The populations of most developed countries are growing older. The number of people aged 65 years and older is projected to double in the next 25 years, thanks to better diets as well as better health and health care (Easterlin 1996). The growth of the older population and their increasing needs will have an impact on every aspect of society.

Second, because of filial obligations supported by laws, traditions, and present-day norms, older people represent a group whose needs continue to be the responsibility of families and the State. However, as older people live longer, and as financial and time constraints place a burden on families and government programs, the ability to continue to meet these obligations is in some doubt.

Third, age is a social category and is related to **status** and **role**, which serve as two of sociology's more fundamental sociological concepts. Typical roles include patient, physician, grandmother, and daughter. Age determines a role, 'independent of capacities and preferences' of the role incumbent (Moen 1996, p. 171). Status represents the prestige or respect accorded to individuals occupying those social positions. Similar to roles, the respect that such an individual receives for performing a role is somewhat independent of actual performance; simply occupying the position itself accords a certain amount of prestige. 'Age', 'ageing', and 'elderly' are all words with supposed biological meanings, yet each represents a socially defined category. In fact, much of what passes as biological wisdom in defining older people has more to do with socially generated beliefs and norms. In addition, because age is a social category, it contains an evaluative component. The terms 'age', 'ageing', and 'elderly' are all associated with negative expectations about abilities, quality of life, and the like (Palmore 1990). Ageing is also viewed as a process of declining status; it is seen as biologically driven downward mobility. This is, in part, true. Many older people experience decline in their health as they continue to age, and many face declining incomes in the form of retirement reimbursements. But ageing is also a negative status because of its relationship to what is currently one of the most desirable statuses in Western society: youth. There is considerable evidence that older people experience **ageism**, or prejudice and discrimination based on age.

Because of the increasing size of the ageing population and the difficult economic circumstances that many older people face, sociologists and nutritionists have turned their attention to older people's food habits and nutritional status or health. Several important themes have emerged from these studies. The first is that of **socioeconomic status (SES)**. It is widely believed that inadequate resources are the reason for food insecurity and risk of malnutrition (McIntosh 1996; Weddle et al. 1996).

A second theme is **social isolation**. Isolation from others is thought to deprive the individual of help, companionship, and motivation for self-care.

The third theme represents the obverse of isolation: social integration and **social support**. A multiplicity of ties to others not only increases contacts with other human beings, but also ensures companionship and access to resources such as transportation or help with cooking. A debate has developed, however, around the degree of importance of social ties, the actual provision of aid, and the subjective assessment of that aid. Some believe that the nature of the **social network** has greater consequences for older people than the help those networks provide; others have argued that the greatest impact of help from others lies in how it is perceived by its recipients.

The fourth, and most recent, theme to emerge in the sociology of nutrition literature is that of stressful life events. All human beings undergo change; some of these changes are upsetting and disrupting (Thoits 1995). Older people are not immune to such events, and they are most likely to experience events such as the death of a close loved one. Such stressors have a negative impact on health, including nutritional status. The debate here centres on whether some stressors have a more deleterious effect than others have, and whether some individuals are better equipped than others to deal with negative life change. Others are able to cope with the help of their social support network. Such aid comes into play for another kind of crisis that confronts many older people: reduced functional capacity.

Disability, its effects, and the social responses to it represent a fifth theme. As people age, the probability of contracting one or more chronic illnesses increases (Verbrugge 1990). A number of such illnesses include side effects that limit mobility or some other aspect of body functioning (Manton 1989). Again, some older people are able to cope with these threats to independence through their own efforts. Self-care involves those changes that individuals choose to make as a means of improving health and dealing with symptoms of illness. These include dietary and exercise modifications. Certain limitations, however, may make it more difficult for the individual to engage in self-care. In such cases the social network's services become vitally important.

Sixth, sociologists have renewed their interest in the body as a reflection of various socially defined attributes of worth. These play a major role in determining individuals' images or perceptions of themselves. Sociologists refer to this self-perception as 'the self'. Body image or body self has increased in its importance in the formation of the self. Anthony Giddens (1991) and others have argued that individuals find it increasingly difficult to affect their political and economic environments, and so have turned increasingly to the self and the body as things upon which they can have an impact. Much of this concern is directed at manipulating body weight in an attempt to achieve physiologically improbable goals.

Finally, it should be noted that sociological approaches to food and nutrition tend to take a 'social problems' orientation. Concerns centre on the social causes and consequences of food insecurity, hunger, malnutrition, over-nutrition, and so on.

This chapter reviews the literature that has developed around the themes mentioned above, beginning with the notion that food and nutrition problems may be conceived of as social problems as well.

Ageing and associated food and nutrition problems

A number of nutritional problems confront older people, and are usually presented in biological terms. In fact, these nutritional problems have clear biological causes and consequences. However, unless social and economic factors are also considered, our understanding of older people's nutrition is incomplete.

One nutritional concern associated with ageing is changing nutritional need (Fiatarone & Evans 1993). Older people have a lessened need for energy, but greater protein requirements. General concerns here have focused on the inability of some older people to meet nutrient needs and on the effects of nutrient deficiency on immune function, for example (Kubena & McMurray 1996). This inability is partly the result of the decreased income that some experience as they age, but it is also the consequence of misperceptions within this age group itself regarding the need for nutrients. A source of these misperceptions can be found in consumer society. Products and advertisements both provide a contradictory array of information regarding the way that nutrition, health, and ageing are related.

Loosely associated with the declining ability of some older people to meet their nutritional needs are the issues of hunger and food insecurity. In the USA these terms are less rooted in biology than they are in norms. Hunger is defined and measured in terms of the inability to buy all the food one would like or of sending one's children to bed hungry. For some, hunger is an acute, emergency situation, the result of a temporary shortfall in resources. For others, the situation may be chronic. Some older people, for example, have reported that they commonly run short of money to purchase food during the last week of every month. There is no evidence, however, that this leads to malnutrition. However, the United States Food Research and Action Committee has found that 20 per cent of the poor older people they interviewed had involuntarily lost weight because of insufficient food (Lieberman 1998). While there is no evidence that such food insufficiency increases the likelihood of chronic disease, there is evidence that it increases the likelihood of infections such as pneumonia.

Food insecurity is a broader concern, affecting those who believe that hunger is just around the corner. The insecure are those who anticipate deprivation or the inability to achieve a diet that they consider adequate. Once again, inadequate resources appear to be the driving force behind food insecurity. The health consequences, however, remain unknown. We could hypothesise that food insecurity represents a stressor, as we will below, and stressors have known consequences for health. Researchers, however, have yet to investigate this possibility. We suggest that, while those who concern themselves with hunger and food insecurity may have negative biological consequences in mind, it is, once again, a normative interpretation that has led others to define these conditions as problems. Hunger and food insecurity are thought to be the result of the inequitable distribution of resources by some and the denial of inalienable rights by others. All people, including older people, have the 'right to food', which is said to incorporate 'the right of everyone to an adequate standard of living' and 'the right to be free from hunger' (Alston 1994, p. 209).

Declining abilities may also result from changes in body size. Both being overweight and being underweight, and the associated health problems, may make it more difficult for older people to perform their various roles. In addition, there is strong evidence that body weight affects the probability of death. Older people who are greatly over or under the weight standard for their age, height, and gender have a greater risk of dying than older people closer to standard (Flegal 1996).

Weight, however, is also a highly salient social marker, partly because of its association with youth. But it is also salient because what is defined socially as excessive body weight connotes a negative social status. To begin with, the weight itself is considered unattractive. In addition, the weight is perceived as a marker of more deep-seated undesirable traits, such as greed, dishonesty, and lack of ambition and self-control (see chapter 11).

Finally, both chronic illnesses and medications affect appetite, the sense of taste, the absorption of nutrients, and the need for nutrients. There are social issues here as well regarding the decline in social relationships that occur as individuals become disabled, on one hand, and the effect that this decline might have on the individual's ability to shop, prepare meals, and ingest those meals, on the other hand. Furthermore, there is some evidence that older people are overmedicated because they may play too passive a role when confronting medical authority.

Access to resources

Socioeconomic status

Individuals' socioeconomic status (SES) depends upon their access to wealth, prestige, and power; differential access to these leads to differences in lifestyles and **life chances** (Gerth & Mills 1946). Those with greater wealth and status enjoy better life chances than those with less of these, simply because of access to better health practices and health care. Differential resources also permit greater lifestyle choices in such areas as dwellings, food purchases, clothing, and vacations. An individual's SES is usually conceptualised and measured by that individual's education, occupation, and income. Education and occupation are primary determinants of income, but they are also sources of prestige. In addition to these, gender, ethnicity, and age also provide individuals with status. Each of these characteristics affects access to wealth, prestige, and power, and each is associated with distinctive aspects of lifestyles and life chances.

Until recently, in the USA, old age was commonly associated with poverty in that as much as 25 per cent of older people were classified as poor (Crystal 1996, p. 394). Increases in social security benefits and other changes have halved this proportion. But great inequities remain among retired people in the USA, with former white-collar workers generally in a better financial position than former blue-collar workers. Furthermore, many of those in the lowest 20 per cent of incomes were still considered to be above the poverty line (Crystal 1996, p. 397). Those in this group tend to lack health insurance, but are not considered poor enough to qualify for means-tested programs like Medicaid or food stamps. Janet Poppendieck (1998) observes that while only 10 per cent of the poor are older, this group constitutes 22 per cent of soup-kitchen clientele.

As previously mentioned, malnutrition exists among poor older people (Weddle et al. 1996). In fact, low SES is related to low levels of nutrition knowledge, poorer eating habits, inadequate diets, and poorer nutritional status (Quinn et al. 1997: Wolinsky et al. 1990). However, in our own study of 424 independent, non-institutionalised older people, we found those with higher SES reported better appetites but had lower body weight and less muscle mass, lower dietary adequacy, and were at risk of riboflavin deficiency (McIntosh et al. 1989a).

Ethnicity and class

Ethnicity is a social status that has implications for the distribution of resources. Social scientists argue that the combination of low income and ethnicity constitutes 'double jeopardy'. While others have used this same argument to claim that older people who are members of minorities experience double jeopardy, it is a relatively short logical leap to argue that poor older people who are minorities are subject to triple jeopardy. Poverty rates have remained highest among older Black people (Quadagno 1994). The effects of double and triple jeopardy are reflected in older people's nutrition. Nancy Schoenberg and her colleagues (1997), for example, found rural Black people to be at greater **nutritional risk** than urban Black people or White people in general.

Class conflict

Social class position is no mere marker of the distribution of resources. Because resources are scarce, struggles ensue over their redistribution, usually along class lines. Food and medical care are two such resources that the politicians frequently consider redistributing according to social categories, such as those of children, older people, women, and veterans. In an era of declining social-welfare funding, struggles over food stamp eligibility and access to subsidised medical care once again reflect class, generational, and ethnic group interests, among others.

In the past, after a great deal of political struggle, a number of programs to benefit older people were promulgated. Meals on Wheels and Congregate Meals were designed to provide one meal per day containing at least one-third of the recommended daily allowances of most nutrients. Critics have sparked considerable debate over the efficacy of these programs, and some have even questioned their fairness.

Debates aside, budget cuts and decentralisation have left many states unable to fund feeding programs to meet current needs. Forty-one percent of Meals on Wheels programs report, for example, that they now maintain lengthy waiting lists (Lieberman 1998). Many food-pantry and soup-kitchen participants report their inability to access programs such as food stamps as their reason for using such food charities.

Ageism and stigma

Social statuses contain evaluative as well as cognitive components: not only do we hold certain beliefs about persons with particular statuses, but we also make judgments regarding the worth of persons holding those statuses. Age is a social status, and various age groups reflect differentially valued statuses. Groups accorded negative status and negative evaluations frequently encounter prejudice and discrimination. When it comes to race or gender, these are referred to as 'racism' and 'sexism', respectively. Ageism is their counterpart when it comes to negative evaluations of old age. At present, younger age is generally regarded as more valuable in Western societies, and so younger persons are accorded more status than older persons. Perhaps one of the most undesirable statuses to inhabit is that of old age. Numerous negative evaluations are attached to this status. As with many negatively evaluated statuses, the basis of the negative evaluations is socially determined.

The stereotypes associated with ageism are similar to those associated with racism and sexism in that they question the abilities of the status-holder relative to the abilities of others. Those holding negatively evaluated statuses are usually judged, in a biological sense, as having lesser physical and mental abilities, and this negative evaluation is thus considered to be both natural and immutable. Many believe that because some older people have physical or mental limitations, all older people are so limited. These assumptions lead to a denigration of older people's capabilities and worth. It is assumed that older people are unable to care for themselves. Such negative evaluations hinder older people's ability to obtain employment and result in intergenerational struggles over the allocation of resources. Much of the debate over the extent to which current and future resources should be devoted to retirement benefits and to subsidised access to food and medical care has reflected a continuing debate over the worth of older persons. This debate is cast in either equality or equity terms. Equality arguments have emphasised the sharing of resources based on need (Poppendieck 1998). Equity arguments, by contrast, centre on the sharing of resources with a set of individuals commensurate with the amount of contributions they make or have made to society at some earlier point in time (Gokhale & Kotlikoff 1998).

The unequal distribution of resources is brought about by social as well as economic and political factors. Those persons eligible for aid, including older people, often refuse it because of the stigma associated with poverty and welfare. Simply put, those who are less well-to-do are less admired than those who are better off. In the USA, where poverty is thought to be the result of irresponsible behaviour rather than resource distributions, the working poor are accorded more respect than the non-working poor. The poor who get by on charity and/or welfare receive the least respect. The public associates a wide range of negative characteristics with welfare recipients, culminating in the assessment of 'the undeserving poor'. Those who provide benefits such as food stamps, for example, hold many of these stereotypes, as do a number of those who work for private charities such as food pantries and soup kitchens (Poppendieck 1998).

Social resources

Social networks

A person's social network consists of friends, relatives, spouses, children, co-workers, neighbours, fellow members of voluntary organisations, and fellow church members. These tend to be the individuals with whom a person has the most contact or from whom the person receives the most support or help (Lin 1986). Social support refers to instrumental aid (goods and services) and expressive aid (emotional support, companionship). Social support also includes efficacious social control (Umberson 1987)—that is, network members may attempt to persuade or cajole the individual to engage in desirable behaviour, such as reducing dietary fat.

People who receive social support become ill less frequently and recover more quickly and successfully when they do become ill. The most striking effect of social support appears to be the lessening of the risk of death. Numerous studies have found that those with social support are less likely to die than those who lack it (Yasuda et al. 1997; Schoenbach et al. 1998; Seeman et al. 1993). More recently we and our colleagues (1989a; 1989b; 1995) have found a connection between social support and nutritional health.

Social support results in part from the very structure of the social network. There is considerable debate, however, between social-support researchers as to the degree to which network characteristics such as size or density are more important than the aid received or recipients' subjective evaluations of that aid. Network structure includes the network's size (number of people in it) and density (the degree to which network members know and interact with one another). Thus, networks that contain a small number of persons who are well acquainted with one another provide greater intimacy and emotional support. In our Houston study, older people with larger sized social networks tended to receive more social support, although men received greater benefits from network size than did women. Older men with larger sized networks got more advice about food and cooking, more help with grocery shopping and cooking, and more mealtime companionship than men with smaller networks, and their iron status was better than those with smaller networks. Older women with denser networks tended to have more company during meals.

Social support

Certain kinds of social support appear to be associated with nutritional health, particularly that of older people. Instrumental aid such as transportation for grocery shopping, help with meal preparation, companionship during meals, loans of food, or advice about cooking, diets, or food have the potential of maintaining or improving the nutritional health of individuals. It is precisely this sort of help that older people frequently need. In Houston, older people with a greater number of companions in their networks had better appetites and more muscle mass (McIntosh et al. 1989a). Those who received help with shopping, cooking, and housekeeping were at lower nutritional risk than were those older people who received little or no such help. And those who had more persons in their social networks giving them advice about food and nutrition tended to have higher vitamin B-6 status.

Social isolation and loneliness

Living alone (social isolation) represents a clear trend among older people. In 1960, about 20 per cent lived alone, but by 1984 the proportion had increased to one-third (Moody 1994). This is partly the result of the mortality differential between males and females: women, on average, live longer than men. Our own data on older people in Houston indicate that 12 per cent of the men and 50 per cent of the women lived alone, and that the propensity to live alone increased with age, especially for women. Others note, however, that many older people live close to one of their children, and approximately 40 per cent keep in daily phone contact with one of their offspring (Moody 1994). Because many older people live alone, they are frequently thought to be at risk of loneliness and poor nutrition. There are documented health consequences of living alone. Those older people who live alone because of the recent death of their spouse, for example, have an increased risk of mortality (Rogers 1996).

Nutrition researchers have argued that without the social contact typical of shared living arrangements, the motivation to cook food or to eat regular meals may be reduced. Maradee Davis and her colleagues (1985) found that older people who lived alone were more likely to eat an inadequate diet than those living with a spouse. Similarly, Susan Murphy and others (1990) observed that older women had higher energy intakes if they lived with a spouse. Dellmar Walker and Roy Beauchene (1991) found among older people in Georgia that the greater the loneliness experienced, the poorer the diet in terms of iron, protein, phosphorous, riboflavin, niacin, and ascorbic acid (vitamin C). In New York, older men skipped more meals if they lived alone (Frongillo et al. 1992). In Houston, we measured dietary adequacy by determining the degree to which the dietary intake of older people over a three-day period met 67 per cent of the recommended dietary allowances (RDAs) for this age group. We found that both older women and older men were likely to fall below 67 per cent of the RDA for a number of nutrients if they lived by themselves.

Disability and functioning

All human beings are susceptible to impairments caused by chronic illness, injury, or accident; impairments involve bodily abnormalities that may limit movement of limbs or cause generalised muscular weakness (Jette 1996). These can limit the ability of a person to perform social roles and are often referred to as '**disabilities**'. Older people are more prone to chronic illnesses than other age groups, and thus their rates of impairment are higher. Furthermore, as they grow older, greater percentages of older people experience these limitations. Some impairments are associated with functional limitations or restrictions in performing what are considered to be everyday activities. In the USA, 39 per cent of people aged 70 years and older have one or more disabilities that limit **activities of daily living**. Eleven per cent of older people experience difficulties shopping for groceries; 4 per cent have trouble preparing meals; 2 per cent experience problems with eating food (Jette 1996, p. 100).

Disabilities are directly associated with the potential for poor nutritional status, and thus some of the tools devised to measure nutritional risk include measures of disability, such as difficulty chewing or swallowing. Certain foods may be avoided as a result, as a study by Mary-Ellen Quinn and others (1997) demonstrates. Others have found a relationship between inadequate diet and level of disability (Walker & Beauchene 1991). The Houston study found that older people with difficulties in using their upper bodies or with difficulties in walking tended to have more body fat and less muscle mass. Such people also tended to be less physically active and have less adequate diets.

There is considerable debate regarding whether disability leads to an increase or decrease in social support. Some studies provide evidence of a shrinking social network and increased social isolation, with the only help with daily activities supplied by remaining kin. Furthermore, as the burden of such help grows, the care giver is in danger of experiencing resentment and burn-out. Others argue that disabilities actually mobilise social networks into action, increasing the level of support supplied. Our own Houston data confirm the latter hypothesis. The greater the level of disability, the more help with grocery shopping, cooking, and other activities of daily living the older person received, regardless of gender (McIntosh et al. 1988). In addition, persons with disabilities were less likely to experience the nutritional problems mentioned above when they had social support from others. For example, those with limited mobility were less likely to eat breakfast and to have lower muscle mass but more body fat. However, these negative effects were offset, to a degree, by having a higher percentage of friends in the social network and by receiving help with activities of daily living.

Stress, strain, and health

Human beings experience a great number of changes in their lives (Thoits 1995). These include marriage, having children, getting a job, retirement, illness, and so on. A number of such changes are welcomed; others are not. The unwelcome changes are thought to be stressful. A stressor is a threat, demand, or constraint on individuals that 'tax or exceed their resources for managing them' (Burke 1996, p. 146). One kind of stressor is a life event, which is the occurrence of a discrete, observable event that leads to a major change in life. Divorce, job loss, and the death of a spouse all represent such potentially life-shattering changes.

There is a well-established link between poor health and stressors (House et al. 1988). Various forms of illness—such as coronary heart disease, hypertension, cancer, and depression—have been found to be associated with various stressful events such as job loss, marital conflict, and the death of a spouse or close friend (Marmot & Theorell

1988; Umberson et al. 1992). Definitions of stress such as those discussed above often emphasise disequilibrium in the organism, which results from exposure to stressors. William Krehl (1964, p. 4) has described nutrition as 'the sum of all the processes by which an organism ingests, digests, absorbs, transports, and utilizes food substances'. Therefore, anything that disrupts ingestion, digestion, absorption, transportation, or utilisation by the body is a potential stressor.

Existing research suggests that stressful life events do indeed interfere with nutrition. In our study of older Virginians (McIntosh et al. 1989b), we found that financial worries led to depressed appetite, which in turn was associated with lower energy and protein-intake. More recently, H. Payette and others (1995) observed a relationship between a high level of self-assessed stress and a lower intake of protein. We found, in Houston, that the two kinds of events that seemed to have the greatest negative effect on older people's nutrition were financial difficulties and general, unspecified problems in relations with various family members. Financial problems had a negative effect on body fat, muscle mass, iron status, and the frequency of eating breakfast among older women, and older men had higher body fat and snacked more if they had recently experienced family troubles.

Social identity and age

All human beings develop a sense of identity, personae, or self. Much of this sense derives from social interactions with others. Individuals, however, have some control over the perceptions of others and actively attempt to influence those perceptions. While there is disagreement over the degree to which an individual can 'manage the impressions of others', it is clear that, within limits, this management is achievable. Western societies, particularly the USA, place a high value on youthfulness. Mass-media programming and advertising have perhaps exacerbated this emphasis, by mostly featuring younger actors, presenters, and models (Turrow 1997). Furthermore, as the older population has grown and its economic fortunes improved, producers and advertisers have discovered a vast, insufficiently tapped market in older people, especially the so-called 'young-old' (those under 70 years of age). Their approach to older people has been to stress that older people are still as capable, in many ways, as the young. According to Mike Featherstone and Mike Hepworth (1995), this has had a positive effect in that it has helped reduce the perception of older people as less capable human beings. However, it must be pointed out that producers have attempted to market their products in terms of identity manipulation—that is, they have developed products to help older people disguise their age.

Sociologists have increasingly taken the body's social dimensions seriously. Chris Shilling (1994), for example, has put forward the notion that bodies are judged unequally; thus differentials in body size and shape constitute a form of inequality. Linda Jackson's (1992) review of extant research indicates that body appearance has a significant impact on how others judge an individual. Pierre Bourdieu (1984) has posited the idea that bodies reflect social class in that they represent the owner's relationship to the worlds of necessities and taste. Among the lower classes, a heavy body represents a diet high in fat but low in cost. Bourdieu (1984) refers to this as the diet of necessity. Taste makes necessity a virtue. Bodies also reflect 'bodily orientation'. Members of the working class take a more instrumental approach in that they make direct use of their bodies' capacities in making their living. The implication for eating is that heavy foods in large quantities are desirable because of their perceived contribution to strength. The dominant classes, according to Bourdieu (1984), prefer slender bodies and are willing to defer gratification to achieve them.

In old age, working-class individuals may experience a decline in both income and bodily function. The middle-class individual may worry about being replaced by a person with a younger body. Upper class individuals may view middle and old age as a time to enjoy the fruits of their labour and may expect to have not only the money but also the physical capacity to do so.

The body in postmodern society is said to have become more malleable in the sense that it can be manipulated in the quest for a new or altered identity. Surgery, diets, exercise, and drugs have all been called upon in attempts to make the body appear more youthful (see chapter 12). Older people are equally prone to such attempts (Biggs 1997). Older people are slightly less likely to participate in exercise programs, but after differences in disability levels are accounted for, their participation levels are likely to be higher than many other age groups. Featherstone and Hepworth argue, however, that with increasing age, the physical constraints on the ability to alter appearance grow. As they put it, the body becomes an unchanging mask that its occupant can no longer escape.

Conclusion

While much is known about the effects of socioeconomic status on nutrition, research is just beginning on how social networks help older people maintain a healthy diet and avoid nutritional risk. Similarly, the negative impacts of both stressors and disabilities on older people's nutrition are not fully understood. Finally, investigation of the older people's efforts to manage their identities through diet and exercise remains an important, but relatively unexplored, area of sociological research.

Summary of main points

- While older people's energy needs tend to be lower than those of other age groups, their need for nutrients is as high or higher.
- Older people's nutrition can be compromised by chronic illness, disabilities, and interactions between drugs and nutrients.
- Older people's nutrition is also negatively affected by poverty, stressful life events, and social isolation.

- Social networks supply aid such as transportation to buy groceries, help with meal preparation, and companionship during meals. Both network structure and the help it provides have a positive impact on older people's nutrition. Social support helps people overcome the constraints imposed by living alone, functional limitations, and stressful events.
- Older people perceive their weight, as do others in modern society, as a means of recreating their selves. Consumer culture has some impact on the choices that older people and others make when selecting 'selves' to pursue. As they increasingly age, however, their ability to control their appearance declines.

Discussion questions

1 What are the main problems of poor nutrition faced by older people?
2 What are the sources of poor socioeconomic status and isolation among older people?
3 How do stress and disabilities affect older people's nutrition?
4 How does social support help older people overcome problems such as lack of resources, isolation, disability, and stress?
5 Why are older people concerned with their physical appearance, and what do they do to maintain that appearance?

Further reading and resources

Blaxter, M. 1990, *Health and Lifestyles*, Routledge, New York.
Kosberg, J. I. & Kayne, L. 1997, *Elderly Men: Special Problems and Professional Challenges*, Springer, New York.
Litwak, E. 1985, *Helping the Elderly: The Complementary Roles of Informal Networks and Formal Systems*, Guilford Press, New York.
Peters, G. R. & Rappaport, L. R. 1988, 'Food, Nutrition, and Aging: Behavioral Perspectives', *American Behavioral Scientist*, vol. 32, no. 1, special issue, pp. 1–88.
Sokolovsky, J. 1997, *The Cultural Context of Aging: Worldwide Perspectives*, Bergin & Garvey, Westport.

Website
New England Research Institute: <http://www.neri.org>

Relevant journals
The Gerontologist
The Journal of Gerontology
Journal of Nutrition Education
Journal of the American Dietetic Association
Appetite
Journal of Aging and Health
Journal of Nutrition for the Elderly

Journal of Food and Society
Agriculture, Food, and Human Values
Journal of Health and Social Behavior

References

Alston, P. 1994, 'International Law and the Right to Food', in B. Harriss-White & R. Hoffenberg (eds), *Food: Multidisciplinary Perspectives*, Blackwell, New York.

Biggs, S. 1997, 'Choosing Not to Be Old? Masks, Bodies, and Identity Management in Later Life', *Ageing and Society*, vol. 17, September, pp. 553–70.

Bourdieu, P. 1984, *Distinction: A Social Critique of the Judgement of Taste*, Harvard University, Cambridge, Mass.

Burke, P. 1996, 'Social Identities and Psychosocial Stress', in H. B. Kaplan (ed.), *Psychosocial Stress: Perspectives on Structure, Theory, Life-Course, and Methods*, Academic Press, San Diego.

Crystal, S. 1996, 'Economic Status of the Elderly', in R. H. Binstock & L. K. George (eds), *Handbook of Aging and the Social Sciences*, 4th edn, Academic Press, San Diego.

Davis, M. A., Randall, E., Forthofer, R. N., Lee, E. S., & Margen, S. 1985, 'Living Arrangements and Dietary Patterns of Older Adults in the United States', *Journal of Gerontology*, vol. 40, no. 4, pp. 434–9.

Easterlin, R. A. 1996, 'Economic and Social Implications of Demographic Patterns', in R. H. Binstock & L. K. George (eds), *Handbook of Aging and the Social Sciences*, 4th edn, Academic Press, San Diego.

Featherstone, M. & Hepworth, M. 1995, 'Images of Positive Ageing: A Case Study of Retirement Magazine', in M. Featherstone & M. Hepworth, *Images of Ageing: Representations of Later Life*, Routledge, New York.

Fiatarone, M. & Evans, W. 1993, 'The Etiology and Reversibility of Muscle Dysfunction in the Aged', *Journal of Gerontology*, vol. 47, September, pp. 77–83.

Flegal, K. M. 1996, 'Trends in Body Weight and Overweight in the US Population', *Nutrition Reviews*, vol. 54, no. 4 (supplement), pp. 97–100.

Frongillo, E. A., Jr, Rauschenbach, B. S., Roe, D. R., & Williamson, D. F. 1992, 'Characteristics Related to Elderly Persons' Not Eating for 1 or More Days: Implications for Meal Programs', *American Journal of Public Health*, vol. 82, no. 4, pp. 600–2.

Gerth, H. & Mills, C. W. 1946, *From Max Weber: Essays in Sociology*, Oxford University Press, New York.

Giddens, A. 1991, *Modernity and Self-Identity: Self and Society in the Late Modern Age*, Stanford University Press, Stanford, Calif.

Gokhale, J. & Kotlikoff, L. J. 1998, Medicare from the Perspective of Generational Accounting, paper presented at the Medicare Reform: Issues and Answers conference, Bush School of Government and Public Service, College Station, Texas A&M University, 3 April.

House, J. S., Umberson, D., & Landis, K. 1988, 'Structures and Processes of Social Support', *Annual Review of Sociology*, vol. 14, pp. 293–318.

Jackson, L. A. 1992, *Physical Appearance and Gender: Sociological and Sociocultural Perspectives*, State University of New York, Albany, NY.

Jette, A. 1996, 'Disability Trends and Transitions', in R. H. Binstock & L. K. George (eds), *Handbook of Aging and the Social Sciences*, 4th edn, Academic Press, San Diego.

Krehl, W. A. 1964, 'Nutrition in Medicine', *American Journal of Clinical Nutrition*, vol. 15, no. 2, pp. 191–4.

Kubena, K. & McMurray, D. 1996, 'Nutrition and the Immune System: A Review of Nutrient–Nutrient Interactions', *Journal of the American Dietetic Association*, vol. 96, no. 11, pp. 1156–64.

Lieberman, T. 1998, 'Hunger in America', *The Nation*, vol. 266, 30 March, pp. 11–16.

Lin, N. 1986, 'Conceptualizing Social Support', in N. Lin, A. Dean, & W. Ensel, *Social Support, Life Events, and Depression*, Academic Press, Orlando.

McIntosh, W. A. 1996, *Sociologies of Food and Nutrition*, Plenum, New York.

McIntosh, W. A., Kaplan, H. B., Kubena, K. S., & Landmann, W. A. 1995, 'Life Events, Social Support, and Immune Response in Elderly Individuals', in J. Hendricks (ed.), *Health and Health Care Utilization in Later Life*, Baywood, Amityville, NY.

McIntosh, W. A., Kubena, K. S., & Landmann, W. A. 1989a, *Social Support, Stress, and the Diet and Nutrition of the Aged: Final Report to the National Institute on Aging*, Department of Rural Sociology, College Station, Texas A&M University.

McIntosh, W. A., Kubena, K. S., Landmann, W. A., & Dvorak, S. 1988, A Comparative Assessment of the Social Networks of Elderly Disabled and Non-disabled, paper presented at the annual meeting of the American Sociological Association, Atlanta, August.

McIntosh, W. A., Shifflett, P. A., & Picou, J. S. 1989b, 'Social Support, Stress, Strain, and the Dietary Intake of the Elderly', *Medical Care*, vol. 21, no. 2, pp. 140–53.

Manton, K. 1989, 'Epidemiological, Demographic, and Social Correlates of Disability among the Elderly.' *The Milbank Memorial Quarterly*, vol. 67, supp. 2, part 1, pp. 13–58.

Marmot, M. & Theorell, T. 1988, 'Social Class and Cardiovascular Disease', *International Journal of Health Service*, vol. 8, no. 4, pp. 1–13.

Moen, P. 1996, 'Gender, Age, and the Life Course', in R. H. Binstock & L. K. George (eds), *Handbook of Aging and the Social Sciences*, 4th edn, Academic Press, San Diego.

Moody, H. R. 1994, *Aging: Concepts and Controversies*, Pine Forge Press, Thousand Oaks, Calif.

Murphy, S. P., Davis, M. A., Neuhouse, J. M., & Lein, D. 1990, 'Factors Influencing the Dietary Adequacy and Energy Intake of Older Americans', *Journal of Nutrition Education*, vol. 22, no. 6, pp. 284–91.

Palmore, E. 1990, *Ageism: Negative and Positive*, Springer, New York.

Payette, H., Gray-Donaldson, K., Cyr, R., & Boutier, V. 1995, 'Predictors of Dietary Intake in a Functionally Dependent Elderly Population in the Community', *American Journal of Public Health*, vol. 85, no. 5, pp. 667–83.

Poppendieck, J. 1998 (forthcoming), *Sweet Charity? Emergency Food, and the End of Entitlement*, Viking Penguin, New York.

Quadagno, J. A. 1994, *The Color of Welfare*, Oxford University Press, New York.

Quinn, M. E., Johnson, M. A., Poon, L. W., Martin, P., & Nickols-Richardson, S. M. 1997, 'Factors of Nutritional Health-Seeking Behaviors: Findings from the Georgia Centenarian Study', *Journal of Aging and Health*, vol. 9, no. 1, pp. 90–104.

Rogers, R. 1996, 'The Effects of Family Composition, Health, and Social Support Linkages on Mortality', *Journal of Health and Social Behavior*, vol. 37, no. 4, pp. 326–38.

Schoenberg, N. E., Coward, R. T., & Dougherty, M. C. 1998, 'Perceptions of Community-Based Services among African American and White Elders', *Journal of Applied Gerontology*, vol. 17, no. 1, pp. 67–78.

Schoenberg, N. E., Coward, R. T., Gilbert, G. H., & Mullens, R. A. 1997, 'Screening Community-Dwelling Elders for Nutritional Risk: Determining the Influence of Race and Residence', *Journal of Applied Gerontology*, vol. 16, no. 2, pp. 172–89.

Seeman, T. E., Berkman, L. F., Kohout F., LaCroix, A., & Blazer, D. 1993, 'Intercommunity Variations in the Association between Social Ties and Mortality in the Elderly: A Comparative Analysis of Three Communities', *Annual Review of Epidemiology*, vol. 3, pp. 325–35.

Shilling, C. 1994, *The Body and Social Theory*, Sage, Newbury Park, NY.

Thoits, P. A. 1995, 'Stress, Coping, and Social Support Processes: Where are We? What Next?', *Journal of Health and Social Behavior*, vol. 36 (supplement), pp. 53–79.

Turrow, J. 1997, *Breaking up America: Advertisers and the New Media World*, University of Chicago Press, Chicago.

Umberson, D. 1987, 'Family Status and Health Behaviors: Social Control as a Dimension of Social Integration', *Journal of Health and Social Behavior*, vol. 18, no. 3, pp. 306–19.

Umberson, D., Wortman, C., & Kessler, R. 1992, 'Widowhood and Depression: Explaining Low-Term Gender Differences in Vulnerability', *Journal of Health and Social Behavior*, vol. 33, no. 1, pp. 10–24.

Verbrugge, L. M. 1990, 'The Iceberg of Disability', in S. M. Stahl (ed.), *The Legacy of Longevity: Health and Health Care in Later Life*, Sage, Newbury Park, NY.

Walker, D. & Beauchene, R. 1991, 'The Relationship of Loneliness, Social Isolation, and Physical Health of Independently Living Elderly', *Journal of the American Dietetic Association*, vol. 90, no. 12, pp. 1667–72.

Weddle, D., Wellman, N., & Shoaf, L. 1996, 'Position of the American Dietetic Association: Nutrition, Aging, and the Continuum of Care', *Journal of the American Dietetic Association*, vol. 96, no. 10, pp. 1048–52.

Wheaton, B. 1996, 'The Domains and Boundaries of Stress Concepts', in H. B. Kaplan (ed.), *Psychosocial Stress: Perspectives on Structure, Theory, Life-Course, and Methods*, Academic Press, San Diego.

Wolinsky, F., Coe, R. M., McIntosh, W. A., Kubena, K. S., Pendergast, J. M., Chavez, M. N., Miller, D. K., Romeis, J. C., & Landmann, W. A. 1990, 'Progress in the Development of a Nutritional Risk Index', *Journal of Nutrition*, vol. 120, pp. 1549–53.

Yasuda, N., Zimmerman, S. I., Hawkes, D., Fredman, L., Hebel, J. R., & Magaziner, J. 1997, 'Relation of Social Network Characteristics to 5-Year Mortality among Young-Old versus Old-Old White Women in an Urban Community', *American Journal of Epidemiology*, vol. 145, no. 6, pp. 516–23.

Part 3

Self-Rationalisation: *Nutrition Discourses, Food, and the Body*

When you don't have any money, the problem is food. When you do have money, it's sex. When you have both, it's health.

J. P. Donleavy, *The Ginger Man* (1955)

Certainly these days, when I hear people talking about temptation and sin, guilt and shame, I know they're referring to food rather than sex.

Carol Sternhell, as quoted in Rothblum 1994, p. 53

In developed countries, food is abundant, and food manufacturers, through the media, regularly and persuasively encourage the full pleasures of food consumption. Despite this, a competing trend away from food hedonism has emerged in the late twentieth century: the increasing focus on the body has contributed to healthism, an ideology that views health as the primary human goal. The sins of gluttony and sloth have returned and can be seen in secular attitudes of lipophobia (fear of fat). For some people, these attitudes have translated into a lifelong quest for the holy grail of the thin-ideal body, pursued in a process of self-rationalisation. These attitudes are reflected in the health discourses espoused by various health authorities and health 'experts', and adopted by consumers. Calls to adopt regimes of body control, particularly through the regulation of food intake, are now common features of Western culture. The chapters in this section deal directly or indirectly with such nutrition and health discourses, and their social implications. Some discourses construct 'ideal bodies' through a regime of rational body management, particularly through the consumption or non-consumption of certain foods.

In chapter 11, Jeffery Sobal explores the issue of self-rationalisation of the body, using a sociological analysis of the stigmatisation of obesity, whereby 'the general orientation in contemporary society is to hold obese individuals personally accountable for their size'. Obesity is associated with a host of negative social traits and is one of the uniformly held prejudices in Western countries. In times of plenty, high status and self-worth are physically demonstrated and identified through body control. The emergence of anti-fat messages and particularly the increasing popularity of the 'thin ideal' for women are historically recent developments. The desire to attain this thin ideal has led to an increase in dieting behaviour, especially by women in Western society. In chapter 12, Lauren Williams and John Germov explore the reasons for female dieting and how the behaviour is perpetuated and resisted. The social construction of the thin ideal for women also has consequences for the life stage of pregnancy, when it is not possible to conform to this ideal. Lauren Williams and Jane Potter discuss the effects of the expectations placed on the bodies of pregnant women in terms of food consumption and self-identity in chapter 13.

In the final two chapters of this part, the emphasis shifts from the life stage of pregnancy to discourses around feeding children and the family. Elizabeth Murphy, Susan Parker, and Christine Phipps discuss the health-related discourses surrounding the choice of method for infant feeding in chapter 14. John Coveney, in chapter 15, examines the discourse about food in the context of feeding the family.

11

Sociological Analysis of the Stigmatisation of Obesity

Jeffery Sobal

Overview

- *Why is obesity stigmatised?*
- *What sociological approaches are useful in explaining the stigmatisation of obesity?*
- *How do individuals deal with the stigmatisation of obesity?*

Stigmas are attributes of a person that are deeply discrediting, and obesity is highly stigmatised in contemporary post-industrial societies. Obesity is the condition of having high levels of stored body fat. Sociological work on the stigmatisation of obesity can be divided into two major orientations: one focusing on documenting the presence, arenas, extent, and sources of stigmatisation, and the other examining coping strategies for managing and negotiating the stigma of obesity. Prejudice, labelling, stigmatisation, and discrimination based on obesity are very widespread, and occur across many arenas of life (work, family, health, and everyday interactions). Obesity is stigmatised more than some conditions, but less than others. A variety of coping mechanisms are used by obese individuals, including denial, concealment, avoidance, mutual aid, and redefinition of situations. Eating is an especially problematic act for obese individuals to manage because of the potential for stigmatisation. The coping strategies that obese people use to explain their food choices include providing several types of accounts, making disclaimers, and discounting some eating behaviours. Obese individuals often adopt 'fat' identities as they deal with the stigmatisation of obesity. Sociologists have examined the stigmatisation of obesity using several mainstream disciplinary perspectives, and yet many aspects of the stigmatisation of obesity remain unresolved and need further attention.

Key terms	disclaimer	obesity
	discounting	post-industrial society
accounts	discrimination	prejudice
attribution	identity	self-fulfilling prophesy
culture-bound syndrome	marginality	stigma
deviance	master status	stigmatising act

Introduction

A stigma is 'an attribute that is deeply discrediting' and that disqualifies a person from full social acceptance (Goffman 1963, p. 3). Stigmatised individuals are seen as blemished, disgraced, and tainted, and for them routine and comfortable social interactions become problematic. Types of **stigma** include physical deformities, character blemishes, and group stigma (Goffman 1963). **Obesity** has become a stigma in contemporary **post-industrial societies**, and sociological perspectives on the stigmatisation of obesity will be the focus of this chapter.

It has been 35 years since Erving Goffman (1963) brought the concept of stigma to the forefront of sociological attention with his classic book *Stigma: Notes on the Management of Spoiled Identity*. Since Goffman's insightful explication of the concept of stigma, the term and idea have diffused widely through sociology, other social sciences, and into wider public discourse (Ainlay et al. 1986; Page 1984), with psychologists showing particular interest (Herman et al. 1986; Jones et al. 1984).

In contemporary, post-industrial societies, many conditions and characteristics are socially defined as being **deviant** rather than being dealt with as 'normal'. These conditions are viewed as marginal, labelled as 'deviant', and consequently stigmatised. The **marginality** of an attribute is not necessarily based on its prevalence or functionality, but instead is established by the social norms and values attributed to that particular trait or condition. Individuals who are marginal with respect to one attribute are not necessarily marginal in other respects (Emmons & Sobal 1981; Sobal & Hinrichs 1986). Marginal conditions that are stigmatised in contemporary society include those that are medical (AIDS, cancer, leprosy, physical deformities, infertility, disability), economic (poverty, unemployment, use of welfare, homelessness), sociocultural (ethnicity, homosexuality, prostitution, criminality, illiteracy, substance abuse, divorce), and many other types of conditions. Obesity is a stigma that has received the regular attention of social scientists.

Obesity is the condition in which people have high levels of stored body fat. The amount of body fat that people possess varies across a wide continuum. The leanest individuals carry only a few per cent of their total body weight as stored fat, while the majority of the fattest people's body weight is made up of stored fat. There is no absolute and universally agreed upon cut-off point for establishing obesity, although many standards are used in practice (Dalton 1997). For the sociological purpose of discussing stigmatisation, obesity can simply be considered as the condition in which an individual has relatively high amounts of body fat (Sobal & Devine 1997). Quantitative definitions that specify exactly the levels of fat that constitute obesity are not necessary for examining sociological patterns and processes, despite their emphasis in biomedical work. A relative definition of obesity permits variation among different groups (such as dancers or construction workers) in their evaluations about how much body fat is excessive.

Public beliefs about the cause of obesity tend to focus on the assumption that obese people overeat and consume too much caloric energy, with less attention and emphasis on the role of low activity levels and low energy expenditure in producing obesity. The strong linkage between food, eating, and weight occurs in contemporary, post-industrial societies, where the food system provides ample access to a wide variety of foods, many of which are high in fat and are calorically dense. Sociologists have commented on how the social system provides easy access to many calories of inexpensive food, with a consequently high prevalence of obesity and the parallel development of a fear of fatness (Beardsworth & Keil 1997; McIntosh 1996; Mennell 1985).

The stigmatisation of obesity reflects the extent to which high body weight is socially defined as either central or marginal to what is collectively agreed upon and accepted as 'normal' in society (or a portion of society). Thus a person with lower body weight than the average may be defined as socially normal, while someone with a body weight equally far from the average may be regarded as marginal and be stigmatised. Where negative and prejudicial attitudes about obesity exist, obesity is treated as a physical deformity, and obese people are discredited and discriminated against.

Cultural and historical factors

The cultural and historical location of the current stigmatisation of obesity is important to consider in order to gain a broader, relative perspective on how the stigma of obesity is socially constructed. Traditional societies, which have not been involved in the modernisation associated with the industrial revolution, tend to appreciate and value at least moderate, if not larger, amounts of body fat (Brown & Konner 1987). Traditional cultures view stored body fat as a sign of health and wealth, particularly for women (Sobal & Stunkard 1989). The harsher survival conditions of traditional societies involve food supplies that may be uncertain; concentrated fat sources are less available in usual foods, and everyday life involves considerable energy expenditure. Consequently, people who can attain at least a moderate degree of fatness are viewed as attractive; they are clearly not afflicted by a wasting disease or intestinal parasites, and appear to have access to the social resources necessary to obtain food. Cross-cultural data about body preferences for women reveal that 85 per cent of cultures prefer a plump shape (Anderson et al. 1992; Brown & Konner 1987). The value of fatness in many African and Pacific cultures is evidenced by the operation of fattening huts, where women and men engage in ritualistic ingestion of huge amounts of food and avoid activity to gain large amounts of weight to enhance their beauty and social status (Gaurine & Pollock 1995). The high prevalence of obesity and the strong rejection of body fat in Western, post-industrial nations is very different from most other cultures, and anthropologists have described obesity as a **culture-bound syndrome** unique to Western societies (Ritenbaugh 1982).

Historical changes in the evaluation and prevalence of obesity also provide important perspectives on the current patterns of stigmatisation of obesity. Just as in traditional cultures, most Western societies until the late nineteenth century valued at least moderate levels of body fat (Brumberg 1988; Seid 1989; Stearns 1997). At the beginning of the twentieth century, a transformation in values about fatness was under way, as modern ideals of thinness were established, promulgated, and widely applied (Stearns 1997). Emphasis on thinness intensified in the second half of the twentieth century, particularly for women. Evidence for this is seen in the increasingly thinner body shapes of women in idealised social roles, such as beauty pageant winners (Garner et al. 1980; Wiseman et al. 1992) and fashion models (Morris et al. 1989). As pressures towards slimness escalated and intensified, fatness moved from being a social ideal to being rejected as a marginal, deviant, and stigmatised attribute. Most concern about body weight is motivated by appearance, not health (Hayes & Ross 1987).

Attribution of responsibility for a stigma is a crucial consideration, with stigmas that are not considered the 'fault' of an individual being treated differently from those for which personal 'blame' can be attributed (DeJong 1980, 1993; DeJong & Kleck 1986; Menec & Perry 1995; Weiner et al. 1988). The causes of high levels of body weight are currently not established with certainty, with claims and counterclaims about whether obesity is the result of overeating, lack of activity, or genetic/hormonal conditions (Sobal 1995). These disputes about the causes of obesity remain unresolved in the scientific and medical community, as well as among the general public. Stigmatising claims about gluttony and sloth are counterpoised with de-stigmatising claims about inheritance and metabolism. Overall, the general orientation in contemporary society is to hold obese individuals personally accountable for their size, and to discredit and reject them as personal failures.

An important aspect of stigma is that it is often incorporated into individuals' **identities** and involved in their self-evaluations. The pervasiveness of a stigma varies, with some stigmas being of only minor importance while others overwhelm a person and become a **'master status'** (Goffman 1963). Obese people are often characterised more by their size than by any of their other attributes, being typified as simply 'fat' rather than being dealt with on the basis of other qualities. The effects of stigmatisation of obesity are often internalised, particularly by women (Crocker et al. 1993; Sobal & Devine 1997). Negative social stereotypes relating to obesity often become **self-fulfilling prophesies** for obese individuals. Such stigmatisation of obesity is much more problematic for women because they are evaluated more on the basis of their appearance and weight than are men. The gendered nature of the stigmatisation of obesity makes weight much more important to women (Germov & Williams 1996; Tiggemann & Rothblum 1988; see also chapter 12).

Ever since Steven Richardson and others' (1961) pioneering quantitative research and Werner Cahnman's (1968) interactionist analysis, sociologists have been examining the stigma of obesity. Sociological analysis of the stigma of obesity has two mainstream theoretical perspectives—functionalism and symbolic interactionism—and has rarely applied other theoretical orientations, such as Marxism or rational choice theory. While a variety of research methods are applied to stigmatisation of obesity, the bulk of existing studies use the two major sociological data-collection methods of surveys and participant observation. Overall, sociological work on the stigma of obesity has followed two major paths, reflecting the two most powerful paradigms in the discipline of sociology (Ritzer 1980).

Functionalist analysis documents and describes as social facts the presence, arenas, extent, and sources of the stigmatisation of obese individuals. This stream of analysis has involved many disciplines and takes a positivist approach in examining stigma as a barrier to access to social roles or privileges. Analyses are often quantitative, using psychological experiments or survey research to analyse the frequency and extent of stigmatisation.

Interactionist analysis examines the strategies that obese individuals use to manage their stigma and to negotiate their way in a world that values thinness. It does so while considering the construction of social definitions of obesity. These analyses are primarily done by sociologists and follow an interpretivist, symbolic-interactionist tradition, often appealing to dramaturgical analyses grounded in the work of Goffman (1959;1963). These investigations employ ethnographic techniques, such as participant observation and in-depth interviews, to investigate stigmatisation as a socially constructed, negotiated, and managed process. These two lines of analysis will be reviewed in the following sections.

The presence, arenas, extent, and sources of stigmatisation of obesity

The consensus within the published literature is that severe stigmatisation of obese people exists in contemporary post-industrial societies (Allon 1981; Goode 1996; Sobal 1984a; 1991). However, some reviews suggest that the negative effects of the stigmatisation of obesity have not been clearly demonstrated (Jarvie et al. 1983). In addition to establishing the presence of stigmatisation of obesity, the arenas, extent, and sources of stigmatisation also have been examined.

Stigmatisation operates in many arenas, occurring broadly across most domains of an obese person's world—such as at work, at home, and in public life (Gortmaker et al. 1993). This observation supports the concept that obesity becomes a 'master status' (Goffman 1963) that pervades all aspects of life. Studies of stigmatisation have focused on some areas more than others, with much research having been carried out on stigmatisation in formal roles, such as that of employee. But less research has been done on stigmatisation in informal roles, such as that of friend. The major arenas where stigmatisation of the obese has been documented are education and work, marriage and family, health and medical care, and interpersonal and social interactions.

Obese individuals in the USA are less favourably evaluated for admission to the higher education that is essential for entry and advancement in many careers, and receive less financial support when they are admitted to college (Benson et al. 1980; Canning & Mayer 1966; 1967; Crandall 1991; 1995). People who are obese are also less successful in gaining employment and entering the labour force (Larkin & Pines 1979; Matusewitch 1983; Roe & Eickwort 1976). Obese individuals who do become employees receive lower wages than comparable co-workers, are less likely to receive promotions, and experience more **discrimination** on the job (Averett & Korenman 1996; Loh 1993; McClean & Moon 1980; Register & Williams 1990; Rothblum et al. 1988; 1990). Overall, stigmatisation of obese individuals consistently occurs across the span of educational and work roles.

Weight is an important criterion for dating and mate selection, and obese individuals (women in particular) have a more difficult time dating and finding marital partners (Gortmaker et al. 1993; Kallen & Doughty 1984; Sobal 1984b; Sobal et al. 1995; 1992). Most obese people eventually marry, but their choices of partners are restricted because of their stigmatised condition (Garn et al. 1989a; 1989b). Once obese individuals are married, obese women may feel that they have less value on the marriage market (Sobal et al. 1995). These findings consistently reveal that stigmatisation of obese individuals occurs in the entry and maintenance of marital and family roles.

Health professionals frequently stigmatise obese individuals, holding prejudicial attitudes and exhibiting them in discriminatory actions. Health care professionals of many types (including physicians, nurses, counsellors, dietitians, psychologists, health administrators, and others) at many stages of their careers (as students, interns, practitioners, and educators) have negative attitudes and beliefs about obese individuals (Agell & Rothblum 1991; Benson et al. 1980; Blumberg & Mellis 1985; Brotman et al. 1984; Maiman et al. 1979; Rand & MacGregor 1990). The antipathy exhibited by student health practitioners towards obesity suggests that their attitudes are based on wider societal values about obesity rather than on actual problems that they have experienced in dealing with obese individuals as patients. Prejudicial attitudes towards obese individuals among health care professionals are exhibited as they discriminate by size in providing health care services such as diagnosis and treatment (Adams et al. 1993; Allon 1979; Young & Powell 1985). Health care providers are not immune to the stigmatisation of obese individuals as they carry out their professional roles, providing unequal health care service on the basis of body weight.

Everyday interactions of obese individuals also may be hampered by stigmatisation (Pauley 1989). Compared with their thinner counterparts, obese individuals are discriminated against in basic transactions such as renting apartments (Karris 1977). Some investigations report that obese individuals have fewer friends (Harris & Smith 1983), although other studies find this not to be the case (Jarvie et al. 1983; Miller et al. 1995a). Overall, stigmatisation operates as a multidimensional burden on obese individuals, spanning work, family, health, and interpersonal arenas.

A classic series of sociological investigations compared the stigmatisation of physical disabilities and that of obesity by showing participants a series of pictures of people with a variety of disabilities as well as an obese child (Alessi & Anthony 1969; Giancoli & Neimeyer 1983; Goodman et al. 1963; Maddox & Liederman 1968; 1969; Richardson 1970; 1971; Richardson et al. 1961, Richardson & Royce 1968, Richardson & Emerson 1970). The striking findings revealed that both adults and children consistently preferred disabled people to obese people, providing clear evidence that obesity 'is more stigmatised than physical disabilities such as blindness, crippling disease, amputations, and facial disfigurements.

Some broader comparative analyses of stigmatisation of different forms of deviant conditions have been done. Several studies reveal that obesity is seen as being as stigmatised as many other deviant conditions, such as AIDS, drug addiction, criminal behaviour, and homosexuality (Schwarzer & Weiner 1990; Spiegal & Keith-Spiegel 1973; Weiner et al. 1988). Stigmatisation of obesity is more severe than that of eating disorders (Brotman et al. 1984; Sobal et al. 1995), although eating disorders are stigmatised and carry negative evaluations (Sobal & Bursztyn 1998; Way 1995). It is notable that in recent years legal measures and social norms have greatly reduced the stigmatisation of many racial, religious, gender, or sexual groups, while **prejudice** against obesity and the derogation of obese individuals are tolerated and even treated as socially acceptable (Stunkard & Sobal 1995).

Myriad sources of stigmatisation permeate the lives of obese individuals. In interpersonal interactions, obese individuals are stigmatised by others in a variety of social roles and relationships. The public at large stigmatises obese individuals in informal interactions of many types. The mass media stigmatise obese individuals actively by negatively representing those large people who do appear on television, and passively by not including large people in significant numbers or in numbers proportional to their presence in the general population (Dyrenforth et al. 1980). The mass media also present extremely thin people as ideals, which leads to negative comparisons of obese individuals with media images (Silverstein et al. 1986; Myers & Biocca 1992; Waller et al. 1994). Overall, stigmatisation of obese individuals exists, is prevalent and often intense, occurs in multifaceted ways, and emanates from a variety of sources.

Coping with the stigma of obesity

Goffman (1963) used the concept of stigma within a broader theoretical examination of the interpersonal interaction process, revealing the development and management of deviant identities as stigma. The development of the concept of stigma complemented his other sociological work on the presentation of self, dramaturgical role analysis, and impression management (Goffman 1959; 1961; Ditton 1980; Drew & Wootton 1988). Based on the perspectives used by Goffman, many sociologists have examined how obese individuals who are stigmatised construct their identities and manage their interactions with others in order to cope with the stigma of obesity.

Stigmatising acts may be verbal (teasing, joking, negative comments, and so on) or non-verbal (such as staring, making gestures, and avoidance). Stigmatisation may be active (operating through overt negative behaviours) or passive (occurring by avoiding interactions with stigmatised individuals).

Everyday life involves the performances of a variety of activities in the presence of various other people, with individuals operating as actors presenting themselves to actual or imagined others, who constitute audiences for their behaviours (Goffman 1959). Stigmatised individuals recognise that their performances of various tasks may be disrupted by negative treatment as a result of their stigma, and attempt to prevent or deal with problems resulting from their stigma. Obese people are treated negatively in social interactions because of their body size and so develop many strategies for dealing with the stigmatising acts of others (Sobal 1991).

Gaining and maintaining acceptance is a central feature of a stigmatised person's life, and although legitimacy in interpersonal interactions is claimed by individuals, it is conferred by others (Elliott et al. 1990). A variety of coping mechanisms exist for individuals with various types of stigma. These include denial, concealment, avoidance, mutual aid, and redefinition of situations, among others (Elliott et al. 1990).

Some obese people, particularly men, use denial to deal with interactional challenges associated with their body weight (Millman 1980). Denying that they are 'really' fat, or denying that the fat they have is their fault, ignores the stigma of obesity and offers one way of coping for particular individuals in specific situations. This type of management of stigmatising acts typically involves claims that large size or weight is caused by muscle, large bones, or genetics.

Concealment is a form of strategic impression management whereby a stigma is hidden, disguised, or modified to make it less obtrusive and therefore less likely to be attended to or focused upon in a social encounter. Obese individuals make considerable efforts in relation to concealment, including hiding parts of their bodies by wearing loose or heavy clothing to mask their size. One form of concealment is deflection or distraction, whereby other aspects of appearance, such as hair or jewellery, are used to refocus attention away from an obese person's body. 'Passing' occurs when stigmatised individuals successfully conceal their stigma and are accepted as 'normal' (Goffman 1963), which may or may not be possible for obese individuals to enact, depending on the extent of their weight and ability to conceal it.

Avoidance and withdrawal are common methods of coping with stigmatisation, and many stigmatised individuals arrange their lives to avoid or minimise stigmatising contacts because of uncertainty about how 'normals' will receive and deal with them (Goffman 1963). Many obese individuals practise selective or widespread avoidance of social settings and individuals where they perceive a likelihood of being stigmatised. This involves outright refusal to enter some situations, particularly those in which a person's entire body will be on display, such as on a beach, at a swimming pool, or in a locker room. Management of the frequency, content, and extent of interactions with particular individuals is another form of avoidance, with obese individuals eschewing contact with some people who have stigmatised them in the past or who are thought to be likely to engage in future stigmatising acts. Self-segregation (Schur 1979) occurs where stigmatised individuals interact with, and accept as 'insiders', only those who are obese or are 'wise' (Goffman 1963) to the plight of overweight people.

By redefining situations, the topic or subject of interactions is refocused away from a stigmatised condition to other more neutral or safe areas. Obese individuals often develop strategies for deflecting or shifting the focus of interactions away from their size to other topics or issues as a coping tactic (Sobal 1991). The threat of stigmatisation leads some obese individuals to present themselves in a comedic role, using humour to facilitate and negotiate interactions with people who could potentially discredit them because of their size.

Mutual aid is a strategy whereby communities of stigmatised individuals are developed in order to share feelings, resources, and provide social support for one another (Goffman 1963). Mutual aid ranges from the exchange of stories and ideas between obese friends to the establishment of national or international organisations to promote size acceptance. While the manifest goal of weight-loss programs is to become thinner through diet and exercise, the latent services often sought and provided through such groups are the sharing of emotional support and the exchange of coping strategies for dealing with being overweight (Allon 1975; Laslett & Warren 1975). Collective behaviour often results from the establishment of advocacy groups and organisations, and the size-acceptance movement has established itself as an important force in contemporary public discourse on obesity (Sobal 1995).

Eating is an especially problematic act for obese people to manage (English 1991), because it carries so much potential for critique and criticism by others (Zdrodowski 1996). Several sociological concepts help us to identify some of the special coping methods used by stigmatised individuals when their eating behaviours are scrutinised by others. Even when an obese person eats the same things as a 'normal'-weight companion, the obese person faces the threat of being attacked and criticised for overeating. Stigmatising acts include challenges to, and criticisms of, the eating behaviours of obese individuals. Obese people may avoid food events entirely as a way to cope with the threat of being discredited. Alternatively they may attend but eat nothing, or they may eat selectively and be prepared to explain their food choices.

Obese individuals may defend the legitimacy of eating by providing what Marvin Scott and Stanford Lyman (1963) term '**accounts**' (Orbuch 1997). Accounts can be divided into justifications and excuses, with several sub-types of excuses (Scott & Lyman 1963). Justifications accept responsibility but deny the negative qualities of the behaviour, as when an obese person eating confectionery claims that it is the only thing that has been eaten all day. Excuses admit the negative qualities of an action, but deny responsibility, and include several types. Accident excuses deny fault because a behaviour was beyond personal control, as when an obese individual eating ice-cream claims that it was the only food available. Defensibility excuses state that insufficient information was available, as when an obese person claims to have believed that the food being eaten was a reduced-calorie version. Biological drive excuses explain actions in terms of a lack of control over a behaviour, as when an obese person claims that hormones led him or her to eat a particular item.

Other ways of managing eating are related to accounts. '**Disclaimers**' (Hewett & Stokes 1975) anticipate challenges to legitimacy, as in claims by obese people that they have adhered to a restricted diet earlier in anticipation of a particular food event. '**Discounting**' (Pestello 1991) includes several strategies. Coercion discounting occurs when a violation of personal principles is outside a person's control, as when an obese person claims that someone else prepared high-calorie foods. Exception discounting involves compromises that are seen as serving a greater purpose, as when an obese person claims not to have wanted to offend someone by refusing to eat special foods that were prepared. Denial discounting makes no admission of a behaviour or its meaning, as when an obese person eats what is served at a dinner and makes no comments or explanations about the food. Concealment discounting entails accepting responsibility for a behaviour but disbelief that the behaviour is negative, as when an obese person reports having eaten a chocolate dessert but claims that the chocolate prevents other food cravings. All of these techniques are used to socially manage eating. They help obese individuals to negotiate a path through potentially precarious social interactions and to ward off threats to their selves.

Often obese individuals will develop 'fat identities' as they accept their weight and as they establish and elaborate social selves that incorporate weight as a personal attribute (Degher & Hughes 1991; Hughes & Degher 1993; McLorg & Taub 1987; O'Brien & Bankston 1990). Attempts to lose weight also involve aspiration to a new, thinner identity. Many obese people perceive this as the attainment of a 'normal' weight status, which will free them from stigmatisation. Often people who do change their weight have to reconcile their social identities with their bodies (English 1993; Rubin et al. 1993). Thinner identities may be seen as desirable in that they avoid stigmatisation, but they may also carry undesirable consequences, such as the need to deal with unwanted sexual advances, which did not occur before (Sobal 1984a).

While obese individuals are stigmatised in contemporary post-industrial society and suffer from the pain of obesity (Millman 1980), they employ many strategies in order to cope with their stigma and to establish functional life patterns in spite of negative societal attitudes towards them. Psychological strategies are used to compensate for stigma (Miller et al. 1995b), and social relationships are established to buffer negative experiences (Millman 1980). Organisations and groups help to empower individuals by validating and valorising their struggles against the weight prejudices of many people in the larger society (Sobal 1995). Struggles with negative attitudes and with social avoidance and ostracism are often required throughout an obese individual's life, requiring coping efforts that deeply shape their identities. Sociological analyses that examine how obese individuals construct, negotiate, and manage their lives provide a portrait of the stigmatisation of obesity that differs from, but complements, work describing the prevalence and types of stigmatisation (see chapter 12).

Conclusion

Over the past several decades, stigma has emerged as an important sociological concept, grounded in the pioneering work of Goffman (1963). The concept of stigma has been widely applied to a variety of conditions, stretching and testing the boundaries of its conceptual coverage. Obesity was mentioned as a stigmatised condition in Goffman's seminal book, and it remains as a clear case of a stigma in contemporary society.

The examination and elaboration of the concept of stigmatisation in relation to obesity has involved some work in a positivist tradition in psychological social psychology and functionalist sociology. Simultaneously, constructionist work based in the symbolic interactionist traditions of sociological social psychology continued on the lines of analysis begun by Goffman. The existing literature on the stigma of obesity reflects a consensus in some areas, but it leaves other aspects of the topic to be addressed in future investigations.

Obesity has become a highly stigmatised condition in contemporary post-industrial societies, with obese individuals being subject to negative labels and risking a variety of defiling and degrading prejudicial attitudes and discriminatory actions. The social position of obesity relative to other deviant conditions is not currently very clear. Obese individuals employ several types of coping mechanisms to manage their social interactions with others. However, the frequency and success of different strategies for coping with the stigmatisation of obesity is not well elaborated. Clearly, obesity is a stigma in contemporary society, but it is not clear how obese people can most effectively deal with stigmatisation based on their size.

Summary of main points:

- Stigmas are discrediting attributes, and obesity is often stigmatised in post-industrial societies.
- Stigmatisation of obesity is widespread, frequent, and often severe.
- Stigmatisation of obesity occurs in work, family, health, and everyday arenas.
- Mechanisms used to cope with the stigmatisation of obesity include denial, concealment, avoidance, mutual aid, and redefinition of situations.
- Eating is problematic for obese individuals, who use accounts, disclaimers, and discounting to explain their food choices.

Discussion questions:

1 How is stigmatisation of obesity similar to and different from stigmatisation of other 'deviant' attributes?

2   How would obese individuals be treated in a culture that did not stigmatise either fatness or thinness, or in a culture that valued fatness highly?

3   What types or categories of people in society are least likely to stigmatise obese individuals, and what types are most likely to do so?

4   How do different approaches to sociological analysis (such as functionalist theory using quantitative methods, or constructionist theory using qualitative methods) provide both incompatible and compatible perspectives on the stigmatisation of obesity?

5   How could society change in order to reduce stigmatisation of obese individuals, and how can obese individuals better deal with stigmatisation?

Further reading

Bryant, C. D. (ed.) 1990, *Deviant Behavior: Readings in the Sociology of Norm Violations*, Hemisphere, New York.

Gaurine, I. & Pollock, N. J. (eds) 1995, *Social Aspects of Obesity*, Gordon & Breach, New York.

Goffman, E. 1963, *Stigma: Notes on the Management of Spoiled Identity*, Simon & Schuster, New York.

Maurer, D. & Sobal, J. (eds) 1995, *Eating Agendas: Food and Nutrition as Social Problems*, Aldine de Gruyter, New York.

Millman M. 1980, *Such a Pretty Face: Being Fat in America*, Norton, New York.

Sobal, J. & Maurer, D. 1999, *Interpreting Weight: The Social Management of Fatness and Thinness*, Aldine de Gruyter, Hawthorne, NY.

—— (eds) 1999, *Weighty Issues: The Construction of Fatness and Thinness as Social Problems*, Aldine de Gruyter, Hawthorne, NY.

References

Adams, C. H., Smith, N. J., Wilbur, D. C., & Grady, K. E. 1993, 'The Relationship of Obesity to the Frequency of Pelvic Examinations: Do Physician and Patient Attitudes Make a Difference?', *Women and Health*, vol. 20, pp. 45–57.

Agell, G. & Rothblum, E. D. 1991, 'Effects of Clients' Obesity and Gender on the Therapy Judgements of Psychologists', *Professional Psychology: Research and Practice*, vol. 22, pp. 223–9.

Ainlay, S. C., Becker, G., & Colemen, L. M. (eds) 1986, *The Dilemma of Difference: A Multidisciplinary View of Stigma*, Plenum, New York.

Alessi, D. F. & Anthony, W. A. 1969, 'The Uniformity of Children's Attitudes toward Physical Disabilities', *Exceptional Children*, vol. 35, pp. 543–5.

Allon, N. 1975, 'Latent Social Services of Group Dieting', *Social Problems*, vol. 23, pp. 59–69.

—— 1979, 'Self-Perceptions of the Stigma of Overweight in Relationship to Weight-Losing Patterns', *American Journal of Clinical Nutrition*, vol. 32, pp. 4770–80.

—— 1981, 'The Stigma of Overweight in Everyday Life', in B. J. Wolman (ed.), *Psychological Aspects of Obesity: A Handbook*, Van Nostrand Reinhold, New York, pp. 130–74.

Anderson, J. L., Crawford, C. B., Nadeau, J., & Lindberg, T. 1992, 'Was the Duchess of Windsor Right? A Cross-Cultural Review of the Socioecology of Ideals of Female Body Shape', *Ethnology and Sociobiology*, vol. 13, pp. 197–227.

Averett, S. & Korenman, S. 1996, 'The Economic Reality of the Beauty Myth', *Journal of Human Resources*, vol. 31, pp. 304–30.

Beardsworth, A. & Keil, T. 1997, *Sociology on the Menu: An Invitation to the Study of Food and Society*, Routledge, London.

Benson, P. L., Severs, D., Tatgenhorst, J., & Loddengaard, N. 1980, 'The Social Costs of Obesity: A Non-Reactive Field Study', *Social Behavior and Personality*, vol. 8, pp. 91–6.

Blumberg, P. & Mellis, L. P. 1985, 'Medical Students' Attitudes toward the Obese and Morbidly Obese', *International Journal of Eating Disorders*, vol. 4, pp. 169–75.

Brotman, A. W., Stern, T. A., & Herzog, D. B. 1984, 'Emotional Reactions of House Officers to Patients with Anorexia Nervosa, Diabetes, and Obesity', *International Journal of Eating Disorders*, vol. 3, pp. 71–7.

Brown, P. J. & Konner, M. 1987, 'An Anthropological Perspective on Obesity', *Annals of the New York Academy of Sciences*, vol. 499, pp. 29–46.

Brumberg, J. 1988, *Fasting Girls: The History of Anorexia Nervosa*, Harvard University Press, Cambridge, Mass.

Cahnman, W. J. 1968, 'The Stigma of Obesity.' *Sociological Quarterly*, vol. 9, pp. 282–99.

Canning, H. & Mayer, J. 1966, 'Obesity—Its Possible Effect on College Acceptance', *New England Journal of Medicine*, vol. 275, pp. 1172–4.

—— 1967, 'Obesity: An Influence on High School Performance', *American Journal of Clinical Nutrition*, vol. 20, pp. 352–4.

Crandall, C. S. 1991, 'Do Heavyweight Students Have More Difficulty Paying for College?', *Personality and Social Psychology Bulletin*, vol. 17, pp. 606–11.

—— 1995, 'Do Parents Discriminate against Their Heavyweight Daughters?', *Personality and Social Psychology Bulletin*, vol. 21, pp. 724–35.

Crocker, J., Cornwall, B., & Major, B. 1993, 'The Stigma of Overweight: Affective Consequences of Attributional Ambiguity', *Journal of Personality and Social Psychology*, vol. 64, pp. 67–70.

Dalton, S. 1997, 'Body Weight Terminology, Definitions, and Measurement', in S. Dalton (ed.), *Overweight and Weight Management*, ASPEN Publishers, Gaithersburg, Md, pp. 1–38.

Degher, D. & Hughes, G. 1991, 'The Identity Change Process: A Field Study of Obesity', *Deviant Behavior*, vol. 12, pp. 385–401.

DeJong, W. 1980, 'The Stigma of Obesity: Consequences of Naive Assumptions Concerning the Causes of Physical Deviance', *Journal of Health and Social Behavior*, vol. 21, pp. 75–85.

—— 1993, 'Obesity as a Characterological Stigma: The Issue of Responsibility and Judgments in Task Performance', *Psychological Reports*, vol. 73, pp. 963–70.

DeJong, W. & Kleck, R. E. 1986, 'The Social Psychological Effects of Overweight', in C. P. Herman, M. P. Zanna, & E. T. Higgins (eds), *Physical Appearance, Stigma, and Social Behavior: The Ontario Symposium*, vol. 3, Lawrence Earlbaum Associates, Hillsdale, NJ, pp. 65–87.

Ditton, J. (ed.) 1980, *The View from Goffman*, St Martin's, New York.

Drew, P. & Wootton, A. (eds) 1988, *Erving Goffman: Exploring the Interaction Order*, Northeastern University Press, Boston.

Dyrenforth, S. R., Wooley, O. W., & Wooley, S. C. 1980, 'A Woman's Body in a Man's World: A Review of Findings on Body Image and Weight Control', in J. R. Kaplan (ed.) *A Woman's Conflict: The Special Relationships between Women and Food*, Prentice-Hall, Englewood Cliffs, NJ.

Elliott, G. C., Ziegler, H. L., Altman, B. M., & Scott, D. R. 1990, 'Understanding Stigma: Dimensions of Deviance and Coping', in C. D. Bryant (ed.), *Deviant Behavior: Readings in the Sociology of Norm Violations*, Hemisphere, New York, pp. 423–43.

Emmons, C. & Sobal, J. 1981, 'Paranormal Beliefs: Testing the Marginality Hypothesis', *Sociological Focus*, vol. 14, pp. 49–56.

English, C. 1991, 'Food is My Best Friend: Self-Justifications and Weight-Loss Efforts', *Research in the Sociology of Health Care*, vol. 9, pp. 335–45.

—— 1993, 'Gaining and Losing Weight: Identity Transformations', *Deviant Behavior*, vol. 14, pp. 227–41.

Garn, S., Sullivan, T. V., & Hawthorne, V. M. 1989a, 'The Education of One Spouse and the Fatness of the Other Spouse', *American Journal of Human Biology*, vol. 1, pp. 233–8.

—— 1989b, 'Educational Level, Fatness, and Fatness Differences between Husbands and Wives', *American Journal of Clinical Nutrition*, vol. 50, pp. 740–5.

Garner, D. M., Garfinkel, P. E., Schwartz, D., & Thompson, M. 1980, 'Cultural Expectations of Thinness in Women', *Psychological Reports*, vol. 47, pp. 483–91.

Gaurine, I. & Pollock, N. J. (eds) 1995, *Social Aspects of Obesity*, Gordon & Breach, New York.

Germov, J. & Williams, L. 1996, 'The Sexual Division of Dieting: Women's Voices', *Sociological Review*, vol. 44, pp. 630–47.

Giancoli, D. L. & Neimeyer, G. J. 1983, 'Liking Preferences toward Handicapped Persons', *Perceptual and Motor Skills*, vol. 57, pp. 1005–6.

Goffman, E. 1959, *The Presentation of Self in Everyday Life*, Anchor, New York.

—— 1961, *Asylums*, Doubleday, New York.

—— 1963, *Stigma: Notes on the Management of Spoiled Identity*, Simon & Schuster, New York.

Goode, E. 1996, 'The Stigma of Obesity', in E. Goode (ed.), *Social Deviance*, Allyn & Bacon, Boston, pp. 332–40.

Goodman, N., Richardson, S. A., Dombusch, S., & Hastort, A. H. 1963, 'Variant Reactions to Physical Disabilities', *American Sociological Review*, vol. 28, pp. 429–35.

Gortmaker, S. L., Must, A., Perrin, J. M., Sobol, A. M., & Dietz, W. H. 1993, 'Social and Economic Consequences of Overweight in Adolescence and Young Adulthood', *New England Journal of Medicine*, vol. 329, pp. 1008–12.

Harris, M. B. & Smith, S. D. 1983, 'The Relationships of Age, Sex, Ethnicity, and Weight to Stereotypes of Obesity and Self-Perception', *International Journal of Obesity*, vol. 7, pp. 361–71.

Hayes, D. & Ross, C. E. 1987, 'Concern with Appearance, Health Beliefs, and Eating Habits', *Journal of Health and Social Behavior*, vol. 28, pp. 120–30.

Herman, C. P., Zanna, M. P., & Higgins, E. T. (eds) 1986, *Physical Appearance, Stigma, and Social Behavior: The Ontario Symposium*, vol. 3, Lawrence Earlbaum Associates, Hillsdale, NJ.

Hewett, J. P. & Stokes, R. 1975, 'Disclaimers', *American Sociological Review*, vol. 40, pp. 1–11.

Hughes, G. & Degher, D. 1993, 'Coping with Deviant Identity', *Deviant Behavior*, vol. 14, pp. 297–315.

Jarvie, G. J., Lahey, B., Graziano, W., & Framer, E. 1983, 'Childhood Obesity: What We Know and What We Don't Know', *Developmental Review*, vol. 2, pp. 237–73.

Jones, E. E., Fanna, A., Hastort, A. H., Markus, H., Miller, D. T., & Scott, R. A. 1984, *Social Stigma: The Psychology of Marked Relationships*, W. H. Freeman & Company, New York.

Kallen, D. & Doughty, A. 1984, 'The Relationship of Weight, the Self Perception of Weight, and Self Esteem in Courtship Behavior', *Marriage and Family Review*, vol. 7, pp. 93–114.

Karris, L. 1977, 'Prejudice against Obese Renters', *Journal of Social Psychology*, vol. 101, pp. 159–60.

Larkin, J. C. & Pines, H. A. 1979, 'No Fat Persons Need Apply: Experimental Studies of the Overweight Stereotype and Hiring Preference', *Sociology of Work and Occupations*, vol. 13, pp. 379–85.

Laslett, B. & Warren, C. A. B. 1975, 'Losing Weight: The Organizational Promotion of Behavior Change', *Social Problems*, vol. 23, pp. 69–80.

Loh, E. S. 1993, 'The Economic Effects of Physical Appearance', *Social Science Quarterly*, vol. 74, pp. 420–38.

McClean, R. A. & Moon, M. 1980, 'Health, Obesity, and Earnings', *American Journal of Public Health*, vol. 70, pp. 1006–9.

McIntosh, W. A. 1996, *Sociologies of Food and Nutrition*, Plenum, New York.

McLorg, P. A. & Taub, D. E. 1987, 'Anorexia and Bulimia: The Development of Deviant Identities', *Deviant Behavior*, vol. 8, pp. 177–89.

Maddox, G. L. & Liederman, V. R. 1968, 'Overweight as Social Deviance and Disability', *Journal of Health and Social Behavior*, vol. 9, pp. 287–98.

—— 1969, 'Overweight as a Social Disability with Medical Implications', *Journal of Medical Education*, vol. 44, pp. 214–20.

Maiman, L. A., Wang, V. L., Becker, M. H., Findlay, J., & Simonson, M. 1979, 'Attitudes toward Obesity and the Obese among Professionals', *Journal of the American Dietetic Association*, vol. 74, pp. 331–6.

Matusewitch, E. 1983, 'Employment Discrimination against the Overweight', *Personnel Journal*, vol. 62, pp. 446–50.

Menec, V. H. & Perry, R. P. 1995, 'Reactions to Stigmas: The Effects of Targets' Age and Controllability of Stigmas', *Journal of Aging and Health*, vol. 7, pp. 365–83.

Mennell, S. 1985, *All Manners of Food: Eating and Taste in England and France from the Middle Ages to the Present*, Blackwell, Oxford.

Miller, C. T., Rothblum, E. D., Brand, P. A., & Felicio, D. M. 1995a, 'Do Obese Women Have Poorer Social Relationships than Nonobese Women? Reports by Self, Friends, and Coworkers', *Journal of Personality*, vol. 63, pp. 65–85.

Miller, C. T., Rothblum, E. D., Felicio, D. M., & Brand, P. A. 1995b, 'Compensating for Stigma: Obese and Nonobese Women's Reactions to Being Visible', *Personality and Social Psychology Bulletin*, pp. 1093–106.

Millman, M. 1980, *Such a Pretty Face: Being Fat in America*, Norton, New York.

Morris, A., Cooper, T., & Cooper, P. J. 1989, 'The Changing Shape of Female Fashion Models', *International Journal of Eating Disorders*, pp. 593–6.

Myers, P. N. & Biocca, F. A. 1992, 'The Elastic Body Image: The Effect of Television Advertising and Programming on Body Image Distortions of Young Women', *Journal of Communication*, vol. 42, pp. 108–33.

O'Brien, M. S. & Bankston, W. B. 1990, 'The Moral Career of the Reformed Compulsive Eater: A Study of Conversion to Charismatic Conformity', in C. D. Bryant (ed.), *Deviant Behavior: Readings in the Sociology of Norm Violations*, Hemisphere, New York, pp. 774–83.

Orbuch, T. L. 1997, 'People's Accounts Count: The Sociology of Accounts', *Annual Review of Sociology*, vol. 23, pp. 455–78.

Page, R. M. 1984, *Stigma*, Routledge & Kegan Paul, Boston.

Pauley, L. L. 1989, 'Customer Weight as a Variable in Salespersons' Response Time', *Journal of Social Psychology*, vol. 129, pp. 713–14.

Pestello, F. 1991, 'Discounting', *Journal of Contemporary Ethnography*, vol. 20, pp. 27–46.

Rand, C. S. W. & MacGregor, A. M. C. 1990, 'Morbidly Obese Patients' Perceptions of Social Discrimination before and after Surgery for Obesity', *Southern Medical Journal*, vol. 83, pp. 1390–5.

Register, C. A. & Williams, D. R. 1990, 'Wage Effects of Obesity among Young Workers', *Social Science Quarterly*, vol. 71, pp. 130–41.

Richardson, S. A. 1970, 'Age and Sex Differences in Values toward Physical Handicaps', *Journal of Health and Social Behavior*, vol. 11, pp. 207–14.

—— 1971, 'Research Report: Handicap, Appearance, and Stigma', *Social Science and Medicine*, vol. 5, pp. 621–8.

Richardson, S. A. & Emerson, P. 1970, 'Race and Physical Handicap in Children's Preference for Other Children: A Replication in a Southern City', *Human Relations*, vol. 23, pp. 31–6.

Richardson, S. A. & Royce, J. 1968, 'Race and Physical Handicap in Children's Preferences for Other Children', *Child Development*, vol. 39, pp. 467–80.

Richardson, S. A., Hastorf, A. H., Goodman, N., & Dornbusch, S. M. 1961, 'Cultural Uniformity in Reaction to Physical Disabilities', *American Sociological Review*, vol. 26, pp. 241–7.

Ritenbaugh, C. 1982, 'Obesity as a Culture-Bound Syndrome', *Culture, Medicine and Psychiatry*, vol. 6, pp. 347–61.

Ritzer, G. 1980, *Sociology: A Multiple Paradigm Science*, Allyn & Bacon, Boston.

Roe, D. & Eickwort, K. R. 1976, 'Relationships between Obesity and Associated Health Factors with Unemployment among Low Income Women', *Journal of the American Medical Women's Association*, vol. 31, pp. 193–204.

Rothblum, E. D., Miller, C. T., & Garbutt, B. 1988, 'Stereotypes of Obese Female Job Applicants', *International Journal of Eating Disorders*, vol. 7, pp. 277–83.

Rothblum, E. D., Brand, P. A, Miller, C. T., & Oetjen, H. A. 1990, 'The Relationship between Obesity, Employment Discrimination, and Employment-Related Victimization', *Journal of Vocational Behavior*, vol. 37, pp. 251–66.

Rubin, N., Shmilovitz, C., & Weiss, M. 1993, 'From Fat to Thin: Informal Rites Affirming Identity Change', *Symbolic Interaction*, vol. 16, pp. 1–17.

Schur, E. 1979, *Interpreting Deviance*, Harper & Row, New York.

Schwarzer, R. & Weiner, B. 1990, 'Die Wirkung von Kontrollierbarkeit und Bewaltigungsverhalten auf Emotionen und Sociale Unterstutzung', *Zeitschrift fur Socialpsychologie*, vol. 21, pp. 118–25.

Scott M. B. & Lyman, S. 1963, 'Accounts', *American Sociological Review*, vol. 33, pp. 44–62.

Seid, R. P. 1989, *Never Too Thin*, Prentice-Hall, New York.

Silverstein, B., Perdue, L., Peterson, B., & Kelly, E. 1986, 'The Role of the Mass Media in Promoting a Thin Standard of Bodily Attractiveness for Women', *Sex Roles*, vol. 14, pp. 519–33.

Sobal, J. 1984a, 'Group Dieting, the Stigma of Obesity, and Overweight Adolescents: Contributions of Natalie Allon to the Sociology of Obesity', *Marriage and Family Review*, vol. 7, pp. 9–20.

—— 1984b, 'Marriage, Obesity and Dieting', *Marriage and Family Review*, vol. 7, pp. 115–40.

—— 1991, 'Obesity and Nutritional Sociology: A Model for Coping with the Stigma of Obesity', *Clinical Sociology Review*, vol. 9, pp. 125–41.

—— 1995, 'The Medicalization and Demedicalization of Obesity', in D. Maurer & J. Sobal (eds), *Eating Agendas: Food and Nutrition as Social Problems*, Aldine de Gruyter, Hawthorne, NY, pp. 79–90.

Sobal, J. & Bursztyn, M. 1998, 'Dating People with Anorexia Nervosa and Bulimia: Attitudes and Beliefs of University Students', *Women and Health*, vol. 27, no. 3, pp. 73–88.

Sobal, J. & Devine, C. 1997, 'Social Aspects of Obesity: Influences, Consequences, Assessments, and Interventions', in S. Dalton (ed.), *Overweight and Weight Management*, ASPEN Publishers, Gaithersburg, Md, pp. 289–308.

Sobal, J. & Hinrichs, D. 1986, 'Bias against 'Marginal' Individuals in Jury Wheel Selection', *Journal of Criminal Justice*, vol. 14, pp. 71–89.

Sobal, J. & Stunkard, A. J. 1989, 'Socioeconomic Status and Obesity: A Review of the Literature', *Psychological Bulletin*, vol. 105, pp. 260–75.

Sobal, J., Nicolopoulos, V., & Lee, J. 1995, 'Attitudes about Weight and Dating among Secondary School Students', *International Journal of Obesity*, vol. 19, pp. 376–81.

Sobal, J., Rauschenbach, B., & Frongillo, E. 1992, 'Marital Status, Fatness, and Obesity', *Social Science and Medicine*, vol. 35, pp. 915–23.

Spiegal, D. & Keith-Spiegel, P. 1973, *Outsiders USA*, Rinehart Press, San Francisco, pp 570–3.

Stearns, P. N. 1997, *Fat History: Bodies and Beauty in the Modern West*, New York University Press, New York.

Stunkard, A. J. & Sobal, J. 1995, 'Psychosocial Consequences of Obesity', in K. D. Brownell & C. G. Fairburn (eds), *Eating Disorders and Obesity*, Guilford Press, New York, pp. 417–21.

Tiggemann, M. & Rothblum, E. D. 1988, 'Gender Differences in Social Consequences of Perceived Overweight in the United States and Australia', *Sex Roles*, vol. 18, pp. 75–86.

Waller, G., Shaw, J., Hamilton, K., Baldwin, G., Harding, T., & Sumner, T. 1994, 'Beauty is in the Eye of the Beholder: Media Influences on the Psychopathology of Eating Problems', *Appetite*, vol. 23, p. 287.

Way, K. 1995, 'Never Too Rich … or Too Thin: The Role of Stigma in the Social Construction of Anorexia Nervosa', in D. Maurer & J. Sobal (eds), *Eating Agendas: Food and Nutrition as Social Problems*, Aldine de Gruyter, Hawthorne, NY, pp. 91–113.

Weiner, B., Perry, R. P., & Magnusson, J. 1988, 'An Attributional Analysis of Reactions to Stigmas', *Journal of Personality and Social Psychology*, vol. 55, pp. 738–48.

Wiseman, C. V., Gray, J. J., Mosimann, J. E., & Ahrens, A. H. 1992, 'Cultural Expectations of Thinness in Women: An Update', *International Journal of Eating Disorders*, vol. 11, pp. 85–9.

Young, L. M. & Powell, B. 1985, 'The Effects of Obesity on the Clinical Judgements of Mental Health Professionals', *Journal of Health and Social Behavior*, vol. 26, pp. 233–46.

Zdrodowski, D. 1996, 'Eating Out: The Experience of Eating in Public for the "Overweight" Woman', *Women's Studies International Forum*, vol. 19, pp. 665–74.

12

The Thin Ideal:
Women, Food, and Dieting
Lauren Williams and John Germov

Overview

- *What structural and cultural factors contribute to the thin ideal for women in Western societies?*

- *Why do so many women succumb to the pressure of the thin ideal by dieting?*

- *How do some women resist the pressure of the thin ideal?*

This chapter applies a sociological perspective to investigate the topic of women, food, and dieting, answering the question of why dieting is predominantly a female behaviour. The chapter uses the sociological imagination template outlined in chapter 1 to investigate the topic of women and dieting. We examine aspects of the historical, structural, cultural, and critical factors that have contributed to the development of, and resistance to, the thin ideal in Western society.

Key terms

agency
gender socialisation
patriarchy
post-structuralist
social construction
structuralist
structure–agency debate
thin ideal

Introduction: the sexual division of dieting

Dieting is the conscious manipulation of food choice and eating patterns to lose or maintain weight. It is a common behaviour in developed countries, especially among women. In an Australian study conducted in the 1980s, David Crawford and Tony Worsley (1988) found that 38 per cent of the Australian women surveyed had dieted in the year prior to participating in the study. Another study of Australian women conducted a decade later found 49 per cent of 11 000 participants aged 18–22 years and 44 per cent of 14 000 participants aged 45–50 years reported having dieted in the previous twelve months (Research Institute for Gender and Health 1996). Australia is similar to other developed countries such as the USA, where studies indicate that a majority of American women fear becoming overweight and so continually diet (Banks 1992; Huon et al. 1990).

Many women who diet are actually within the medically defined 'healthy weight range'[1] and therefore, according to current medical orthodoxy, do not have health reasons to lose weight (Tiggemann &Pennington 1990; Huon et al. 1990; Banks 1992). Successive surveys in Australia throughout the 1980s and 1990s have shown that more men than women are above the healthy weight range, even though more women diet (National Heart Foundation 1990; Australian Bureau of Statistics 1997). Other research indicates that women diet in the pursuit of the '**thin ideal**', at least when they are younger, when the desire for weight loss leads some women to consciously adopt unhealthy dieting practices to achieve the goal of slenderness (Germov & Williams 1996b).

Dieting for weight loss requires a considerable investment in time and money, as well as emotional and physical resources. Kelly Brownell and Judith Rodin (1994) note that the unsuccessful nature of diets can lead to a cycle of 'yo-yo' dieting or 'weight cycling', with detrimental physiological and psychological consequences. Dieting can thus result in a lifelong 'tug of war' with food, and female food consumption can be wrought with feelings of guilt, anxiety, and deprivation. Women often perceive food for its dieting value, dividing foods into 'dieting' (good) and 'fattening' (bad) foods (Sobal & Cassidy 1987; McKie et al. 1993; Germov & Williams 1996b).

Several feminist authors have described the relationship between gender, food, and the social context of eating (Charles & Kerr 1988; Burgoyne & Clark 1983; Murcott 1983). The relationship between gender, food, and the body is epitomised by the sexual division of dieting, since dieting is primarily a female act. Thus it is important to ask questions about why dieting is a gendered behaviour and about the thin ideal that

---

1   We recognise that the terms 'healthy weight range', 'overweight', and 'obesity' are social constructions and are problematic, especially considering debates within the medical literature over the extent to which excess weight causes health problems. But we have adopted theses terms because of their wide use in the literature. The issues of conflicting medical findings, stigmatisation, and medicalisation are discussed by Kelly Brownell and John Rodin (1994), and John Germov and Lauren Williams (1996a), and in chapter 11 of this volume.

promulgates this behaviour. However, the answers obtained will depend very much on the theoretical framework from which the questions are developed. The **structuralist** and **post-structuralist** perspectives are the two theoretical frameworks used most commonly by feminist authors to investigate questions about the female body. To help understand these perspectives, we must first consider and clarify the **structure–agency debate**.

As discussed in chapter 1, sociology is concerned with the relationship between society and the individual, and many key issues centre on the structure–agency debate. The pressure to conform to the thin ideal clearly has a structural basis, perpetuated by various social institutions and material interests such as the media, fashion, and cosmetics industries. The health sector has also played a part, with anti-fat messages often equating health with thinness. These structural factors have clear antecedents in the historical development of **patriarchy**, particularly as represented in various forms of social regulation of the female body (see Schwartz 1986; Turner 1992). However, structural factors alone do not provide a complete picture of the contemporary reproduction and pervasiveness of the thin ideal and gendered eating patterns. Post-structural factors, which represent female subjectivity and **agency**—that is, the way women respond to the social pressure of the thin ideal on a daily basis—also play an important role.

What interests sociologists is the study of this interplay between a patriarchal social structure and female agency: how the thin ideal shapes women's attitudes to food and eating, and how women adopt, modify, or reject these social pressures. The controversial question is why so few women resist the thin ideal, making it so pervasive. Feminist writers have generally approached this vexed question from the opposing philosophical perspectives of structuralist feminist theories (liberal, Marxist, and radical feminism) and post-structuralist feminism. Structuralist theories assume that individuals are primarily *determined* by the society in which they live. The focus is on the large-scale features of society such as the economy, political system, or dominant culture, and on how they shape individual and group behaviour. Post-structuralist perspectives developed as a critique of structuralist approaches that failed to adequately theorise how individuals shape society. Post-structuralist approaches generally abandon the search for universal, original causes, or for any form of 'objective reality' or an overriding logic of social change (Annandale & Clarke 1996). Post-structuralist theorists focus on human agency and **social construction**, rather than social determinism. Women are not conceived of as passive recipients of the dominant thin ideal discourse, but rather 'It is women themselves who practise this discipline on and against their own bodies … This self-surveillance is a form of obedience to patriarchy … [a woman becomes] a body designed to please or excite' (Wearing 1996, p. 88).

Before exploring these perspectives further, we will discuss the historical antecedents and cultural determinants of the female thin ideal, which necessarily involve a focus on structural factors.

Thin ideal antecedents: a brief historical overview

How and why did the thin ideal eventuate, and why were women singled out as its subjects? While the thin ideal is a relatively recent phenomenon, the historical antecedents of the social control of the female body are well documented (see Rubin 1975; Ehrenreich & English 1979; Turner 1992; Michie 1987; Eisenstein 1988; Corrigan & Meredyth 1994). In the nineteenth century, 'women's appearance norms' (Rothblum 1994) acted to reinforce patriarchal beliefs about female sexuality and to limit women's participation in public life. For example, corsetry and head-to-toe fashion literally constricted the bodies and mobility of women, which was obviously of advantage in maintaining a patriarchally dominated society. Therefore, the establishment of an ideal shape and size for women as an instrument of social control is not a new phenomenon. The socially desired body ideal may change over time, in terms of size and shape, but the existence of an ideal for women to aspire to has remained constant.

The female ideal of the nineteenth century was a large, curved body, which connoted fertility, wealth, and high status (Seid 1994; Bordo 1993). While poor women were occupied with physical work, the voluptuous women of the middle and upper classes were often viewed as objects of art, luxury, status, virtue, and beauty. The voluptuous ideal female body is the direct opposite of today's thin ideal. Fatness was linked to emotional stability, strength (stored energy), good health, and refinement in a display of leisure rather than labour. The undergarment industry came to the rescue of the naturally thin woman with products such as inflatable rubber attachments (complete with dimples) to give that rounded, full-figure look(!) (Seid 1994).

The first break with the voluptuous tradition of the nineteenth century began in the 1920s with the 'flappers'—a term used to describe skinny women who were financially and sexually independent, partly as a result of the First World War, which left many women to manage their dead husbands' estates. The word 'flapper' was used to trivialise the 'new independent woman', as Banner states:

> On the one hand, she indicated a new freedom in sensual expression by shortening her skirts and discarding her corsets. On the other hand, she bound her breasts ... and expressed her sensuality not through eroticism, but through constant, vibrant movement ... The name 'flapper' itself [was drawn] from a style of flapping galoshes popular among young women before the war; it connoted irrelevant movement and raised the spectre of a seal with black flapping paws (1983, p. 279).

Thus these women rejected the dominant patriarchal ideal of feminine appearance and the passivity that went with it, and assumed a more masculine ideal; the new liberated woman was to dress, act, and look more like a man (thin and without curves) (Hesse-Biber 1991). However, when women lose their curves they tend to become physically smaller and apparently weak. This era of redefining women's bodies arose during a time of female political activism in the USA and the United Kingdom, as the suffragette movement pressed for the vote for women. As women entered the public sphere and increased their profile and power, the ideal female body inversely decreased in size.

Other factors contributed to the emergence of the thin female ideal. The onset of the Great Depression in 1929, followed by the Second World War, led to austerity measures as a result of food shortages and a subsequent concern with the link between food and health. These decades marked the start of calorie-counting and using food for its energy value (Schwartz 1986). These measures thus imposed a dieting mentality on the population, especially for women as the then primary gatekeepers of food in the family.

The contemporary thin ideal

The contemporary thin ideal was born in the 1960s and was epitomised by the model Twiggy (whose name was coined as a result of her slight frame). By this time, the Western world was enjoying an era of prosperity and plenty. As prosperity grew and food consumption increased, concern also grew over the increasing weight of the population as medical and epidemiological studies began to find links between obesity and premature mortality. By the 1970s, a rare coalescence of factors emerged to reinforce the thin ideal: medical science, government authorities, and the fashion industry all adopted an anti-fat stance. In chapter 11, Jeffery Sobal discusses the changing social attitudes towards 'fat' and the growing stigmatisation of obesity. While dieting and the cultural aversion to 'fat' have historical underpinnings that existed before the advent of contemporary health warnings (see Schwartz 1986), the well-intentioned actions of health professionals and government agencies in promoting anti-fat messages may have reinforced and legitimised the 'thin ideal' and encouraged unnecessary dieting (Germov & Williams 1996a).

Roberta Seid (1994) argues that the second wave of feminism in the 1970s initially embraced the super-fit, thin ideal as a celebration of women's strength and control. Such body control was regarded as a positive symbol of femininity, in contrast to the aesthetics of previous centuries, which conceptualised women as invalids. Jane Fonda was a vocal feminist of this time, and promoted health and beauty through physical fitness. Marjorie Ferguson's content analysis of women's magazines (1983, p. 113) notes the influence of the self-help movement on contemporary femininity, bringing about a shift in editorial emphasis 'towards greater self-realisation, self-determination, and the presentation of a more independent and assertive femininity'. Such a development paralleled the growth of consumerism and individualism in advanced capitalist societies, reflecting a successful marketing strategy on the part of the magazines to increase profitability. As Jane Fonda and various imitators discovered, the focus on female self-help and independence through body discipline tapped into a new market of consumers from which to profit.

The rise of mass production and consumption led the body-image industries to develop a 'sure-fire' formula for success: promote a thin ideal of beauty that the majority of women can never attain, which will result in a virtually infinite market of consumers. In the early 1990s, the United States diet industry was estimated to be worth

US$55 billion per year, with more than 65 million Americans dieting to lose weight (Brownell 1993). Australian figures are proportionately similar, with over A$500 million per year spent on commercial weight-loss programs (Lester 1994).

As a number of authors have noted (Beller 1977; Mennell 1985), when food is scarce, cultural ideals favour a large body, whose 'abundance' symbolises wealth and status. Conversely, in times of plenty, social mores shift towards disciplining food intake, and the thin body becomes the ideal. In today's advanced capitalist societies, food is easily available and social worth is increasingly measured by a person's ability to resist excess. This reassertion of 1950s morality regarding sloth and gluttony are remnants of earlier Christian values that focused on purifying the soul and disciplining the body through abstinence and penance, and on purging oneself of excess (Schwartz 1986; Turner 1992). Some authors have also made links between religion and the self-starvation diet regimen that is seen at its most extreme in eating disorders (see Bynum 1987; Bell 1985; Brumberg 1988).

Susan Faludi (1991) and Naomi Wolf (1990) see a parallel between female sexual liberation and the thin ideal, where part of the backlash against the social gains made by women since the 1960s have been a renewed emphasis on women's appearance. As Faludi and Wolf argue, it is no accident that the current thin ideal emerged during the second wave of feminism—a period of increased female sexual and socioeconomic liberation. As in the era of the flappers, the rise of women's political and social status resulted in a female body ideal that was diminutive, weak, and physically powerless. The increased entry of women into the public sphere directly challenged male dominance but resulted in a female ideal of physical size that emphasised weakness as opposed to physical strength—the ultimate source of male dominance over women.

Popular portrayal of the thin ideal

Models and celebrities have been the overt public face of changes in beauty standards over recent decades. For example, compare the figure of Marilyn Monroe in the 1950s with that of Elle Macpherson in the 1980s and Kate Moss in the 1990s. Content analysis of magazines, beauty pageants, Hollywood movies, and television programs have consistently found that the female beauty ideal has become thinner with time (Silverstein et al. 1986; Morris et al. 1989). Sharlene Hesse-Biber links this trend with the growing equality of women thus: 'when women are "demanding more space" in terms of equality of opportunity, there is a cultural demand that they "should shrink"… Thinness may be considered a sign of conforming to a constricting feminine image, whereas weight may convey a strong, powerful image' (1991, p. 178).

Boxes 12.1, 12.2, and 12.3 show the cover designs of Australia's popular women's magazine *Cleo* to trace the presentation of women by the structural interests of the media, advertising, and fashion industries from the 'self-help days' of the early 1970s to the engineered 'insecurity' of the early 1990s.

The image on the cover of the January 1973 *Cleo* is a sexual presentation of an attractive blonde model with a plunging halter-top. The shot stops just below the

Box 12.1 *Cleo* magazine cover, January 1973

- Meet Don Dunstan, the bright young man of politics
- And Bianca Jagger, the bright young wife of Mick
- Will 1973 be a successful year for you?
- A working girl's guide to working men
- I was a sleep–around girl
- Female fantasies
- Are secretaries substitute wives?
- Your *Cleo* book of bawdy songs
- PLUS our mate of the month

Box 12.2 *Cleo* magazine cover, January 1983

- Make money! How to cash in on your bright ideas
- *The genius factory.* Are super babies the nightmare of the future?
- Personality quiz: Are you much too possessive in love?
- JON VOIGHT The enigma exposed
- *The second hand husband* He may be the answer to your prayers—but learn to read the danger signs
- FIT FOR LIVING Stretch, kick and punch your way to a healthy mind and body
- Hollywood's new breed of raunchy young superstars
- Midsummer health and beauty plan. The clue is care—not camouflage
- The truth about glamour careers
- Sex with a robot? Possible but more likely your computer will be just a friend!
- YOUR STARS FOR 1983 Complete guide to love, health and money
- SEXUAL INCOMPATABILITY Why *his* thrill can be *your* ho-hum. Revealing advice from Australia's leading sex therapist

Box 12.3 *Cleo* magazine cover, January 1993

- 3 top cover girls open their wardrobes
- RETIN A The new cure for stretch marks!
- The workout that transformed Madonna, Demi and Linda Hamilton
- 'I tracked down my daughter's rapist'
- The *one* thing men always fall for in a woman
- Diary of a bulimic
- Are you crazy or is he seeing someone else?
- SEALED SECTION YOUR HOTTEST SEX EVER From the raciest sex book ever written
- STARGUIDE '93 Who's in the stars for you?

breasts. The woman has her hand to her face in a submissive gesture and is smiling into the camera with a 'knowing' look. The cover shot reflects the content of some of the editorial headlines, which have an emphasis on sexual liberation. There is a notable absence of editorial material relating to dieting, exercise, or the body.

The 1983 model is an attractive brunette in a head-and-shoulders shot, turned side on below the shoulders so that we do not see her breasts. She has an almost vacant, expressionless look on her face. The image is one of attractive wholesomeness, rather than sexuality. By the 1980s, the stories no longer focus on sexual liberation, but on the need for a health and beauty plan. The magazine has learned that encouraging insecurity is the best strategy for ensuring a continued market ('Are you much too possessive

Figure 12.1   The Body Shop's 'Ruby' campaign (reproduced with permission of The Body Shop International PLC)

in love?'). The emphasis on money in the headline story reflects both the increased financial independence of women and the rise of the 'decade of greed'.

The January 1993 cover shows a three-quarter body shot, in which the body is exposed but in a stance that is more athletic than sexy. The model is wearing a white bathing costume with quite full pants rather than revealing briefs. By the 1990s, the focus on body insecurity has intensified by exposing readers to the wardrobes of models and the workouts of movie stars, neither of which most readers have any hope of attaining. Thus the thin ideal is glamorised and made apparently accessible (if you just read the health and beauty section!). The outcomes of body insecurity are poignantly reflected in the 'diary of a bulimic'. Encouragement of insecurity about men, sex, and life-management continues (you need to read the 'stars' to know how to meet men, and if you already have a man, you need to ask 'are you crazy or is he seeing someone else?'). The representation of the female body in consumer culture, such as in popular women's magazines, 'encourages the individual to adopt instrumental strategies to combat deterioration and decay (applauded too by state bureaucracies who seek to reduce health costs by educating the public against bodily neglect) … Images of the body beautiful, openly sexual and associated with hedonism, leisure and display, emphasise the importance of appearance and the "look"' (Featherstone 1991, p. 170).

Women are exposed to the thin ideal from childhood through the process of **gender socialisation**, as evidenced by the success of the Barbie doll by Mattel. This doll, with annual sales of US$1 billion (*New York Times Magazine*, 27 May 1994, p. 22; O'Brien 1997), is blonde, tall, thin, long-legged, slim-waisted, and has a flat stomach, square shoulders, large eyes, and curved red lips. Ken Norton and others (1996) undertook a study in which they scaled the anthropometric measurements of the Barbie doll to adult size, finding that the probability of an adult woman having a Barbie-like body shape is less than one in 100 000. Interestingly, they also scaled the Ken doll (the male equivalent of the Barbie doll, which is produced and marketed by the same company), finding it to have a 'more realistic' body shape, likely to be found in one in every fifty males. This makes Barbie 2000 times less attainable than Ken, reflecting the fact that women are encouraged to aspire to a more unrealistic body ideal than men. The Body Shop company produced its own version of Barbie, named 'Ruby', a full-figured doll, as part of its campaign for body diversity. The company was initially forced to withdraw the doll as a result of pressure from the Mattel company, which considered the features to be too similar to that of their idealised blonde best-seller (Benjamin Smith, pers. comm., 27 May 1998). The Body Shop have since released a revised version of Ruby.

Factors influencing the thin ideal today

Structuralist approaches to the thin ideal

In explaining the emergence of the thin ideal, a structuralist approach would argue that the thin ideal is the outcome of a patriarchal society, in which powerful men and the various industries and social institutions they control (structural factors) construct the 'beauty myth' for their own material and political interests (see Bordo 1993; Wolf 1990). These structural factors clearly have an impact on cultural beliefs by constructing and promoting a particular ideal of female beauty, particularly in terms of gender socialisation.

As thinness became synonymous with the powerful combination of 'health and beauty', the female body became an increasingly exploited target of both material interests and government health authorities. Calls to exercise self-control over one's body for the health benefits and for the sake of social conformity expanded upon the cultural values of individualism and self-responsibility. Thus women's magazines became an important sphere of influence for perpetuating the thin ideal. Those maga-zines that do not conform to this strategy may not survive. An Australian example of the extent of this control was reported in the *Sydney Morning Herald* by Pilita Clark and Andrew Hornery (1997). In an interview, the former editor of *New Woman* magazine in Australia, Cyndi Tebbel, claimed to have lost her job because the magazine featured a 'Big Issue', which supported International No Diet Day, used size-16 models, and pro-moted body diversity. According to Tebbel, sales of the magazine were not affected, but advertisers complained and threatened to withdraw, risking up to 50 per cent of the total revenue of the magazine. This meant that the magazine returned to featuring thin models and to stories promoting body insecurity and promised cures. This illustrates the fact that the material interests of the cosmetics, fitness, and fashion industries will not tolerate a message that acts against their commercial interests—that is, a message challenging the dominant ideal of female beauty.

While gender is clearly the major factor in explaining the cultural preoccupation with the thin ideal, the influence of ethnic culture may play a contrary role. A United States study by Sheila Parker and others (1995) examined the body image and dieting behaviours of African-American and White adolescent females. They found that African-American girls exhibited significantly less body dissatisfaction, and greater appreciation of body diversity and of larger sized female bodies, than their White coun-terparts, who tended to be rigid adherents to the thin ideal. While the African-Ameri-can girls studied tended to have a lower prevalence of dieting and were less concerned about body weight and shape than were White girls, this may not apply to all ethnic groups in the USA. A major United States study of over 17 000 adolescent girls found that ethnicity, as opposed to skin colour, does not 'protect' against body dissatisfaction or dieting behaviour, concluding that ethnic subculture is just as affected by the thin ideal as is White mainstream culture (French et al. 1997).

The role of female agency in perpetuating the thin ideal

In contrast to a structuralist analysis, which focuses on the external forces that put pres-sure on women to conform to a thin ideal, feminist post-structuralist theorists are con-cerned with the role played by women in reproducing and resisting the thin ideal (Weedon 1987; Bartky 1990; Barrett & Phillips 1992; Pringle 1995). Post-structuralist theorists do not deny the importance of the historical and cultural factors discussed above, but rather than viewing these factors as all-determining, they stress the importance of theorising female subjectivity and deal with the complex and subtle facets of the social construction of women's bodies.

It is commonly stated that some women use body control as evidence of their control over other aspects of their lives. As the 1993 Cleo cover shows in Box 12.3, the successful woman is financially independent, sexually liberated, *and* thin. However, Sandra Bartky argues that 'a tighter control of the body has gained a new kind of hold over the mind' (1990, p. 81). The thin body has become an essential symbol of modern femininity and a new form of social control of women's bodies; body-regulation is self-inflicted, administered by women on themselves through dieting, starvation, excessive exercise, and, at its most extreme, plastic surgery. Therefore, there is a self-imposed component in the pressure to conform—that is, women are not simply passive sponges of coercive patriarchal structures and cultural stereotypes. In effect, the social control of women's bodies becomes internalised by the women themselves.

In examining female agency, it is important to note that not all women respond to the thin ideal by internalising it so that it becomes an integral part of their identity. Nor do all women perpetuate it by forcing the thin ideal on other women. Some women reject the thin ideal altogether, as we shall see later in the chapter (Germov & Williams 1996b; Orbach 1986; Chernin 1981). Responses to the thin ideal can be categorised on a continuum, as depicted in Figure 12.2. This figure has more to do with whether or not women choose to conform to the thin ideal, and with the subsequent effect on eating, than it has to do with actual body weight. On the left of the continuum are the 'thin-ideal conformers' who diet to lose weight, either on a permanent basis or on an 'on again, off again' basis, which often results in weight cycling. Women who diet or who consciously restrict their eating (by eating low-fat, low-calorie foods, for instance) may be of any weight, but will probably tend to be thinner than women at the other end of the continuum. The women on the right of the spectrum, whom we have called

Figure 12.2 Continuum of responses to the thin ideal

thin-ideal conformers	weight maintainers	size acceptors
• yo-yo dieting	• never dieted	• may have 'failed' at dieting
• restrained eaters	• unrestrained eaters	• unrestrained eating
• weight cycling	• maintain desired body without dieting	• may be any weight but more often overweight
• may be any weight	• neither accept nor reject thin ideal	• reject thin ideal
• conform to thin ideal		

'size acceptors', do not diet, possibly because they have failed to achieve their desired weight and have decided to be unrestrained eaters, or because they have consciously rejected the thin ideal and accepted body diversity. As a group, they will tend towards being heavier than the dieters. In the middle are the 'weight maintainers', who have never had to diet to stay thin and are unrestrained eaters. These are women who have never consciously grappled with whether to conform to the thin ideal or to reject it. It is possible that if their weight were to increase, they may move to the left or right of their neutral position.

The desire to be seen as attractive and the pressure of social conformity are powerful and rational reasons for the prevalence of dieting among women. The social importance placed on women's appearance norms (Rothblum 1994) can be so great that some women value weight loss above success in love or work (Charles & Kerr 1988; Wolf 1990). As Edwin Schur argues, 'physical appearance is much more central to evaluations of women than it is to evaluations of men; this emphasis implicitly devalues women's other qualities and accomplishments; women's 'looks' thereby become a commodity and a key determinant of their "success" or "failure"' (1983, p. 68). Hesse-Biber (1991) argues women are socialised to focus on physical appearance in order to receive social acceptance, while for men, public achievement determines social worth and self-image. As Margaret Duncan states (1994, p. 50), women learn to 'compare their appearance with that of the patriarchal feminine ideal and thus become objects for their own gaze'.

Dieting and pursuit of the thin ideal can thus be viewed as a rational response by women striving for acceptance in the context of dominant ideals of beauty, sexuality, and femininity. The internalisation of patriarchal norms explains the active role women play in perpetuating the thin ideal (Bartky 1990). Women police their own bodies and the bodies of other women in a process of constant body surveillance. In this way, the thin ideal is reinforced and perpetuated without coercion and often with women's consent. We have described this process as the 'body panopticon' effect (see Germov & Williams 1999 (in press); and also Duncan 1994) to refer to women's body monitoring, where the pressure to conform to the thin ideal not only stems from the structural factors and material interests, but also from women acting as 'body police' for themselves and other women.

Our previous research has documented the myriad of responses to the thin ideal exhibited by women (Germov & Williams 1996b). The benefit of a post-structuralist approach is that it sheds light on the active role that women play in the social construction of the thin ideal. While such an understanding helps to explain the pervasiveness of the thin ideal, self-regulation does not occur in a vacuum and is reinforced by structural interests such as the fashion, weight loss, fitness, health, and cosmetic industries.

Towards a synthesis of the structuralist and post-structuralist approaches

Both structuralist and post-structuralist perspectives are important in understanding the pressure on women to diet to attain the thin ideal—but can they be reconciled? On its own, neither perspective offers a complete explanation of why women diet. For example, structuralist explanations tend to imply women are easily duped or even 'brainwashed' by the media, fashion, and men in general to succumb to the thin ideal. However, such a perspective ignores the fact that not *all* men act as oppressors of women (either consciously or implicitly) and that some women consciously and effectively resist the pressure to conform to the thin ideal. In an attempt to bridge these two approaches, we suggest that dieting and the thin ideal must be understood within a theoretical schema that acknowledges structural factors and female agency, but that avoids voluntaristic explanations of dieting behaviour as simply a matter of individual lifestyle choice.

Figure 12.3 provides a helpful starting point for understanding the complex processes involved in the pressure to conform to the thin ideal. It summarises the key structural and post-structural factors and shows how these factors are responsible for the reproduction of the thin ideal and the pressure on women to diet.

Figure 12.3 The social and cultural reproduction cycle of the thin ideal

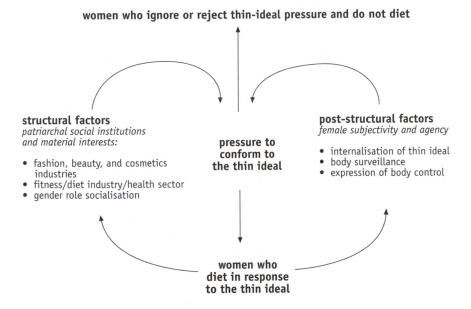

The starting point of Figure 12.2 is the pressure put on women in Western society to conform to the thin ideal. Women can respond to the pressure in one of two ways: by ignoring or actively rejecting the thin ideal, which takes them out of the cycle (as represented by the upward arrow); or, alternatively, by responding to the thin ideal by dieting, which results in gendered food and restrained eating practices. The lists of structural and post-structural factors summarise the key modes by which the pressure to conform to the thin ideal is produced and reproduced (the arrows indicate the direction of influence). Dieting behaviour reinforces both structural interests (for example, the dieting industry) and post-structural factors (for example, self-surveillance), which in turn reinforce pressure to conform to the thin ideal and dieting behaviour, and the cycle continues.

Challenging the thin ideal via size acceptance

Incorporating the concept of female agency to understand the production of the thin ideal also allows the possibility of women rejecting this ideal in favour of an alternative ideal—that of size acceptance. Some women may simply ignore the ideal as irrelevant, while others may have tried to conform to the thin ideal in the past and have chosen at some point to actively reject it. These women move out of the cycle in Figure 12.3, thereby challenging the dominance of the thin ideal. Enough individuals are choosing this option to constitute an emerging social movement, variously termed 'anti-dieting', 'size acceptance' or 'fat rights'. These movements are challenging the dominant discourse of the thin ideal and are providing an alternative form of social acceptance by advocating body diversity. Occasionally, this anti-dieting sentiment is popularised by the mass media. Figure 12.4 depicts the front cover of the Australian *Who Weekly* magazine. It is one of the few examples of the mass media being critical of the thin ideal. This picture was seized upon by the media in Australia as an example of how the then trend towards the 'waif look', promoted by the modelling and fashion industry, had pushed the thin ideal too far. While this was only a transitory development, it may nonetheless reflect the nascent undermining of the thin ideal. Such an example lends support to the possibility that the dominance of the thin ideal can be challenged.

Promotion of size acceptance offers a mechanism for the dismantling of the thin female ideal. In qualitative research conducted with Australian women, we found that size acceptance can be the result of a history of failed dieting to lose weight, or it can be based on the decision to end the pain of the dieting process and the obsession with one's body (Germov & Williams 1996b). The development of a size-acceptance identity poses the analytical question of how some women are able to manage the consequences of rebelling against the thin ideal. Further research into the development of size acceptance is required, as it remains an underconceptualised issue and has been given scant attention in the sociological literature to date.

Some health professionals are recommending the alternative of size acceptance as part of a new health promotion paradigm in recognition of the limited success of weight-loss diets. The paradigm is based on facilitating a healthy lifestyle by promoting body satisfaction and body diversity, healthy eating, and moderate exercise, without recourse to starvation, restrained or disordered eating, or yo-yo dieting in pursuit of an idealised body size and shape (see Box 12.4).

Conclusion

This chapter has outlined the historical, structural, and cultural factors that have contributed to the thin ideal and the role that women have played in reinforcing or rejecting it. We have also adopted a critical approach in arguing that any understanding of gendered eating—particularly an understanding of why women diet and why the thin ideal is so pervasive—requires a conceptual framework that reconciles

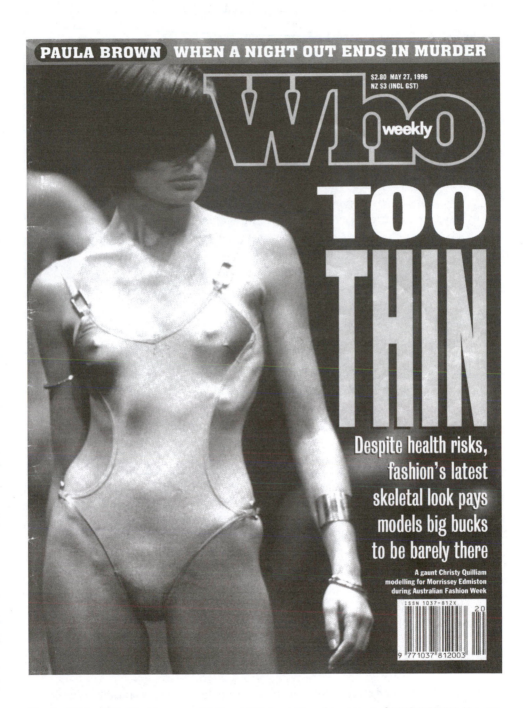

Figure 12.4 *Who Weekly* cover, 27 May 1996 (reproduced courtesy of WHO WEEKLY, May 27, 1996, Issue No. 222)

Box 12.4 Ten basic tenets of size acceptance

1 Human beings come in a variety of sizes and shapes. We celebrate this diversity as a positive characteristic of the human race.
2 There is no ideal body size, shape, or weight that every individual should strive to achieve.
3 Every body is a good body, whatever its size or shape.
4 Self-esteem and body image are strongly linked. Helping people feel good about their bodies, and about who they are, can help motivate and maintain healthy behaviours.
5 Appearance stereotyping is inherently unfair to the individual because it is based on superficial factors which the individual has little or no control over.
6 We respect the bodies of others even though they might be quite different from our own.
7 Each person is responsible for taking care of his/her body.
8 Good health is not defined by body size; it is a state of physical, mental, and social well-being.
9 People of all sizes and shapes can reduce their risk of poor health by adopting a healthy lifestyle.
10 Health promotion programs should celebrate the benefits of a healthy lifestyle. Programs should be accepting of and sensitive to size diversity. They should promote body satisfaction, and the achievement of realistic and attainable health goals without regard to weight change.

Source: Developed by dietitians and nutritionists who are advocates of size acceptance; their efforts were coordinated by Joanne P. Ikeda, Department of Nutritional Sciences, University of California, Berkeley, CA 94720-3104, USA. Comments regarding these tenets may be sent to <jikeda@garnet.berkeley.edu>.

structuralist and post-structuralist approaches. Women are not merely victims of patriarchal and capitalist imperatives, nor are they simply free to adopt or reject the thin ideal as they please. Some women actively participate in the reproduction of the pressure to conform to the thin ideal, while others resist this pressure by constructing alternative discourses such as size acceptance. The rejection of the thin ideal and the promotion of size acceptance as a new body ideal remain possible avenues through which the thin ideal and associated unnecessary and harmful dieting practices can be challenged.

Summary of main points

- A sexual division of dieting exists, in which dieting to lose weight is primarily a female act.
- Sociological explanations of why women diet can be categorised into two broad perspectives: structuralist and post-structuralist.

- An understanding of why women diet and of the persistence of the thin ideal requires a synthesis of structural and post-structural factors.
- The notion of women as victims of patriarchal subordination has been successfully critiqued by feminist post-structuralist theorists through a renewed focus on women's agency and subjective experiences of femininity.
- Women react to the thin ideal in a myriad of ways; accepting, reinforcing, and resisting the dominant discourse.
- Resistance of the thin ideal through size acceptance is an alternative gaining social momentum.

Discussion questions

1 Outline the difference between the structuralist and post-structuralist perspectives of the thin ideal.
2 How did the thin ideal originate, and why did it become so pervasive?
3 How do women act to perpetuate the thin ideal?
4 Are there any responses to the social pressure to conform to the thin ideal that are not encompassed by Figure 12.3? Reflect on where you fit in this schema.
5 Discuss the potential for the size-acceptance movement to dismantle the thin ideal. Do you think this could happen in your lifetime?

Further reading and resources

Corrigan, A. & Meredyth, D. 1994, 'The Body Politic', in K. Pritchard Hughes (ed.), *Contemporary Australian Feminism*, Longman, Melbourne.

Germov, J. & Williams, L. 1996a, 'The Epidemic of Dieting Women: The Need for a Sociological Approach to Food and Nutrition', *Appetite*, vol. 27, pp. 97–108.

—— 1996b, 'The Sexual Division of Dieting: Women's Voices', *The Sociological Review*, vol. 44, no. 4, pp. 630–47.

Hesse-Biber, S. 1998, *Am I Thin Enough Yet? The Cult of Thinness and the Commercialization of Identity*, Oxford University Press, New York.

Rothblum, E. D. 1994, '"I'll Die for the Revolution but Don't Ask Me Not to Diet": Feminism and the Continuing Stigmatization of Obesity', in P. Fallon, M. A. Katzman, & S. A. Wooley (eds), *Feminist Perspectives on Eating Disorders*, Guilford Press, New York.

Schwartz, H. 1986, *Never Satisfied: A Cultural History of Diets, Fantasies and Fat*, The Free Press, New York.

Seid, R. P. 1994, 'Too "Close to the Bone": The Historical Context for Women's Obsession with Slenderness', in P. Fallon, M. A. Katzman, & S. A. Wooley (eds), *Feminist Perspectives on Eating Disorders*, Guilford Press, New York.

Sobal, J. & Maurer, D. (eds) 1999 (forthcoming), *Weighty Issues: Constructing Fatness and Thinness as Social Problems*, Aldine de Gruyder, Hawthorne, NY.

Journals
Body & Society
Feminist Studies
Food and Society
Gender & Society
Healthy Weight Journal
International Journal of Eating Disorders
Sex Roles
Women and Health
Women's Studies International Forum

Websites
To find out more about The Body Shop Ruby campaign:
<http://www.the-body-shop.com/fullvoice/fullvoice1/index.html>
The Body Shop provides some useful information, links, and teaching resources on its website:
<http://www.the-body-shop.com/>
Association for the Health Enrichment of Large People (AHELP):
<http://www.usit.com/ahelp/>
Fat Acceptance weblinks:
<http://www.comlab.ox.ac.uk/oucl/users/sharon.curtis/BF/SSFA/home.html>
Fat Girl:
<http://www.fatso.com/fatgirl/>
Fat!So?:
<http://www.fatso.com/>
Healthy Weight Journal:
<http://www.healthyweightnetwork.com/>
International Size Acceptance Association:
<http://www.size-acceptance.org/>
National Association to Advance Fat Acceptance:
<http://naafa.org/>
Radiance: The Magazine for Large Women:
<http://www.radiancemagazine.com/>
Yahoo Fat Acceptance page:
<http://www.yahoo.com/text/Society_and_Culture/Size_Issues/Fat_Acceptance>

Videos
The Famine Within 1990 (Kandor Productions, Ontario, with Ronin Films, Canberra:, 90 minutes). An excellent discussion of body image and eating disorders.
Fat Chance 1994 (National Film Board of Canada, 50 minutes). A riveting and thought-provoking account of fat prejudice.

References

Annandale, E. & Clarke, J. 1996, 'What is Gender? Feminist Theory and the Sociology of Human Reproduction', *Sociology of Health and Illness*, vol. 18, no. 1, pp. 17–44.

Australian Bureau of Statistics 1997, *National Nutrition Survey Selected Highlights, Australia 1995*, Cat. no. 4802.0, ABS, Canberra.

Banks, G. G. 1992, 'Culture in Culture-Bound Syndromes: The Case of Anorexia Nervosa', *Social Science Medicine*, vol. 34, no. 8, pp. 867–84.

Banner, L. W. 1983, *American Beauty*, Knopf, New York.

Barrett, M. & Phillips, A. (eds) 1992, *Destabilizing Theory: Contemporary Feminist Debates*, Polity Press, Cambridge.

Bartky, S. L. 1990, *Femininity and Domination: Studies in the Phenomenology of Oppression*, Routledge, New York.

Bell, R. 1985, *Holy Anorexia*, Chicago University Press, Chicago.

Beller, A. S. 1977, *Fat and Thin: A Natural History of Obesity*, Farrar, Strauss & Giroux, New York.

Bordo, S. 1993, *Unbearable Weight: Feminism, Western Culture and the Body*, University of California Press, Berkeley, Calif.

Brownell, K. D. 1993 'Whether Obesity Should Be Treated', *Health Psychology*, vol. 12, no. 5, pp. 339–41.

Brownell, K. D. & Rodin, J. 1994, 'The Dieting Maelstrom: Is It Possible and Advisable to Lose Weight?', *American Psychologist*, vol. 49, no. 9, pp. 781–91.

Brumberg, J. J. 1988, *Fasting Girls: The Emergence of Anorexia Nervosa as a Modern Disease*, Harvard University Press, Cambridge, Mass.

Burgoyne, J. & Clarke, D. 1983, 'You Are What You Eat: Food and Family Reconstruction', in A. Murcott (ed.), *The Sociology of Food and Eating*, Gower, Aldershot.

Bynum, C. W. 1987, *Holy Feast and Holy Fast: The Religious Significance of Food to Medieval Women*, University of California Press, Berkeley.

Charles, N. & Kerr, M. 1988, *Women, Food and Families*, Manchester University Press, Manchester.

Chernin, K. 1981, *The Obsession: Reflections on the Tyranny of Slenderness*, Harper, New York.

Clark, P. & Hornery, A. 1997 '"Fat is Fab" Campaign that Ate an Editor', *Sydney Morning Herald*, 18 December.

Corrigan, A. & Meredyth, D. 1994, 'The Body Politic', in K. Pritchard Hughs (ed.), *Contemporary Australian Feminism*, Longman, Melbourne.

Crawford, D. A. & Worsley, A. 1988, 'Dieting and Slimming Practices of South Australian Women', *The Medical Journal of Australia*, vol. 148, no. 7, pp. 325–31.

Duncan, M. C. 1994, 'The Politics of Women's Body Images and Practices: Foucault, the Panopticon and Shape Magazine', *Journal of Sport and Social Issues*, vol. 18, no. 1, pp. 48–65.

Ehrenreich, B. & English, D. 1979, *For Her Own Good: 150 Years of the Experts' Advice to Women*, Feminist Press, New York.

Eisenstein, Z. R. 1988, *The Female Body and the Law*, Berkeley, University of California Press, Berkeley, Calif.

Faludi, S. 1991, *Backlash: The Undeclared War against Women*, Chatto & Windus, London.

Featherstone, M., Hepworth, M., & Turner, B. S. (eds) (1991), *The Body: Social Process and Cultural Theory*, Newbury Park, London.

Ferguson, M. 1983, *Forever Feminine: Women's Magazines and the Cult of Femininity*, Heinemann, London.

Foucault, M. 1979, *Discipline and Punish*, Penguin Books, Harmondsworth.

French, S. A., Story, M., Neumark-Sztainer, D., Downes, B., Resnick, M., and Blum, R. 1997, 'Ethnic Differences in Psychosocial and Health Behavior Correlates of Dieting, Purging, and Binge Eating in a Population-Based Sample of Adolescent Females', *International Journal of Eating Disorders*, vol. 22, no. 3, pp. 315–22.

Germov, J. and Williams, L. 1996a, 'The sexual division of dieting: women's voices', *The Sociological Review,* vol. 44, no. 4, pp. 630-647.

Germov, J. and Williams, L. 1996b, 'The epidemic of dieting women: the need for a sociological approach to food and nutrition', *Appetite*, vol. 27, pp. 97-108.

Germov, J. & Williams, L. 1999 (in press), 'Dieting Women: Self-surveillance and the Body Panoptican', in J. Sobal & D. Maurer (eds), *Weighty Issues: Constructing Fatness and Thinness as Social Problems*, Aldine de Gruyder, Hawthorne, NY.

Hesse-Biber, S. 1991, 'Women, Weight and Eating Disorders: A Socio-cultural and Political-Economic Analysis', *Women's Studies International Forum*, vol. 14, no. 3, pp. 173–91.

Huon, G. F., Morris, S. E., & Brown, L. B. 1990, 'Differences between Male and Female Preferences for Female Body Size', *Australian Psychology*, vol. 25, pp. 314–17.

Lester, I. H. 1994, *Australia's Food and Nutrition*, AGPS, Canberra.

McKie, L. J., Wood, R. C., & Gregory, S. 1993, 'Women Defining Health: Food, Diet and Body Image', *Health Education Research*, vol. 8, no. 1, pp. 35–41.

Mennell, S. 1985, *All Manners of Food: Eating and Taste in England and France from the Middle Ages to the Present*, Basil Blackwell, Oxford.

Michie, H. 1987, *The Flesh Made Word: Female Figures and Women's Bodies*, Oxford University Press, New York.

Morris, A., Cooper, T., & Cooper, P. J. 1989, 'The Changing Shape of Female Fashion Models', *International Journal of Eating Disorders*, vol. 8, pp. 593–6.

Murcott, A. 1983, 'Cooking and the Cooked: A Note on the Domestic Preparation of Meals', in A. Murcott (ed.), *The Sociology of Food and Eating*, Gower, Aldershot.

National Heart Foundation 1990, *Risk Factor Prevalence Study: Survey No. 3 1989*, National Heart Foundation of Australia and Australian Institute of Health, Canberra.

Norton, K. I., Olds, T. S., Olive, S., and Dank, S. 1996, 'Ken and Barbie at Life Size', *Sex Roles*, vol 34, nos 3 & 4, pp. 287–94.

O'Brien, S. 1997, '"I Want to Be Just Like You"—Barbie Magazine and the Production of the Female Desiring Subject', *Journal of Interdisciplinary Gender Studies*, vol. 2, no. 2, pp. 51–66.

Orbach, S. 1986, *Hunger Strike*, Faber & Faber, London.

Parker, S., Nichter, M., Nichter, M., Vuckovic, N., Sims, C., & Rittenbaugh, C. 1995, 'Body Image and Weight Concerns among African American and White Adolescent Females: Differences that Make a Difference', *Human Organization*, vol. 54, no. 2, pp. 103–14.

Pringle, R. 1995, 'Destabilising Patriarchy', in B. Caine & R. Pringle (eds), *Transitions: New Australian Feminisms*, Allen & Unwin, Sydney.

Research Institute for Gender and Health 1996, *Data Book for the Baseline Survey of the Australian Longitudinal Study on Women's Health (Main Cohort)*, Research Institute for Gender and Health, University of Newcastle, Newcastle, NSW.

Rothblum, E. D. 1994, '"I'll Die for the Revolution but Don't Ask Me Not to Diet": Feminism and the Continuing Stigmatization of Obesity', in P. Fallon, M. A. Katzman, & S. A. Wooley (eds), *Feminist Perspectives on Eating Disorders*, Guilford Press, New York.

Rubin, G. 1975, 'The Traffic in Women', in R. R. Rayna (ed.), *Toward an Anthropology of Women*, Monthly Review Press, New York, pp. 157–210.

Schur, E. 1983, *Labelling Women Deviant: Gender, Stigma, and Social Control*, Temple University Press, Philadelphia.

Schwartz, H. 1986, *Never Satisfied: A Cultural History of Diets, Fantasies and Fat*, The Free Press, New York.

Seid, R. P. 1994, 'Too "Close to the Bone": The Historical Context for Women's Obsession with Slenderness', in P. Fallon, M. A. Katzman, & S. A. Wooley (eds), *Feminist Perspectives on Eating Disorders*, Guilford Press, New York.

Silverstein, B., Perdue, L., Peterson, B., Vogel, L., & Fantini, D. A. 1986, 'Possible Causes for the Thin Standard of Bodily Attractiveness for Women', *International Journal of Eating Disorders*, vol. 5, pp. 135–44.

Sobal, J. & Cassidy, C. 1987, 'Dieting Foods: Conceptualizations and Explanations', *Ecology of Food and Nutrition*, vol. 20, no. 2, pp. 89–96.

Tiggemann, M. & Pennington, B. 1990, 'The Development of Gender Differences in Body Dissatisfaction', *Australian Psychology*, vol. 25, pp. 306–13.

Turner, B. S. 1992, *Regulating Bodies*, Routledge, London.

Walby, S. 1990, *Theorizing Patriarchy*, Blackwell, Oxford.

—— 1992, 'Post-Post-Modernism? Theorizing Social Complexity', in M. Barrett & A. Phillips (eds), *Destabilizing Theory: Contemporary Feminist Debates*, Polity Press, Cambridge, pp. 31–52.

Wearing, B. 1996, *Gender: The Pain and Pleasure of Difference*, Longman Australia, Melbourne.

Weedon, C. 1987, *Feminist Practice and Poststructuralist Theory*, Blackwell, Oxford.

Wolf, N. 1990, *The Beauty Myth*, Vintage, London.

13

'It's Like They Want You to Get Fat': *Social Reconstruction of Women's Bodies during Pregnancy*[1]

Lauren Williams and Jane Potter

Overview

- *What influence does society have on the size and shape of the bodies of pregnant women?*
- *How does this influence affect eating during pregnancy?*
- *How do women respond to their reconstructed, pregnant bodies?*

The social construction of women's bodies in Western societies means that, for most of their lives, women are pressured to control their weight to conform to a thin, sexually attractive ideal. However, during the life stage of pregnancy, physiological changes are echoed in societal expectations that women will gain weight to conform to a larger, maternal ideal, and thus their bodies are, briefly, 'reconstructed'. This process relies on women eating differently during pregnancy, and for some women, eating becomes problematic. This chapter uses qualitative research to illustrate the pressure to conform to the maternal ideal during pregnancy, examines how this pressure is applied and reinforced, and looks at how the women themselves respond to this pressure. Research in this area has important implications for health during pregnancy, body image for women, and incorporation of the maternal ideal into female self-identity.

Key terms

maternal ideal	social reconstruction
medicalisation	thin ideal
social construction	

---

1 The data-collection stage of this project was undertaken by Angela Moncrieff, Catherine Offner, and Megan Williams on a fieldwork placement as a partial requirement of the Bachelor of Health Science (Nutrition and Dietetics), University of Newcastle, New South Wales. We would like to thank the women who gave freely of themselves in contributing to this study.

Introduction

The available studies of body changes during pregnancy provide an example of the dominance of the scientific perspective. However, the physiological changes of pregnancy occur in a social context, and the sociological perspective explores how women themselves, and the people they interact with, react to this life stage, including changes in the way that their bodies are defined.

In considering women in Western society, we need to examine the **social construction** of women's bodies. This involves exposing the social values, practices, and institutions that influence the way that women's bodies are perceived, valued, and idealised. For example, in previous centuries the ideal female body was socially constructed as a large, voluptuous figure that would be considered obese by today's standards. Therefore, the current cult of thinness, which is socially rewarded in Western societies, is the result of social construction via various historical, cultural, and structural factors (see chapter 12). The desire for social acceptance drives many people to conform to this ideal. To fail to conform is to risk stigmatisation, with obesity perceived to be one of the worst forms of social deviance (see chapter 11). It has been argued that this societal disapproval of overweight is targeted more directly at women (or is at least experienced more by women) (Wiles 1994). Since the **thin ideal** is only attainable by a small percentage of women, body dissatisfaction is common.

The pressure to be thin is applied to women across most of their life span, although there is some evidence that it is experienced more keenly among younger women (Armstrong & Weijohn 1991). However, there is a notable event during the life span of many women when the direction of this weight pressure shifts. This is the life stage of pregnancy, which results in significant physiological change to women's bodies. During pregnancy, there is also a change in societal expectations, and the usual pressure to lose weight and be slim is actually reversed, becoming a pressure to gain weight and become larger. There is a shift from the usual requirement of the thin ideal, which requires a woman to be androgynous, with an impossibly flat stomach, to the **maternal ideal**, which entails a large body, with 'feminine' breasts and hips, and an obviously protruding stomach. Thus, for the duration of pregnancy, the ideal female body is **socially reconstructed**; women are rewarded for having larger bodies, whereas they are required to look small at all other times in their lives.

The pregnant body shape is an external expression of the developing maternal role. Those conforming to the maternal ideal are rewarded by both the social and biomedical systems, while those who fail to conform are more strongly encouraged to conform. Pregnancy is thus a life event that highlights the ways in which women's bodies are reconstructed to fit a new, maternal ideal. As we shall see, this changes the expectations of the way pregnant women should eat, and thus their relationship to food.

Pregnant women are suddenly exposed to the maternal body ideal at a time when many other factors are changing in their lives. There is some anticipation of these changes, and women embark on the journey of pregnancy equipped with certain expectations (Oakley 1980). They expect to see a change in body shape and to gain weight, and there is also the more subtle expectation of the role changes that are about to occur. These expectations are usually constructed from the information they are given and from their previous experiences (Oakley 1980). Despite these expectations, it is the actual lived experience, rather than the anticipated one, to which women and their significant others will respond.

Qualitative research into the experiences of women's bodies during pregnancy can shed light on how women respond to this redefinition of the socially acceptable female body. The experiences of pregnant women have been studied to a limited extent to date, with most of the available literature focusing on the scientific aspects of the bio-logical processes and medical interventions that occur during pregnancy and child-birth. Sociological research seeks to understand the emotional and social implications of pregnancy; however, sociological literature mostly focuses on **medicalisation**, especially in relation to birth (see Oakley 1980), rather than the results of changes in weight and size. There is little research on women's attitudes and feelings to pre-pregnancy weight satisfaction, pregnancy weight gain, post-partum weight loss, and responses to 'expert' advice on weight and nutrition.

This chapter reviews the literature which does exist about pregnant women and the maternal ideal. It also draws on the results of a qualitative research study into the experiences of pregnant women, designed to explore some of the issues neglected in the literature. Twenty women, aged between 15 and 41, were recruited through ante-natal clinics at the local hospital in a large rural town in New South Wales, Australia, during September 1996. Six women were in the first trimester of pregnancy, four were in the second trimester, and the remaining ten in the third trimester. For six women it was their first pregnancy, seven had experienced one previous pregnancy, with the remainder having multiple pregnancies. The study involved in–depth individual interviews with sixteen of the participants and a focus group for the remainder; both techniques using the same semi-structured interview protocol. Questions were aimed at eliciting information about feelings on weight gain, body image, nutrition advice and eating habits during pregnancy. Responses of participants are reported by self-selected pseudonym in the following discussion. We argue that pressure to conform to a new, larger ideal is applied to the pregnant women by partners, friends and family, and is reinforced and legitimised through the medicalisation of pregnancy and the giving of expert advice.

Social reconstruction of women's bodies

In simplified terms, there are two ideal female bodies that reflect two social constructions of women in modern society. The thin ideal represents the social construction of female sexual attractiveness; the maternal ideal represents the fulfilment of women's biological role—the reproduction of the species and, more specifically, the continuance of male lineage. The maternal ideal has a historical background in many cultures that idealised female sexuality and fertility through images of abundantly bodied goddesses and 'Mother Earth' icons. Therefore, a fecund female body has long symbolised fertility and maternity. This historical image continues today, where for the duration of pregnancy women are rewarded for having a larger body.

The bodies of women increasingly come under biological and social scrutiny as pregnancy progresses. Women lose the right to the physical privacy of their body, through both the medical arena (regular, intrusive inspections) and the social (the touching of the pregnant stomach by people not in a position to initiate such intimate touch at other times). The body of the pregnant woman almost becomes public property. During pregnancy, women are seen as having less knowledge about their own bodies and are subject to all types of advice, both expert and non-expert (Oakley 1980). These processes serve to enhance feelings of lack of familiarity with a rapidly changing body.

During pregnancy the objectification of women's bodies is intensified as women become 'incubators of babies' rather than bearers of their own bodies. Women are expected to eat more and differently during the period of their pregnancy, reflecting the change in status of their bodies and roles (Lupton 1996). The responsibility for the nourishment of children originates in pregnancy, when a woman is expected to nourish her body 'appropriately' to ensure the optimal health and development of her growing foetus. This mechanistic image is illustrated in Deborah Lupton's (1996) analysis of the advice in an American book on pregnancy entitled *What to Eat when You're Expecting* by Arlene Eisenberg and others (1990). The authors use the metaphor of the mother as a factory for the production of the foetus, with food as the raw material of production. Women thus become food producers for their children through their own bodies.

As mentioned in the introduction, family and friends, as well as the providers of scientific advice, convey the shift in what is regarded as acceptable for the female body during pregnancy and thus participate in the social reconstruction of women's bodies. Not surprisingly, then, there are rewards for eating behaviours that contribute to developing this larger body. Some participants in the research discussed how 'significant others' encouraged them to eat more because they were pregnant:

BECKY: It's like they want you to get fat.

Pregnancy is often a time when people encourage food treats that they would not otherwise offer in order to help a pregnant woman achieve the socially desired shape and size:

INGRID: My boyfriend says 'Let's go to McDonald's', and he doesn't
            understand that I'd rather have a salad sandwich ... I don't want to
            be a big blimp.

Medical reinforcement of social reconstruction

The process of childbirth has changed dramatically over the course of the twentieth century. In most industrialised countries, women no longer give birth at home, and nearly all women deliver their babies in the hospital setting. This trend has meant that childbirth has gradually become defined as the doctor's responsibility, with this responsibility extended to the period of pregnancy before childbirth. Thus the 'natural' phenomenon of child-bearing has become medicalised.

Medicalisation is the process whereby non-medical problems are described as medical disorders or illnesses (Conrad 1992). Medicalisation describes a situation in a medical framework and adopts a medical intervention to treat or resolve it. In the medicalisation of pregnancy, the doctor comes from the position of power through knowledge, which necessarily reduces the power of the subjective experience of the woman herself in controlling her own body (Oakley 1980). Some women in the study acknowledged this loss of control of their pregnancy:

> LAURA: I went through the first half of my pregnancy knowing nothing until I changed doctors.

This quote exemplifies how the experience of the woman means 'nothing' without a medical explanation. The doctor holds the power to inform, or to leave the woman in 'ignorance'. Other women mentioned that their doctors had withheld information, especially in regard to safe medications during pregnancy. For example, Vicki was forced to ask 'you think—should I really ask?—I feel silly, but I want to know', and Debbie decided: 'You just have to work it out for yourself'.

It is not the purpose of this chapter to critique medical advancements and technologies, or to take a broad view on how the process of medicalisation impacts on the experiences of pregnant women, which have been extensively reviewed elsewhere (see Oakley 1980). This chapter seeks instead to examine how medicalisation and the giving of expert advice contributes to and reinforces the reconstruction of women's bodies during pregnancy.

Advice from medical and other health professionals can be a direct source of pressure on pregnant women. Expert advice may be created at a policy level, and implemented by local practitioners or through written publications. For example, government guidelines on advisable weight gain and nutrient requirements during pregnancy have been established in Australia by the National Health and Medical Research Council (NHMRC), and by similar organisations in other Western countries. The guideline on weight recommends a gain of 10–13 kilograms during pregnancy (Ash & Allen 1986). This gain is to allow for the weight of the foetus, the maternal fat stores, and the fluids for increased circulation (Ash & Allen 1986).

Thus the amount of weight to be gained during pregnancy becomes medicalised by public health bodies, with adherence to these rules being checked by doctors and other health professionals, who monitor how closely women conform to this range. Despite the fact that this is the only time in the life of a non-underweight adult when weight gain above the usual levels is medically sanctioned, women are expected to quickly adapt to this reversed advice. Recommendations on advisable weight gain may be well intentioned, but they can provide the impetus for feelings of maternal inadequacy if rates of weight gain are higher or lower than the narrowly defined acceptable range (MacIntyre 1983).

BECKY: I've probably gained a couple more kilos than I *should* have (emphasis added).

As Becky illustrates, women may gain more, and sometimes less, than the recommended levels. These women are then subject to criticism, and more strongly advised to adhere to the rules, despite the fact that weight gain is not the most significant factor impacting on pregnancy outcome. In reflection of this, there has been a recent tendency among obstetricians in Australia to not taking regular weight measurements, although general practitioners may still weigh pregnant women. Regardless of this unofficial shift in policy, the women still try to conform to recommended weight gain. To not gain enough weight is seen as putting the baby at risk, setting the woman up as a 'bad mother' before her child is even born, a pressure that Ingrid acknowledges:

INGRID: When it wasn't happening like the book said, you tended to panic.

Another area of expert advice concerning pregnancy is that of food and nutrition. It is thought that women need professional advice on how to feed the maternal body. The medical and dietetic literature defines pregnant women as vulnerable in terms of nutrition (Lupton 1996). This nutritional vulnerability is premised on increased nutrient requirements at a time when adverse physiological changes, such as morning sickness, often mean that pregnant women feel less inclined to eat (MacIntyre 1983). The term 'nutritional vulnerability' reinforces the medicalisation of pregnancy. This view is emphasised in medical literature and popular culture such that a pregnant woman feels the pressure to be the perfect pregnant woman (Stern 1993). If she chooses to drink alcohol or eat the 'wrong' foods, she is constructed as negligent and is criticised for risking the health of her developing baby (Lupton 1996). The responsibility of choosing the 'right' foods during pregnancy reinforces the fact that the woman's role has now become functional, and that eating has become the means to the ideal maternal body image.

Most women in the study reported trying to establish healthy eating patterns after becoming pregnant. They felt an increased amount of pressure to follow expert advice and made conscious dietary changes along recommended lines:

DEBBIE: You do become very conscious of what you're doing.

The changes reported by some of the women included eating breakfast when they previously had not, consuming more fruit and vegetables, increasing their consumption of dairy foods, or taking calcium and iron supplements. Women also tried to eat less foods labelled as 'unhealthy', but noted that cravings for sweet foods and increased appetite made such eating more difficult:

JUDY: It's more important to eat healthy, but harder, too.
SUSAN: I know what I've got to eat—but I've got no will-power.

These quotes illustrate that the women accepted the expert nutritional wisdom, but found it difficult to follow in reality. Some, like Susan, blamed themselves for their inability to meet these standards. This denies the physiological effects of pregnancy, which tend to enhance appetite during the later stages.

Some respondents experienced cravings or aversions for particular foods in pregnancy. Women usually linked food cravings with an increase in appetite and the tendency to overeat, sometimes leading to health problems:

> SUSAN: I eat everything I see.
>
> INGRID: I ate whatever was in the fridge—I'd get stuck into the chockies, and then I'd miss dinner—I'd start skipping meals, so that … I ended up in hospital with high blood pressure.
>
> FIONA: I just eat constantly.

These women, while being encouraged by others to eat and gain weight, saw overeating as a personal failing and expressed guilt when they indulged their cravings for sweet foods, in case they gained weight above the advisable upper limit:

> NATALIE: I feel guilty and depressed—I go for a walk after eating sweet foods.

The provision of expert advice around weight gain and nutritional intake may disempower pregnant women and inflict guilt if they cannot conform to the exacting standards. Medicalisation and the giving of expert advice, while aiding in physiological aspects of pregnancy, may contribute to the pressure women feel to change their body shape and size during pregnancy. The next section of the chapter examines how women respond to this pressure.

Women's responses to the social reconstruction of the female ideal

The argument about the social pressure to conform to a maternal ideal during pregnancy is not intended to imply that women play a passive role in the process. Women actively respond to the maternal ideal in a variety of ways depending on their response to the pressure to conform to the thin ideal before pregnancy, and the extent to which they have redefined their social role during pregnancy. Ellen Stern (1993) reflects on this, stating that women have a variety of self-images during pregnancy, ranging from fat to feminine. Stern states that pregnancy is often a 'turning point' in the way that women relate to their body-image. Some women in the study responded negatively to their changing bodies, others positively, depending on satisfaction with their usual body weights and the extent to which self-perception had shifted with impending motherhood. This affected the way they viewed and consumed food.

Concern with weight gain: pregnant women still striving to conform to the thin ideal

Some women rejected the maternal ideal and continued trying to conform to the thin ideal. That is not to say that they dieted or changed their behaviour to conform to the thin ideal—their bodies underwent the inevitable physiological changes of pregnancy. However, they continued to hold a mental perception of the thin ideal as that to which they should aspire. Many women in the study expressed their dislike of gaining weight during pregnancy, especially because of the loss of control over the gain, given that they would usually control weight gain through dieting. Although they felt unhappy about their pregnancy weight gain, they agreed that they would not diet until after pregnancy for fear of harming the baby.

> ROWENA: You do (think of dieting), but then you'd worry about doing something to the baby.

It would seem that these women still sought to conform to the thin ideal, but bowed to the social and physiological pressure of the maternal ideal, without actually accepting it. Thus they increased their body size, but at the same time, they felt guilty about the weight gain and were dissatisfied with their new bodies.

> JUDY: That's when you get depressed—when you look in the mirror. When I look in the mirror, I think yuck!

Attractiveness and sexuality

One consequence of the social reconstruction of women's bodies during pregnancy is that they become desexualised. Attractiveness and thinness are two ideals that are deeply entwined in Western society, and women are usually expected to be both. The social construction of female bodies reinforces for women that they are accepted and valued according to how they look, which is tied up with being sexually attractive to men. However, during pregnancy it is physically impossible to conform to the thin ideal, resulting in a concomitant inability to conform to the societal definition of attractiveness. While body size gets redefined during pregnancy to new, maternal standards, the common standard of attractiveness does not. This reinforces R. Wiles's (1994) observation that, in a society that equates attractiveness with slimness, women move from being decorative to being functional, or even mechanical, during pregnancy.

Many of the women in the study felt less sexually attractive during pregnancy, because of the weight gain:

> BECKY: I don't think of myself as ugly, but I don't think of myself as sexually attractive ... you don't see yourself as a sexual person any more; it's almost like the roles are different.
> KATIE: I feel less attractive because of my size.

The sexual attractiveness role is obscured by pregnancy, where the 'main function' of the woman is to bear a child. There are many taboos around intercourse with pregnant women, and sexual abstinence may result from the common belief among men in Western society that intercourse will somehow harm the unborn child. This reinforces the message to the woman that she is an incubator of a baby, rather than a sexual being. Some women expressed insecurity about their partners' feelings towards them during pregnancy:

> SUSAN: My boyfriend says I'm beautiful, but I say, 'No I'm not—I'm fat', because I know he thinks I'm big.
>
> TRACEY: It makes you feel good when your husband says that you're beautiful ... but you don't believe it.

Some women even felt that the maternal ideal gave them increased sexual attractiveness, reflected in their partner's admiration:

> JUDY: My husband says, 'Oh you've got big boobs now'.

In Judy's case, the adoption of the maternal ideal was sexually rewarded.

Research has found that women who are concerned about their pre-pregnancy weight are also the most worried about their weight during and after pregnancy (Armstrong & Weijohn 1991). This was borne out in our research study, in which those participants who were unhappy about putting on weight during pregnancy were all dissatisfied with their pre-pregnant weight, despite the fact that they were not medically classified as overweight.

Release from the social pressure to be thin

The situation was different for the women in the study who were medically classified as overweight before pregnancy. In line with R. Wiles's (1994) observations, these women noticed a shift in societal attitudes towards their size. They felt that their large size was now accepted, since it conformed to the dominant (maternal) ideal, whereas before pregnancy they were subject to the stigma associated with overweight in a society obsessed with thinness. This transient release from the social pressures to be thin, to which they had not conformed before pregnancy, allowed these women to feel more positive about their bodies.

> DEBBIE: I love my pregnant body; I feel better about myself.

One woman who had gained a lot of weight during pregnancy expressed the release from social pressures to stay thin that came through liberating her eating:

> INGRID: I look at it like—if I want chockies, I can have chockies—I don't really have to worry about my weight at the moment ... I'll deal with that later.

Thus, Ingrid had relaxed her usual eating restrictions with the removal of pressure to conform to a thin ideal.

Embracing the maternal ideal

Some women used the change in body size over the period of pregnancy to reconstruct their self-identities as mothers, thus taking an active part in assuming the maternal role:

> TRACEY: I love being pregnant.
>
> DEBBIE: You've got a baby growing inside you, so it doesn't really matter what you look like on the outside … if you want a baby, you've got to get the big belly.

Other women showed a resigned acceptance that the physiological changes were a necessary part of the process:

> BECKY: Getting a bit of a stomach I'm feeling OK about; I mean you expect those things to happen.
>
> INGRID: Your boobs sag, you get stretch marks, you gain weight … I mean there's no use complaining about it—it's something that happens.

One of the study participants expressed relief at attaining a body shape that no longer caused any confusion about the reason for her body size:

> ANNA: I hate the stage where you just look fat, but it's not a problem once you look pregnant.

Anna recognises that if she is perceived as merely putting on weight, she would be stigmatised, and is uncomfortable about this prospect. However, as soon as her body makes it clear that the extra size is the result of pregnancy, it ceases to be 'a problem'—that is, she is no longer stigmatised, but will instead be rewarded. The initial increase in body weight and size is identical, whether it be because of fat or pregnancy; it is her own reaction and the reactions of other people that seem to concern Anna, rather than her actual size and shape.

Return of the thin ideal: fear of not being able to lose weight after pregnancy

Understanding the beliefs of pregnant women about losing weight after delivery is another piece of the information needed to understand women's feelings about their bodies during pregnancy, and one that does not appear to have been previously reported in the literature.

The child-bearing years are a time when excess weight gain begins for many women (Smith et al. 1994; Rossner 1992). Recent research in the USA has indicated that rates of weight gain are higher for women than they are for men in the age group 25–34 years (Manson et al. 1994). Women in this age range are twice as likely as are men to experience a weight gain of five kilograms (per squared metre of height). It has been suggested that this can be explained by the number of women in this age group experiencing their first pregnancy. On average, women tend to gain 2–3 kilograms after their first pregnancy (Manson et al. 1994).

Even the women who felt relieved from the pressure to be slim during pregnancy were well-aware that, after delivery, the societal expectation will be for them to revert from child-bearers to sexual beings and therefore to lose the weight. This shows the women were aware of the transitory nature of the shift in social acceptability of an increased weight and shape. Revisiting Ingrid's words:

INGRID: I don't really have to worry about my weight at the moment ... I'll deal with that later.

This quotation shows that Ingrid acknowledges there will be a time when she again has to worry about her weight. Some women feared that they would not be able to return to previous body weight and shape after pregnancy:

KATIE: I hope I'm one of the lucky ones that the weight just drops off.
JUDY: That's what I'm worried about ... going back to my normal weight.
FIONA: I want to try to get back to what [weight] I am now—I just don't know if it's possible.

This was especially true of the younger women interviewed, who appeared to be more concerned about losing weight after the pregnancy because of the social implications:

SUSAN: You feel so self-conscious about what you're going to look like if you don't lose the weight, and you're so young—no one else will be like it.
TRACEY: You think: 'Will I look the same when I finish?' You've still got a social life and trendy clothes and stuff.

Women who had successfully lost weight after previous pregnancies and those who were older were confident that losing the weight would be difficult but possible:

JANE: Now I know I can do it, it's not worrying me.

Women in their first pregnancy and those that had had difficulty losing weight after previous pregnancies tended to express concern about post-partum weight loss:

MAREE: I think it's harder to lose weight after each pregnancy.

The opinions of others about losing weight after pregnancy seemed to have a strong influence on those women who were in their first pregnancy:

INGRID: I know of women who say you won't lose weight or are really negative.

Respondents most often cited dieting and exercise as the main methods by which they would attempt to lose weight after pregnancy. However, many women emphasised that there would be a number of barriers to exercising after pregnancy, such as lack of time because of work commitments, caring for a newborn, and tiredness. Some women believed that breast-feeding would help them to lose the weight:

INGRID: Breast-feeding takes a lot of it [weight], anyway.

Thus they recognised that they would experience pressure to conform to the thin ideal again soon, but that conforming to that ideal would be logistically more difficult.

Conclusion

The bodies of women are socially constructed from an early age in Western society. The social pressure on women to conform to a thin ideal shapes the way that they view their bodies, resulting in widespread body dissatisfaction, dieting, and disordered eating. Despite the fact that for most of their lives women are bombarded with messages about the need to be slim, they are expected rapidly to assimilate the reverse message of weight gain and maternal body shape during the social reconstruction of their bodies in pregnancy. The physiological changes of pregnancy thus take place in a social context. Friends, family, and the health professionals alike expect women to accept and respond positively to adopting the maternal ideal, an ideal that is located outside the usual social standards of sexual attractiveness. This maternal ideal, associated with a long historical tradition of fertility, is socially constructed and medically defined to lie within narrowly defined boundaries.

Women respond to the social reconstruction of their bodies in a variety of ways, which may have significance for the quality of their pregnancies and for their pregnant and non-pregnant body images. A certain amount of weight gain and body-shape change is biologically inevitable. While women may allow, and actively seek, these biological changes, it does not mean that they fully accept their bodies during that period, and some women experience intense body dissatisfaction during pregnancy. This dissatisfaction has the potential to decrease the quality of the pregnancy experience, and may even be symbolic of the rejection of the maternal role. Other women love their pregnant bodies as symbols of their new maternal status, while still others, who were overweight before pregnancy, find a new body acceptance during pregnancy since they conform to the dominant societal ideal, and are released from the usual stigmatisation regarding their size.

The pregnant body is a transitory one, however, and after delivery of their babies, women are expected, and expect themselves, to once again conform to the thin ideal of sexual attractiveness. This view of the social construction of the female body as labile has implications for body acceptance or body dissatisfaction during pregnancy, and for later body image, and requires further exploration.

Summary of main points

- The bodies of women in Western society are socially constructed to conform to an idealised standard of thinness.
- During pregnancy, the desired standard shifts to that of the maternal ideal, in a process termed 'social reconstruction'.

- Pressure to conform to the maternal ideal is mediated by family and friends, and by the medical and health professions.
- Women are encouraged to eat more and differently during pregnancy in order to achieve the maternal ideal, but at a time when many have difficulty with eating.
- Women respond to the maternal ideal in a variety of ways: some reject it and feel dissatisfaction with their bodies during pregnancy; some accept it in embracing the maternal role; while others, who were overweight before pregnancy, find a new social acceptance in their size.

Discussion questions

1 Explain what is meant by the expression 'the social construction of women's bodies'?
2 In what ways is pregnancy medicalised? How can this be a negative experience for women?
3 Explain the authors' concept of the social reconstruction of women's bodies away from the thin ideal and towards the maternal ideal during pregnancy.
4 How is this reconstruction mediated?
5 What influence does this reconstruction have on the way pregnant women eat?

Further reading

Armstrong, J. E. & Weijohn, T. T. 1991, 'Dietary Quality and Concerns about Body Weight of Low-Income Pregnant Women', *Journal of the American Dietetic Association*, vol. 91, no. 10, pp. 1280–4.
Lupton, D. 1996, *Food, the Body and the Self*, Sage, London.
Oakley, A. 1980, *Women Confined: Towards a Sociology of Childbirth*, Martin Robertson, Oxford.
Stern, E. S. 1993, *Expecting Change: The Emotional Journey through Pregnancy*, Bantam, New York.
Wiles, R. 1994, 'I'm Not Fat, I'm Pregnant: The Impact of Pregnancy on Fat Women's Body Image', in S. Wilkinson & C. Kitzinger (eds), *Women and Health: Feminist Perspectives*, Taylor & Francis, London.

References

Armstrong, J. E. and Weijohn, T. T. 1991, 'Dietary Quality and Concerns about Body Weight of Low-Income Pregnant Women', *Journal of the American Dietetic Association*, vol. 91, no. 10, pp. 1280–4.
Ash, S. & Allen, J. 1986, *Nutrition and Pregnancy: A Guide to Nutrition and Lifestyle during Pregnancy and Breastfeeding*, Reed, Sydney.
Conrad, P. 1992, 'Medicalisation and Social Control', *Annual Review of Sociology*, vol. 18, pp. 209–32.
Eisenberg, A., Murcoff, H. E., & Hathaway, S. E. 1990, *What to Eat When You're Expecting*, Angus & Robertson, Sydney

Lupton, D. 1996, *Food, the Body and the Self*, Sage, London.

MacIntyre, S. 1983, 'The Management of Food in Pregnancy', in A. Murcott (ed.), *The Sociology of Food and Eating*, Gower, Aldershot.

Manson, J. E., Colditz, G. A., & Stampfer, M. J. 1994, 'Parity, Ponderosity and the Paradox of a Weight-Preoccupied Society', *Journal of the American Medical Association*, vol. 271, no. 22, pp. 1788–91.

Oakley, A. 1980, *Women Confined: Towards a Sociology of Childbirth*, Martin Robertson, Oxford.

Rossner, S. 1992, 'Pregnancy, Weight Cycling and Weight Gain in Obesity', *International Journal of Obesity*, vol. 16, pp. 145–7.

Smith, D. E., Lewis, C. E., Caveny J. L., Perkins L. L., Burke, G. L., & Bild, D. E. 1994, 'Longitudinal Changes in Adiposity Associated with Pregnancy: The CARDIA Study', *Journal of the American Medical Association*, vol. 271, pp. 1747–52.

Stern, G. S. 1993, *Expecting Change: The Emotional Journey through Pregnancy*, Bantam, New York.

Wiles, R. 1994, 'I'm Not Fat, I'm Pregnant: The Impact of Pregnancy on Fat Women's Body Image', in S. Wilkinson & C. Kitzinger (eds), *Women and Health: Feminist Perspectives*, Taylor & Francis, London.

14

Motherhood, Morality, and Infant Feeding

Elizabeth Murphy, Susan Parker, and Christine Phipps

Overview

- *What are the current trends in infant feeding in industrialised countries?*

- *What role do experts play in influencing mothers' infant-feeding practices?*

- *How can policy responses to concerns about infant feeding be seen as individualising a social problem?*

The decline in the frequency and duration of breast-feeding in industrialised countries during the early part of this century has been a matter of concern to policy-makers. Increases in breast-feeding during the 1970s and early 1980s now appear to have levelled off. Currently one-quarter of mothers in the United Kingdom and less than one-fifth of mothers in the USA breast-feed their babies for the minimum recommended period. Rather more Australian mothers breast-feed, but there is still a significant proportion who do not. This situation causes concern to policy-makers and health professionals because of evidence that breast-feeding promotes the health of babies and protects them against a range of illnesses. In this chapter, we consider the ways in which the 'problem' of infant feeding has been individualised and transformed into a question of maternal morality. We go on to consider recent reforms in hospital practices surrounding infant feeding in the immediate postnatal period, suggesting that, while these are welcome, they run the risk of replacing one expert orthodoxy with another. Finally, we consider how, in infant feeding, as in other aspects of child-rearing, experts have been invested with the power to define what counts as 'good mothering'. Drawing upon data from a current study of infant feeding in Nottingham, England,[1] we show how mothers' accounts of their decisions about infant feeding can be read as displays of morality and responsibility in the face of expectations about what it means to be a good wife or girlfriend and a good woman, as well as a good mother.

Key terms

deviance
medicalisation

Introduction

One of the most immediate decisions facing a new mother in a contemporary industrialised society concerns how her baby is to be fed. In practice, the alternatives are limited to a choice between breast milk or infant formula milk. Medical opinion and health and nutrition policy are unequivocal: 'breast is best'. Internationally, the World Health Organization and the United Nations' Children's Fund are committed to promoting breast-feeding. This pro–breast-feeding stance is reflected in the policies of individual governments. In the United Kingdom, for example, exclusive breast-feeding is recommended for the first four months of a baby's life (DHSS 1988; Department of Health 1994). In the USA in 1979, the American Academy of Pediatrics recommended exclusive breast-feeding for six months (American Academy of Pediatrics 1978). Guidelines from the Australian National Health and Medical Research Council emphasise the 'unequalled value of breast milk as the sole food for infants for the first 4–6 months of life' (National Health and Medical Research Council 1995, p. 3). These recommendations are justified primarily in terms of the perceived health benefits to the breast-fed baby. Breast-feeding, it is argued, protects the baby against infection, allergy, and over- or underfeeding, and reduces the risk of contamination (Quandt 1986). Health benefits may extend beyond the period of infant feeding (Campbell 1996) to include protection against insulin-dependent diabetes, Crohn's disease, and some childhood cancers later in life (Lawrence 1995). The range of proposed non-nutritional advantages to the child includes both improved mother–infant bonding and increased confidence and self-esteem. Some benefits to the mother, such as weight loss, reduced rates of ovarian and breast cancer, and greater self-esteem have also been proposed, but the overwhelming emphasis in the expert literature is upon the baby's welfare.

In this chapter, we shall be considering the extent to which these policy recommendations are or are not reflected in women's feeding practices. We shall discuss the assumptions underpinning the response of policy-makers and health professionals to women's 'failure' to feed their babies as recommended. First, we shall argue that by focusing upon mothers' individual behaviour as the central problem, official perspectives distract attention from the 'working conditions' (Carter 1995) under which women feed their babies and that constrain the decisions that they make. We shall consider the way in which such individualisation transforms a nutritional matter into a problem of maternal morality. A second response to the problem of infant feeding has been the reform of hospital practices that have been associated with early cessation of breast-feeding. We shall argue that, while these reforms are welcome, they risk replacing one expert

1   We are grateful to the women and health professionals who took part in this study and to colleagues in the Department of General Practice at the University of Nottingham who assisted us with sampling and access. This research was funded by a grant from the Economic and Social Research Council (United Kingdom) as part of 'The Nation's Diet' program (Grant Number L209252035).

orthodoxy with another. The power of experts to define 'good mothering' by setting standards for infant feeding will be demonstrated, drawing upon data from our longitudinal study of the choices mothers make in relation to infant feeding. Throughout the chapter we shall show how the ways in which women feed their babies raise issues not only of nutrition, but also of morality and maternal responsibility.

Contemporary patterns of infant feeding

In spite of strong scientific support for breast-feeding, current rates of breast-feeding are relatively low in most of the industrialised world. In both the United Kingdom and the USA, marked increases in rates of breast-feeding were observed between the early 1970s and the mid-1980s. In 1970 only 26 per cent of mothers in the USA initiated breast-feeding, but this had risen to 60 per cent in 1984 (Hartley & O'Connor 1996). Similar, if less extreme, rises occurred in the United Kingdom. In 1975, 51 per cent of mothers started to breast-feed their babies (Martin 1978), but by 1980, this had risen to 67 per cent (Martin & Monk 1982). However, hopes of continued growth in the popularity of breast-feeding have not been fulfilled. A survey of infant-feeding practices in Great Britain, which was carried out in 1990, reported that 63 per cent of babies were initially breast-fed (White et al. 1992). The most recent survey (Foster et al. 1997) shows a significant increase in initial breast-feeding rates between 1990 and 1995, with 68 per cent of British mothers initiating breast-feeding in 1995. However, once these data were standardised for age and occupational class, these differences disappeared. A marked decline is reported in the USA, where the rate of initial breast-feeding had fallen to 51 per cent in 1990 (Hartley & O'Connor 1996). In both countries, the increase in initial breast-feeding in the 1970s appears to have either levelled off or been reversed. In the 1980s Australia had one of the highest rates of initial breast-feeding in the world (85 per cent at hospital discharge) (Palmer 1985).

Official concern about the decline of breast-feeding centres not only on those babies who are never breast-fed, but also on those whose mothers breast-feed for less than the recommended duration. In 1990, only 25 per cent of British mothers were breast-feeding four months after their babies' births (the minimum recommended duration) (White et al. 1992). In the USA, just under 20 per cent of women were still breast-feeding their babies at six months (the minimum recommended duration in that country) (Hartley &O'Connor 1996). Once again, figures for Australia are somewhat higher, with 40–42 per cent of mothers breast-feeding their babies at six months (Palmer 1985).

Infant feeding as a social problem

For health professionals and policy-makers alike, infant feeding is a social problem. In spite of the consensus among experts about how mothers *ought* to feed their babies, and about the risks of not doing so, the majority of women still fail to meet the officially recommended targets. Current concerns about the decline of breast-feeding are not a new phenomenon. However much policy-makers may reminisce about a golden age before the introduction of formula-feeding, there is evidence (Lewis 1990; Arnup 1990; Carter 1995; Fildes 1992) that anxiety about women's failure to breast-feed their babies is not new. In the eighteenth century concern focused upon women who sent their babies out to be wet-nursed rather than feeding them themselves (Maher 1992; Carter 1995). In 1747 William Cadogan, an influential physician, berated women who did not feed their own babies, ascribing the refusal to do so to a woman's reluctance to 'give up a little of the Beauty of her Breast to feed her off-spring' (Cadogan , as quoted in Carter 1995, p.7). While Cadogan attributed the popularity of wet-nursing to women's vanity, other contemporary sources suggest that it had more to do with the insistence of husbands on their sexual privileges. Vanessa Maher (1992) describes how, in the sixteenth, seventeenth, and eighteenth centuries, it was believed that sexual intercourse would 'spoil the milk', and so men prevented their wives from breast-feeding rather than give up their sexual rights.

As Katherine Arnup (1990), Jane Lewis (1990), and Valerie Fildes (1992) all show, the failure of women to breast-feed was a particular source of public and professional anxiety in the early twentieth century in both the United Kingdom and Canada. Fildes (1992) reports doctors' concerns about the decline of breast-feeding in the United Kingdom in the late nineteenth and early twentieth centuries. Arnup (1990) relates this preoccupation with mothers who did not breast-feed their babies to wider public anxieties about national adequacy. In the United Kingdom the discovery, during recruitment for the Boer War, that a substantial proportion of working-class men were unfit for military service provoked concerns about the state of the nation's health. In Canada, similar issues arose during the First World War. In both countries, attention focused upon evidence of high rates of infant mortality, and in turn these were attributed to women's failure to breast-feed their babies.

In Canada the policy response was to establish a complex public health bureaucracy (Arnup 1990). The emphasis was upon prevention, and the experts were adamant that most infant deaths could be avoided. However, the concept of prevention was a somewhat limited one. While these reformers acknowledged that a range of factors, including poverty, overcrowding, and malnutrition, were all associated with infant mortality, they focused their efforts on the reform of maternal behaviour and, in particular, the promotion of breast-feeding. As Arnup acknowledges, the reformers were undoubtedly right in viewing breast-feeding as the safest form of infant feeding. However, their exclusive focus upon maternal behaviour served to distract attention from the social and material causes of infant mortality and placed the responsibility for infant survival entirely upon mothers' shoulders.

Lewis (1990) describes how similar concerns arose in England during the same period. Working class women were seen as a particular problem, and their education and reform was presented as the key to improving the health of the nation. Once again, by focusing upon the supposed 'ignorance and carelessness of mothers' (G. Newman 1906, as quoted in Carter 1995, p. 41), such policies distracted attention from the wider causes of infant mortality. As Lewis remarks, 'The fault lay not in offering mothers information on child rearing, which they welcomed, but in subordinating the material conditions of their lives—the poverty and unsanitary living conditions—which were also at the root of the problem and which early twentieth century medical reports adequately diagnosed, to an individualist solution' (Lewis 1990, p. 6).

Research into contemporary patterns of infant feeding shows that both the initiation and the duration of breast-feeding are consistently associated with the mother's social and economic location. Women who are older, better educated, from higher occupational classes, and who are living with partners on higher incomes are more likely to start breast-feeding and to continue breast-feeding for longer (Wright & Walker 1983; Florack 1984; Simopoulos & Grave 1984; Hitchcock & Coy 1988; Martin & White 1988; Bailey & Sherriff 1993; Lowe 1993; White et al. 1992; Cooper et al. 1993; Pesssl 1996; Piper & Parks 1996; Foster et al. 1997). From the perspective of policy-makers and health professionals, these patterns are paradoxical. Those women who can least afford to buy infant formula, and whose babies are in greatest need of the protection and health promoting qualities of breast milk, are least likely to breast-feed.

The professional and policy response to evidence of such socioeconomic variations in infant-feeding practices has largely been restricted to 'targeting'. Having identified the population groups who are least likely to breast-feed, health professionals are encouraged to direct their educational and promotional activities towards these groups, in an attempt to persuade such mothers to breast-feed their babies. Educational programs sometimes include more 'support' for women in the most disadvantaged groups. However, such support is generally seen as verbal encouragement and advice, rather than any attempt to modify the conditions under which women feed their babies. Once again the problem of infant feeding is individualised. While the research informing such targeting exercises frequently refers to the 'determinants' of infant-feeding practices (for example, Salt et al. 1994), these tend to be seen as immutable. Little attention has been paid to uncovering the processes by which material and social disadvantage operate to constrain the decisions that mothers make about how they will feed their babies, and even less to how such disadvantages might be overcome, other than by encouraging individual mothers to compensate for them. Yet, the establishment of successful breast-feeding, which often initially involves frequent feeding sessions throughout the day and night (Quandt 1986), makes heavy demands on a mother's time and energy (Murphy et al. 1998b). Securing optimal infant nutrition is only one of the (sometimes competing) tasks in which women are involved as they feed their babies (Murphy et al. 1998a). A mother's capacity to meet such demands will be inextricably linked to the availability of other human and material resources. For example, the new mother who is supported by her partner, family members, or friends can breast-feed her baby while others take on responsibility for running the home and provide her with the essential time for both feeding and rest. In later weeks, when time between feeds is at a premium, breast-feeding will also be easier for those women who have access to a car and can make necessary journeys to the supermarket or the health centre quickly, rather than by public transport. Breast-feeding is a form of work to which a mother may not be able readily to commit herself if it conflicts with other tasks for which she has responsibility.

The individualising of social problems is not restricted to infant feeding. Naomi Aronson (1982) has shown how the rise of nutritional science in the late nineteenth century was characterised by the attribution of malnutrition to the shortcomings of the poor rather than to poverty per se. By presenting the cause of poor living standards as the poor's extravagance and mismanagement, rather than their limited access to resources, nutritionists offered politicians an expedient response to the 'labour problem'. The nutritional problems of the poor were to be solved not by relieving poverty, but by educating the poor to shop and cook more economically. Emphasising the contribution that individual behaviour, whether it be household management or breast-feeding, makes to health can be seen to be politically expedient. In the case of breast-feeding, by emphasising the one aspect of the situation over which mothers might, superficially at least, be said to exercise control, other sources of infant morbidity and mortality are rendered less visible. Infant feeding becomes a problem of individual morality and responsibility.

The impact of hospital practices on infant feeding

One area where women's individualised obligation to feed their babies in approved ways is tempered by the recognition that what others do can be significant relates to what happens in the period immediately after a baby's birth. In particular, hospital management of infant feeding is seen as either obstructing or facilitating breast-feeding. Experts recognise that, in the past, hospital practices have undermined breast-feeding. Current policies can be seen as a self-conscious recantation of former practices. The discovery that women who stay longer in hospital are more likely to give up breast-feeding than those who leave hospital early has contributed to this change of heart (White et al. 1992). National surveys of infant feeding in the United Kingdom show that certain hospital practices affect the likelihood of successful breast-feeding. In particular, early termination of breast-feeding has been associated with delay in putting the baby to the breast after delivery, operative deliveries, having a general anaesthetic, the baby's admission to special care, offering supplementary feeds of formula milk, and feeding at set times rather than 'on demand'. The link between hospitalisation and early termination of breast-feeding was observed as long ago as 1943, when a government report noted that babies born in British hospitals were less likely to be breast-fed than those who were born at home (Ministry of Health 1943, in Carter 1995).

Experts attribute the negative impact of traditional hospital practices on breast-feeding to wrong advice and mismanagement. The solution proposed is to give good advice and better management. A significant response to mounting evidence of iatrogenic practices has been the Baby-Friendly Hospitals Initiative. This program was launched by the World Health Organization and the United Nations' Children's Fund in 1991, with the aim of 'ensuring health care environments where breast feeding is the norm' (Saadeh & Akre 1996, p. 154). Hospitals have been urged to change policies and discard practices that have discouraged breast-feeding. Such changes may be seen as a helpful response to evidence of the negative impact of previous hospital practices upon breast-feeding rates. However, as we discuss below, these reforms do not challenge, and indeed may reinforce, the fundamental assumption that experts should have the authority to define and control hospital practices in relation to infant feeding.

These reforms of hospital lactation policies are analogous to contemporary responses to criticisms of the **medicalisation** of childbirth and of interventionist obstetric management (also mentioned in chapter 13). Just as the appropriateness of traditional hospital practices in relation to breast-feeding has been challenged, so too the effectiveness (and humanity) of the so-called 'active management of childbirth'—through such procedures as caesarean section, induction of labour, and foetal monitoring—has been called into question (see, for example, Foster 1995; Tew 1995). It has been argued that these and other routine practices, such as the shaving of pubic hair, the administration of enemas, and the routine use of episiotomies, have all had distressing and even harmful consequences for women in childbirth. Here the criticism is that obstetric practices have failed to live up to the claims that their advocates and practitioners make for them. As in infant feeding, the problem is seen to be one of misinformation and mismanagement, and the response has been to advocate 'evidence-based' practices and policies.

There is, however, a more fundamental, and explicitly feminist, critique of expert interventions in childbirth, which might be extended to apply to infant feeding. Rather than simply questioning the effectiveness of particular practices, critics argue that the rise of interventionist obstetrics represents the exercise of male domination and professional power. Experts (usually male) have succeeded in taking control of women's bodies and have replaced a natural process with interventionist strategies. Obstetricians are condemned for turning a 'normal' process into a technological event or, as Ann Oakley has described it, 'an expert mystery' (1993, p. 124). Feminists have argued that such obstetric practices represent the exercise of patriarchal power and the imposition of passivity on women. From this perspective, recent moves towards humanising hospital childbirth, however welcome, miss the point. Merely being nicer to women in childbirth does no more than conceal the iron fist of medical control within a velvet glove.

Similarly, reforms of hospital lactation policies can be seen as no more than changing one set of expert directives for another. While specific hospital practices have undergone radical transformation, in response to evidence that they were undermining rather than promoting breast-feeding, there has been no fundamental break with the assumption that experts should define and control infant feeding. Breast-feeding, too, has become an 'expert mystery' (Oakley 1993, p. 124). Randa Saadeh and James Akre, technical officers with the World Health Organization, present 'ten steps' that hospitals aspiring to be designated as 'Baby Friendly' must take (Saadeh & Akre 1996). These steps espouse the rhetoric of maternal choice. For example, we are told, 'Mothers should be counselled correctly, and enabled to make and carry through informed choices' (Saadeh & Akre 1996, p. 155). However, it is clear that such 'correct counselling' is defined as that which will promote 'a positive attitude towards breast feeding' (p. 155). Some of the 'ten steps' can be seen as compatible with a commitment to promote maternal choice. For example, step 3 requires professionals to 'inform all pregnant women about the benefits and management of breast feeding' (p. 155). Here the emphasis is upon giving women accurate information on which to base their decision. However, other recommended steps appear to demand more active professional control of how babies are fed while they are in hospital. For example, step 6 states that newborn infants should be given 'no food or drink other than breast milk, unless medically indicated'. This directive is justified in terms of the evidence that supplementary feeding is associated with an increase in early cessation of breast-feeding. It presents the decision about whether supplementary drinks of water or infant formula should be offered as one that professionals rather than mothers are mandated to take.

Just as current attempts to reform obstetric practices do not represent a 'de-medicalisation' of childbirth, so the changes in hospital infant-feeding practices, reflected in the Baby-Friendly Hospitals Initiative, do not challenge the assumption that experts should decide how babies should be fed. In spite of the rhetoric of women's choice, the object of the Baby-Friendly Hospitals Initiative is to 'manage' the hospital environment in such a way that mothers will make and sustain the 'right' (that is, expert-defined) choice. In that sense, the reforms represent the substitution of one expert orthodoxy for another. Clearly, the extent to which such directives actually limit maternal autonomy in practice will depend upon the spirit in which they are implemented. However, there is evidence that some health professionals are uneasy about the potentially coercive implementation of the Baby-Friendly Hospitals Initiative in some British hospitals, recently described in the nursing press as a 'dictatorial drive that denies mothers their right to choose' (Casey 1996, p. 1).

Expert advice and infant feeding

The medicalisation of infant feeding can be seen as just one aspect of the growing involvement of professional experts in all aspects of child rearing and family life throughout the twentieth century. Dorothy Chunn (1990) describes the impact of the new 'cadre of experts': 'Good mothering, parenthood, marital sex were not simply a matter of following biological instinct: they were activities requiring the most specialized knowledge and training' (p. 92). Thus, as Lynn Jamieson and Claire Toynbee (1990) have argued, the needs of children are now defined by professionals rather than by parents, and experts have acquired the power to overrule parents' definitions of reality. Parents, and in particular mothers, bear the responsibility of meeting such expert-defined needs, in expert-approved ways, rather than identifying and interpreting their children's needs for themselves. More traditional sources of information, such as family and friends, have been displaced (Arnup 1990). Harriette Marshall shows how modern child-care manuals warn mothers about the dangers of the 'many old wives' tales, horror stories and unfounded advice which continues to surround motherhood' (Gordon Bourne 1979, as quoted in Marshall 1991, p. 73). The dominance of science and technology has led to an assumption that lay people, particularly parents, are in need of expert guidance. In infant feeding, as elsewhere, the child's needs and the optimal means of meeting those needs are now defined by experts (see chapter 15 for an alternative viewpoint).

While recognising that infant feeding has become an 'expert domain', we should not exaggerate the power of experts to control infant feeding. Women are not simply passive recipients of expert directives. Particularly once they have left the hospital environment, their exposure to surveillance and control is limited. While, as we have suggested above, women's feeding practices may be subject to both social and material constraints, nevertheless, it is mothers who are in day-to-day control of how babies are fed (Maher 1992). Experts may advise exclusive breast-feeding, but its implementation depends on mothers' readiness to follow such advice. In this respect, the analogy of childbirth with infant feeding begins to break down. Although, in principle, medical intervention in childbirth requires a woman's cooperation, insofar as she must give her consent, such cooperation is of a rather different order to that required for breast-feeding. Since over 90 per cent of British births now take place in hospital, women in childbirth are physically located in the arena where the power of doctors is greatest. By contrast, infant feeding largely takes place outside hospital, and the impotence of doctors to impose their recommendations upon women is reflected in the relatively small numbers of women who actually meet current recommendations for exclusive breast-feeding. Mothers are able to resist the attempts of health professionals to direct how their babies are to be fed and, in many cases, do so.

Nevertheless, it would be a mistake to assume, just because women do not always follow expert recommendations, that those who make such recommendations do not exercise power. Their power lies not in their ability to *make* women follow their advice, but in their right to define the standards by which mothers' feeding activities are to be judged, by others and indeed by the women themselves.

The categorical nature of expert advice on the benefits of breast-feeding makes a woman's failure to follow it particularly transparent. Either a baby is exclusively breast-fed for the recommended period or she or he is not. Failure to breast-feed one's child lays one open to the charge that one is a 'poor mother' (Carter 1995). However, simply breast-feeding one's child is not in itself constitutive of good motherhood. 'Good mothers' not only have to breast-feed their babies, but they must do so in a way that ensures that the baby thrives. As Oakley commented: 'A baby that is feeding and grow-ing "well" is ... a tangible token of her love and work. Conversely, a baby who gains weight more slowly than it "should", and who perhaps cries a lot and seems unsatisfied is ... a sign of maternal failure' (1979, p. 165). Women may reject expert advice on infant feeding, but they can rarely ignore it. Infant feeding, like other ways in which mothers provide food for their families, is not simply a practical activity; it is a moral undertaking. As Deborah Lupton (1996) observes, the way in which a mother feeds her baby becomes a symbol of her wider ability to care for her child.

The force of expert definitions of breast- and formula-feeding as 'good' and 'bad' respectively, and the implications of such definitions for the self-evaluations of moth-ers, are illustrated in our current longitudinal study of the decisions that mothers make about how, when, and where to feed their babies. As part of this study, we carried out in-depth interviews with thirty-six first-time mothers, living within a 10-mile radius of Nottingham, England, at six fixed intervals between late pregnancy and their babies' second birthdays. Quota sampling was used to ensure heterogeneity in terms of both age and the women's own occupational class. The data discussed below are drawn from the first interview with each woman, which was carried out shortly before the birth of her baby.

Antenatally, the majority of women intended to breast-feed their babies (29 out of 36 women); six intended to formula feed, and one woman intended to combine breast- and formula-feeding. At this stage, then, four-fifths of the women we interviewed planned to follow expert recommendations about infant feeding. The women who intended to breast-feed explained their decision in terms of the health benefits to the baby, in ways that reflect current expert opinion. For example, one woman said, 'I just think it's healthy for the baby; it gets all the, the goodness from the breast ... because at the beginning the first lot of milk, it's got all the extra vitamins and nourishment which the baby needs and also, er whatever it is, antibodies, whatever to protect it from dis-eases and bugs'. These women are able to present themselves unproblematically as 'good mothers' who are acting and will act in ways that prioritise their babies' needs. Their decisions are entirely in keeping with expert definitions of appropriate maternal behaviour, and their explanations of their decisions can be read as straightforward claims to responsible motherhood. There is no indication that they feel obliged to defend their decision to breast-feed.

By contrast, five of the six women who had decided to formula-feed accounted for their intended behaviour in ways that suggest that they see the morality of their deci-sion to formula-feed as called into question. In spite of the self-consciously neutral stance adopted by the interviewers, these women's accounts appear to be formulated in response to the putative charge that formula-feeding is an irresponsible or inappropri-ate choice and hence evidence that the woman will be a 'bad mother'. These women treated their decision to formula-feed their babies as an 'untoward act' (Lyman & Scott 1989), and they engaged in defensive accounting as they explained it to the interviewers. The sixth woman's discussion of her feeding intentions was significantly different from that of all the other women in the study. This woman acknowledged that breast-feeding was 'supposed to be more good for the baby than bottle feeding' but did not appear to see her decision to formula-feed, or indeed any of the other decisions that she made in relation to her baby, as requiring to be justified.

The remaining five women who intended to formula-feed acknowledged that their decision deviated from expert recommendations and sought to justify it, so countering any potential allegation that they were not 'good mothers'. The justifications take a number of different forms. First, the women specifically challenged expert claims that 'breast is best'. Such challenges were often presented in the quasi-scientific language of 'nutrients' and 'vitamins'. For example, one woman said, 'There's the same nutrients in both … they say breast milk is better because it's yours and it's nature … there's definitely the same nutrients in both'. Formula-feeding is presented as more reliable, because 'at least you know how much it's getting'. Breast-feeding mothers run the risk of underfeeding their babies:

> Like sometimes a woman's had a poor diet through pregnancy or if she has a poor diet when she's had a baby because probably she is rushing around after the baby, then her milk could be poor if she was breast-feeding the baby. So the baby might be starving you know. It might not be getting the right, or gaining weight properly. So I think it's better bottle.

Here, the 'good mother' is implicitly redefined as one who ensures that her baby receives sufficient milk, rather than insisting on a particular type of milk. The women bolster their claims that formula-feeding is a legitimate choice for the responsible mother by pointing to other babies who have been formula-fed and who are 'all perfectly healthy'.

The second way in which this same group of women countered the implied charge of irresponsibility was to challenge the authority of experts to define what is in the best interests of their particular child. They appealed to their own authority as mothers, for example—'I don't care what everybody else says, it's what I feel is better for my child'—and to the expertise of their family and friends: 'I know that might sound a bit daft, but I think my family knows best'.

These women also justified their decision to formula-feed in terms of their responsibilities to others. They argued that breast-feeding would exclude their partners or other members of the family. One woman explained, 'But you see, if I was breast-feeding he'd feel left out because he wouldn't be able to feed his baby'. This reminds us that the moral responsibilities of mothers extend to their partners as well as to their babies. Not only did these women feel called upon to demonstrate that they are 'good mothers', but they are also expected (and expect themselves) to be good wives. Marshall's analysis of child-care manuals shows how women are required not only to take responsibility for the needs of the new baby, but also to ensure both that her partner plays his new role as father adequately and that he does not feel neglected. For example, she cites Gordon Bourne, who advised women, 'It should be remembered that men are sometimes neglected when their wives are pregnant and therefore require just as much attention as the new arrival. Every woman should make sure that the new member of the family does not mean that her husband has less of her love, time and affection' (Bourne 1979, as quoted in Marshall 1991, p. 77). Thus, women are required to meet the needs of their babies, but they must do so in ways that keep their partners happy. Babies' fathers must be insulated from any negative consequences arising from the babies' arrival. It is for women to ensure that both babies' and fathers' interests are safeguarded, however much these are in conflict with one another.

While, as noted above, those women who intended to breast-feed their babies did not appear to feel called upon to justify this decision per se, a number were at pains to point out that the *way* in which they would breast-feed would allow them to meet their responsibilities to both partners and babies. In particular, they addressed themselves to the possible charge that the decision to breast-feed would act to exclude their partners. Thus, the factor that women intending to formula-feed invoked to justify their decision became, for some breast-feeding women, a challenge that needed to be addressed. A number of these women described how they planned to express breast milk so that the baby's father would not feel 'left out'. For example, one woman said, 'I intend, as early as possible, to start expressing and giving it bottles of breast milk so that Ray [partner] can have that [the opportunity to feed the baby]'. Another said, 'I was worried he'd feel a bit left out, but I've bought a breast pump anyway and I've got some bottles and a sterilising unit'.

Not only do new mothers have to deal with the moral injunction to be 'good mothers' and 'good partners', but they must also be 'good women'. The 'sexualisation' of women's breasts (Newson & Newson 1963) means that breast-feeding women risk being seen as immodest or indiscreet. Thus, those women who intended to formula-feed appealed to modesty to justify their decision not to breast-feed. For example, one woman explained, 'I'm self-conscious about my body ... I'm not going to have to get my boobs out in the middle of Nottingham.' Another referred to a recent experience when she had observed a woman breast-feeding in public and had been 'quite put off by it'. She insisted that women who wanted to breast-feed their babies should 'hide away'.

Conversely, a number of the women who intended to breast-feed their babies were concerned to distance themselves from any suggestion of brazenness or immodesty. These women stressed the measures they would take to avoid giving offence to others:

When I'm out in public, I don't like the idea of that ... I couldn't just openly do it in public ... I'd have to be in a corner somewhere tucked away where nobody can see. I won't feed in public like on a bench in a park or anything like that … I think I'd probably, what do you call it, suction it out … I'd feel conscious if I was out and the baby wanted to feed, and I'd want some kind of privacy, because it's like flashing your flesh to everyone.

As we have seen, women who decide not to breast-feed their babies at all are vulnerable to the charge that they are 'bad' mothers. The reasons they give for their decisions to formula-feed can be read as a rebuttal of a potential charge of **deviance**. However, it is not only mothers who 'fail' to breast-feed their babies who are faced with the possibility of being considered deviant. There is evidence from a number of studies to suggest that women who prolong breast-feeding, particularly into the baby's second year, are likely to incur social disapproval (Hills-Bonczyk et al. 1994; Kendall-Tackett & Sugarman 1995). Once again, while breast-feeding in itself is not an activity that women in our study felt required to justify, a number of the women we interviewed appeared to be engaged in distancing themselves from the charge that they might be the 'sort of woman' who would prolong breast-feeding. They referred to such behaviour as 'not very dignified' and 'very, very distasteful'. One woman said, 'Our midwife told us that somebody breast-feeds when they are three. That to me is absolutely revolting, for mother and child, because it's not natural. Well not the way, in the society I've been brought up with. You don't do that sort of thing'.

In order to be a good mother, then, one must breast-feed one's baby. To be a good mother who is also a good partner, one must breast-feed one's baby in such a way that one's husband or boyfriend does not feel neglected or displaced. To be a good mother and a good wife who is also a good woman is even more demanding. One must avoid giving offence to others by breast-feeding in public or prolonging breast-feeding beyond the age when it is socially acceptable to do so. The space within which one can simultaneously be a good mother, a good partner, and a good woman is therefore limited indeed.

Conclusion

As sociologists, we have been concerned in this chapter with the 'problem of infant feeding' from a particular perspective. We have examined the ways in which nutritional concerns have been translated into a problem of maternal behaviour, where issues of morality and individual responsibility have come to preoccupy not only policy-makers, but also mothers themselves. For policy-makers and practitioners, the problem may appear to be a simple one. Babies should be breast-fed, but too few mothers actually do so for long enough. Solutions which have been advocated include the education of supposedly ignorant mothers and the reform of unhelpful hospital practices. The former has met with little success, and the latter has raised significant concerns about compromising mothers' autonomy. We would argue that those developing policies to encourage breast-feeding need to recognise that infant feeding is a moral as well as a nutritional matter and that simply trying to change the knowledge or behaviour of individual women, without due attention to the broader cultural and material contexts in which they act, is likely to meet with limited success.

Summary of main points

- Current rates of breast-feeding are low in most of the industrialised world, and this causes concern to policy-makers because of evidence of the health benefits of breast-feeding.
- Policy responses have tended to individualise the problem, distracting attention from the 'working conditions' under which women opt to feed their babies in particular ways.
- It is now recognised that, in the past, hospital practices have obstructed the establishment of successful breast-feeding. The response to such evidence has been to reform hospital practices. This is welcome, but does not challenge the assumption that experts should control infant feeding.
- Infant feeding, like other aspects of child rearing, has increasingly become an 'expert domain'. While experts are not able to control how mothers actually feed their babies, they are able to set standards by which women may be judged and may judge themselves.
- Infant feeding is a highly moral enterprise and failure to breast-feed leaves women vulnerable to the charge that they are not good mothers. However, women who breast-feed must demonstrate that they do so in ways that do not cause offence or cause their husbands or boyfriends to feel neglected.

Discussion questions

1 What are the current trends in infant feeding in the industrialised world, and why do these cause concern for medical experts and policy-makers?
2 How can policy-makers' responses to concerns about infant feeding be seen as individualising a social problem?
3 In what ways can infant feeding be seen as an example of medicalisation?
4 How do infant-feeding experts influence mothers' self-evaluations?
5 In what ways does women's talk about their feeding choices suggest that they are concerned with presenting themselves as 'good mothers', 'good partners', and 'good women'?

Further reading

Arnup, K., Levesque, A., & Roach Pierson, R. 1990, *Delivering Motherhood: Maternal Ideologies and Practices in the 19th and 20th Centuries*, Routledge, London.
Carter, P. 1995, *Feminism, Breasts and Breast Feeding*, Macmillan, Basingstoke.
Maher, V. 1992, 'Breast Feeding in Cross-Cultural Perspective: Paradoxes and Proposals', in V. Maher (ed.), *The Anthropology of Breast Feeding: Natural Law or Social Construct*, Berg, Oxford.
Murphy, E., Parker, S., & Phipps, C. 1998, 'Food Choices for Babies', in A. Murcott (ed.), *The Nation's Diet: The Social Science of Food Choice*, Addison Wesley Longman, London, pp. 250–66.

Oakley, A. 1993, 'Birth as a "Normal" Process', in A. Oakley (ed.), *Women, Medicine and Health*, Edinburgh University Press, Edinburgh, pp. 124–138.

References

American Academy of Pediatrics 1978, 'Breast Feeding', *Pediatrics*, vol. 62, pp. 591–601.

Arnup, K. 1990, 'Educating Mothers: Government Advice for Women in the Inter-War Years', in K. Arnup, A. Levesque, & R. Roach Pierson (eds), *Delivering Motherhood: Maternal Ideologies and Practices in the 19th and 20th Centuries*, Routledge, London, pp. 190–210.

Aronson, N. 1982, 'Nutrition as a Social Problem: A Case Study of Entrepreneurial Strategy in Science', *Social Problems*, vol. 29, pp. 474–87.

Bailey, V. F. & Sherriff, J. 1993, 'Reasons for Early Cessation of Breastfeeding in Women from Lower Socio-Economic Groups in Perth, Western Australia', *Breastfeeding Review*, vol. 11, pp. 390–3.

Campbell, C. 1996, 'Breastfeeding and Health in the Western World', *British Journal of General Practice*, vol. 46, pp. 613–17.

Carter, P. 1995, *Feminism, Breasts and Breast Feeding*, Macmillan, Basingstoke.

Casey, N. 1996, Editorial, *Nursing Standard*, vol. 10, p. 1.

Chunn, D. 1990, 'Boys Will Be Men, Girls Will Be Mothers', in P. Adler & P. Adler (eds), *Sociological Studies of Child Development*, JAI Press, Greenwich, Conn., pp. 87–110.

Cooper, P., Murray, L., & Stein, A. 1993, 'Psychosocial Factors Associated with Early Termination of Breast Feeding', *Journal of Psychosomatic Research*, vol. 37, pp. 171–6.

Department of Health 1994, *Weaning and the Weaning Diet: Report of the Working Group on the Weaning Diet of the Committee on Medical Aspects of Food Policy*, no. 45, HMSO, London.

Department of Health and Social Security 1988, *Present Day Practice in Infant Feeding: Third Report*, no. 32, HMSO, London.

DHSS. See Department of Health and Social Security.

Fildes, V. 1992, 'Breast Feeding in London, 1905–19', *Journal of Biosocial Science*, vol. 24, pp. 53–70.

Florack, E. 1984, 'Breast-Feeding, Bottle-Feeding and Related Factors', *Acta Paediatrica Scandanavica*, vol. 73, pp. 789–95.

Foster, F., Lader, D., & Cheesbrough, S. 1997, *Infant Feeding 1995*, The Stationery Office, London.

Foster, P. 1995, *Women and the Health Care Industry: An Unhealthy Relationship?*, Open University Press, Buckingham.

Hartley, B. & O'Connor, M. 1996, 'Evaluation of the 'Best-Start' Breast Feeding Education Program', *Archives of Pediatric and Adolescent Medicine*, vol. 150, pp. 868–71.

Hills-Bonczyk, S., Tromiczak, K., Avery, M., Potter, S., Savik, K., & Duckett, L. 1994, 'Women's Experiences of Breast Feeding Longer than 12 Months', *Birth*, vol. 21, pp. 206–12.

Hitchcock, N. E. & Coy, J. F. 1988, 'Infant Feeding Practices in Western Australia and Tasmania: A Joint Survey, 1984–85', *Med J Aust*, vol. 148, pp. 114–47.

Jamieson, L. & Toynbee, C. 1990, 'Shifting Patterns of Parental Authority, 1900–1980', in H. Corr & L. Jamieson (eds), *Politics of Everyday Life: Continuity and Change in Work and the Family*, Macmillan, London, pp. 86–113.

Kendall-Tackett, K. & Sugarman, M. 1995, 'The Social Consequences of Long-Term Breast Feeding', *Journal of Human Lactation*, vol. 11, pp. 179–83.

Lawrence, R. 1995, 'The Clinician's Role in Teaching Proper Infant Feeding Techniques', *The Journal of Pediatrics*, vol. 126 (supplement), pp. 112–17.

Lewis, J. 1990, '"Motherhood Issues" in Late Nineteenth and Twentieth Centuries', in K. Arnup, A. Levesque, & R. Roach Pierson (eds), *Delivering Motherhood: Maternal Ideologies and Practices in the 19th and 20th Centuries*, Routledge, London, pp. 1–19.

Lowe, T. 1993, 'Regional and Socio-Economic Variations in the Duration of Breastfeeding in Victoria', *Breastfeeding Review*, vol. 2, pp. 312–15.

Lupton, D. 1996, *Food, the Body and the Self*, Sage, London.

Lyman, S. & Scott, M. 1989, *A Sociology of the Absurd*, General Hall, Dix Hills, NY.

Maher, V. 1992, 'Breast Feeding in Cross-Cultural Perspective: Paradoxes and Proposals', in V. Maher (ed.), *The Anthropology of Breast Feeding: Natural Law or Social Construct*, Berg, Oxford, pp. 1–36.

Marshall, H. 1991, 'The Social Construction of Motherhood: An Analysis of Childcare and Parenting Manuals', in A. Phoenix, A. Woollett, & E. Lloyd (eds), *Motherhood: Meanings, Practices and Ideologies*, Sage, London, pp. 66–85.

Martin, J. 1978, *Infant Feeding 1975: Attitudes and Practices in England and Wales*, Office of Population Censuses and Surveys, London.

Martin, J. & Monk, J. 1982, *Infant Feeding 1980*, Office of Population Censuses and Surveys, London.

Martin, J. & White, A. 1988, *Infant Feeding 1985*, Office of Population Censuses and Surveys, London.

Ministry of Health 1943, *The Breast Feeding of Infants*, report of the Advisory Committee on Mothers and Young Children, HMSO, London.

Murphy, E., Parker, S., & Phipps, C. 1998a, 'Competing Agendas in Infant Feeding', *British Food Journal*, vol. 100, no. 3, pp. 128–32.

—— 1998b, 'Food Choices for Babies', in A. Murcott (ed.), *The Nation's Diet: The Social Science of Food Choice*, Addison Wesley Longman, London, pp. 250–66.

National Health and Medical Research Council 1995, *Dietary Guidelines for Children and Adolescents*, AGPS, Canberra.

Newson, J. & Newson, E. 1963, *Patterns of Infant Care in an Urban Community*, Penguin Books, Harmondsworth.

Oakley, A. 1979, *Becoming a Mother*, Martin Robertson, Oxford.

Oakley, A. 1993, 'Birth as a "Normal" Process', in A. Oakley (ed.), *Women, Medicine and Health*, Edinburgh University Press, Edinburgh, pp. 124–138.

Palmer, N. 1985, 'Breastfeeding: The Australian Situation', *Journal of Food and Nutrition*, vol. 42, pp. 13–18.

Pesssl, M. 1996, 'Are We Creating Our Own Breast Feeding Mythology?', *Journal of Human Lactation*, vol. 12, pp. 271–2.

Piper, S. & Parks, P. 1996, 'Predicting the Duration of Lactation: Evidence from a National Survey', *Birth*, vol. 23, pp. 7–12.

Quandt, S. 1986, 'Patterns of Variation in Breast Feeding Predictors', *Social Science and Medicine*, vol. 23, pp. 445–53.

Saadeh, R. & Akre, J. 1996, 'Ten Steps to Successful Breast Feeding: A Summary of the Rationale and Scientific Evidence', *Birth*, vol. 23, pp. 154–60.

Salt, M., Law, C., Bull, A., & Osmond, C. 1994, 'Determinants of Breast Feeding in Salisbury and Durham', *Journal of Public Health Medicine*, vol. 16, pp. 291–5.

Simopoulos, A. & Grave, G. 1984, 'Factors Associated with the Choice and Duration of Infant-Feeding Practice: Task Force on Infant-Feeding Practices', *Pediatrics*, vol. 74 (Supp.), pp. 603–14.

Tew, M. 1995, *Safer Childbirth: A Critical History of Maternity Care*, 2nd edn, Chapman & Hall, London.

White, A., Freeth, S., & O'Brien, M. 1992, *Infant Feeding 1990*, HMSO, London.

Wright, H. & Walker, P. 1983, 'Prediction of Duration of Breast Feeding in Primiparae', *Journal of Epidemiology and Community Health*, vol. 37, pp. 89–94.

15

The Government of the Table:
Nutrition Expertise and the Social Organisation of Family Food Habits

John Coveney

Overview

- *How have changing social attitudes towards childhood affected the nature of nutrition advice about children's eating patterns?*

- *In what ways can nutrition advice be seen as a form of power?*

- *Does current nutrition advice result in positive outcomes for children and parents?*

In this chapter, the area of child nutrition is analysed in relation to changing views about family life in Australia over the past 60 years. Pre-war advice from experts contained little, if any, reference to the management of feeding children, concentrating instead on timetables, recipes, and amounts. By contrast, the problems posed by 'picky' or 'fussy' eaters—and strategies for dealing with these difficulties—are widely discussed in modern texts on child nutrition. The changing attitudes towards feeding children are situated in a wider context in which modern social views accord children the status of citizens with rights, responsibilities, and autonomy. The new social space that children now occupy has been reproduced and reinforced in the advice of nutritionists. The importance of encouraging choice in the eating habits of children is especially foregrounded in texts that advise parents how to feed the family. However, independence and autonomy for children in choosing food comes at a price, and the widespread problem of children not choosing nutritious foods is considered to be an inevitable part of growing up. The tensions that these new views of childhood bring to the process of feeding children are examined through interviews with families. It is suggested that expertise in family relationships establishes a code of conduct for parents, which guides them in the management of children's behaviour. Feeding children is made problematic by new social practices for 'good' parenting, which privilege independence for children, a belief that food and mealtimes should be enjoyable, and an imperative that food for children should be nutritious.

Key terms

government	ethics
normality	ethical responsibilities

Introduction

One important aspect of the sociology of food and nutrition is the examination of the nexus between the nutritional sciences and the social sciences. In this sense, 'sociology' is handled differently across these different disciplinary divides. For example, nutritionists commonly focus on social sciences in order to try to explain why people's knowledge of nutrition is not always put into practice (Mennell et al. 1993, p. 36). And social scientists have, among other things, examined nutrition as an example of how development of scientific knowledge (in this case, about food) has developed within a specific social milieu (see Aronson 1982a, 1982b). Along these lines, a number of recent Australian texts have examined nutrition from a social or a historical point of view (Walker & Roberts 1988; Santich 1995; Crotty 1995). These texts further emphasise the truism that nutrition, as a scientific discipline, has never existed in a sociocultural vacuum. They show that social and cultural priorities have flowed over into nutrition.

However, this is not a one-way street. Expert knowledge, in the form of nutritional advice, has also shaped certain expectations around eating, especially in the assessment of what are considered to be 'normal' eating patterns. In this chapter, an aspect of nutrition—that of child nutrition—is examined to illustrate the relationship between developments in social views of childhood and nutritional knowledge and advice in this area.

Expert advice and feeding children

The Australian National Health and Medical Research Council guidelines on healthy diets for children (NHMRC 1994) represent the latest in a long line of advice from health and nutrition experts about the kinds of food that infants and children should eat. Indeed, expert advice on what children should eat has a long history, the Australian branch of which has been well documented by Nancy Hitchcock (1989a, 1989b). By contrast, expert recommendations about the management of children's social behaviour in relation to food—for example, how to cope with 'difficult' or 'fussy' eaters—has a much shorter history. To be sure, books, articles, and papers on children's nutrition published earlier this century often contained sections in which these matters were briefly discussed. This advice, however, was quite different, in terms of both nature and detail, from that provided today. Current manuals on parenting contain information designed to prepare parents for, and advise them about, what now appears to be an inevitable aspect of childhood: anti-social habits associated with food and feeding difficulties. This is not to say, of course, that children have only recently become what is often described as 'fussy' or 'picky' eaters. Rather, it is to say that the recognition of this phenomenon as a problem, and its management, has become part of expert advice to parents only relatively recently.

The role of the expert in advising parents about the social management of children is not, of course, confined to feeding. According to Nikolas Rose (1990, p. 129), the whole field of family life in general, and parenting in particular, has become governed by expertise. Expert advice now infuses and shapes the personal investments of parents, especially the ways in which they regulate and evaluate their actions and their goals. Through this process, expert opinion not only informs parents but also provides them with an index of what is considered to be the 'proper' way of managing children. Expertise thus becomes the benchmark against which parental behaviour is judged by others and, importantly, by parents themselves. In other words, parents know they are doing a 'good' job by reference to expert opinion. Expertise outlines and facilitates the production of **'normality'** in childhood, which, in the end, is what most parents aspire to. The popularity of books, journals and articles, and electronic media coverage concerned with parenting skills is an indication of these aspirations. In trying to understand this popularity, we should not see parents as cultural or 'judgemental dopes' (Heritage 1987) who are beguiled by expert advice against their will or better nature. On the contrary, we should recognise that parents *actively* seek out this information in order to better handle the complex and often difficult process of bringing up children. And even when parents do not find expert advice especially useful, it is still recognised as having a certain validity. Comments like 'They say you should [do such and such], but I find that … ' are frequently heard from parents, indicating the recognised authority with which expertise speaks.

It is the nature of 'doing it right', especially with regard to the feeding of children, that is the topic of this chapter and which demonstrates the reification of the social management of eating, with its inherent problems in modern family settings. The area is examined in a number of ways. First, expert advice in the area of feeding children from earlier this century is compared with that available today. Second, the nature of such advice is situated within the larger context of the changes in Australian social life with respect to the family—especially attitudes to raising children—over the last 60 years. This comparison illustrates the new considerations that parents are required to take into account in relation to feeding children. Third, in order to ground the recognition of these changes—and the tensions they bring—in concrete experiences, interviews with families in which feeding children was discussed are examined.

Setting an analytical context: government and the family

The theoretical framework of this analysis is drawn from Michel Foucault, especially as his work has been used by Jacques Donzelot (1980) and Rose (1990). Briefly, this work acknowledges that the development of the 'modern family', as we know it today (small, private, independent), began in the early part of the last century. This happened through a process that culminated in the State eventually making possible certain advantages and privileges for families which went beyond the provision of regulation and legislation. As Rose says, ' "Familialization" was crucial to the means whereby personal capacities and conducts could be socialised, shaped and maximised in a manner that accorded with the moral and political principles of liberal societies' (Rose 1990, p. 126). In this process, however, the state should not necessarily be seen as a centralised bureaucracy from which power emanated. As Nikolas Rose and Peter Miller (1992) note, it is more productive to analyse political power from the point of view of **government** rather than state apparatus. The difference is that government may be understood as a range of practices, 'tactics, strategies, techniques, programmes, dreams and aspirations of those authorities who shape the beliefs and conduct of the population' (Nettleton 1991, p. 99). Clearly such authorities need not belong only to State bureaucracies. Techniques or technologies of government are also the domain of non-political organisations with or without religious affiliations (now sometimes known as non-government organisations or 'NGOs'). As Rose and Miller state, 'in Europe for many centuries economic activity was regulated, order was maintained, laws promulgated and enforced, assistance provided for the sick and needy, morality inculcated, if at all, through practices that had little to do with the state' (Rose & Miller 1992, p. 176).

Indeed, much of the work in the early formation of the domesticated modern family was undertaken through philanthropic activity, especially that concerning health, welfare, and hygiene (Donzelot 1980, p. 55). This assistance was almost always conditional upon families adopting 'good' moral principles, especially marriage, good housekeeping, sobriety, and the moral supervision of children (Rose 1990, p. 127). As such, charitable organisations often worked more closely with families who had middle-class tendencies and aspirations. Even in the working classes, it was the 'deserving' families— those who, despite economic and social hardships, displayed certain moral principles— who were the main targets of middle-class philanthropy. Charitable organisations would not assist the 'undeserving' poor, whose plight was a product of 'drunkenness, laziness, roving dispositions, and dishonesty' (Finch 1993, p. 44).

Central to the technologies of government is knowledge—expertise or 'know how'. This knowledge can be transferred into programs that specify objects to be governed or managed and the ends to which these objects are to be put. By laying claim to certain knowledge, programs map out the problems that are to be addressed. Thus programs, through knowledge, become problematising activities that attempt to direct or control the behaviour of others. It is through such technologies of government that power is exercised. As Foucault says, 'power and knowledge directly imply one another; there is no power relationship without the correlative constitution of a field of knowledge, nor any knowledge that does not presuppose and constitute at the same time power relations' (Foucault 1979, p. 27). In other words, people conduct themselves in relations of power. However, it is important to note that relationships of power are not necessarily negative. On Foucault's understanding, power can be positive: 'It [power] needs to be considered as a productive network which runs through the whole social body, much more than as a negative instance whose function is to repress' (Foucault 1980, p. 119). One aspect of the productive nature of power is in creation of socially desirable or ethical categories. We can see this in the development of family ideals during the last century, when expert advice from philanthropic organisations was available in the areas of health, hygiene, and normality. The latter quality was especially important for the promotion of happy, healthy family lives. Normal families were those that had high standards of ethical conduct. Unsociable behaviours—debauchery, viciousness, masturbation, insanity—were considered to be detrimental to the health and harmony of family life (Rose 1990, p. 128). But normality was not merely an observation—it was a valuation that defined a situation as 'that which should be', and the justification of which was increasingly made according to medical, psychological, and other scientific knowledges. A number of proto-State services were established in this way. It was, for example, through establishing categories of 'normality' that child health and welfare services first made an appearance earlier this century. In Australia, as in other countries, the early child-welfare movement began as a philanthropic venture (Reiger 1986, p. 130). Attendance at the infant welfare clinic—then as now—became an exercise in examining children against a range of normal criteria for feeding, growth and development, and behaviour.

Today it is the reification of what is considered to be 'normal'—in family life in general, and childhood in particular—that provides parents with an obligation *and* a commitment to produce hygienic homes and to raise happy, healthy children. It is in the attainment of the 'normal' that parents are judged by *others* and, importantly, judge *themselves* in terms of doing the 'right thing'. And it is in the quest for the 'normal', especially in relation to childhood, that requires parents to *seek out* expert advice for reassurance or correction of parenting practices. It is important to stress again that it would be a mistake to view this understanding of the construction of the modern family as implying some kind of domination or repression on the part of the State. On the contrary, parents actively seek out expert advice about the 'proper way' of raising children, and they do not do so under some misguided notion of 'false consciousness'. They do it as a way of bringing about their ethical completion as parents, although the characteristics of this subject position are multiple and continually changing in light of expert opinion. We should regard **'ethics'** as referring to the obligations that individuals feel compelled to fulfil, especially in relation to moral codes defined by their social groups. Foucault sees the development of ethics as a:

> process in which the individual delimits that part of himself [*sic*] that will form the object of his moral practice, defines his position relative to the precepts he will follow, and decides on a certain mode of being that will serve as his moral goal. And this requires him to act upon himself, to monitor, test, improve, and transform himself (Foucault 1992, p. 28).

Moral conduct has, since the seventeenth century, become increasingly governed by expertise in the human sciences. We should thus understand the expert advice examined in this chapter as a form of 'control at a distance' (Rose & Miller 1992); it is a kind of control that requires families to be autonomous from, and yet cooperative with, the State. This control functions through the production and valorisation of specific conducts, developed and outlined by experts, to which parents will *want* to aspire in order to recognise themselves as 'good', 'responsible', and 'committed' mothers and fathers, thus fulfilling their ethical responsibilities. This short summary sets the context for the analysis that follows.

The changing nature of family life

Reporting on a survey of Australian family life undertaken in 1954, Harold Fallding notes that parents at this time saw themselves as pioneering a new era of child-rearing. This new form of parenting had four main elements:

> a belief that one had to be equipped with knowledge in order to deal with children effectively, not simply repeat the methods used by one's own parents; a belief that one should be affectionate and companionable towards children, not the remote authorities that parents had been in previous generations; a desire to produce a self-regulated rather than an obedient child; and an aim to ensure the full development of the child's capacities rather than prepare him [sic] to be devoted to duty (Fallding 1957, p. 71).

Fallding notes that, compared with the position of children in families before the Second World War, the status of postwar childhood had radically changed. Blind obedience was replaced by cooperation and negotiation between parents and children.

The nature of these changes in family life is very noticeable in the different obligations parents had in the area of feeding children in the pre- and postwar eras. We can examine these changes by reference to expert advice to parents on the 'correct' ways of feeding children. In the early part of the century, parental advice about feeding children focused almost exclusively on rules and regimes around foods. *The Australian Mothercraft Book* (Mothers and Babies' Health Association 1938), used by infant welfare nurses in the 1930s, lists the sequence in which foods should be introduced into a child's diet on weaning. Also special instructions are given for 'correctly' cooking the food and achieving the 'right' consistency. Specimen diets for older children are also provided, listing those foods that should be given and the times at which they must be offered. However, little is written about the ways in which parents should manage the social arrangement of mealtimes or about the correct course of action should meals be refused by uncooperative children.

Another book of the day offering advice about the management of children in the nursery states that 'As a rule it is wise not to coax an unwilling child to take its food … [but f]addiness about food should in no case be encouraged … The food provided should always be suitable and it should be *assumed that it will be eaten.* (Bennett & Issacs 1931, emphasis added)

Truby King's pre-war book on *Feeding and Care of Baby* (King 1933), which was used extensively by infant welfare nurses in Australia, goes into great detail about refusal at the breast and the kinds of foods to give older children. It offers a range of timetables and menus, listing the foods that should be given. However, it offers little guidance about the social management of feeding—that is, what to do if food is disliked and refused. Instead, King's advice takes on a rather 'no nonsense' approach, with the assumption that feeding children will be an unproblematic affair.

We should contrast this advice with that given in manuals written in the postwar period, where potential problems of feeding children start to surface. In his book *Baby and Child Care*, Ben Spock (1955) devotes almost a whole chapter to the feeding problems in children. Spock starts by noting that 'You don't see feeding problems in puppies or among young humans in places where mothers don't know enough about diet to worry' (Spock 1955, p. 448). He continues by stressing the importance of patience, offering choices, and encouraging independence in eating. As a postwar text on child management, Spock's book stands in stark contrast to those written earlier in so far as feeding children is now a recognised problem. Another topic—that of fatness in children, which was not mentioned to any great degree in earlier texts—is also given special treatment by Spock. He provides advice on how to cope with fat children who 'crave large amounts of rich foods [cakes, biscuits, and pastry]' (Spock 1955, p. 457). Obesity in children is now seen as a health problem requiring intervention by parents and doctors. Stressing the difficulties that beset the management of children's overweight problems, Spock points out that:

> A child has less will-power than an adult. If the mother serves the child less fattening foods it means either that the whole family must go without the richer dishes or that the fat child must be kept from eating the very things his heart craves while the rest of the family enjoy them. There are few fat children reasonable enough to think that's fair (Spock 1955, p. 459).

Note that Spock stresses children's ability to reason and that their views should be respected. According to Spock, if a child shows willingness to cooperate in dieting, then the child should be encouraged to visit the doctor, preferably alone. 'Talking to the doctor, man to man, may give him [*sic*] a feeling of running his own life like a grown up' (Spock 1955, p. 459). Uppermost in Spock's advice, then, is an assumption that reason, independence, and self-regulation in children should all be encouraged. Children should not be merely obedient.

The importance of fostering dietary freedom and independence in children becomes explicit in the recommendations of contemporary nutritionists. For example, in her book *The Complete Guide to Feeding your Child*, Audrey Stewart-Turner (1986) points out that children should be given a choice of nutritious foods to encourage independence in eating. She puts children's capricious attitude to eating on the same footing as the food preferences of adults, saying 'remember that there are some foods [parents] like to eat more than others or feel like at certain times and not other times!' (Stewart-Turner 1986, p. 67). We are, then, invited to rationalise children's eating behaviours by comparing them with those of adults who, presumably, know when they are hungry and when they are not, and have recognisable and distinct food preferences.

A second example of contemporary advice is a book on child nutrition by S. Baker and R. Henry (1987), who recognise that many children are 'picky' eaters. In dealing with this problem, parents should show encouragement rather than use force. According to the authors, negative encounters with food should always be avoided and 'parents should respect children's food preferences and not try to dictate them' (Baker & Henry 1987, p. 135).

A more recent example is the nutrition book by Susan Thompson (1995), which points out that 'Finding the balance between self-expression and freedom on the part of your child, and meeting [parents'] ideas of a healthy diet can be difficult' (Thompson 1995, p. 14). Thompson paraphrases Ellen Satter—another child nutrition expert in the area—who believes that 'The parent is responsible for what is presented to eat. The child is *responsible* for how much is eaten and even whether he [sic] eats' (Satter 1987, emphasis added). It is the recognition of the rights of children to choice and their social responsibility to eat if they want to that is so apparent in modern texts. Such a recognition assumes that children be accorded a degree of autonomy and social freedom, a notion that is utterly missing from earlier advice by experts.

One of the driving forces for encouraging self-expression and independence in modern children's food choices is the importance of harmony and happiness when eating. Parents are reminded that the child's happiness around food and eating should be preserved because unpleasant social experiences around food in childhood can lead to eating problems. As Thompson puts it, 'Studies have shown that if parents are rigid and authoritarian about food [amounts], children will lose their ability to control intake. There is a good chance that your child will become overweight, or even underweight if the battle becomes more important than eating' (Thompson 1995, p. 70). This kind of advice reaches something of an apogee in the work of J. Hirschmann and L. Zaphiropoulos. Arguing for a more child-centred approach to the management of eating, these authors believe that 'by allowing the child to decide when to eat, what to eat, and how much to eat, we can strengthen her [sic] self-confidence, self-esteem, and sense of dignity and also avoid the kinds of eating difficulties that have plagued many of us for life' (Hirschmann & Zaphiropoulos 1985, p. 13). Thus, the social organisation of the feeding of children, mostly taken for granted by experts at an earlier time, now becomes somewhat precarious. It requires sensitivity so as to avoid rigidity and authoritarianism, the pathological consequences of which are now based on scientific fact.

In postwar nutrition texts, then, the new responsibilities parents have concerning food in the family explicitly recognise and valorise an emotional investment in eating. Managing this problematic process requires judgment and skill, the acquisition of which turns an inexperienced parent into a competent one. Coping with children's eating habits becomes another opportunity for individuals to display prowess in the art of good parenting. This skill is 'in theory intellectually exciting, a test of personal capacities, virtually a profession in its own right; in practice [parenthood] is the site of a constant self-scrutiny and self-evaluation [by the parent] in relation to the norms of responsibility to one's child' (Rose 1990, p. 198). It is through this self-scrutiny of ethical conduct that parents recognise themselves as 'good' mothers and fathers.

However, the concept of children *choosing* food—especially nutritious food—is itself somewhat problematic, and encouraging self-expression and independence in children comes at a price. Commenting on this, Rosemary Stanton says that 'In Australia and New Zealand, we cannot assume that giving children a free choice of foods will produce an ideally balanced intake of nutrients' (Stanton 1990, p. 6). Nevertheless, as described earlier, the idea that children should be given certain choices in their diets endures. Stanton continues: 'Whatever your age it makes sense to follow the principles of a balanced diet. With this scheme, nothing is forbidden, but some foods are given a greater or lesser place than others' (Stanton 1990, p. 8). And yet, the issue of balancing diets and choice in eating is not easily managed. As we have seen, nutrition experts recognise this as 'difficult' because of the need to match the importance of encouraging the child's self-expression with the parent's responsibility to provide a healthy diet. The difficulty of managing this delicate balance has been readily recognised by the food industry, which often promotes certain foods to children as both 'nutritious' and 'enjoyable'. In reality, while many such foods are certainly enjoyable, they are not necessarily nutritious (Australian Consumers Association 1993, p. 21). Thus the freedom to choose—so much a part of postwar consumer ethos—becomes problematic because of the sheer variety of food in the market-place, and because many foods now fall short of current nutritional guidelines. The responsibility now falls to parents, teachers, and others who are expected to instil in children the notion of 'correct' or 'incorrect' food choices.

Children as citizens

Postwar attitudes to choice did not, of course, arrive unannounced purely in the area of children, food, and nutrition. Instead, the recognition given to the new ways in which parents should interact with children can be seen as a manifestation of a new social view of childhood that emerged in the second half of the twentieth century. The growing importance of children in postwar families dramatically influenced their visibility and status. This new status can be seen in a number of developments. For example, in 1959 the United Nations unveiled a *Declaration of the Rights of the Child*, (United Nations 1960), which was reformulated and re-released in 1989 as the *United Nations International Convention for the Rights of the Child* (Greenwood 1993). Under this new Convention, the Australian government has to report to the United Nations every two years on how it is complying with the Convention's principles. The emergence of children's rights in the postwar period required that family life be opened up to closer scrutiny to ensure that these rights were being addressed. The granting of rights to children amounted to extending to them a form of citizenship, not in the sense that they could participate in the execution of political power, but in the sense that they now had the right to liberty and they had social rights (Rose 1990, p. 122). These rights provided for the exercising of choice by children. Pre-war expert discourses on parenting emphasised the importance of avoiding 'molli-coddling' or 'spoiling' children. Frequent parent–child interactions, through play or even just cuddling, were believed to lead to overstimulation of the nervous system, which was considered to be detrimental to proper development (Reiger 1986, p. 148). However, with advances in postwar understandings, especially in child psychology, emotional and cognitive development were to be strongly encouraged through play, discovery, and frequent 'quality' interactions between adults and children. The home itself was believed to be the best place for these activities. The norms of good parenting were less predicated on the amount of discipline and control metered out to children, and more on the extent to which parents maximised their children's learning and developmental potential: 'With the aid of books, games, toys, records, and other aids now made available for purchase, the intimate environment of the home was to be transformed into a veritable laboratory of cognitive growth' (Rose 1990, p. 196). We might note here that the recognition of children's choice and freedom went hand in hand with the greater economic and material possibilities of the so-called postwar 'boom'. Choice and variety became key themes in the postwar consumerism.

On another level, children now had the right to be heard, and they had opinions that were to be taken seriously. The idea of choice and freedom for children in family life was played out in a number of regimes of new parenthood. As we have seen, the eating habits of children became an important site for encouraging the development of choice, self-expression, and eventual independence of children. Thus the notion of choice for children became an important part of family food events.

In the next section, we will examine the experiences of individuals who are negotiating the role of parent. On the one hand, this role requires that their children are provided with foods they will enjoy, and foods with which they can display autonomy and self-expression. On the other hand, it requires that they provide a nutritious diet to their children.

A study of family food experiences

This small study involved twelve families with young children from different parts of Adelaide, Australia. Although these families were randomly enlisted in this study, they are not presented here as representative of all families. They are, instead, used to illustrate examples of family life concerned with food. Briefly, the material presented here was collected and compiled in the following way. In each family the father and mother were interviewed—sometimes together, but sometimes individually. An interview schedule was developed to guide the discussions with participants. The schedule consisted of open-ended questions about everyday routines concerning food preparation, shopping, and other aspects of family food decision-making. All the interviews were audio-taped (with permission) and transcribed. All transcriptions were reviewed and summarised with field notes so that, for each family, an overall description of the couple's responses was produced. The interview transcripts were then 'thematised' using NUDIST (version 3.0.4, QSR Melbourne), a software package for handling qualitative data. Reported here are some of the themes that were developed regarding the parents' food experiences during their own childhood compared with those of today, the management of the social arrangements of family meals, and the obligations faced by parents in relation to nutrition and health.

The interview extracts begin with a reference to the differences between arrangements in family eating when the parents were children and those of today:

STELLA: I know my parents struggled and I remember eating the same meal night after night because that's all there was.

ANGUS: I think when I was a kid I was served meat and two veg …

HILARY: The same thing every night virtually.

ANGUS: And I was expected to pretty much eat it, and if I didn't eat it I wouldn't get dessert. And that would be legit, like if I didn't eat it I wouldn't get dessert. Whereas these days … you serve meat and two veg or three veg and you say 'If you don't eat it you won't get dessert' and they don't eat it but they still get dessert. And it's not just us …

HILARY: But we're not strict like, we're just not strict.

ANGUS: It's not just us that are soft, I think it's just like everything shifts to the left, you know, society is just a bit more malleable whereas when I was a kid it was a bit more black and white.

These examples are typical of many respondents who remembered childhood mealtimes to be more restricted than those of their own children. Many also remembered the hardships that their parents endured where money was often limited. This required that food be eaten and not wasted. The lack of mealtime rigidity that now exists for these families ('We are just not strict') may therefore result from a more affluent climate, in which choice is not only desirable but a material possibility. In some cases, current family food arrangements were influenced by parents' own food experiences as children, as the following extracts indicate:

GREG: Well I think I quite often believe that a lot that I went through and was made to eat and whatever, that I don't believe you've got to … modern day children, or my children should be forced to do that.

WENDY: OK, when I was growing up you ate whatever you got the first time, you didn't have to ask for seconds but you finished what was on your plate. Anyway my mother would serve this god awful stuff, stewed tomatoes on toast with cheese and its nauseating … and we would have this I would say at least twice a month, and we had to eat it and I swore I would never do that to my children and I don't.

However, the different expectations parents have of mealtimes today are also the result of a difference in parental attitudes; as Angus said, 'society is just a bit more malleable whereas when I was a kid it was a bit more black and white'. Parents today are *expected* to be more flexible and to offer their children certain freedoms.

The extent of the change may be judged by the influence children have over the family menu. These influences are brought out in the following extracts:

> STELLA: No. I had virtually no say in what meals went on the table as a child, whereas my kids do have a say in what does go on the table.
>
> GREG: We [parents] try to I suppose change our own [food preferences] around to suit the children always.

The need to keep children happy and to provide an enjoyable meal for them is often a priority for many of these families. Mealtimes together were expected to be occasions when the family came together to share not only food but also pleasant experiences. And respondents often justified the choice and freedom they gave to children by reference to a need to avoid unpleasant experiences:

> WENDY: I don't see turning the mealtimes into a battleground anyway.
>
> DIANA: I always try to cook something that I know that [husband] is going to get a good meal and at least [son] will have something that he will like.

Sometimes, in order to ensure that mealtimes were positive occasions, the food preferences of children were specifically catered for and a separate meal was prepared, even if this meant extra work for the cook:

> ALISON: It's a nuisance. It's a great nuisance but I tend to do the things, when I'm cooking two separate things, I'll do things that I know the children will definitely eat. So at least I don't feel I've gone to all this trouble to do two separate things and find that they don't eat what I gave them anyway.
>
> JACK: He [son] has been spoilt by his grandmother and [mother]; he quite often gets different things cooked for him because he doesn't like this and he doesn't like that.

For these families, then, the principles that informed meal preparation and presentation were based on the importance of providing children with a certain degree of choice and freedom. They were also informed by the need to provide a happy and harmonious environment in which the family eats, thus avoiding a 'battleground' at mealtimes. A third obligation—that of providing nutritious foods—was often believed to be a necessary mealtime consideration. However, because this obligation often jeopardised harmony and choice, it was referred to as problematic:

> ROSE: We try, I mean if you can get them to eat [healthy food]. Yeah, I would like them to eat meat and three vegetables every night, but they don't always.
>
> CASSIE: I mean, you go to the trouble of trying to prepare something different and something nutritious possibly, you know, and you sort of think 'God, this is a waste of time'.

Some parents took a broader view of the problems that confronted them in feeding the family. Below, Alison recognises the change in the status of children and the way that this has been cultivated in a number of institutions, especially the school.

ALISON: I've been trying to work out why [our children are difficult to feed], and I suspect that they seem to grow up a lot more quickly these days and I think partly because school encourages them to think a lot more for themselves and they are taught that they have rights as children and so they question what we tell them far more, and that includes things like what they're going to eat and what they're not going to eat and how they're going to eat it and where.

As Alison says, the child's rights are dealt with explicitly at school, thereby providing children with notions of autonomy and choice. In the next extract, May, who arrived in Australia from Vietnam 10 years ago, contrasts the attitudes to children in Australia with those she remembers in Vietnam:

MAY: Maybe I [take notice of my children] because I think Vietnamese people you know, their children, when they upset about parent they don't want to say [anything] about them, only keep inside. Because now the children learn Australian school they have their opinion and I think I have to hear [pauses] listen to them, you know, in Vietnam parents very rarely listen to the children.

INTERVIEWER: Is that right?

MAY: Yeah, the children only do what the parent say [and] they have to obey, or have to do anything that the parent wants them to do, you know, and now maybe my children is better than in Vietnam.

Children in Australia are thus constructed by discourses of freedom or choice, which May sees as preferable to the position of children she believed prevailed in Vietnam. She makes the point that children now have to be listened to; their views have to be considered. Autonomy and choice not only construct children as modern subjects, but also assist in the production of 'good parents'—ones who can show the right ethical concern for their children's views. The relationship between the correct way of feeding children and views of good parenting was demonstrated recently in a study by Heather Morton and others (1996). Mothers of two-year-olds considered themselves to be 'good' parents if, first, they gave their children the 'right' foods and, second, if the children ate with visible pleasure and enjoyment. Parental responsibilities concerning the provision of family foods are, then, informed by what is believed to be 'right'. Mealtimes and menus that are influenced by children's preferences, as was the case for many of the families examined earlier, should not therefore be seen as *passive* capitulation by parents. Instead, they should be considered as examples of parents *actively* seeking to do the 'right' thing by implementing child-rearing strategies that recommend negotiation and cooperation, which are designed to encourage autonomy and independence in children and promote happy and harmonious occasions in relation to food.

Conclusions

This chapter set out to examine the way that nutrition advice has mirrored certain social expectations in family life over the course of this century. It has looked at the changing nature of expert advice on feeding children over the last 60 years and has situated these changes within larger social trends in which the relationship between children and parents has undergone a profound change. The influence of expert knowledge has been granted an important role in this analysis since changes in social attitudes have generally followed the standards and norms set by expertise, itself a technology of government. As such, expert knowledge can be seen to inform everyday ethical conduct in terms of the 'right' and the 'wrong' thing to do: it provides the network—the power relationship—within which people conduct themselves. The area of parenting, which is thoroughly imbued with the psychology of child development and family relationships, is a good example of this kind of power, and the examination of expert advice allows for an understanding of the way that specific conducts are articulated so as to shape the desires and aspirations of parents. Of course, this does not mean that parents always do what experts say. What is suggested here is that expert discourse, often reified by science, becomes the moral fabric out of which normality is fashioned. This is not to suggest, however, that expertise is wrong or ill informed: the examination presented here attempts to describe what is, not what should be. It is therefore explanatory rather than critical or judgmental.

The interviews with families reported here highlight a number of changes regarding that which is 'normal' and the labile nature of social phenomena. Participants were able to clearly articulate the changing nature of family life around food and the increasing centrality of children in that process. The rigid and often authoritarian nature of family food practices that these parents experienced as children were entirely consistent with the expert advice of the time. Less well articulated—though still identifiable—were the reasons given by parents for the change to a more flexible approach to family meals. Statements like 'We are just not strict' and phrases such as 'Gone soft' highlight the way that parenting has undergone a change in direction. The new approach—which recognises the need for self-expression and freedom in childhood—assumes that children have autonomy, and attributes to them the responsibility for choosing to eat or not to eat. As shown earlier, this is either explicit or implicit in the advice of experts, who are both reflecting and reinforcing the new approaches to raising children. In reality, however, granting children a sense of independence can often be problematic since the training of children in proper dietary habits can be fraught with difficulties. This is especially the case in light of the parental obligations to promote happy, positive mealtimes. Thus the way out of this dilemma is not the traditional authoritarian approach, the pathological consequences of which have been outlined by experts. On the contrary, as in other areas of family difficulty, parents are encouraged to negotiate and reason with children. Such practices are, in fact, part of the role of today's 'good' parent: the listener, the reflective adviser, the 'sounding board' for children's thoughts, desires, and beliefs (Gordon 1975).

The area of child nutrition, then, provides a way of understanding the process by which social priorities influence nutrition advice. The production of children as self-reflecting, self-regulating individuals is encouraged through the act of choosing 'good' food. But nutrition expertise can also be seen to inform cultural practice by virtue of the fact that it defines which foods are 'good'. Expertise—in its many guises—thus produces 'good' parents: ones who can recognise themselves as having acquired the modern skills of parenting, in which enjoyment, health, and, importantly, choice are central to the management of feeding the family. As this chapter has shown, this societal development is a relatively recent phenomenon, and is perfectly illustrated through a cultural analysis of 'good food' and the 'good child'.

Summary of main points

- Social attitudes to childhood have changed over the last 60 years so that children are now expected to have choice, autonomy, and independence.
- The changing nature of the expectations of childhood is reflected and reinforced in modern advice by nutrition experts about how children's eating habits, in relation to nutritious foods, should be managed.
- Expert advice on feeding the family can be analysed in terms of its government of daily conduct or ethics.
- Expert knowledge on nutrition can, following Foucault, be regarded as a form of power.
- As an example of Foucauldian power, nutrition advice can be seen as positive and productive in that it outlines proper and correct ways of behaving that can fulfil the **ethical responsibilities** of parents.

Discussion questions

1 What are the advantages of analysing the function of the State as 'technologies of government' rather than as a centralised bureaucratic power?

2 Apart from nutritionists, who else may have been important in dispersing notions regarding the management of the proper feeding of children to parents?

3 Brief mention was made in this chapter about the role of the food industry in the provision of food directed at children. Comment further on the sociological impact of food industry practices in this area.

4 Compare and contrast Foucault's understandings of power with those of a more traditional position in social theory (for example, a Marxist position). Highlight the implicit assumptions in each position. Comment on the explanatory possibilities that each position provides for the social actor.

5   This chapter has combined historical data and empirical data collected through interviews. Discuss the current debates that relate to the collection of qualitative research
data, in particular the 'crisis of representation' and the 'crisis of legitimation' (see
Altheide & Johnson 1994). How are the solutions proposed expected to overcome some
of the purported problems in qualitative research?

Further reading

Altheide, D. & Johnson, J. 1994, 'Criteria for Assessing Interpretive Validity in Qualitative
Research', in N. Denzin & Y. Lincoln (eds), *The Handbook of Qualitative Research*, Sage,
Thousand Oaks, Calif.

Charles, N. & Kerr, M. 1988, *Women, Food and Families*, Manchester University Press,
Manchester.

Donzelot, J. 1980, *The Policing of Families*, Hutchinson, London.

Nettleton, S. 1991, 'Wisdom, Diligence and Teeth: Discursive Practice and the Creation of
Mothers', *Sociology of Health and Illness*, vol. 13, pp. 98–111.

Rose, N. 1990, *Governing the Soul: The Shaping of the Private Self*, Routledge, London.

Rose, N. & Miller, P. 1992, 'Political Power beyond the State: Problematics of Government',
British Journal of Sociology, vol. 43, no. 2, pp. 173–205.

References

Altheide, D. & Johnson, J. 1994, 'Criteria for Assessing Interpretive Validity in Qualitative
Research', in N. Denzin & Y. Lincoln (eds), *The Handbook of Qualitative Research*, Sage,
Thousand Oaks, Calif.

Aronson, N. 1982a, 'Nutrition as a Social Problem: A Case Study of Entrepreneurial Strategy in
Science', *Social Problems*, vol. 29, pp. 474–87.

—— 1982b, 'Social Definitions of Entitlement: Food Needs 1885–1920', *Media, Culture and
Society*, vol. 4, pp. 51–61.

Australian Consumers Association 1993, 'Fruit Substitutes for Children', *Choice Magazine*, vol.
34, no. 3, pp. 21–3.

Baker, S. & Henry, R. 1987, *Parents' Guide to Nutrition: Healthy Eating from Birth through
Adolescence*, Addison-Wesley, Reading, Mass.

Bennett, V. & Issacs, S. 1931, *Health and Education in the Nursery*, George Routledge & Sons,
London.

Crotty, P. 1995, *Good Nutrition? Fact and Fashion in Dietary Advice*, Allen & Unwin, Sydney.

Donzelot, J. 1980, *The Policing of Families*, Hutchinson, London.

Fallding, H. 1957, 'Inside the Australian Family', in A. Elkin (ed.), *Marriage and the Family in
Australia*, Angus & Robertson, Sydney.

Finch, L. 1993, *The Classing Gaze: Sexuality, Class and Surveillance*, Allen & Unwin, Sydney.

Foucault, M. 1979, *Discipline and Punish: The Birth of the Modern Prison*, Peregrine Books
(Penguin), London.

—— 1980, 'Truth and Power', in C. Gordon (ed.), *Power/Knowledge: Selected Interviews and Other Writings 1972–1977*, Pantheon Books, New York.

—— 1992, *The History of Sexuality: The Use of Pleasure*, vol. 2, Penguin Books, Harmondsworth.

Gordon T. 1975, *Parent Effectiveness Training: The Tested New Way to Raise Responsible Children*, New American Library, New York.

Greenwood, A. 1993, *Children's Rights: The United Nations Convention on the Rights of the Child*, Australian Early Childhood Association, Canberra.

Heritage, J. 1987, 'Ethnomethodology', in A. Giddens & J. Turner (eds), *Social Action Today*, Stanford University Press, Stanford, Calif.

Hirschmann, J. & Zaphiropoulos, L. 1985, *Solve your Child's Eating Problems*, Fawsett Columbine, New York.

Hitchcock, N. 1989a, 'Infant Feeding in Australia: An Historical Perspective Part 1: 1788–1900', *Australian Journal of Nutrition and Dietetics*, vol. 46, pp. 62–6.

—— 1989b, 'Infant Feeding in Australia: An Historical Perspective Part 2: 1900–1988', *Australian Journal of Nutrition and Dietetics*, vol. 46, pp. 102–8.

King, T. 1933, *Feeding and Caring of Baby*, Macmillan & Co., London.

Mennell, S., Murcott, A., & van Otterloo, A. 1993, *The Sociology of Food: Eating, Diet and Culture*, Sage, London.

Morton, H., Santich, B., & Worsley, T. 1996, 'Mothers' Perception on the Eating Habits of Two-Year-Olds: A Pilot Study', *Australian Journal of Nutrition and Dietetics*, vol. 53, pp. 100–5.

Mothers and Babies' Health Association 1938, *The Australian Mothercraft Book*, Rigby, Adelaide.

National Health and Medical Research Council 1994, *Dietary Guidelines of Children and Teenagers*, AGPS, Canberra.

Nettleton, S. 1991, 'Wisdom, Diligence and Teeth: Discursive Practice and the Creation of Mothers', *Sociology of Health and Illness*, vol. 13, pp. 98–111.

NHMRC. See National Health and Medical Research Council.

Reiger, K. 1986, *Disenchantment of the Home: Modernising the Australian Family 1880–1940*, Oxford University Press, Melbourne.

Rose, N. 1990, *Governing the Soul: The Shaping of the Private Self*, Routledge, London.

Rose, N. & Miller, P. 1992, 'Political Power beyond the State: Problematics of Government', *British Journal of Sociology*, vol. 43, no. 2, pp. 173–205.

Santich, B. 1995, *What the Doctors Ordered: 150 Years of Dietary Advice in Australia*, Hyland House, Melbourne.

Satter, E. 1987, *How to Get your Child to Eat … but Not Too Much*, Bull Publishing Co., Palo Alto.

Spock, B. 1955, *Baby and Child Care*, Bodley Head, London.

Stanton, R. 1990, *Foods for Under Fives*, Allen & Unwin, Sydney.

Stewart-Turner, A. 1986, *The Complete Guide to Feeding your Child*, Science Press, Sydney.

Thompson, S. 1995, *A Healthy Start for Kids: Building Good Eating Patterns for Life*, Simon & Schuster, Sydney.

United Nations General Assembly 1960, *Declaration of the Rights of the Child*, HMSO, London.

Walker, R. & Roberts, D. 1988, *From Scarcity to Surfeit: A History of Food and Nutrition in New South Wales*, New South Wales Press, Sydney.

Part 4

Future Directions

Good to eat, and wholesome to digest, as a worm to a toad, a toad to a snake, a snake to a pig, a pig to a man, and a man to a worm.

Ambrose Bierce, *The Enlarged Devil's Dictionary* (1967)

In this part we focus on future directions for exploring the social appetite in terms of research, public policy, and sociological analysis. Anne Murcott discusses the background of 'The Nation's Diet', a £1.6 million British program aimed at researching food from the perspective of the social sciences. Murcott discusses the wider political context of funded policy research in the social sciences and the potential for the politicisation of research findings. 'The Nation's Diet' provides an example of how the political context shapes research, just as research can shape public policy. Murcott's chapter also raises important questions of inter-sectoral collaboration in the study of food and nutrition in terms of 'territorial disputes, professional rivalries, scientific controversy, and sectoral interests'. The final chapter provides a theoretical synthesis of the three food themes discussed in this book and proposes a hyper-rational social appetite as an umbrella concept to explain the social patterning of food production and consumption.

16

'The Nation's Diet' and the Policy Contexts

Anne Murcott

Overview

- *What is 'The Nation's Diet' program? How was it established? What part might the policy contexts have played in its creation?*

- *What kinds of information are needed to start understanding the relationship between food policy, nutrition policy, and science policy?*

- *Why might the public policy contexts need to be considered when undertaking sociological research?*

This chapter introduces the sociological analysis of the relationship between sociological research and its broader, particularly policy, contexts. It takes as its example the 6-year 'The Nation's Diet' research program funded by the Economic and Social Research Council (UK), which is still being completed. The first section outlines the program itself, both by describing the manner in which its various contexts were already having an influence in the early stages of its development and by highlighting sociology's involvement in this multidisciplinary research effort. The second section sketches developments in nutrition policy, food policy, and science policy that both preceded the program and unfolded during its lifetime. By providing a necessarily simplified chronological account of relevant developments from a long-term historical perspective, the chapter aims to give readers a preliminary and distinctively sociological grasp of the dynamic between sociological research in food and nutrition, and the sociopolitical background against which it is conducted.

Key terms

food choice
food safety
public health
public policy
sociological research

Introduction

This chapter introduces a sociological topic that is too often left on the margins of the discipline: the sociological analysis of the relationship between **sociological research** and its broader, particularly policy, contexts. It does so by taking the British 'The Nation's Diet' research program as its example, outlining the program itself, and then moving on to sketch policy developments that unfolded during its lifetime. Taking a distinctively sociological perspective, it introduces the reader to the dynamic between sociological research in food and nutrition and the sociopolitical background against which it is conducted. The moment 'dynamic' or 'relationship' is mentioned, the passage of time is implicated, thus posing awkward questions about how time can be adequately incorporated into this distinctively sociological understanding.

Sociological research and time—exposing a difficulty

Even though sociology is rarely, if ever, experimentally based, sociological research nevertheless shares with the experimental sciences a studious lack of attention to time. Unless the research is expressly designed to study change, projects and their results are usually interpreted as though they have no duration. So to all intents and purposes, the period of data collection is regarded as a single instant and the data analysed as if they are coincident. The write-up pauses properly to record the length of the project along with other specifics of location, scope, and so on, but then often proceeds to report as if they are irrelevant. Though recording the date or scope places due limits on the study, it also—and not so incidentally—constitutes its unique signature, distinguishing it from all other research projects. Even if the project is treated as having duration, its background—that is, all else in the social world—is liable to be treated as static until the study is completed. Almost paradoxically, the tacit conventions of writing up simultaneously incline the record and publication of the research to claim a status that transcends the coordinates of time and space. For there is an implicit and arguably legitimate claim that, in principle, research findings have some universal character. Not only does the presentation of research tend to eclipse the passage of time; it also tends to omit the social organisation of its origins and form.

This characterisation of sociological research is, of course, something of a caricature. Yet, like most caricatures, it does convey an element of truth in its description of the ordinarily workable convention that governs our work. This convention, however, is liable to be seriously exposed as a fiction, either by projects that last longer than the average 3 years or by great and/or rapid changes in the background. Both of these factors are at issue in outlining 'The Nation's Diet' research program and its **public policy** location.[1] This

---

1   I am grateful to the Economic and Social Research Council (UK) for supporting 'The Nation's Diet' research program. I also wish to thank the following: members of the 'Islington Seminar' for discussions about the sociologies and geographies of food; Elizabeth Murphy and Martin Hughes for many insightful comments about the management of research; Keara Hooper and Elizabeth Marshall for a friendly interlude more timely than they could have realised; and Magali Douillet and David Charlesworth for preparing the figures.

major, and perhaps unique, program just happened to be British (although, in the future there may be a case to be made that a conjunction of antecedent forces define it as peculiarly British). And its 6-year life just happened to begin in 1992.

It will not be known for a long while yet whether 1992–98 will be judged as lying in the midst of the most dramatic decade for food, eating, and nutrition in the United Kingdom since the Second World War (when the food supply was threatened). It might just as well turn out that, in hindsight, the events of the 1990s pale in comparison with startling events to come. Naturally, such future events cannot be accurately foretold, even if some might be imagined—or feared, such as an epidemic of fatalities from new-variant Creutzfeld-Jacob disease (nv-CJD) caused by bovine spongiform encephalopathy (BSE). In the meantime, there is plenty of sociological work to be done—some of which is discussed in this chapter. More broadly, the chapter seeks to lay some of the foundations for future analysis of the relationship between sociological research and public policy in food and nutrition.

A select chronology as a preliminary aid to thinking

In order to portray the program and its policy contexts, while simultaneously trying to avoid premature judgments about the period in which it has been running, a long historical perspective of fifty or so years has been adopted. While it is not appropriate to discuss that history in any detail here, a sketch is provided in the selected chronology, set out in Tables 16.1 and 16.2.[2] Representing multiple dimensions and intensely complex social realities in so simple a form runs the risk of being misleading. Treated with circumspection, however, it can serve as a preliminary aid to thinking—but no more than that.

Table 16.1 spans the postwar period up to the end of the 1980s. Note that one of the 1989 entries is a proposal to develop a 'Research Initiative on Health and Nutrition'. This was the first stage in the gestation of what became 'The Nation's Diet'—impertinently classified under the heading Sociology (Social Anthropology) despite, as will be seen, its being a multidisciplinary social science effort. Note too that its title changed, as will also be seen.

The chronology is designed to distinguish various elements of social change from one another, in order to offer a basis for future analyses. On the extreme left are classified socioeconomic trends, which, for the purposes of studying certain selected aspects of food sociologically, were treated as happening 'by themselves'. This is untrue, of course. Human agency is anything but absent from unemployment rates, the innovations of self-service stores and supermarkets, the recruitment of Jamaican migrants to the British labour force, or the invention, production, and marketing of freezers or

---

2   The tabular representation of the chronology is adapted from a chronology devised for a 1990 conference paper (Murcott 1990a) on 'Nutrition and Health in Post-War Britain', but not included in an abbreviated, published version (Murcott 1994). Table 16.2 provides a partial update of the original chronology.

Table 16.1 Selected entries from table showing developments in nutrition and health in postwar Great Britain, 1945–89

Year	Socioeconomic changes	Social movements	Market & market-related research	Social nutrition	Policy	Policy analysis, commentary, & official monitoring	Social history	Sociology (Social Anthropology)
1945	Bird's Eye begin frozen-food processing				Wartime rationing continues			
1951	21.74% of married women in labour force	1st edn of The Good Food Guide						
1966	38.08% of married women in the labour force			Barker & McKenzie (eds), Our Changing Fare	Minister of Health rules against preservation of food by irradiation		Burnett, Plenty and Want; Barker & McKenzie (eds), Our Changing Fare	Garron, Captive Wife; Levi-Strauss, The Culinary Triangle; Wilmott, Adolescent Boys
1974	26% of expenditure on income out at take-aways & pubs	1st postwar edn of Michelin Red Guide to Great Britain				AFRC/ Medical Research Council, Food & Nutrition Research		Douglas & Nicod, Taking the Biscuit
1986	66% of households own a freezer; Over 25% of households own a microwave oven. Total frozen-food expenditure in UK is £1193 million	Alan Davidson begins compiling Oxford Companion to Food		McKenzie, Consumer's View of Healthy Diet	Labour Party's 'Food Policy' released	Wenlock et al., The Diets of British School Children OPCS; Anderson, A Diet of Reason (Social Affairs Unit)	Society for the Social History of Medicine (SSHM) annual conference is on nutrition for the first time	
1989	ESRC proposes research initiative on health & nutrition							

Table 16.2 Nutrition and health in postwar Great Britain, 1989–97

Year	Socioeconomic changes	Social movements	Social nutrition	Policy	Policy analysis, commentary, & official monitoring	Social sciences	Science Policy
1989		BNF initiate 'Food—a factor of life' campaign for schools		MAFF, Food Safety—Protecting the Consumer (White Paper)	Department of Health, The Diets of British Schoolchildren		
1990		10th Oxford Symposium is on 'Feasting & Fasting'		Food Safety Act	50th anniversary of the National Food Survey		
				Department of Health, HEA, & MAFF, Eight Guidelines for a Healthy Diet	Gregory et al., The Dietary and Nutritional Survey of British Adults		
1991		BDA & HEA 'Food Network' conference		COMA, Dietary Reference Values… nomenclature changed: increased number of nutrients from 10 to 40		2nd Symposium of the International Commission for Research into European Food History, held at Brunel University	
				Health of the Nation Green Paper			
1992				Health of the Nation White Paper		First Food Choice conference (Psychology)	
				Initiation of Nutrition Task Force		Launch of ESRC research program 'The Nation's Diet' (multidisciplinary social sciences)	

Year	Socioeconomic changes	Social movements	Social nutrition	Policy	Policy analysis, commentary, & official monitoring	Social sciences	Science Policy
1993	Vegetarian cheese made with genetically modified bacterium goes on sale	*Nutritional Guidelines for School Meals* (Caroline Walker Trust report)				Second SSHM conference on Nutrition (Glasgow)	*Realising our Potential* White Paper
1994				COMA, *Nutritional Aspects of Cardiovascular Disease* (includes recommendations in terms of portions of types of food) Nutrition Task Force Action Plan			Technology Foresight (TF) program launched Food & Drink is one of the initial foresight sector panels National Health Survey research & development initiative—'Priority Setting in Nutrition'
1995	Tesco stops selling European veal	Social Affairs Unit, *A New Diet of Reason* NCH Actions & Maternity Alliance report on poverty and under-nourishment in pregnancy	Death of John Yudkin	'Balance of Good Health' diet information campaign launched by HEA			

Year	Socioeconomic changes	Social movements	Social nutrition	Policy	Policy analysis, commentary, & official monitoring	Social sciences	Science Policy
1996	NFS records lowest ever level of whole-milk purchases			Nutrition Task Force progress report		LINK research program—'Eating, Food and Health'—proposed by BBSRC, ESRC, & MAFF	ESRC, MRC, BBSRC asked to nominate members to TF Food & Drink Panel
	E Coli 0157 outbreak in central Scotland			Nutrition Task Force low income project team report			
	Import to UK of genetically modified maize from USA			Diet Action Plan for Scotland			
	Mass-media coverage of 'Olestra' (fat-free fat)						
	Genetically modified tomato puree on shelf						
1997	New E Coli 0157 outbreak in Scotland	Royal Society of Arts, Cooking Counts (food in schools)		EC Green Paper on food law in the European Union			
	Chocolate-flavoured carrots launched	Information on Sugars report on misleading claims of 'sugar free'		James Report on a food standards agency			
	Co-op announces ban of sale of 'alcopops' in its stores	Which report on inaccuracies in nutritional labelling		Black Report to be updated			
				Excellence in Schools White Paper recommends reinstatement of minimum nutritional standards for school meals			
				Pennington recommendations on E Coli to be implemented in full			

microwave ovens. But it is self-evident that such phenomena can be classified separately from other intentional human activity, such as:

1 public policy about food and nutrition
2 efforts to influence public policy about food and nutrition—such as by social movements, lobbies, and pressure groups
3 the study of food and nutrition as market or market-related research—that is, tightly specified, heavily focused research for commercial clients
4 the compilation of official statistics about, and/or the study of, food and nutrition in order to support or monitor activity 1 or 2—that is, applied or strategic research
5 university-based science, including basic (pure or 'blue skies') research in the social sciences of food and nutrition (compare the distinction between basic, strategic, and applied nutrition set out in James 1993).

Although this list is not exhaustive, any examination of the relationship between research and public policy would need to keep these five types of activity in view. Academic disciplines are lined up on the right hand side of the table broadly to signal that they stand apart from their subject matter. This is not to claim that all disciplines or subjects found in universities are of this type—only that the university has a high concentration of them and is a social location in which they are legitimately entitled to flourish. This classificatory arrangement reflects the view that academic disciplines are somehow to be disengaged from food and nutrition as their object of study. And they are to steer clear of alignment with particular sets of values associated with that object of study. The rationale for these disciplines' interest in the field of nutrition is not solely, or even predominantly, the amelioration of human nutritional status or ensuring the security of the food supply. In this respect, a defining quality of the academic is that, for the purposes of enquiry, the unpopular or the controversial is to be analysed in its own terms and taken as seriously as the popular or uncontroversial. Such an approach is not to be misunderstood as endorsing any one position or any other relevant set of values.

This view, of course, reflects a particular liberal position on the nature of knowledge and the role of the academic. It is one that, in rough-and-ready terms, draws a distinction between understanding the world and changing the world; the former is, in principle at least, to be the realm of (social) science, and the latter of engagement in political activity. In practice, the distinction is not straightforward, and remains perpetually perilous and in tension. Even so, the self-same liberal position insists that care should be taken not to confuse such necessary academic disinterest with some amoral indifference or lack of commitment to attempts to improve the human condition. It simply signals an approach that differs from, and exists in addition to, specifically 'targeted' applications of knowledge, such as those used by those seeking to improve nutritional status, to support health promotion practice, or to sell more chocolate bars.

The chronology and its classification is used as a sketch map of an extensive terrain, serving as a very broad background against which to look more closely at the specifics of 'The Nation's Diet' and at its policy contexts. In doing so, the reader should bear in mind that, although this chapter stands as a contribution to the sociology of food and nutrition, the discussion is not a full-blown sociological analysis of either the research program or the policy backgrounds.[3] It is still far too early to begin anything of the kind. It is not too early, though, to indicate some of the elements that such an analysis will need systematically to take into account—which is what is attempted here.

'The Nations' Diet': its origin and form

This section describes the inception and nature of the program. It illustrates influences connecting the wider policy context with the shaping of the program, as well as briefly spotlighting the location of sociology in a multidisciplinary research enterprise.

ESRC programs and the profile of 'The Nation's Diet'

The UK Economic and Social Research Council (ESRC) committed £1.6 million to its 6-year coordinated research program '"The Nation's Diet": the social science of food choice'. The program consists of sixteen research projects (in two phases of eight each) and two research fellowships. These are based in universities (and one independent research institute) in England, Scotland, and Wales. Three of the eighteen studies are exclusively sociological (see Table 16.3). Each project was designed independently of the others, which obviously means that they are self-contained and that each could stand alone. So the location, disciplinary identities, and topics of the projects range very broadly. In certain critical respects, their combined 'profile' is arbitrary—a feature that derives from the distinct character of ESRC programs—although commissioning panels seek to balance the projects supported across the main themes of each program.

At any one time, the Research Council has a portfolio of some twenty research programs. Its programs are typically multidisciplinary, spanning a range of the social sciences. The ESRC deploys over 30 per cent of its budget for research through programs. Among other things, these programs support research in specific areas that are underinvestigated, relevant to policy, or otherwise deserving of special attention. Unless cross-nationality is

---

3   This chapter takes off from the editors' original brief to provide a summary of program findings to date, to cover their implications for public policy, and to give an overview of its management—but it is none of these. For one thing, at the time of writing, the program still has well over a year to run. In any case, the findings are now far too extensive to be sensibly summarised in a chapter (but see the chapters 7 and 14 in this volume; Murcott 1997; Murcott 1998a; and the program's website, <http://www.sbu.ac.uk/~natdi>, which provides both summaries for non-specialists and a list of publications). Also, a summary would be a little out of place in this volume, given that 'The Nation's Diet' is multidisciplinary rather than exclusively sociological. As to running the program, this chapter is not about its management, although it is a view from the very peculiar vantage point of the Director (see Table 16.1 and see Hughes 1998).

Table 16.3   Projects and fellowships in 'The Nation's Diet' program, indicating their main social scientific disciplinary bases*

	Topic of project or fellowship	Disciplinary base
Phase 1	Concepts of healthy eating: a comparative anthropological investigation (phase 1)	social anthropology
	Dietary change among South Asians and Italians in Glasgow	sociology
	Teaching and learning about food and nutrition in schools	education
	The effect on the family of one member's change in diet	economics/sociology
	The effects of life stress on food choice	psychology
	The psychological determinants of children's food preferences	psychology
	The role of the media in the emergence of food 'panics'	media studies
	What we eat and why: a socioeconomic study of standard items in food consumption	economics
Phase 2	Ambivalence about health-related dietary change	psychology
	Concepts of healthy eating: a comparative anthropological investigation (phase 2)	social anthropology
	Constructing the consumer interest: retailing, regulation and food quality	human geography
	Consumption, diet and ageing: the construction of food choice in later life	psychology
	Eating out and eating in: households and food choice	sociology
	Food choices made by mothers on behalf of babies and young children	sociology
	The decision not to eat meat: an analysis of changing preferences	economics
	The marriage menu—food and diet in transition after marriage	sociology
Research fellowships	After the store wars: return to the high street?	human geography
	Changing conditions of competition and regulation in UK food retailing	
	Employment status, domestic situation, and food choice	sociology

* Brevity requires an over-simplified listing, which fails to do justice to the collaborations of some of the projects; for fuller exposition, see Murcott 1998a.

integral to the topic, this research tends to be national rather than international. A specialist in the field concerned is appointed as part-time Director (compare Hughes 1998). The Director's role is to coordinate the academic work of the separate projects (competitively funded and peer-reviewed in the usual way) that make up each program and to help draw the attention of that work to potential users of the research outside the academy.

During the period when 'The Nation's Diet' was developed, the ESRC's internal procedure involved two stages of bidding to compete for funds with other proposals for initiatives (as they were then known). The Stage I proposal was approved by Council in October 1989 (see Table 16.1). The development work was the responsibility of a small sub-group of the ESRC's Human Behaviour and Development Group, which was responsible for psychology and education, with sociology, politics, economics, and so on being the responsibility of other development groups. (The Council has since been reorganised, replacing development groups with new board structures). The sub-group was composed of representatives of three social science disciplines: health economics, psychology, and social policy and administration.

In order to work up the Stage II bid, two academic reviews were commissioned— on the psychology of nutrition (Wardle 1990) and on the economics of nutrition (Ensor 1990)—to augment and support the sub-group's appreciation of the state of work in the field at that time. As part of the ESRC's very long-established policy that programs have relevance and utility beyond the academic community, the usual proce- dure was followed in commissioning an academic as a very short-term consultant to conduct a series of 'wide ranging consultations with relevant institutions and individu- als' (Murcott 1990a).[4]

Sociological aspects of a multidisciplinary social science program

Obviously, the approach that implicitly informs any such series of consultations will be influenced to some extent by the disciplinary identity and professional biography of whoever is appointed to do the work. So in this instance, key elements of the think- ing were inevitably closer to sociology than to other relevant social science disciplines, and were derived from my earlier observations of the field. One of these elements relied on familiarity with the well-established sociological (social anthropological) lit- erature in health and illness (for instance, Freidson 1970; and see Nettleton 1995 for a recent introduction) as well as with the far sparser work in food and eating (Murcott 1988b). The reading of both these literatures enabled not only the definition of health but also the social organisation of nutritional, **public health**, and health promotion practice to be treated as integral to the field to be investigated. That is, nutrition, pub- lic health, and health promotion could be problematised and treated as data, as distinct from being disciplines with which to investigate the field. This is not to deny the sci- entific standing or professional status of these disciplines, any more than it is to lay imperialistic claim to their intellectual territory. It is simply to include them as part of the terrain to be studied.

A second observation that informed the consultation work was that, in key respects, many of the varied interests in the field are more than just independent of each other; they are so separate as to constitute segments wholly insulated from each other's influ- ence (Murcott 1988a). Consequently, it was thought to be particularly important to try to avoid confining the consultations to some segment or another, or, worse, being cap- tured by any vested interest. So the range was intentionally wide. Thus, in addition to government departments, pressure groups, professional associations, and the academic community, the consultation included representation that covered the length of the food chain from 'production to consumption'—including agriculture through to man- ufacturing, retailing, and consumers' spokespersons.

---

4   It should be noted that it is by no means automatic that the consultant undertaking such devel- opment work will be later appointed Director should the program be funded, even though this was eventually the case for 'The Nation's Diet'.

The process of developing the program led to its being recast to extend beyond and encompass (rather than be confined to) research in the social sciences on 'Health and Nutrition', as had been initially envisaged. This significant shift in emphasis was reflected in the title of the program that was eventually funded in 1991. This extension of the program's range resulted from bringing together a grasp of the existing academic literature with an appraisal of the non-academic background. The development group took the view that an artificial boundary could not and should not be drawn between, on the one hand, *health and nutrition*—including notably the public policy concerns— and, on the other, the effect of different sectors, notably industrial and commercial sectors engaged in the provision of *food*. To this extent, it catered for a sociological perspective, which recognises, among other things, that:

- human activities with implications for health are not always embarked on expressly in the name of health
- human beings eat food not nutrients
- what counts as food is as much socially as biologically defined
- there may be 'good' reasons for 'bad' nutritional habits.

Such scope is not peculiarly sociological; rather, peculiarly sociological approaches were thus made possible—although even a 6-year program such as 'The Nation's Diet' cannot hope to exhaust the opportunities for worthwhile sociological investigation that it creates. In any case, such scope encompasses what is shared and distinctive about *all* the social sciences' attitude towards the field of study.

The consultation work—and this is the third observation—also served as a reminder, if it was needed, that the terrain in which the program was to be set is not only colonised by the wide variety of interests noted above but also, on occasion, heavily contested. As was stressed in the initial consultant's report:

> In proposing such an Initiative, the ESRC is moving into a territory already heavily colonised by numerous other sciences, a range of health and other service practitioners and a wide diversity of government, industrial and consumer interests and responsibilities. A territory of fruitful collaborations and well-established alliances, it also serves, from time to time, as something of a battleground for scientific controversy, professional rivalries, sectoral interests and irreconcilable philosophical attitudes to public policy (Murcott 1990a, p. 1).

Nonetheless, one question emerged as being of common concern to all: 'What makes people eat what they do?' Altering this question slightly to become 'Why do people eat what they do?', this was adopted as the central question to be addressed by the program. Though collected under the sub-heading of 'food choice', the program is highly diverse. Indeed, this diversity is its hallmark and is evident throughout, not least in the wide variation among its projects' interpretations of, and methodological approaches to, 'food choice' itself (Murcott 1998a).

As is illustrated, for instance, by Rory Williams (Williams et al. 1998), Alan Warde (Warde & Martens 1998), and Elizabeth Murphy (Murphy et al. 1998), this variation tends to run along disciplinary lines, with sociology's stance set some considerable distance from other approaches, such as that of economics (See Fine et al. 1996, for instance). Sociologists (and social anthropologists) are less likely to proceed by adopting a definition of food choice that is operationalised, a measure devised and then studied as a dependent variable. Sociologists are more likely to want to 'problematise' food choice. Furthermore, they may prefer to see their stance as sceptical and/or as one that leaves open the question of whether choice even exists—along the lines perhaps of 'beggars can't be choosers'. They are likely to regard certain questions as integral to their object of study, such as whether choice is:

1 evenly spread through a population
2 varies according to social status or occasion
3 is itself a value that then can be analysed in relation to some hierarchy of values, and so on.

They may also want to ask, as does Warde (Warde & Martens 1998), whether choice can be usefully regarded as an appropriate notion in the study of human activity and social life, particularly when something as intensely personal and individual as suicide, for instance, can be subject to systematic social variation and can be regarded as displaying socially constructed motivation. All these distinctively sociological characterisations of food choice and approaches to its investigation are pursued in the program's work, tending to set these approaches apart from other disciplines' contributions.

The policy contexts: food policy, nutrition policy, science policy

Although the work of the program itself has naturally claimed much of the attention of those associated with it, the external contexts have had to be registered nonetheless. This task forms part of an ESRC director's remit, albeit more as publicist and manager than as a scholar or academic researcher. This section outlines how the general public-policy background to activities concerned with the population's food intake has continued to be the subject of shift and debate.

On one hand—with probably unintended consequences for changing British food habits—there are proposals and policies at the European (Common Agricultural Policy, the single market, and so on) and international levels—for example, the General Agreement on Tariffs and Trade (GATT). These international developments clearly require sociological investigation to complement work in economics and political science—investigation that, it seems, is still to be initiated. Although the international dimension is vital to a fuller understanding of the nation's diet, further consideration falls outside the scope of this chapter—and, it should be said, the Director's remit. On the other hand, there are movements within the United Kingdom, some of which are considered below beginning with the nutritional features of public health policy.

Nutrition policy: 'multi-sectoral' working

The nutritional features of public health policy have seen sustained activity since the landmark events of the early 1980s, when attention broadened from concentrating on selected groups at so-called nutritional risk to encompass the diet of the whole population (see Murcott 1994). Developments in the nutritional features of public health policy in the 1990s illustrate one aspect that, it is proposed here, distinguishes the policy contexts of the 1990s from those of earlier postwar decades. This aspect is a trend towards what has come to be referred to (at least in health promotion circles) as 'multi-sectoral working'. One of its recent and major expressions in England (with counterparts in other regions of the United Kingdom) is a 1992 White Paper entitled 'The Health of the Nation' (Department of Health 1992).

As will be seen in a moment, multi-sectoral involvement is integral to this 1992 document, but it is not introduced by it. Any policy development is probably traceable not just to preceding documentation—formal and informal—but also to oral exchanges (whose details may only be captured by chance in memoirs or political diaries, or if a special study is mounted that duly records them). So, in noting two antecedents to the White Paper, I am not claiming that they represent all the thinking that went before. Indeed, only one, the Green Paper (that is, the document that ordinarily precedes a White Paper), can strictly be regarded as a formal antecedent. Appearing in June 1991 (Department of Health 1991b), and sharing the same name as its successor White Paper, it is a 'consultative document for health', and more than 2000 organisations and individuals submitted their comments on it.

Reflecting the considerable debate surrounding nutrition policy (as well as health policy), the Green Paper's publication prompted a statement by the Labour Party (then in Opposition) that was reported in the press (*The Independent*, 4 June 1991). The statement promised that Labour would address the link between poor income and poor health, and that an action plan, rather than targets, would be put in place—a plan that included the labelling of foodstuffs to show their sugar, fat, and salt content. Surprising as it may seem, what *distinguishes* the White Paper is its creation of the first-ever strategy for public health (for England, with parallels for the rest of the country), focusing especially on the prevention of ill health and the promotion of good health, along with the reduction of avoidable disease and premature death. All the same, it continues the theme established in 1976 (under a Labour government), which stresses that the onus is on individuals to take responsibility for their own health. The Green Paper identifies a set of sixteen possible 'key areas', which include diet (and alcohol), under the heading of 'contributing factors to both mortality and morbidity and to healthy living', and food safety, which is listed along with HIV/AIDS and other communicable diseases under the heading of 'areas where there is a great potential for harm' (1991b, p. 35). A year later, the White Paper adopted five initial key areas to 'represent the beginning of a rolling programme for priority action' (1992, p. 15).

Its status as the first public-health policy in the United Kingdom, and its continuity with the earlier view that members of the public have a responsibility for looking after their own health are clearly two important historical features of the White Paper. But as important is the planned involvement of different sectors—public, private, and voluntary—in the support of the policy's intentions. The promotion of a principle of 'co-ordinated action ... from a range of interested parties' had already been enunciated in a meeting held the year before the Green Paper was published; this meeting is the other antecedent to explicit approbation of multi-sectoral working to be noted here.

This meeting was the Food Network conference, which the 1990 program consultation work (described earlier) had identified in the meeting's planning stages. It was duly held in March 1991 and later reported in a publication of the same name (Hurren & Black 1991). This occasion was intended not only to bring together 'different (and often conflicting) interests' but to improve on discussions of the previous decade by including all parts, not just some, of what they described as the 'food network' (Hurren & Black 1991, p. 7). The network encompasses processors, producers, caterers, retailers, education and media, and government, with consumers at the centre of the network. The task was to 'open up a debate on nutrition and health' with the novel idea of the network at its centre: 'Instead of a food chain with perhaps inflexible links and set relationships, the meshes of a net are inter-connected and a pull on one will affect the shape of all' (Hurren & Black 1991, p. 1).

Such multi-sectoral coordination is evident in the provisions of the White Paper. For, in its wake, the Nutrition Task Force was created to develop and coordinate a program of action to implement the nutritional aspects of its strategy. With Professor Dame Barbara Clayton in the chair, the task force was a substantial presence, consisting of twenty-four members, five observers, and a secretariat of five. Intended to work up until October 1995, the task force brought a number of government departments—the Department of Health, the Ministry of Agriculture, Fisheries and Food (MAFF), the Department for Education and the Department of Employment (now merged into a single department), and the Department of Social Security—together with representatives from food producers, manufacturers and retailers, caterers, health and local authority services, the voluntary sector, the media, and advertising (Department of Health 1992, pp. 53–4). By January 1994 there were four working groups in operation:

1 information and education (public, schools, and media)
2 catering
3 food chain
4 National Health Service (NHS) services and health care professionals.

Each had membership cutting across the various sectors and was designed to collaborate in 'healthy alliances'. And, in the same year, an Action Plan was produced (Department of Health 1994a).

This sort of cross-cutting liaison in the nutrition policy arena may possibly strike the reader as commonplace. If it does, then it is arguably all the more remarkable. For, as indicated earlier, when the consultation that formed part of the development work for 'The Nation's Diet' was undertaken, a defining quality of the field was a strong tendency to subdivision into insulated segments, rather than overlap in any kind of intermeshed network—to use Caroline Hurren and Alison Black's vocabulary. It would seem that attempts within the policy community at least to develop dialogues across the subdivisions, if not to dissolve them, had paid off. Moreover, the change that those within the policy community sought to engineer appears to have been achieved in little more than a decade.

Further and fuller analysis is, of course, needed to confirm any suggestion that these cross-sectoral dialogues have indeed been newly established on a larger scale in the postwar period. And any such analysis will also have to take account of two further features of the policy background against which 'The 'Nation's Diet' program has been running. One of these lies, unresolved, at the heart of nutrition and food policies in the United Kingdom (as elsewhere).

Nutrition policy, food policy: circles to be squared

In essence, the current policy questions and the practical activities that flow from them appear to centre on reconciling potentially conflicting public health and food policies. The circumstances may be summarised as the desire for simultaneously:

- achieving nutritional targets measured by modifications in the whole population's dietary intake
- remaining faithful to the principle of freedom of consumer choice, coupled with continued efforts to make that choice informed
- pursuing regulatory policies that optimise commercial (capitalist) freedom of supply, including new product development and the exploitation of novelty in genetic and biotechnology.

Illustration of this tension-ridden position was provided when underlying disagreements surfaced with the publication in autumn 1994 of a new Committee on Medical Aspects (COMA) report on diet and heart disease by the Cardiovascular Review Group. The focus of comment, and of some dissent, appears to have been the report's attempt to translate dietary modification that is protective against heart diseases, previously expressed in nutritional terms, into recommended intake in terms of foods. Leaked before publication, the report apparently sparked behind-the-scenes lobbying of government departments, public divisions of opinion between representatives of industry, and efforts to restore 'consensus' in the following weeks.

Policies for the sciences themselves

The third aspect distinguishing the 1990s policy contexts of 'The Nation's Diet' concerns science policy in the United Kingdom. In addition to the events described above, this period has seen activities that lie on the margins between policy and practical efforts aimed at changing food habits, on the one hand, and (social science) research about food choice, on the other. Such activities have had far reaching effects on the policy contexts of 'The Nation's Diet' program. Their influence has stemmed from two directions, which have inevitably also interlocked. First, they sustained a 'multi-sectoral' character as well as reproducing those unresolved tensions between nutrition policy and food policy already indicated. Second, they led to what many in the academic community experienced as a major upheaval in the organisation of research, its funding, and its ethos. Of course, major change was intended. Whether the intended consequences have been achieved and what, if any, costs have been incurred in the process can only be adequately answered at some point in the future.

These changes were triggered by the publication of a separate White Paper, this time on science policy (OST 1993). It provided for an overhaul of the research councils' governance and organisation, marked by giving them new mission statements. So far-reaching was this overhaul that those involved in managing research needed to devote a good deal of time and care to working through its implications with principal investigators and their research staffs. In the process, the attention of all concerned needed to be drawn to the manner in which the government's strategy was geared towards 'improv[ing]' the nation's competitiveness and quality of life' by, among other things, 'developing stronger partnerships with and between the science ... communities [and] industry' and continuing to promote the public understanding of science (OST 1993, p. 68). As a consequence, the relationship between the academic and the non-academic was thrown into sharp focus. This was evident in the revised mission statements set out in the White Paper for all the research councils (bar the Particle Physics and Astronomy Research Council), not just the ESRC, which placed 'special emphasis on meeting the needs of the users of its research ... output, thereby enhancing the UK's industrial competitiveness and quality of life' (OST 1993, p. 29). Among the research users on the ESRC's list are business, government, non-profit organisations, the media, and the general public, as well as academic researchers. Renewed and stronger emphasis was thereby placed on continuing to engage the attention of key 'contacts' concerned with the production and consumption of food in these various sectors who had already been made aware of 'The Nation's Diet' program's existence.

A second and overlapping set of consequences flowing from the 1993 science White Paper included a series of exercises, notably the creation of a British Technology Foresight Programme to develop a view of the nation's needs in science, technology, and so on over the next 10–20 years. Self-evidently related to the increased emphasis on engagement between researchers and the users of research beyond the academic community, its purpose includes 'identifying and prioritising markets and technologies of future importance for wealth creation and quality of life in the UK'. Accordingly, fifteen panels of experts in different areas were established to develop detailed reviews.

One of these panels, formed in the spring of 1994, was devoted to food and drink. In the second phase of its work, this panel carried out consultation among the various interests across the country, both through regional workshops and by post (OST 1995).

Among the panel's recommendations are some relating to what it describes as 'consumer science'. It reports that 'sensory perception of product quality; the psychology of consumer choice; and risk perception associated with the acceptance of novel technologies all require further research' (OST 1995, p. 2). And it recommends that a program of work in this area be jointly developed by two research councils—the Biology and Biotechnology Research Council (BBSRC) and the ESRC—and a government department (naming MAFF, rather than the Department of Health). By 1996 these two research councils, together with the Medical Research Council (MRC) were asked to nominate members to join the Food and Drink Panel. And by 1997, proposals funded under 'LINK' rules, which require co-sponsorship with an industrial partner, were in place for a new research program, likely to be entitled 'Eating, Food and Health', with £1 million support from each of the BBSRC and the ESRC, together with a further probable £0.5 million from MAFF. There is likely to be support from the Department of Health.

A new government, 'New Labour': a new start?

A selection of other policy landmarks of the period from 1989 is included on the Tables 16.1 and 16.2, but for present purposes, they are left to speak for themselves. For, by way of conclusion, this abbreviated exposition now moves ahead 'fast forward' to 1997 and the weeks following the general election on 1 May to add a short epilogue to this section's overview of 'The Nation's Diet' policy contexts.

Commentators had a field day well into May drawing parallels between the celebration surrounding the landslide victory of 'New Labour' and the public euphoria associated with another new Labour government elected in 1945. As the publicists and journalists expressed it at the time, the new Labour government 'hit the ground running'. A good many proposals and measures were speedily announced very soon after Labour came to power, a number of which presage major changes in nutrition and food policy. These include four significant items. First, the government intends to restore the requirement that school meals meet defined nutritional specifications (Department for Education and Employment 1997)—a requirement that had been abolished under Margaret Thatcher's government in the Education Act of 1980. Then, with the creation of the Independent Inquiry into Inequalities in Health, set up by the Minister for Public Health and chaired by a former chief medical officer, provision has been made for the Black Report, 'Inequalities in Health' (Department of Health and Social Security 1980), to be updated. This report reviewed the existing evidence that showed consistent correlations between lower socioeconomic position and premature death. It encompassed the question of the place of diet, noting that the lower the social class, the greater the likelihood that the diet will depart from current nutritional advice. In addition, the new government announced its intention to implement all thirty-two of the recommendations proposed by Professor Hugh Pennington (Professor of Bacteriology at the University of Aberdeen), who chaired the group set up following the 1996 outbreak of *E Coli* O157 in central Scotland.

Much the most prominent event of those heady early summer days, however, was the release of the 'James Report'. Amid the unresolved attempts to square the circle of food versus nutrition policy, various pressure groups (see, for example, Lang et al. 1996) have levelled the criticism that MAFF cannot be the government department charged with championing the industrial interests of agriculture and simultaneously bear responsibility for food safety and consumer protection (compare Mills 1992). As if the mounting problem of BSE were not bad enough, the Scottish *E Coli* outbreak had become notorious as one of the most severe on record anywhere in the world, making matters for the government and its ministries worse. Faced with the need to restore public confidence, and with the continuing economic consequences of the European Community (EC) ban on exports of British beef, the then Conservative government was obliged, or so it seemed, to capitulate to criticism. By January 1997 it announced proposals for the appointment of a food safety adviser, along with plans for a new Food Safety Council.

Historians may eventually judge the proposals to have been too little, too late. At the beginning of March 1997, while they were still in Opposition, but with the opinion polls more and more certainly predicting a change of government, the Labour Party requested Professor W. P. T. James, Director of the Rowett Institute in Aberdeen, to 'propose the function and structure of a Food Standards Agency'. James put his signature to the report on 30 April 1997, and within days of coming to power, the new government made it available—duly initiating the conventional period of consultation.

Concluding observations

Accepting the invitation to discuss 'The Nation's Diet' has produced an unusual chapter for an introductory textbook. It has been specially written in the belief that, however new the reader is to sociology, they should, from the outset, have an appreciation of what lies at the heart of any discipline—that is, research. Moreover, as sociologists, it behoves us, from time to time, to regard the manner in which our research is organised—including its sociopolitical contexts—as itself open to sociological investigation. Were we to neglect such investigation, we would be failing to live up to what we profess.

It was with all this in mind that the crude classification of this chapter's selected chronology (Tables 16.1 and 16.2) is presented. It provides, among other things, a means of identifying the relation between sociology and other activities exemplified in the chronology. Socioeconomic changes are already, obviously, the object of sociological investigation. But by comparison, the nature of the relation between sociology and the other spheres is more intricate. For instance, sociologists might be employed to work alongside social nutritionists, or sociological studies might be drawn upon by those active in one or other nutrition-related social movement or pressure group. Sociologists might be interested in discovering ways of engaging more closely with those in market research, and sociologists, along with activist and market researchers, draw on the output of official statistical monitoring.

A great deal of research remains to be done. I will focus on just one glaring omission as an example.[5] In the British context at least, organisations such as the industry-funded British Nutrition Foundation, and activists and pressure groups—such as Action and Information on Sugars, The Social Affairs Unit, or the group now based at the Centre for Food Policy, Thames Valley University in London (see, for example, Lang 1997)—have been particularly prominent, especially in the last two decades. Yet, we can search in vain for the sociological literature on this extraordinarily influential form of social activity—even though, *prima facie*, it exactly conforms to early stages of Herbert Blumer's now classic definition of social movements 'as collective enterprises to establish a new order of life' (Blumer 1951, p. 199).

Newcomers to sociology are already likely to appreciate that they ought to think about the implications of research for public policy. But they also need to appreciate that there is a continuing relation between policy and research, which is neither simple nor one-way. Further, they are to be encouraged to reflect sociologically on the social, political, and economic organisation of this complex, two-way relation. And if any reader has been inspired to embark on further development of the as yet understated sociology—a 'meta-sociology'—of the policy contexts of sociological research in food and nutrition sketched here, then this chapter will have succeeded in one of its main aims.

Summary of main points

- The case of the ESRC's research program 'The Nation's Diet' and the changes in the policy contexts illustrate the suggestion that a *sociological* examination of the relation between sociological research and policy contexts is needed.
- Attention to the passage of time is required—that is, time does not stand still, and nor do relevant events cease to occur while a research project is being carried out.
- As a means of thinking reflexively about the matter, a chronology summarising selected relevant events in public policy about food and about nutrition, the associated activities of pressure groups, key publications from government departments, and socioeconomic changes (for example, in the acquisition of food-related consumer goods) has been devised. It juxtaposes these events with the evolving history of the (sociological) research effort.
- The 'Nation's Diet' research program was designed to address a commonly posed question—'Why do people eat what they do?'—against a background known to represent a

---

5   This example conveniently illustrates a second sociological advantage of the classification system used in Tables 16.1 and 16.2: it caters for the use of entries under each heading as *both* a 'topic' for sociological investigation and a 'resource' to support sociological study (see Zimmerman & Pollner 1971). Sociologists can use documents produced by pressure groups and activists, for instance, as a source of information (that happen to have a distinctive slant), but they can also extend their scrutiny to examination of such material as an object of study in its own right (compare Scott 1990).

wide diversity of interests, alliances, and collaborations, as well as controversies, rivalry, and (at times) irreconcilable attitudes to public policy.

• Recent trends appear to perpetuate nutrition and food policies in tension with one another—allegiance to the freedom of consumer choice may not be readily aligned with achieving nutritional targets requiring the whole population to modify its dietary intake—while developments in science policy have resulted, among other things, in the creation of an innovative research program on 'Eating food and health', providing for co-funding between the public and private sectors.

Discussion questions

1 Comment critically on the classification used to present the selected chronology of events (Tables 16.1 and 16.2).
2 What are the strengths and weaknesses of the view that academic disciplines are to be disengaged from food and nutrition as their object of study?
3 Why has establishing a relation between British food policy and nutrition policy been described as 'squaring a circle'. Is this description analytically useful?
4 What types of evidence would be required to:
   a assess whether the intended consequences of revisions to the British science policy had been achieved?
   b monitor whether any unintended consequences had occurred?
5 Identify the differences and similarities between the British case and that of any nation with which you are familiar by reflecting on parallel events in nutrition and health over the last 50 years.

Further reading

Burnett, J. & Oddy, D. J. (eds) 1994, *The Origins and Development of Food Policies in Europe*, Leicester University Press, London.

Smith, D. F. (ed.) 1997, *Nutrition in Britain: Science, Scientists and Politics in the Twentieth Century*, Routledge, London.

References

Blumer, H. 1951, 'Social Movements', in A. M. Lee (ed.), *New Outline of the Principles of Sociology*, Barnes & Noble, New York.

Commission of the European Communities 1997, *The General Principles of Food Law in the European Union*, Commission Green Paper, Commission of the European Communities, Brussels.

Conning, D. 1995, *A New Diet of Reason: Healthy Eating and Government Policy*, The Social Affairs Unit, London.

Department for Education and Employment 1997, *Excellence in Schools*, White Paper HMSO, London.

Department of Health 1989, *The Diets of British Schoolchildren*, HMSO, London.

—— 1991a, *Dietary Reference Values for Food Energy and Nutrients for the United Kingdom*, (COMA) HMSO, London.

—— 1991b, *The Health of the Nation: A Consultative Document for Health in England*, Green Paper, HMSO, London.

—— 1992, *The Health of the Nation: A Strategy for Health in England*, White Paper, HMSO, London.

—— 1994a, *Eat Well: An Action Plan from the Nutrition Task Force to Achieve the Health of the Nation Targets on Diet and Nutrition*, Department of Health, London.

—— 1994b, *Nutritional Aspects of Cardiovascular Disease*, Department of Health, London.

—— 1996, *Eat Well II: A Progress Report from the Nutrition Task Force on the Action Plan to Achieve the Health of the Nation Targets on Diet and Nutrition*, Department of Health, London.

Department of Health and Social Security 1980, *Inequalities in Health: Report of a Research Working Group*, Department of Health and Social Security, London.

Ensor, T. 1990, The Economics of Nutrition, unpublished report to the ESRC.

Fine, B., Heasman, M., & Wright, J. 1996, *Consumption in the Age of Affluence*, Routledge, London.

Freidson, E. 1970, *Profession of Medicine*, Dodd Mead, New York.

Hughes, M. 1998, 'More than the Sum of its Parts? Coordinating the ESRC Research Programme on "Innovation and Change in Education"', in G. Walford (ed.), *Doing Research about Education*, Falmer Press, Sussex.

Hurren, C. & Black, A. 1991, *The Food Network: Achieving a Healthy Diet by the Year 2000*, Smith-Gordon, London.

James, W. P. T. 1993, 'Challenges for Applied Nutrition Sciences for the 1990s', in D. G. van der Heij & T. Ockhuizen (eds), *Food and Nutrition Policy in Europe*, Pudoc Scientific Publishers, Wageningen.

—— 1997, Food Standards Agency: An Interim Proposal, proposal submitted to the Labour Party, 30 April.

Lang, T. 1997, *Food Policy for the 21st Century: Can It Be Both Radical and Reasonable?*, Discussion Paper no. 4, Centre for Food Policy, Thames Valley University, London.

Lang, T., Millstone, E., Raven, H., & Rayner, M. 1996, *Modernising UK Food Policy: The Case for Reforming the Ministry of Agriculture, Fisheries and Food*, Centre for Food Policy, Thames Valley University, London.

Low Income Project Team 1996, *Low Income, Food, Nutrition and Health: Strategies for Improvement*, Nutrition Task Force, Department of Health, London.

MAFF. See Ministry of Agriculture, Fisheries and Food.

Mills, M. 1992, *The Politics of Dietary Change*, Dartmouth, Aldershot.

Ministry of Agriculture, Fisheries and Food 1989, *Food Safety—Protecting the Consumer*, White Paper, HMSO, London.

Murcott, A. 1988a, 'A Finger in Every Pie', in A. S. Truswell & M. L. Wahlqvist (eds), *Food Habits in Australia*, René Gordon, Melbourne.

—— 1988b, 'Sociological and Social Anthropological Approaches to Food and Eating', *World Review of Nutrition and Dietetics*, vol. 55, pp. 1–40.

—— 1990a, Consultant's Report: Proposed Research Initiative on *Health and Nutrition*, unpublished report to the ESRC.

—— 1990b, 'From "Government Orange" to "No Milk, Unless It's Skimmed": Nutrition and Health in Post-War Britain', paper delivered to the Institute of Contemporary British

History Conference 'Understanding Post-War British Society', London School of Economics, 17–18 September.

—— 1994, 'Food and Nutrition in Post-War Britain', in J. Obelkevich & P. Caterall (eds), *Understanding Post-War British Society*, Routledge, London.

—— 1997, '"The Nation's Diet": An Overview of Early Results', *British Food Journal*, vol. 99, no. 3, pp. 89–96.

—— 1998a, 'Introduction: Food Choice, Social Sciences and "The Nation's Diet" Research Programme', in A. Murcott (ed.), *'The Nation's Diet': The Social Science of Food Choice*, Longman, London.

—— (ed.) 1998b, *'The Nation's Diet': The Social Science of Food Choice*, Longman, London.

Murphy, E., Parker, S., & Phipps, C. 1998, 'Food Choices for Babies', in A. Murcott (ed.), *'The Nation's Diet': The Social Science of Food Choice*, Longman, London.

Nettleton, S. 1995, *The Sociology of Health and Illness*, Polity Press, Oxford.

Obelkevich, J. & Caterall, P. 1994, 'Introduction: Understanding British Society' in J. Obelkevich & P. Caterall (eds), *Understanding Post-War British Society*, Routledge, London.

Office of Science and Technology 1993, *Realising Our Potential, a Strategy for Science, Engineering and Technology*, HMSO, London.

—— 1995, *Progress through Partnership: 7 Food and Drink*, HMSO, London.

OST. See Office of Science and Technology.

Scott, J. 1990, *A Matter of Record*, Polity Press, Cambridge.

Scottish Office 1994, *The Scottish Diet*, The Scottish Office Home & Health Department, Edinburgh.

—— 1996, *Eating for Health: A Diet Action Plan for Scotland*, The Scottish Office Home & Health Department, Edinburgh.

Sharp, I. 1992/93, *Nutritional Guidelines for School Meals*, The Caroline Walker Trust, London.

Warde, A. & Martens, L. 1998, 'A Sociological Approach to Food Choice: The Case of Eating Out', in A. Murcott (ed.), *'The Nation's Diet': The Social Science of Food Choice*, Longman, London.

Wardle, J. 1990, The Psychology of Nutrition, unpublished report to the ESRC.

Williams, R., Bush, H., Lean, M., Anderson, A. S., & Bradby, H. 1998, 'Food Choice and Culture in a Cosmopolitan City: South Asians, Italians and Other Glaswegians', in A. Murcott (ed.), *'The Nation's Diet': The Social Science of Food Choice*, Longman, London.

Zimmerman, D. H. & Pollner, M. 1971, 'The Everyday World as a Phenomenon', in J. D. Douglas (ed.), *Understanding Everyday Life: Toward the Reconstruction of Sociological Knowledge*, Routledge & Kegan Paul, London.

17

The Hyper-Rational Social Appetite: *Towards a Synthesis of Food Trends*

John Germov and Lauren Williams

Overview

- *How do McDonaldisation, social differentiation, and self-rationalisation contribute to the food choice of individuals?*

- *Is a theoretical synthesis of these three trends possible?*

- *What is the hyper-rational social appetite?*

This chapter reviews the themes of the book: McDonaldisation, social differentiation, and self-rationalisation. Some preliminary conclusions are drawn from the various chapters as a basis for establishing a theoretical synthesis of the three social trends. A neo-Weberian perspective is presented through the concept of hyper-rationalisation as a way forward in explaining why we eat the way we do.

Key terms

agency	rationalisation
cultural capital	reflexive modernity
figurations	social appetite
hyper-rationality	self-rationalisation
Marxism	social construction
McDonaldisation	social differentiation
modernity	social structure
postmodernism	structure–agency debate

Introduction

The purpose of this book has been to demonstrate the importance of studying the **social appetite.** The benefit of applying a sociological perspective to food is the ability to conceptualise the connections between individual experience and wider social patterns to explore why we eat the way we do. In addressing this question, we have argued that the dominant social patterns of food production and consumption are represented by three trends: **McDonaldisation, social differentiation,** and **self-rationalisation** (see chapter 1 and the introductions to parts 1–3 of this book). As mentioned in the chapter 1, these trends reflect the **structure–agency debate** that is conducted as we attempt to understand how the **social structure** shapes our actions and how we, in turn, shape it. This concluding chapter will review the relative contributions of structure and **agency** to the social appetite, and will present a new synthesis of the three trends discussed in this book.

First, it is important to note that structure and agency are inextricably linked. The social structure consists of 'recurrent social practices' (Giddens 1989, p. 252), or as George Ritzer puts it, '[a]ll social action involves structure, and all structure involves social action' (1996b, p. 529). The interdependence of structure and agency is succinctly expressed by Norbert Elias's (1978) concept of **figurations**, which are patterns of social, cultural, economic, and political arrangements. As Ritzer (1996b, p. 512) states: 'Figurations are social processes involving the "interweaving" of people. They are *not* structures that are external to and coercive of relationships between people; they *are* those relationships'. Elias argued that figurations were part of a 'civilising process', whereby social regulation of individual behaviour was no longer achieved through external coercion, but rather through moral self-regulation. A parallel can be drawn here between the concept of figurations and Foucault's (1979) notion of discourse and self-surveillance as the basis for the internalisation of social control (see Germov & Williams 1998; Petersen & Bunton 1997). Whether we use the language of figurations or of self-surveillance, such an approach is based on a concept of power as diffused, localised, and operating at the micro-level through its institutionalisation in daily practices and routines (see Turner 1997). Figurations are contingent on the particular time and culture in which they occur, often changing in response to conflict and competition between social groups, and to wider socioeconomic and political factors.

Stephen Mennell, in *All Manners of Food* (1996), adapts Elias's approach by using the notion of the 'civilising of appetite' to explain trends in food consumption. For Mennell (1996, p. 322, original italics), **globalisation** and **rationalisation** processes result in an overarching trend towards *'diminishing contrasts and increasing varieties'* in food production and consumption, similarly characterised by what George Ritzer (1996a) has labelled the process of McDonaldisation. The increasing rationalisation or McDonaldisation of social life is further detailed by Ritzer (1996a), who states that it is made up of four interrelated features:

1 calculability: the quantification of production processes, such as the explicit timing of the cooking of various ingredients
2 efficiency: the best means to achieve a desired end (for example, drive-through service)
3 predicability: a production process that always operates the same way and produces the same good, irrespective of the individual worker or the geographic location of the food venue
4 control: the increasing use of technology to minimise human judgment and error, where unskilled cooks follow detailed instructions and assembly-line methods, and use machines to produce food.

Another implication of the McDonaldisation trend in industrialised countries is the issue of food products that are modified genetically or chemically to enhance health benefits for consumers (see chapter 4). Take, for example, the introduction of the pseudo-food 'Olestra', the brand name for a fat substitute available in the USA. Olestra has similar chemical properties to traditional fats and can be used for frying and general cooking. It is available as oil and can be used in the production of 'fat-free' products such as potato chips. Olestra is not digested or absorbed into the body and therefore is excreted from the body unchanged. The product has significant side-effects when the product has been consumed in large amounts, such as abdominal cramping, anal seepage, and malabsorption of essential nutrients, not to mention the fact that once excreted the product is non-biodegradable (Kantor 1996; Burros 1996). Further concerns have been raised about the implications such products may have for people's nutritional intake, where the implicit message is that you can have 'all you can eat' of certain products without any consequences. The example of Olestra reflects the impact of mass production, distribution, and marketing of food products in shaping food choices.

Ritzer (1996b) notes that the process of rationality produces its own forms of irrationality, such as the side-effects of Olestra noted above. Examples are detailed by Bill Whit and Terry Leahy in chapters 2 and 3, which demonstrate how rational production methods can contribute to the displacement of workers in underdeveloped countries by using capital-intensive, rather than labour-intensive, farming practices. Furthermore, efficient agricultural production methods can also wreak environmental devastation, with implications for future generations. While the McDonaldisation process refers to the way in which structural factors on a macro level influence why we eat the way we do, other trends clearly operate.

Social differentiation refers to the nexus of the social shaping of food choice and the food choices that individuals actually make. While the social structure clearly affects the production, distribution, and consumption of food, a sole focus on structural determinants obscures the agency of people and the counter-trend away from rationalisation, represented by the concept of social differentiation. This concept acknowledges that food 'consumption communicates social meaning, and is the site of struggles over social distinction' (Corrigan 1997, p. 32). Social differentiation through food consumption is discussed in this section of the book in terms of vegetarianism, eating out, class, culture, and ageing. Deidre Wicks's discussion of vegetarianism clearly shows that individuals can make the choice not to eat meat for a variety of reasons, including as part of an ethical stance. Not only can vegetarianism be the choice of an individual, but it can also be an indicator of membership of a new social group, bound together through common interests and values—in this case a vegetarian ethic that forms the basis of a social movement. The trend to vegetarianism may also have been influenced by recent food scares, since food-borne disease usually affects high protein foods such as meat. While food production and handling standards have generally greatly improved during the twentieth century, more recent pressure from mass production and deregulation of food manufacturing has undermined public trust in 'the system'. Threats such as 'mad cow disease', for example, have devastated public confidence in British meat production and food safety in general. When Oprah Winfrey made the statement on United States national television that she would not be eating hamburger meat again, the consumption and market price of beef dropped to the extent that Texan meat producers took her to court for defaming their product (but lost their case and possibly further public support through their actions). Other food trends, such as the consumption of organic foods, have been developed in response to consumer demand for a 'return to nature', based on a scepticism of food-processing techniques and chemical additives, various food scares, and ethical concerns about mass production techniques. The media has fuelled the various food scares by highlighting food-borne disease as a significant health concern.

A further example of social differentiation is provided by Pat Crotty, who explains in chapter 8 that, while class-based food consumption patterns are diminishing, they are still discernible. Pierre Bourdieu's (1984) notion that consumption patterns are used to create social distinction is relevant here, particularly with regard to food choices based on **cultural capital**, which can be used to denote social class membership. Yet some social patterns regarding food choices are not simply attempts at social differentiation; rather they are attempts at social conformity. Such social patterns are the result of the third trend—self-rationalisation—which refers to a micro-sociological form of rationality that parallels the macro-sociological McDonaldisation process (see Figure 17.1). Health, nutrition, and beauty discourses reflect attempts to manage the human body rationally. This is epitomised by the well-known company and phrase 'Weight Watchers', which symbolises the notion of body discipline and surveillance—by the individual themselves and by others—to conform to a socially acceptable notion of beauty. Furthermore, as we argue in chapter 12, attempts to regulate the body are gendered through the **social construction** of the thin female ideal. While external pressures play a significant role in the construction and maintenance of such discourses, they are also internalised and reproduced by individuals. The self-rationalisation process therefore involves the role that human agency plays in adopting and perpetuating various food and body regimes.

The interrelationship of the three dominant social trends that affect food consumption are illustrated in Figure 17.1. The emphasis for each theme shifts from the macro-

Figure 17.1 The social trends of food production and consumption

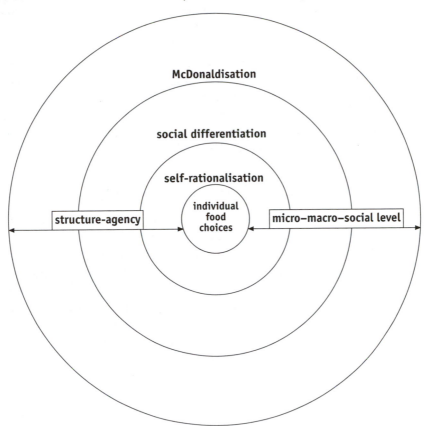

sociological trend of McDonaldisation to the micro-sociological trend of self-rationalisa-tion, which sees many of the principles of McDonaldisation applied at the level of the individual. In between these two trends lies social differentiation, which reflects the nexus of the influence of structure and agency based on social group membership and the con-struction of social identity through particular consumption practices.

The interrelatedness of these three social trends—McDonaldisation, social differen-tiation, and self-rationalisation—sets the scene for a pluralisation of food and nutrition regimes that influence why people eat the way they do (see Germov 1998). The three trends coexist, overlap, and have multiple effects on an individual's food consumption. Because of this overlap, we should not be surprised to find contradictory beliefs and practices among individuals, who may be subscribing to a number of food and nutri-tion discourses, while also responding to the structural influences of the wider society. Fat-modified foods provide an example of the complexity of food choice. Low-fat foods are designed to present 'healthy choices' to consumers and are used by women for dieting purposes.

Despite the consumption of low-fat foods, the average degree of overweight of the population in the USA has also increased, cautioning against any simplistic notions that low-fat foods result in weight control (Allred 1995). While people may use light foods for this reason, Claude Fischler (1995) argues that people seek increased pleasure through the inclusion of light foods in addition to, rather than as a replacement for, other foods in the diet. For example, it is not uncommon for people to use artificial sweetener in their coffee so that they can have a slice of mud cake; or purchase diet cola with a hamburger—giving a sense of dietary 'balance'. The common-sense notion of a 'balanced' diet is highly variable, but is often defined as a balance between 'good' and 'bad', or healthy and unhealthy, food (see Fischler 1988).

Food consumption in the age of reflexive modernity

In the Foreword, Stephen Mennell noted the rise of **postmodernism** as one of the factors responsible for the growing interest in the sociology of food. The 'postmodern turn' (Seidman 1994) in social theory has focused attention on social construction, agency, and consumption practices as the prime influences on social life. As noted above, following the trend of social differentiation, particular food consumption choices can be used as social markers to construct particular social identities and lifestyles (see Bauman 1991, 1992; Lupton 1996). This theoretical concern with consumption can be traced to the notion that, in the late nineteenth century, the middle and upper classes used 'conspicuous consumption' as a way of designating social distinction —an idea that was first discussed by Thorstein Veblen (1975). Peter Corrigan (1997, p. 17) describes this approach as one that views social groups as being in competition for social status through consumption patterns and use of particular goods. He observes that 'there is a permanent tension between "distinguished" goods and the popularization which threatens their distinguished status. Goods, then, are involved in endless definitions and redefinitions of social status'. According to some postmodern accounts of food consumption, we do, in a sense, become what we eat. Therefore, the availability of a wide range of consumption choices is taken as evidence of the growing fragmentation of social life (as long as you have the means to exercise choice), with consumption no longer viewed as the product of traditional social cleavages such as social class.

Rather than giving way to the emergence of a postmodern society, both Anthony Giddens and Ulrich Beck argue that **modernity** is alive and well, but has developed into a '**reflexive modernity**' (see Beck et al. 1994). As Giddens states, we live in a time when 'social practices are constantly examined and reformed in the light of incoming information about those very practices, thus constitutively altering their character' (Giddens 1990, p. 38). Since everything is open to reflection, modification, questioning, and change, people live in an age of uncertainty. As Giddens (1991, p. 5) states, 'because of the "openness' of social life today, the pluralisation of contexts of action and the diversity of "authorities", lifestyle choice is increasingly important in the constitution of self-identity and daily activity'.

While Giddens (1991) recognises that the poor are excluded or marginalised in their lifestyle choices, he maintains that it is a mistake to view such social changes as only having an impact on privileged social groups. The poor are not immune from social change; even in severe hardship, there are lifestyle choices to be made. In terms of food consumption, 'what to eat' becomes a daily and individual decision—yet this is not a decision devoid of social determinants. For example, 'Plurality of choice is in some substantial part the very outcome of commodified processes ... Yet standardisation can often be turned into a mode of creating individual qualities ... Mass produced clothing still allows individuals to decide selectively on styles of dress' (Giddens 1991, p. 200).

Similarly, mass produced food has brought increased consumption choices through the number of food outlets and the availability of certain cuisines at all times of the day. Therefore, the emerging era of reflexive modernity does not imply an overarching trend towards rampant individuality, but rather a socially derived plurality of lifestyles involving multiple food discourses. While Beck describes this trend to 'lifestylism' as a process of individualisation, he recognises that:

> Individualization means market dependency in all dimensions of living ... mass consumption of generically designed housing, furnishings, articles of daily use, as well as opinions, habits, attitudes and lifestyles [means that] individualization delivers people over to an external control and standardisation that was unknown in the enclaves of familial and feudal subcultures (1992, p. 132).

In terms of the three food trends discussed above, the question remains whether it is possible to provide a conceptual synthesis of the social patterning of food choice, an issue that is taken up in the next section.

The hyper-rational social appetite

We propose that there is an overriding logic to current trends in the social appetite and have adapted the neo-Weberian concept of **hyper-rationality** (Ritzer & LeMoyne 1991; LeMoyne et al. 1994) as a useful concept for explaining the plurality of food consumption patterns discussed above. The social patterning of food consumption is based on identifiable sets of 'food rationales', which people use to guide their food choices. While we have suggested three main social trends responsible for the social appetite, these trends coalesce in an overarching logic of rationality, which explains the plural and contradictory food practices that individuals may adopt.

Stephen Kalberg (1980) identifies four types of rationality in Max Weber's writings, as shown in Table 17.1, which couples them with the three dominant food trends that we have discussed throughout this book.

These four forms of rationality can be applied to McDonaldisation (formal rationality), social differentiation (substantive rationality), and self-rationalisation (theoretical rationality). The coexistence of all three trends in influencing individual food consumption practices in daily life is termed 'practical rationality'. We are all exposed to

Table 17.1 Typology of rationality as applied to food

Rationality types	Definition	Food trend
Formal	procedure- and rule-based	McDonaldisation
Substantive	value-based	social differentiation
Theoretical	knowledge-based	self-rationalisation
Practical	expedient management of daily life	pluralisation of trends

Source: Adapted from LeMoyne et al.1994, p. 223.

various forms of food rationales by which we can consume food. Alan Beardsworth and Teresa Keil (1997) use the concept of 'menus' in a similar way as we use food rationales. They claim that 'menu pluralism' is evident, in which individuals may change from one menu to another, and even adopt multiple menus (or food rationales) depending on the social situation in which food is consumed. In such a conceptualisation, the nexus of structure and agency is emphasised, as in Elias's use of figurations (discussed above); however, hyper-rationality remains the overriding logic.

Therefore, we use hyper-rationality as an umbrella concept to encapsulate the apparently contradictory social trends of food consumption and production. This neo-Weberian concept offers a way forward for understanding food trends, rather than viewing current developments as a pastiche of food discourses that are used to constitute self-identity and 'lifestylism'. Instead we argue that these trends can more appropriately be conceptualised as part of the neo-rationality of reflexive modernity. While individual differences in food habits have always existed, the relaxation of social mores and the increasing commodification of social life mean that the images of lifestyle and choice are manufactured and promoted by the logic of capitalism. Frederick Jameson's (1990) blend of **Marxism** and postmodernism posits the growth of materialism and consumerism in advanced capitalist societies as the basis of the theoretical shift towards lifestyle diversity, evidenced by consumption choices. The concept of hyper-rationality reveals the social patterning of such a development. Rather than being viewed as evidence of fragmentation and uncertainty, it is evidence of the contrary: an expansion of rationalisation at both the macro- and micro-sociological levels. While we have only been able to provide a brief sketch of the hyper-rational social appetite, we view it as a helpful conceptualisation to explain the rationality of the social trends of food production and consumption at both the macro and micro levels.

Conclusion

There is clearly more to the sociological study of food and nutrition than the recognition of cultural differences, the role played by socialisation in food consumption, and the social implications of food for health. As this book attests, the sociology of food has a much wider scope and has an impact on sociological concerns such as class, gender, environment, and public policy. The production and consumption of food involves many sectors of society; from agriculture to food processing, from the restaurant to the home, and from the individual to the social group. Therefore, the social context of food is too large a topic to be covered by one discipline or one book. We trust we have whetted your appetite to further explore the social context of food with a sociological menu in hand.

Further reading and resources

Corrigan, P. 1997, *The Sociology of Consumption: An Introduction*, Sage, London.
Social Appetite website: <http://www.newcastle.edu.au/department/so/socialappetite.htm>

References

Allred, J. 1995, 'Too Much of a Good Thing?', *Journal of the American Dietetic Association*, vol. 95, pp. 417–18.
Bauman, Z. 1991, *Modernity and Ambivalence*, Polity Press, Cambridge.
—— 1992, *Intimations of Postmodernity*, Routledge, London.
Beardsworth, A. & Keil, T. 1997, *Sociology on the Menu*, Routledge, London.
Beck, U. 1992, *Risk Society: Towards a New Modernity*, Sage, London.
Beck, U., Giddens, A., & Lash, S. 1994, *Reflexive Modernization: Politics, Tradition and Aesthetics in the Modern Social Order*, Polity Press and Blackwell Publishers, Cambridge.
Bourdieu, P. 1984 (1979), *Distinction: A Social Critique of the Judgement of Taste*, Harvard University Press, Cambridge, Mass.
Burros, M. 1996, 'Illness Cited as a Reason for Fat Substitute Ban', *New York Times*, vol. 145, 2 July, p. B9.
Corrigan, P. 1997, *The Sociology of Consumption: An Introduction*, Sage, London.
Elias, N. 1978, *The Civilizing Process*, Blackwell, Oxford.
Germov, J. 1998, 'Whetting the Appetite: A Taste of the Sociology of Food and Nutrition', *Annual Review of Health Social Sciences*, vol. 7, pp. 35–46.
Fischler, C. 1988, 'Food, Self and Identity', *Social Science Information*, vol. 27, no. 2, pp. 275–92.
—— 1995, 'Sociological Aspects of Light Foods', in P. D. Leathwood, J. Louis-Sylvestre, & J.-P. Mareschi (eds), *Light Foods: An Assessment of their Psychological, Sociocultural, Physiological, Nutritional, and Safety Aspects*, International Life Sciences Institute Press, Washington, DC.
Foucault, M. 1979, *Discipline and Punish: The Birth of the Prison*, Penguin Books, Harmondsworth.
Giddens, A. 1989, 'A Reply to My Critics', in D. Held & J. B. Thompson (eds), *Social Theory of Modern Societies: Anthony Giddens and His Critics*, Cambridge University Press, Cambridge, pp. 249–301.
—— 1990, *The Consequences of Modernity*, Polity Press, Cambridge.
—— 1991, *Modernity and Self-Identity: Self and Society in the Late Modern Age*, Stanford University Press, Stanford, Calif.
Jameson, F. 1990, *Postmodernism, or the Cultural Logic of Late Capitalism*, Duke University Press, Durham, NC.
Kalberg, S. 1980, 'Max Weber's Types of Rationality: Cornerstones for the Analysis of Rationalization Processes in History', *American Journal of Sociology*, vol. 85, pp. 1145–79.

Kantor, M. A. 1996, 'Olestra: Questions Still Unanswered', *Journal of Nutrition Education*, July–August, vol. 28, no. 4, pp. 191–3.

LeMoyne, T., Falk, W. W., & Neustadtl, A. 1994, 'Hyperrationality: Historical Antecedents and Contemporary Outcomes within Japanese Manufacturing', *Sociological Spectrum*, vol. 14, pp. 221–40.

Lupton, D. 1996, *Food, the Body and the Self*, Sage, London.

Mennell, S. 1996, *All Manners of Food*, 2nd edn, Illini, Chicago.

Peterson, A. & Bunton, R. (eds) 1997, *Foucault, Health and Medicine*, Routledge, London.

Ritzer, G. 1996a, *The McDonaldization of Society*, revised edn, Pine Forge Press, New York.

—— 1996b, *Sociological Theory*, 4th edn, McGraw-Hill, New York.

Ritzer, G. & LeMoyne, T. 1991, 'Hyperrationality: An Extension of Weberian and Neo-Weberian Theory', in G. Ritzer (ed.), *Metatheorizing in Sociology*, Lexington Books, Lexington, Mass.

Seidman, S. 1994, 'Introduction', in S. Seidman (ed.), *The Postmodern Turn: New Perspectives on Social Theory*, Cambridge University Press, New York, pp. 1–23.

Turner, B. S. 1997, 'From Governmentality to Risk: Some Reflections on Foucault's Contribution to Medical Sociology', in A. Petersen & R. Bunton (eds), *Foucault, Health and Medicine*, Routledge, London, pp. ix–xxi.

Veblen, T. 1975 (1899), *The Theory of the Leisure Class*, Augustus M. Kelly, New York.

Glossary

accounts
The making of specific claims about the reasons for particular behaviours in order to manage interactions and to gain or maintain acceptance.

active micro-organisms
Organisms that are not visible to the human eye and that have biological activity in humans.

activities of daily living
Activities considered fundamental to an individual's independent existence, including getting out of bed, cooking and eating food, and shopping for groceries.

ageism
A term like 'sexism' and 'racism', denoting discrimination based on age.

agency
The ability of people, individually and collectively, to influence their own lives and the society in which they live.

alienated workers/alienation
'Alienation' is a Marxist term that refers to the experience of people who have to work for a monetary wage to live. They are alienated from—in that they have no control over—their conditions of work, the process of production, what they produce, and the ownership and distribution of their products.

alternative lifestyle/new age
A cultural alternative to mainstream culture in developed countries, it usually includes some subsistence production and the rejection of some elements of puritan and mainstream culture, such as the work ethic, puritan sexual morality, or consumerism.

anti-vivisection
A movement that is against the use of animals for laboratory experiments.

attribution
Ascribing a characteristic, quality, causation, or character to some other factor.

biological determinism
An unproven belief that individual, group, and organisational behaviours are ultimately determined by biology.

biomedicine/biomedical model
The conventional approach to medicine in Western societies. It seeks to diagnose and explain ill health in terms of a malfunction of one of the body's internal biological mechanisms. The biomedical approach of most medical services focuses attention on the internal workings of the body and generally precludes consideration of social, economic, and other environmental factors.

cash crops

Crops produced to be exchanged for cash.

capitalist/capitalism/capitalist society

An economic and social system in which a relatively small capitalist class own almost all the productive property of a society. A capitalist is someone who owns productive property, employs labour, and markets the product. (Capitalists include shareholders, who jointly own the property and have the functions of ownership performed on their behalf.) Most people either work for a wage or are part of the world's poverty-stricken unemployed classes.

class (or social class)

A concept used by sociologists to refer to a position in a system of structured inequality based on the unequal distribution of power, wealth, income, and status. People who share a social class position typically share similar life chances.

colonial period

The period when most developing countries were governed directly by imperial powers.

coping

Contending or dealing with issues or problems.

commodity economy

The cash economy, as opposed to the subsistence economy.

commodity/commodity production

Goods produced to be bought and sold. In terms of food production, a commodity is food that is produced to be exchanged for cash.

community farms

Farms that are owned cooperatively by community groups.

community-supported agriculture

An organic farming enterprise that is supported by a community group of consumers. The community group is organised to give financial or labour support to the enterprise, which in turn produces food for them.

competitive private ownership

In capitalist societies, land is a commodity that can be bought and sold. Agriculture is carried out to make a profit by selling farm products on the market, and farms compete locally and internationally to make the highest possible profit. Farms that make lower profits usually have to be sold by their owners.

conservatism

A political ideology that favours the status quo and a hierarchical society governed by power élites, based on the assumption that social inequality is natural, inevitable, and necessary for social order. Such beliefs often support strict moral regulation of individual behaviour.

cross-cultural competency

The ability to work effectively with people from another culture based on understanding and accepting the values, assumptions, beliefs, and practices of members of that culture.

culture
> The values, assumptions, and beliefs shared by a group of people, which structure the behaviour of group members from birth until death.

cultural relativism
> The concept that social values and beliefs are culturally specific and are not universal or absolute.

culture-bound syndrome
> A health or medical condition that only occurs in particular cultures and is not universal or culture-free.

cultural capital
> A concept that implies that culture can be treated like an economic asset upon which hierarchies in society are founded.

cultural sensitivity
> Understanding and accepting the values, assumptions, beliefs, and practices of a cultural group other than one's own without needing to pass judgment on it.

developed world/developing world
> The developed world comprises the rich countries of the world, in which industrial development is long-standing, and the developing world comprises the poorer countries of the world, in which industrial development is more recent.

deviance
> Behaviour or activities that violate social expectations about what is normal.

disabilities
> Limitations on the ability to fulfil role obligations as a result of physical impairments; impairments include limited motion of limbs or generalised muscular weakness, which are usually the result of injury or illness.

disclaimer
> An explanation provided in anticipation of challenges to a person's or a behaviour's legitimacy.

discounting
> Techniques for dealing with violations of personal principles without threatening internal self-definitions or identity.

discrimination
> Unfavourable treatment of a person or rejection of a person based on distinctions between that person and others.

dichotomous view
> A view that stereotypes the dietary quality and food choices of the affluent and better educated as 'healthy' and the diets of low-income and less educated groups as 'unhealthy'.

Dietary Guidelines for Australians
> Dietary advice for the Australian population. The guidelines are aimed at reversing trends in the Australian diet, which contribute to chronic disease and disorders.

economic liberalism/economic rationalism

A general term used to describe a political philosophy based on small government and market-oriented policies, such as deregulation, privatisation, reduced government spending, and lower taxation.

ethics

Socially or culturally patterned codes of conduct that form the basis of the relationships that individuals develop with themselves.

ethical responsibilities

Obligations that individuals are required to fulfil on the basis of their cultural or societal position. For example, individuals who are parents have ethical responsibilities concerning the duty of care for their children. These form the standards by which individuals judge themselves to be 'good' parents.

ethnocentric

The belief that one's own cultural practices are admirable, sensible, and right in comparison with those of other cultures; the inability to understand and accept the values, assumptions, beliefs, and practices of other cultures as being appropriate for members of those cultures.

ethnography

A research methodology based on qualitative experience, detailed observations, and in-depth description of the daily social life of people under study.

family commensality

The process of family members preparing, serving, and sharing meals together.

feeding relationship

The complicated set of interactions that occur between child and parent as they select, eat, and regulate food.

figurations

A concept developed by Norbert Elias as an alternative to structure and agency. Figurations represent the nexus of structure and agency, and can be conceived of as networks of people in interdependent relationships. They are the product of individuals but beyond the control of any single individual or group. Elias suggested that figurations could best be imagined as a game in which people must depend on one another within the confines of the rules. Social conflict or competition may result in the rules changing or may cause new forms of figurations to develop.

food choice

An active part of eating behaviour, in which people choose which foods to eat at which time. This process of food choice is influenced by food availability, and by cultural, economic, and psychological factors.

food insufficiency

Can refer to total amount of food related to nutritional needs or capacity to work, to lack of desired foods, or to intermittent periods of shortage.

food safety

Refers to whether food is 'safe' for human consumption—that is, lacking in biological or chemical contaminants that have the potential to cause illness.

food security
A situation in which an adequate amount of accessible, affordable, nutritious, and culturally acceptable food is available to all individuals all of the time.

foodways
Food habits and practices with respect to food acquisition, food preparation, food storage, distribution of food among family members, meal and snack patterns, food combinations, uses of food, beliefs about food, and identification of core, secondary, and peripheral foods in the diet.

Fordism
A society in which a system of mass production and consumption is the dominant system of producing goods. It is derived from principles first developed by Henry Ford in making the Model T Ford motor car (that is, the use of the automated assembly line).

functional foods
Food products that allegedly deliver a health benefit beyond providing nutrients.

gender socialisation
The process by which males and females learn the socially constructed behaviour patterns of masculinity and femininity (the cultural values that dictate how men and women should behave).

gift economy
A proposed utopia in which goods and services are produced by collectives of people and either consumed by the collective or given to other community groups or to the community at large. There is no money and no wage labour: community groups have effective ownership of productive property; individuals, families, or households have effective ownership of personal property.

global capitalist class
The global social class consisting of substantial capitalists.

global consuming class
The world's middle class, made up of affluent workers and professionals in developed countries and of the middle class of developing countries.

global poor
The unemployed of developed countries, peasants, low-wage workers, and the unemployed in developing countries.

globalisation
The influence of international factors on the political system, economy, and culture of nation states and their citizens.

government
In general sociological terms, it is understood as a wide range of practices, strategies, techniques, and programs that influence the beliefs and conduct of the population, rather than simply as centralised state bureaucracies.

greenhouse effect
The gradual, but significant, increase in the temperature of the planet resulting from an increase in the proportion of carbon dioxide present in the atmosphere because of human and natural activities (also referred to as 'global warming').

health claims

Claims made by food manufacturers that their product or an ingredient in their product directly induces health or combats illness when consumed by individuals.

health lifestyles

Collective patterns of health-related behaviours based on choices from options available to people according to their life chances.

healthism

An extreme concern with personal health, which has now become a major preoccupation for many people.

hyper-rationality

A neo-Weberian concept that refers to the synthesis of four types of rationality—formal, substantive, theoretical, and practical—which, when acting in concert, produce a whole greater than its parts.

ideological contest

Conflicting views of social processes, which reflect the goals and interests of different organisations (for example, public health professionals or food producers).

identity

The self-conception or self-definition that a person has and portrays for him- or herself.

individualism

A belief that we can explain social phenomena in terms of individual ideas, attributes, and behaviour.

liberalism

A political philosophy that emphasises individual freedom in all spheres of social life. Meanings of the term tend to differ markedly between countries and contexts—for example, social liberalism supports state intervention to enhance and protect individual freedoms, while economic liberalism views state intervention as an encroachment on individual liberty. See 'economic liberalism/economic rationalism'.

life chances

The probability of people realising their lifestyle choices.

life choices

People's choices in their selection of lifestyle.

marginality

The socially constructed definition of a characteristic as 'out of the mainstream' or abnormal.

Marxism

A political philosophy and social theory based on the writings of Karl Marx. It is founded upon a critique of capitalism in which capitalist society is dominated by a conflict of interest between two dominant social classes: the capitalist class and the working class. Much of Marx's theory has been reinterpreted and modified, and is now often referred to as 'neo-Marxism'. For example, one version of neo-Marxism is critical theory, which has produced critiques of communist regimes and emphasises the importance of culture rather than the traditional focus on the economy.

master status

The dominant social label applied to an individual and according to which the individual is automatically attributed with a host of stereotyped personality traits commonly associated with the particular status (for example, criminal or homosexual) irrespective of the person's individual personality.

materialist

A cultural belief that places great value on material goods (and particularly their accumulation). A second meaning refers to comprehending social life as founded in the real, tangible, observable, material reality of everyday life.

maternal ideal

Refers to the social construction of the female body that reinforces the desirability of the physiological changes of pregnancy. To conform to the maternal ideal, women should have a large body size when pregnant (as opposed to the thin ideal of female beauty that dominates most Western societies). See 'social reconstruction'.

McDonaldisation

A term coined by George Ritzer to expand Max Weber's notion of rationalisation, defined as the standardisation of work processes by rules and regulations based on increased monitoring and evaluation of individual performance akin to the uniformity and control measures used by fast-food chains.

medical model of diet

The conception of food and eating as a process of sustaining the body as a biological organism by using the nutrients that medical science considers to be most effective.

medical–food–industrial complex

A term that refers to the combination of manufacturing interests, medical scientists, and certain government agencies that have a vested interest in the development and introduction of functional food for the purposes of profit maximisation.

medicalisation

The process by which the influence of medicine is expanded by defining non-medical problems as medical issues, usually in terms of illnesses or disorders.

modern foods

Those foods for which overall consumption is increasing and that are consumed more by higher status groups than by lower status groups.

modernity

A particular view of society that is founded upon rational thought and the belief that objective realities can be discovered and understood through rational and scientific means—a view rejected by postmodernists.

monoculture

When a piece of land is used to produce a single crop.

multinational oligopolies

The control of markets by a small number of international companies, which often have budgets that are larger than that of a small country. Such companies are able to act together in pursuit of their mutual vested interests, thereby limiting competition.

neo-Marxism

See Marxism.

'new' public health

An approach that aims to minimise the effects of illness, injury, and death by addressing the social and economic conditions under which they are produced. It adopts a structural, rather than individualistic, model of health and illness.

niche market

A market demand for a particular specialised product that can be sold at a higher price than similar products. The higher price makes up for the fact that the product requires more expensive inputs or more labour to produce, which relates to the view of economists that prices are lowest with the economies of scale that go with a mass market.

non-government organisations (NGOs)

Non-government groups, including those that work to assist development in poor countries—such as local self-help groups or charity organisations based in rich countries.

normality

Behaviours, procedures, and practices that conform to certain socially or culturally patterned standards or goals.

nutritional risk

Factors thought to increase the probability that an individual will develop under-nutrition or malnutrition; risk factors include social isolation and disabilities such as difficulty chewing or swallowing food.

obesity

The condition of having high levels of stored body fat.

organic

Agriculture that makes no use of artificial chemicals for fertilisers, pesticides, or herbicides.

patriarchy

A system of power in which males dominate households. Feminists use the concept more broadly to argue that society is dominated by patriarchal power, which functions to subordinate women and children.

permaculture

A system of permanent, sustainable agriculture.

phytochemicals

Chemicals derived from plants that have biological activity in humans.

polyculture

When a piece of land is used to produce a diversity of crops.

post-Fordism

A disputed term that refers to new forms of production based on the rise of information and computer technology. These new forms have allegedly resulted in more democratic management techniques and small-scale batch production aimed at niche markets.

post-industrial society

A society in which information replaces property as the prime source of power and social control; in such societies, professionals become powerful social groups, and employment is increasingly in service industries rather than manufacturing industries.

postmodernism/postmodern society

A social condition that follows modernity, where the social is fragmented as a result of high levels of social and cultural diversity.

post-structuralism

Opposed to the view that social structure determines human action, this theoretical framework emphasises the local, the specific, and the contingent in social life.

prejudice

An unfavourable opinion or evaluation based on preconceived attitudes rather than on evidence or reasoning.

psychological well-being

Dimensions of self-acceptance, positive relationships with other people, autonomy, environmental mastery, purpose in life, and personal growth.

public health

Assessment of health needs and services aimed at the population level.

public policy

Policy made by the government or government agencies.

rationalisation

See 'McDonaldisation'.

rational individualism

This characterises social life as consisting of the rational choices of individual actors, each motivated to act in his or her own interest.

reflexive modernity

The present social era in developed societies, when social practices are open to reflection, questioning, and change. Therefore, social traditions no longer dictate people's lifestyles.

role

Behavioural expectations (including duties and rights) associated with a position in social space.

self-fulfilling prophecy

A concept derived from interactionist theory, in which a predicted series of events unfolds as a reaction to the actual prediction. For example, the labelling of a young child as of low intelligence may result in a self-fulfilling prophecy, whereby the child chooses to fulfil these low expectations.

self-rationalisation

A concept that draws on Michel Foucault's (1979) ideas of surveillance as a form of social control, and which particularly refers to discourses that attempt to rationally manage and regulate the human body.

shaman
A healer who practices traditional medicine; sometimes described as a physician-priest.

social appetite
The social patterns of food production and consumption.

social class
See 'class'.

social control
Mechanisms that aim to induce conformity, or at least to manage or minimise deviant behaviour.

social construction/socially constructed
A position that holds that all phenomena, including those that appear 'natural', are in fact constructed by humans. Specifically, it can refer to social action perspectives that focus on the idea that society is actively constructed by people, and that therefore reality is invented by humans—rather than just existing—and should not be taken for granted.

social differentiation
The emergence of diverse food consumption patterns in developed societies—a trend towards social diversity based on the creation of social distinction and self-identity through particular food choices and social group membership.

social isolation
The condition in which an individual both lives alone and has little facility for social contact.

social network
The persons with whom an individual normally has the most contact. These can include friends, immediate family members, more distant relatives, neighbours, co-workers, fellow members of voluntary organisations, and fellow church members.

social reconstruction
A term coined to connote the change in societal expectations regarding women's bodies during the period of pregnancy. It is based on the notion of the social construction of women's bodies to conform to the thin ideal at all other stages of their lives. These expectations are redefined during pregnancy, thereby reconstructing women's bodies to conform to the maternal ideal.

social structure
Recurring patterns of social interaction by which people are related to each other through social institutions and social groups.

social support
Instrumental aid (goods and services) and expressive aid (companionship, comfort, advice about personal matters) provided by members of a social network.

socialism
A political ideology based on the elimination of social inequality and the promotion of altruistic values, where wealth is not accumulated by individuals but is appropriated and distributed by the State.

socioeconomic status (SES)
Wealth, status, and power possessed by individuals; SES is usually measured by determining the individual's education, occupation, and income.

sociological imagination

A phrase coined by Charles Wright Mills (1959) to describe the sociological approach to analysing issues. A sociological perspective on the world can be 'imagined' by making a link between personal problems and social issues.

sociological research

Methods used in sociological enquiry and guided by the sociological imagination (see 'sociological imagination').

spiritual well-being

Dimensions of meaning and purpose in life; self-awareness, and connectedness with self, others, and a larger reality.

status

The respect or prestige associated with a particular position in social space.

stigma

An attribute of a person that is deeply discrediting and that disqualifies that person from full social acceptance.

stigmatising act

The behaviour of a 'normal' individual that devalues another person.

structuralism

Theories maintaining that individuals are primarily *determined* by the society in which they live, emphasising that language, culture, and economic organisation pre-exist the individual and limit the possibilities for thought and action.

structure–agency debate

A key debate in sociology regarding the extent to which human behaviour is determined by the social structure.

subsistence production

Production of food for local consumers; moneyless exchange of food by barter, gifts, and so on.

technological determinism

The assumption that technological intervention shapes society in an apolitical, objective, and predictable way.

thin ideal

The dominant aesthetic ideal of female beauty in Western societies, which refers to the social desirability of a thin body shape.

traditional foods

Those foods for which overall consumption is decreasing and which are consumed more by lower status groups than by higher status groups.

unproblematised

Treated as natural and therefore not requiring research or examination.

Appendix

Key Web Resources, Books, Journals, Videos, and Associations

Websites

While we have aimed to be as accurate as possible, it is common for Web addresses to change. Therefore, we maintain an updated and expanded list of all the websites mentioned below on the *Social Appetite* website.

Social Appetite website: <http://www.newcastle.edu.au/department/so/socialappetite.htm>

Sociological Approaches to Nutrition and Eating (SANE):
   <http://www.newcastle.edu.au/department/so/tasa/tasa16.htm>

Eco-Village Information Service: <http://www.gaia.org/>

McSpotlight: <http://www.McSpotlight.org>

The Hunger Site: <http://www.thehungersite.com/chi-bin/WebObjects/HungerSite>

Institute of Food Science and Technology: <http://www.ifst.org>

Health Sociology home page:
   <http://www.newcastle.edu.au/department/so/tasa/tasa8.htm>

New England Research Institute: <http://www.neri.org>

New Internationalist: <http://www.oneworld.org/ni/>

Permaculture International: <http://www.nor.com.au/environment/perma/>

Vegetarian Resource Group (VRG): <http://www.vrg.org/>

World Health Organization: <http://www.who.ch/>

Agriculture, Food, and Human Values Society:
   <http://www.clas.ufl.edu/users/rhaynes/afhvs/>

Body Image and Health: <http://www.rch.unimelb.edu.au/BIHInc>

Association for the Health Enrichment of Large People (AHELP):
   <http://www.usit.com/ahelp/>

International Size Acceptance Association: <http://www.size-acceptance.org/>

National Association to Advance Fat Acceptance: <http://naafa.org/>

Yahoo Fat Acceptance page:
   <http://www.yahoo.com/text/Society_and_Culture/Size_Issues/Fat_Acceptance/>

Australia New Zealand Food Authority: <http://www.anzfa.gov.au>

United States Food and Nutrition Information Center: <http://www.nal.usda.gov/fnic/>
Public Health Nutrition: <http://www.hbs.deakin.edu.au/nutpub/natspec/>
Slow food: <http://www.slowfood.com/main.html>

E-mail discussion groups

Food-for-thought is a multidisciplinary discussion list on all aspects of food and eating, acting as a bridge between the social and natural sciences. To subscribe, send an e-mail to <mailbase@mailbase.ac.uk> and leave the subject line blank. In the body of the message, type the text 'Subscribe Food-for-Thought [First name] [Last name]'.

Socnut is an Australia-based electronic discussion list for those interested in the social aspects of nutrition. To subscribe, send an e-mail to <majordomo@daa.net> and leave the subject line blank. In the body of the message type the text 'socnut subscribe'.

Videos and films

The Politics of Food 1987 (Yorkshire Television, Leeds, four 52-minute episodes). A critical analysis of world hunger, aid, and development.

Influences on Food Choices 1995 (Video Education Australia, Bendigo, Vic., 40 minutes). Covers thirteen influences on food choice through interviews, including interviews with a family, a psychologist, a marketing executive, a teacher, a vegetarian, and a technology consultant.

Global Gardener 1991 (Australian Broadcasting Corporation, 120 minutes). Tony Gailey, Julian Russell, and Bill Mollison talk about permaculture in different parts of the world.

Eat your Garden (Australia, 56 minutes). A step-by-step guide to small-scale permaculture gardens.

'Lisa the Vegetarian' 1995 (episode of *The Simpsons*, approximately 24 minutes). An amusing look at the vegetarian debate.

The Famine Within 1990 (Kandor Productions, Ontario, and Ronin Films, Canberra, 90 minutes). An excellent discussion of body image and eating disorders.

Fat Chance 1994 (National Film Board of Canada, 50 minutes). A riveting and thought-provoking account of fat prejudice.

Babette's Feast (*Babette's Gaestebud*) 1987 (A. S. Panorama Film International in cooperation with Nordisk Film and the Danish Film Institute, Denmark, 109 minutes, Danish dialogue with English subtitles). Adapted from a short story by Karen Blixen writing under the pseudonym 'Isak Dinesen'.

Eat the Rich 1987 (directed by Peter Richardson, United Kingdom, 89 minutes).

Eat, Drink, Man, Woman 1994 (directed by Ang Lee, Taiwan, 123 minutes).

Like Water for Chocolate 1993 (directed by Alfonso Arau, Mexico, 113 minutes).

The Cook, the Thief, his Wife and her Lover 1989 (written and directed by Peter Greenaway, 119 minutes).

The Wedding Banquet 1993 (directed by Ang Lee, Taiwan, 111 minutes).

Associations

Association for the Study of Food and Society (ASFS)

The ASFS is an interdisciplinary international organisation interested in the relationship between food and society. It publishers a newsletter, the *Journal of Food and Society*, and holds annual conferences. Contact Marion Newman, ASFS, Department of Family, Nutrition, and Exercise, Queens College—CUNY, Flushing, NY 11367, USA.

Agriculture, Food and Human Values Society (AFHVS)

Contact Richard Haynes, AFHVS, Agriculture and Human Values Inc., PO Box 114938, Gainsville, FL 31604, USA. Internet: <http://www.clas.ufl.edu/users/rhaynes/afhvs/>.

International Association for the Psychology of Food and Nutrition

Contact Professor D. A. Booth, School of Psychology, University of Birmingham, Edgbaston, Birmingham, B15 2TT, UK.

International Commission on the Anthropology of Food and Food Problems

Contact Dr Claude Fischler, International Commission on the Anthropology of Food and Food Problems, Directeur de recherche CNRS, CETSAH (EHESS), 14 rue Corvisart, 75013, Paris, France.

The British Sociological Association Sociology of Food Study Group

This study group publishes a newsletter and organises seminars and conferences such as the annual Food Choice Conference. Contact Kathryn Backett-Milburn, e-mail <k.milburn@ed.ac.uk>.

The Research Committee on Food and Agriculture (RC-40)

RC-40 exists under the auspices of the International Sociological Association. Its goal is the study of contemporary food and agricultural systems. RC-40 sponsors the International Journal of the Sociology of Agriculture and Food (IJSAF). Visit the RC-40 web page at <http://www.ssc.msu.edu/~soc/foodag2.html>.

The Foodways Section of the American Folklore Society holds seminars and conferences, and produces a newsletter and a journal—*Digest: An Interdisciplinary Study of Food and Foodways*. Contact Lucy M. Long, Department of Popular Culture, Bowling Green State University, Bowling Green, Ohio 43402, USA. E-mail: <lucy@bgnet.bgsu.edu>. Internet: <http://afsnet.org/sections/foodways/>.

The Vegetarian Resource Group (VRG)

The VRG provides information on vegetarian and vegan nutrition, cookbooks, *Vegetarian Journal* excerpts, and links to most things vegetarian. Visit the website at <http://www.vrg.org/>.

Permaculture International, PO Box 6039, South Lismore, NSW 2480, Australia. Visit the website at <http://www.nor.com.au/environment/perma/>.

Books on food from a social science perspective

Beardsworth, A. & Keil, T. 1997, *Sociology on the Menu*, Routledge, London.
Bell, D. & Valentine, G. 1997, *Consuming Geographies: You Are Where You Eat*, Routledge, London.

Bread for the World Institute, *Hunger 1995: Causes of Hunger: Fifth Annual Report on the State of World Hunger*, Bread for the World Institute, Washington, DC.

Caplan, P. 1997, *Food, Health and Identity*, Routledge, London.

Charles, N. & Kerr, M. 1988, *Women, Food and Families*, Manchester University Press, Manchester.

Crotty, P. 1995, *Good Nutrition? Fact and Fashion in Dietary Advice*, Allen & Unwin, Sydney.

Fieldhouse, P. 1995, *Food and Nutrition: Customs and Culture*, 2nd edn, Croom Helm, Kent.

Fine, B., Heasman, M., & Wright, J. 1996, *Consumption in the Age of Affluence: The World of Food*, Routledge, London.

Finkelstein, J. 1989, *Dining Out: A Sociology of Modern Manners*, Polity Press, Cambridge.

Grigg, D. 1993, *World Food Problem*, Blackwell, London.

Keane, A. & Willetts, A. 1995, *Concepts of Healthy Eating: An Anthropological Investigation in South East London,* Goldsmith College, London.

Lester, I. H. 1994, *Australia's Food and Nutrition*, AGPS, Canberra.

Lupton, D. 1996, *Food, the Body and the Self*, Sage, London.

Maurer, D. & Sobal, J. (eds) 1995, *Eating Agendas: Food and Nutrition as Social Problems*, Aldine de Gruyter, New York.

McIntosh, Wm A. 1996, *Sociologies of Food and Nutrition*, Plenum Publishing, New York.

Mennell, S. 1996, *All Manners of Food*, 2nd edn, Illini, Chicago.

Mennell, S., Murcott, A., & van Otterloo, A. H. 1992, *The Sociology of Food: Eating, Diet, and Culture*, Sage, London.

Murcott. A. (ed.) 1983, *The Sociology of Food and Eating*, Gower, Aldershot.

—— (ed.) 1998, *'The Nation's Diet': The Social Science of Food Choice*, Longman, London.

Pendergrast, M. 1993, *For God, Country and Coca-Cola*, Phoenix, London.

Riddell, R. 1989, *Food and Culture in Australia*, Longman Cheshire, Melbourne.

Ritzer, G. 1996, *The McDonaldization of Society*, revised edn, Pine Forge Press, New York.

Santich, B. 1995, *What the Doctors Ordered: 150 Years of Dietary Advice in Australia*, Hyland House, Melbourne.

Schwartz, H. 1986, *Never Satisfied: A Cultural History of Diets, Fantasies and Fat*, The Free Press, New York.

Tansey, G. & Worsley, T. 1995, *The Food System: A Guide*, Earthscan, London.

Visser, M. 1989, *Much Depends on Dinner*, Penguin Books, London.

—— 1995, *Why We Eat the Way We Do*, Penguin Books, London.

Warde, A. 1997, *Consumption, Food and Taste*, Sage, London.

Whit, W. C. 1995, *Food and Society: A Sociological Approach*, General Hall, New York.

Worsley, A. (ed.) 1996, *Multidisciplinary Approaches to Food Choice*, Department of Community Medicine, University of Adelaide, Adelaide.

Introductory sociology books

Bilton, T., Bonnett, K., Jones, P., Skinner, D., Stanworth, M., & Webster, A. 1996, *Introductory Sociology*, 3rd edn, Macmillan, Houndsmills.

Germov, J. (ed.) 1998, *Second Opinion: An Introduction to Health Sociology*, Oxford University Press, Melbourne.

Giddens, A. 1997, *Sociology*, 3rd edn, Polity Press, Cambridge.

Henslin, J. M. 1996, *Essentials of Sociology: A Down to Earth Approach*, Allen & Bacon, Boston.

Jureidini, R., Kenny, S., & Poole, M. (eds) 1997, *Sociology: Australian Connections*, Allen & Unwin, Sydney.

Kellehear, A. (ed.) 1996, *Social Self, Global Culture: An Introduction to Sociological Ideas*, Oxford University Press, Melbourne.

Lemert, C. 1997, *Social Things: An Introduction to the Sociological Life*, Rowman & Littlefield, Lanham.

Macionis, J. J. 1995, *Sociology*, 5th edn, Prentice-Hall, Englewood Cliffs, NJ.

Macionis, J. J. & Plummer, K. 1997, *Sociology: A Global Introduction*, Prentice-Hall, New York.

Osborne, R. & van Loon, B. 1996, *Sociology for Beginners*, Icon Books, Cambridge.

Ruggiero, V. R. 1996, *A Guide to Sociological Thinking*, Sage, Thousand Oaks, Calif.

Willis, E. 1995, *The Sociological Quest*, 2nd edn, Allen & Unwin, Sydney.

Sociological dictionaries

Johnson, A. G. 1995, *The Blackwell Dictionary of Sociology*, Blackwell, Oxford.

Marshall, G. (ed.) 1994, *The Concise Oxford Dictionary of Sociology*, Oxford University Press, Oxford.

Essay and research skills

Germov, J. 1996, *Get Great Marks for Your Essays*, Allen & Unwin, Sydney.

Germov, J. & Williams, L. 1999, *Get Great Information Fast*, Allen & Unwin, Sydney.

General sociological theory

Haralambos, M., van Krieken, R., Smith, P., Holborn, M., Davis, A., & Habibis, D. 1996, *Sociology: Themes and Perspectives*, Australian edn, Addison Wesley Longman, Sydney.

Ritzer, G. 1996, *Sociological Theory*, 4th edn, McGraw-Hill, New York.

—— 1997, *Postmodern Social Theory*, McGraw-Hill, New York.

Tong, R. 1989, *Feminist Thought: A Comprehensive Introduction*, Routledge, London.

Turner, B. S. (ed.) 1996, *The Blackwell Companion to Social Theory*, Blackwell, Oxford.

Turner, S. T. (ed.) 1996, *Social Theory and Sociology: The Classics and Beyond*, Blackwell, Cambridge.

Wearing, B. 1996, *Gender: The Pain and Pleasure of Difference*, Addison Wesley Longman, Melbourne.

Relevant journals

Agriculture, Food, and Human Values
Alternatives
Appetite
British Food Journal
Body & Society
Digest: An Interdisciplinary Study of Food and Foodways
Food and Society
Gender and Health
Gender and Society
Healthy Weight Journal: <http://www.healthyweightnetwork.com/>
International Journal of the Sociology of Agriculture and Food (IJSAF)
    <http://www.ssc.msu.edu/~soc/foodag2.html>
Journal of the American Dietetic Association
Journal of Health and Social Behavior
Journal of Public Health Policy
    <http://www.pitt.edu/~jphp/jphp.html>
New Internationalist
    <http://www.oneworld.org/ni/>
Journal of Nutrition Education
Permaculture International Journal
    <http://www.nor.com.au/environment/perma/>
Sex Roles
The Sociological Review

Index